Cambodia 1975–1978: Rendezvous with Death

CAMBODIA 1975-1978

Rendezvous with Death

KARL D. JACKSON

Princeton University Press, Princeton, New Jersey

Copyright © 1989 by Princeton University Press

Published by Princeton University Press, 41 William Street, Princeton, New Jersey 08540
In the United Kingdom: Princeton University Press, Guildford, Surrey

All Rights Reserved

This book has been composed in Linotron Aldus

Clothbound editions of Princeton University Press books are printed on acid-free
paper, and binding materials are chosen for strength and durability. Paperbacks, although
satisfactory for personal collections, are not usually suitable for library rebinding

Printed in the United States of America by Princeton University Press,
Princeton, New Jersey

Library of Congress Cataloging-in-Publication Data
Cambodia, 1975–1978 : rendezvous with death / [compiled by] Karl D. Jackson.
p. cm.
Bibliography: p.
Includes index.
ISBN 0–691–07807–6
1. Cambodia—History—1975–   I. Jackson, Karl D.
DS554.8.C357 1989
959.6′04—dc19   88–26764

This book is dedicated to

Lucian W. Pye

Teacher, Scholar, and Friend

Contents

Preface

A year of sabbatical leave in Thailand, generously financed by the Henry Luce Foundation, led to this volume. During 1977–1978 the Khmer Rouge frequently raided Thai villages and simultaneously involved themselves in a war with Vietnam. However, the single most interesting topic that year derived from the sense of mystery concerning what was transpiring within Democratic Kampuchea. *Cambodia: Starvation and Revolution* by Gareth Porter and George Hildebrand (1976) contended that the tales of political bestiality and economic catastrophe were a hoax. In contrast, *Murder in a Gentle Land* by John Barron and Anthony Paul (1977) and *Cambodia: Year Zero* by François Ponchaud (1978) depicted an extremely violent and perhaps autogenocidal revolution. Clearly both versions could not be true. What, in fact, was happening just beyond the Thai-Cambodian border?

Upon returning to the United States I realized that the task of explaining the Cambodian revolution exceeded my own knowledge and that, if possible, I should gather together a group of persons with unique experience and expertise. This led to the selection of the authors whose chapters comprise this study. Rather than asking them merely to contribute their latest writing on Cambodia, I sought to design a book that would illuminate the most salient dimensions of revolutionary Cambodia: how the revolutionaries came to power, what they believed in, their organizational structure, the economic system, social and religious life, and the pattern and origins of the violence of their rule.

Timothy Carney had lived in Cambodia from 1972 to 1975, while serving as a political officer at the American Embassy. After 1975, he published a monograph on the communist party in Kampuchea—before the Kampuchean communists had even admitted their adherence to that doctrine. By experience and expertise, he seemed the logical choice for composing the chapters on how the Khmer Rouge came to power and the resulting party structure. Another foreign Service officer, Charles Twining, came to my attention because of the careful work he had done in interviewing Khmer refugees in Thailand. The knowledge he garnered made him ideal for describing and explaining Kampuchean economic life. Kenneth Quinn spent two years in Vietnam living just across the border from Cambodia and composed a remarkably prescient report for the U.S. State Department in 1974, a time when many Americans and Cambodians alike were reluctant to accept the reality described to Quinn by those early Cambodian refugees from Khmer Rouge rule. His interest in the patterns and intellectual origins of violence led not only to his chapters in this book but also to a dissertation. François Ponchaud's unique knowledge of Cambodian society and culture made his contribution essential to the volume. My own chapters grew from a fascination with what the Khmer Rouge leaders were attempting to achieve. What peculiar brand of ideology and circumstance minted the alloy of history's most violent revolution? Words alone bear insufficient witness to the human toll exacted by history. For this reason David Hawk's photographic essay describes, perhaps with greater intensity than other chapters, the impact of the revolution on the Cambodian people. Finally, primary source documents on the Khmer Rouge remain scarce, at least in English translation, and I therefore included several hitherto unavailable articles provided by Timothy Carney.

THIS STUDY would not have been possible without a grant from the Henry Luce Foundation to the Institute of East Asian Studies of the University of California, Berkeley. The project greatly benefited from the advice and help of Martha Wallace and Robert Armstrong, executive directors of the Luce Foundation, and Robert A. Scalapino, director of the Institute. In addition, numerous colleagues at Berkeley provided advice, including A. James Gregor, Kenneth Jowitt, William Muir, and Aaron Wildavsky. Finally, I would like to thank Rhonda Brown, Gerard Maré, Susan Barnes, and Steve Denney, who served ably as research assistants during various phases of the project.

THROUGHOUT the manuscript Kampuchea and Cambodia have been used interchangeably. When the Khmer Rouge ruled Cambodia, between 1975 and early 1979, the world conformed to their usage, Kampuchea, whereas Cambodia was the country's accepted name before 1975 and resumed its place after 1979.

THE PHOTOS and illustrations in Chapter 7 are from the collection of David Hawk. Unless otherwise indicated, they were taken by Hawk himself and are reproduced here with his permission.

Table 1 in Chapter 3 is reproduced, by permission of the publisher, from Laura Summers, "The CPK Secret Vanguard of Pol Pot's Revolution," *Journal of Communist Studies* 3 (March 1987), pp. 14–15.

Cambodia 1975–1978: Rendezvous with Death

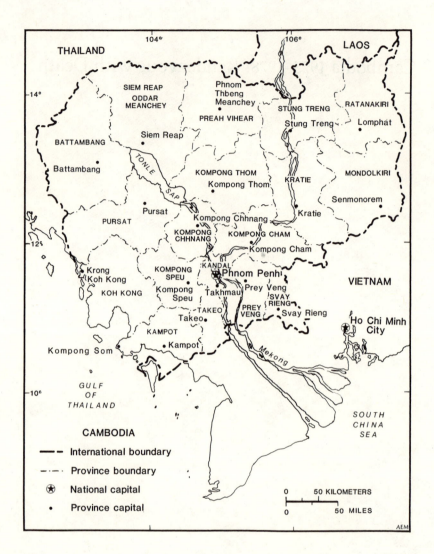

THAILAND

LAOS

104°

106°

14°

SIEM REAP

ODDAR
MEANCHEY

Phnom
Thbeng
Meanchey

RATANAKIRI

STUNG TRENG

PREAH VIHEAR

Stung Treng

Lomphat

Siem Reap

BATTAMBANG

Battambang

TONLE

SAP

KOMPONG THOM

Kompong Thom

KRATIE

MONDOLKIRI

Senmonorem

Pursat

PURSAT

12°

Kompong Chhnang

KOMPONG
CHHNANG

KOMPONG CHAM

Kratie

Kompong Cham

Krong
Koh Kong

KOH KONG

KOMPONG
SPEU

Kompong
Speu

KANDAL

Phnom Penh

Takhmau

Prey Veng

VIETNAM

SVAY
RIENG

TAKEO

Takeo

PREY
VENG

Svay Rieng

Ho Chi Minh
City

KAMPOT

Kompong Som

Kampot

Mekong

10°

GULF
OF
THAILAND

SOUTH
CHINA
SEA

CAMBODIA

— — International boundary

—·— Province boundary

⊛ National capital

• Province capital

0   50 KILOMETERS

0   50 MILES

AEM

Introduction. The Khmer Rouge in Context

by Karl D. Jackson

More than one million people are dead to begin with. Included are not only the victims of Pol Pot's killing fields, where members of the former ruling elite were cut down, but also, hundreds of thousands of men, women, and children who died from disease and starvation directly resulting from the regime's misguided and draconian policies.

Out of 7.3 million Cambodians said to be alive on April 17, 1975, less than 6 million remained to greet the Vietnamese occcupiers in the waning days of 1978.[1] Although precise figures may never be known, present calculations suggest that in the Cambodian revolution a greater proportion of the population perished than in any other revolution during the twentieth century. Not only were the highest echelons of the Lon Nol bureaucracy and army quickly dispatched, but, in addition, the killing and the dying endured throughout the revolution's forty-four-month tenure. As time passed, it devoured its own, especially at the infamous Tuol Sleng prison, where communist cadres and their families were being executed down to the last days of Khmer Rouge rule (see Chapters 6 and 7 and Appendix D). Pol Pot's regime purged and repurged itself in a fratricidal search for ideological purity and internal security. In the end, striving for security at any price proved counter-productive; the government fundamentally alienated its people, frightened critical cadres into an alliance with Vietnam, and weakened the country to the point that it could offer little organized resistance when Democratic Kampuchea faced the third and conclusive invasion from Vietnam in late December 1978.

Starvation and pestilence stalked the land because the regime's pursuit of complete independence led it to sever access to most aid and trade, thereby insuring death-dealing shortages of food, pesticides, and modern medicine. Successful communist revolutions emphasize national sovereignty and self-reliance, but no other movement has applied the academic theory of dependency in such a doctrinaire and literal manner, thereby inflicting on Cambodia severe diplomatic isolation, economic devastation, and massive human suffering. Likewise, aspiring revolutionaries have been wont to dis-

---

[1] This estimate assumes 600,000–700,000 war-related deaths before the Khmer Rouge victory and a middle range-estimate of 5.8 million survivors at the beginning of 1979. The only professional demographic estimates available were prepared by the U.S. Central Intelligence Agency (1980). If there had been neither war nor the Pol Pot regime, U.N. population projections would have led us to expect a total population of 8.7–9.0 million on December 1, 1979. Most journalists estimated the total population at 5–6 million at the beginning of 1979. (For a radically different assessment, see Vickery 1984.)

place ruling bureaucratic and military elites of the ancien régime; however, no previous revolutionary elite has moved so relentlessly to hunt down and kill as many as possible of the trained and educated manpower necessary to staff a state. Standard revolutionary practice has been to establish the regime first, eliminating the prerevolutionary elite only after revolutionary replacements have been trained; instead, the Khmer Rouge eliminated the functional elite or drove them out of the land, disregarding the absence of replacements. Similarly, revolutionaries have often cursed the clergy, but political pragmatism has usually precluded the type of policies adopted by the Khmer Rouge, namely, immediate disestablishment of the national religion, death to its elders, and desecration of its revered monuments.

Since the European industrial revolution, romantics, as well as some revolutionaries, have perceived cities as dens of iniquity, but only the Khmer Rouge emptied every city in the land immediately after victory. Finally, proponents of revolution have been known to predict that streets, of necessity, must run red with blood in order that the last should be first in the celestial city of the revolution; however, precious few have looked so positively on bloodshed as to use the word blood more frequently than any other in their national anthem, thereby conferring sanctity on tragedy (see Chapter 2).

It is not extraordinary that the Khmer Rouge, prior to victory, might have fantasized about ending Cambodian dependence on the international markets, killing their opponents to the last man, disestablishing religion and the monarchy, and instituting a total social revolution. What is extraordinary is that the experience of power did not sober the Khmer Rouge. Instead their swift sword applied untried revolutionary theories with an appalling literalism that left room for neither pragmatism nor compassion.

How can we explain such an outcome? Authors in this volume seek not only to describe who did what to whom, but to explain how and why these events transpired. Thus our purpose has not been to chronicle particular policies but to describe in the broadest sense how the revolutionary elite came to power (Chapter 1), the nature of its ideology (Chapter 2), how it organized itself (Chapter 3), how it ran an economy without money or markets (Chapter 4), the transformation of everyday social life (Chapter 5), the pattern of revolutionary violence (Chapters 6 and 7), and the intellectual origins of the Khmer Rouge (Chapters 8 and 9). In addition, a set of appendixes supplies basic documents for understanding the Cambodian revolution.

Given the complex and, one hopes, rare nature of the phenomena being explained, neither unanimity nor certitude is appropriate. At the most general level, however, the essays supply raw data for a tentative explanation. The civil war between the Khmer Republic (1970–1975) and the Khmer Rouge was a conflict between two divergent political cultures that had flowered within the Cambodian elite during the postcolonial era, the hierarchic political culture of the Lon Nol and Sihanouk regimes and the radical egalitarian political culture of the Khmer Rouge.

The Khmer Republic of Lon Nol, like its more regal predecessor under Norodom Sihanouk, represented the type of hierarchic political culture that underpins most governments in Southeast Asia to this day. In a political culture descended from the Hinduized kingdoms of Southeast Asia's first millennium, neither equality of opportunity nor equality of attainment represented predominant social values or expected outcomes for the majority of the citizenry. All men were inherently unequal and society was hierarchically organized. Social roles were largely determined by birth, casting the individual into particular social classes or ethnic groups. Inequality was sanctified by the Buddhist concept of karma (Spiro 1970). There was a definite ruling class, and the governed, by and large, had few illusions that they would one day become the governors. Rewards were distributed unequally, according to particularistic and ascriptive criteria. Legal and economic justice was dispensed on the basis of group membership and according to one's place in the group. It was accepted and understood that advancement occurred through the manipulation of the personal channels open to each individual, given his ascribed characteristics of religion, ethnic group, and family ties. Charges of corruption, favoritism, and nepotism were irrelevant in a culture founded upon the assumption that rewards were distributed unequally according to group membership and one's place in the hierarchy of the group. The prime form of organization was the patron-client grouping, through which wealth was redistributed; those with God-given high status, patrons, were expected to lead, teach, educate, and provide for their clients. Politics in the society was largely a competition, *not* between ideologies, but among patron-client groupings, each of which was bound together by the sinews of personal reciprocity.

In the traditional kingdoms of Southeast Asia, antedating the European presence, being perceived as powerful had little to do with exercising power to enact changes in the larger society. Traditionally, power was a matter of status rather than an active seeking out, ordering, and energizing of subordinates in the pursuit of concrete organizational goals. In the precolonial era, kingdoms were nonterritorial theater states dedicated to the glorification of god-kings while peasants were left to participate only vicariously in the great tradition represented by the capital city.

In the postcolonial era, governments in Burma, Cambodia, Indonesia, and Thailand have continued to share many of these traditional aspects. Governments have not, by and large, been noted for either efficiency in raising military power or commitment to solving the problems of their rural masses. As bureaucratic polities, they have existed by and primarily for the benefit of the official class (including the officer corps) that comprised the only meaningful political participants in the national decision-making mechanism (see Jackson 1978b; Riggs 1966; Girling 1981). Anticorruption campaigns often were attempts by political "outs" to oust the "ins" rather than to change the system of selective distribution of the benefits of government. In bureaucratic polities the military and the bureaucracy have not been held accountable to other political forces such as political parties, interest groups, or even organized communal groups. Actions designed to influence government decisions usually have originated entirely from within the elite itself. Political parties, to the extent that they exist at all, neither control the central bureaucracy nor effectively organize the masses at the local level. By and large, such governments remain dependent on international support, isolated from the peasantry, incapable of consistent penetration beyond the urban centers, preparticipatory, and basically administrative rather than political states.

The governments associated with names such as Ne Win (Burma), Sihanouk and Lon Nol (Cambodia), and Suharto (Indonesia), and most Thai governments since 1932, have been bureaucratic polities existing within hierarchic political cultures. They have endured throughout the period in spite of the fact that they remain relatively weak, "soft authoritarian" states usually incapable of executing policies if such initiatives are dependent on the cooperation of large numbers of persons outside the cities. Like bureaucracy in general, bureacratic polities tend to define all policy issues as administrative problems, effectively depoliticizing them. The bureaucracy itself (be it military or civilian) is comprised of multiple subunits competing for control of limited resources (the budget). Competition is relatively genteel because units endure and today's rivals may be tomorrow's allies in the jockeying among the competing patron-client groupings that constitute the core of polity. Pragmatism predominates; the goal is survival in position rather than radical transformation of the surrounding society. The favored strategies are compromise, cooptation, and corruption.

"Loners," elite members "who won't play the game," are imprisoned or otherwise deprived of their civil liberties, whereas non-elite members (because they are not truly participant) are normally exempt from anything other than ordinary forms of government coercion (routine law enforcement and tax collection). In bureaucratic polities, utilization of violence against whole social categories is the exception rather than the rule because social transformation of the masses is not an important goal. Authoritarian but weak governments are tolerated because they are incapable of interfering in most spheres of life, and hence they coerce the general population in limited and relatively "acceptable" ways. Government is often disorganized and usually ineffectual but not generally pernicious; it bumbles but it lacks the kind of grand ideological vision that might countenance killing whole groups of people to transform a society.

Nothing could be more different from the Khmer Rouge. The civil war (1970–1975) pitted Lon Nol's bureaucratic polity against a revolutionary sect bent upon implementing a radical egalitarian revolution. The bedrock of the old bureaucratic order was inequality, whereas the thrust of the Khmer revolution was the complete eradication of Phnom Penh's "cognac and concubine circuit" (Carney 1977). When the Khmer Rouge seized power in April 1975, they did so with the intention of obliterating its hierarchic political culture in order to reconstruct Cambodian society from ground zero as the world's most egalitarian, and therefore revolutionary, social order.

Although it is useful to search for the intellectual antecedents of the Khmer Rouge—be they Maoist, Marxist, Fanonist, or Stalinist (see Chapters 8 and 9)—the ferocity and literalism with which they pursued these ideals cannot be explained merely by reference to abstract formal ideologies. Marxists have frequently discussed the desirability of doing away with the exploiters, and yet only the Khmer Rouge sought literally to exterminate the entire class. Likewise, theoreticians like Fanon might condemn the evils of "neo-colonialist" cities, but only the Khmer Rouge actually destroyed all of their cities. The proclivity toward violence, the fear of contamination by outsiders, the moral self-righteousness, and the literal and doctrinaire way of pursuing goals are what separate the Khmer Rouge from comparable revolutionary phenomena. To understand the Khmer Rouge, it is necessary to comprehend the psychological driving force that transformed commonplace ideological nostrums into the century's most extreme revolution. The Khmer Rouge devotion to violence, xenophobic fear of contamination, righteousness, and literalism derive their peculiar pyschological force from the dictates of sectarianism.

Sectarians throughout history have been radical egalitarians (see Douglas and Wildavsky 1982; Talmon 1952 and 1960; and Huntington and Dominguez 1975). Differences between people are perceived as the root of evil. Sectarians believe that if society can rid itself of customs that produce distinctions, then society can return to an earlier, morally pristine state. The cardinal assumption is that man is inherently good and only become[s] evil through contact with the institutions of a corrupt society; singled out as most reprehensible are the marketplace, technology, the division of labor, and resulting distinctions of birth, wealth, and social class. Perfection is to be attained either through abandoning the social order (like religious sects in Western society) or by destroying the existing order (like the Khmer Rouge).

In a structural sense, sectarian movements are exclusive rather than inclusive. People are born into churches but must join a sect. The act of affiliating is individual, voluntary, and often involves withdrawing from life in society because society is percieved as morally bankrupt. Religious sects remain exclusive because they dread spiritual pollution from contact with those who are less holy than the chosen few. Sectarian movements espouse moral rejuvenation through the creation of a new grouping with its own set of institutions.

Finally, sectarian movements are characteristically doctrinaire. They demand 100 percent participation from their members. Their world view remains sharply dichotomous: it is divided into believers, who are good, and nonbelievers, who are evil. Pragmatic compromise with the outside world is to be avoided, and the world beyond the sect is percieved as a hostile place. Literalism is the birthright of sectarian movements everywhere because membership is limited strictly to the morally pure. Politics is the pursuit of "absolute virtue," the application of a preexisting philosophy to the organization of society, a perfect doctrine supplying the moral rationale for ideological absolutism (see Talmon 1952).

If we conceive of the Khmer Rouge as a revolutionary sect, how does this help us to understand the pattern of their violence and the way in which their movement evolved? The Khmer Rouge were obviously radical egalitarians (see Chapter 2). They were doctrinaire in word and deed and rejected the marketplace, division of labor, and most aspects of modern technology (see Chapter 4). What differentiates the Khmer Rouge from other radical egalitarian movements are the circumstances in which they came to power. In most societies sectarian movements remain marginal, isolated from power and often persecuted by the central authorities. By the mid-1970s Khmer society had been fundamentally destabilized by civil war as well as armed intervention by North Vietnam, South Vietnam, and the United States. If anything, the field of Khmer politics between 1970 and 1975 was overcrowded with alternative sources of politico-military power. Lon Nol and the Khmer Rouge were both very weak militarily in 1970, although the Khmer Rouge grew rapidly enough to defeat the Khmer Republic after American assistance had been suspended (see Chapter 1). U.S. economic and military assistance, including a massive aerial bombardment (1969–1973), supplied conditions that made possible the temporary survival of an inherently weak, corrupt, and incompetent bureaucratic polity that was facing the combined onslaught of the Khmer Rouge as well as mainforce units of the Vietnamese army. The Vietnamese army had moved against the Lon Nol government in its infancy, making the first major move toward Phnom Penh before, rather than after, the May 1970 American invasion of Cambodia. During the first two years of the Cambodian civil war, most of the fighting against Lon Nol's army was accomplished by Vietnamese regulars who provided a military shield behind which the Khmer revolutionary army grew.

One by one, and for different reasons, the external participants withdrew from Cambodia, leaving the field to Pol Pot and Lon Nol. South Vietnamese and American troops withdrew after their "joint incursion" during the spring of 1970. Most North Vietnamese regulars withdrew from Cambodia in 1972 to partake of the Easter Offensive inside South Vietnam. American bombing ended in 1973 by Congressional mandate. The size of the American mission on the ground in Cambodia was limited by law to 200, virtually precluding any direct U.S. military involvement during the climax of the Cambodian civil war. Finally, American military assistance was terminated by Congress in 1975, severing the last remaining lifeline of Lon Nol's encircled government in Phnom Penh.

When the Khmer Rouge assumed power on April 17, 1975, no significant foreign sources of power remained inside Cambodia. A vacuum of foreign intervention (both North Vietnamese and American) combined with the complete collapse of the Khmer Republic to present the Khmer Rouge with virtually unconstrained political domination. The Khmer revolutionary army consisted of only sixty thousand men out of more than seven million people, but in late April 1975 they were the only organized coercive force in Cambodia. At that point they were the only significant player on the Cambodian politico-military stage. However, there were ominous signs indicating that this period of domination would end unless they moved swiftly to consolidate their power. Prior to the capture of Phnom Penh, the Khmer Rouge were already at war with their Vietnamese communist brethren (see Quinn 1976). Furthermore, there were far too few trained and educated cadre within the movement for the Khmer Rouge to hope to dominate permanently the corrupt but relatively sophisticated elite of the acien régime. Unless drastic actions were taken, the old elite, simply by dint of its mass and sophistication, would reassert dominance. Therefore, the talents of the Phnom Penh elite were not only superfluous but positively dangerous to the goal of a peasant-led, completely egalitarian revolution. The ferocity of the initial onslaught against the elite of the Khmer Republic may have derived from a Khmer Rouge perception that the opportunity for total revolution was fleeting and might slip away unless actions were executed immediately and with zealotry. These political circumstances combined with the Khmer Rouge's sectarian view of the world as sharply divided between peasant-workers and all other classes. The peasant-workers and the revolutionary soldiers represented hope for future greatness, whereas all other social classes were exemplars of the very inequalities that the Khmer Rouge were bent upon extinguishing. A large proportion of the elite, as well as skilled laborers and many common urbanites, were marked for elimination because they had been contaminated by Western education or exposure to the evils of Phnom Penh. In devising their new social order, the revolutionaries were very reluctant to allow the unpurified masses of city dwellers to join the new Cambodia, classifying them instead as *bannheu* (depositees) who had no rights whatsoever, not even the right to food (see Heder 1980a:

1–4 and Chapter 2). The moral exclusivity of the Khmer Rouge as a revolutionary sect might also explain at least partially the reluctance to welcome back into the Communist Party those Khmer who had been trained in Hanoi and returned south to join the revolution in 1970. Instead of welcoming these communist cadres, the Khmer Rouge began purging them, well in advance of the victory of April 1975.

The sectarian pursuit of "a society of equal saints" (Talmon 1952: 9–10) created tensions within the Khmer Rouge that drove it to devour its own while simultaneously aggressing against all of its neighbors. When radical egalitarians achieve power in a vacuum and succeed almost immediately in destroying all of their traditional domestic opponents, they are faced with a dilemma. Sects require enemies, or at least percieved enemy forces, to feed on. In the political religion of radical egalitarianism the existence of a leadership class is evidence of rebirth of the invidious distinctions characteristic of the morally bankrupt ancien régime. The existence of a formal leadership violates the principle of strict equality and hence is morally reprehensible. And yet, in a society of equal saints, some are obviously more equal than others. One way to rationalize the existence of a formal leadership is to base its claim to authority on extraordinary circumstances, a threat from within or fear of invasion from without. When the revolution has already come to pass and when the institutions that caused evil in the old society have already been destroyed, how does one explain the continued absence of a perfect society in which all are supposed to be equal? Religious and political sects blame the continued absence of social perfection on enemies within who are secretly conspiring to sabotage the new order. The sect can only remain strong in the face of challenge if it remains monolithically unified; therefore, anyone judged not to be a true believer must be expelled, and the movement cannot rest until it has rooted out all of the fainthearted from its midst. Expulsion from the sect is the primary means of insuring more than mere ideological purity. In addition, the ever-present possibility that further cleansing may be needed supplies a continuing rationale for the existence of leaders in a completely equal society (Douglas and Wildavsky 1982). By analogy to the terror of the French revolution, only when the imperfect have been expelled, when the Dantons have been defeated, and all power yielded to incorruptibles like St. Just and Robespierre, can the perfect vision begin to be realized. Some such rationale may have converted the pursuit of absolute equality into a witchhunt resulting in the execution of a bevy of Khmer Rouge founding fathers. The Khmer Rouge obsession with internal security led them to seek out, and if necessary invent, conspiracies within their own inner circle. Paradoxically, the search for radical egalitarianism (under these special circumstances) lead to permanent purge in order to rationalize the inherently illegitimate and supposedly temporary nature of the leadership's own position.

No one has yet gained meaningful scholarly access to the top level of the Khmer Rouge leadership. Hence, all conclusions must remain tentative and interpretations primarily speculative. One can only wish that phenomena such as the Khmer Rouge will remain sufficiently rare as to preclude the kind of scientific certitude that multiple cases might afford.

1. The Unexpected Victory

by Timothy Carney

On April 17, 1975, troops of the revolution's "Northern and Eastern Regions" captured the Cambodian capital of Phnom Penh. The Communist Party of Kampuchea (PKK) had capped its twenty-four-year history with a stunning victory, anticipating the Vietnamese communist capture of Saigon some two weeks later. The Cambodian movement was almost totally unknown five years earlier, when Prince Norodom Sihanouk, Cambodia's one-time king and then head of state, was overthrown. By 1975, the party had built a tough, innovative armed force of a dozen battle-tested brigades and defeated the army of the rival Khmer Republic.

The process did not start with Sihanouk's 1970 overthrow and his subsequent alliance with the (PKK) in the National United Front of Kampuchea (NUFK). The PKK success begins with its spawning by the Vietnamese during the First Indochina War. In addition to the creating hand of the Indochinese Communist Party, which Ho Chi Minh founded in 1930 and which was almost wholly Vietnamese, the Cambodian communist movement itself recognized both French and Thai communist influences.[1] The party's vicissitudes included a search for an identity from 1951 to 1959, a period of self-examination and contact with other Asian communist centers from 1960 to 1967, the opening of armed struggle against Prince Sihanouk's government from 1968 to 1970, an alliance with the deposed prince and massive Chinese and Vietnamese communist support for a successful war against the American-backed, incompetently led Khmer Republic from 1970 to 1975.

The PKK won the war because: (a) Norodom Sihanouk provided an enormously popular drawing card to recruit troops into the (NUFK), which the party came to control. The prince also helped isolate the Khmer Republic diplomatically and gave the PKK-dominated front credibility among opinion makers in the West; (b) the North Vietnamese army, the People's Army of Vietnam (PAVN), formed a two-year shield in eastern Cambodia behind which the party developed its infrastructure and the army trained its troops;

THE ANALYSIS, opinions, and conclusions here expressed are mine alone and do not necessarily reflect those of the U.S. Government.

[1] The major source on party history in the 1950s and 1960s is a captured document entitled, "Summary of Annotated Party History" (see Appendix A). The document's internal evidence dates it to 1973 when it was written by the party's Eastern Region military political service as part of celebrations for the twenty-second anniversary of the founding of the PKK. Henceforth cited as "Democratic Kampuchea 1973." See also Ben Kiernan's study of early Cambodian communism that adds many new details from interviews with both Khmer and Vietnamese survivors of this early period (Kiernan 1981b).

13

(c) the adversary Khmer Republic was generally afflicted with an unimaginative set of political and military leaders whose personal corruption undercut the genuine enthusiasm among the elite that had followed the prince's March 18, 1970, deposition; (d) the PKK and its army had the toughness, resolution, and discipline to prevail, and their vision of a new society attracted a dedicated core of followers; (e) China and North Vietnam backed the PKK to the finish, but the United States ended its massive assistance to the Khmer Republic.

Part of the tactical success of the revolution included the PKK decision to remain clandestine throughout the war. Only in September 1977 did the party publicly emerge to claim credit for its leading role in the establishment of a new order. Such a tactic is not unknown to other successful communist movements. In Cambodia, the special importance of remaining clandestine was due to the major campaign Prince Sihanouk had waged in the 1950s and 1960s to equate communism with antimonarchism and antinationalism. By 1977, however, the party believed itself sufficiently in control of the nation it had rechristened Democratic Kampuchea to emerge publicly. At the same time, the PKK's public unveiling probably also aimed to encourage other communist states to pressure the Socialist Republic of Vietnam to desist in the name of communist solidarity. The Vietnamese were even then, in the wake of deteriorating relations since their 1975 accession to power, preparing the first stages of major military action across the border with Kampuchea.

The Khmer case is unusual less in the process that led to victory than in the obscurity surrounding the war. What had looked like a straightforward PAVN invasion in 1970, launched partly in reaction to political change in Phnom Penh and the subsequent U.S. incursion into Vietnamese sanctuaries in Cambodia, had become a Cambodian civil war by early 1973. The active diplomatic operation Prince Sihanouk ran from Beijing masked some of the developments on the ground in Cambodia. The domestic American political battle over a U.S. role in Indochina also helped to hide the realities. In addition, the American focus on Vietnam gave Cambodia short shrift.

Nor did the Khmer communists do much to enlighten us. Khmer documents were rare: first person accounts like those of Vietnam's senior general, Van Tien Dung, still do not exist. Party history, as brought out in connection with the public unveiling of the PKK in 1977 and in propaganda concerning the war with Vietnam in 1978, needs very careful handling to separate the fact from the myth. The creation of a Vietnamese client regime in Phnom Penh since 1979, however, has given scholars access to many documents of the Pol Pot period. Former mid-level leaders of his regime now form part of the Phnom Penh regime and have talked candidly to scholars about party history.

For more than three years Cambodia lived in an era of "socialist revolution, socialist construction and defense of Democratic Kampuchea," as Prime Minister and Party Secretary Pol Pot described the post-victory period in his speech announcing the reality of the party role in Cambodia's revolution (FBIS IV October 4, 1977). What the leaders did with their people after victory demands attention, all the more so because the treatment of the population after April 1975 had a firm base in wartime population control policy.

Even more stunning, although prefigured to a certain degree by Soviet action in Czechoslovakia, was the Vietnamese offensive launched December 25, 1978, after a long buildup. The successful Vietnamese capture of Phnom Penh, January 7, 1979, on behalf of a "Solidarity Front for the Salvation of the Kampuchea Nation," has sought to return Cambodia to the paths traced by Ho Chi Minh's Indochinese Communist Party. That front is led by a coalition of obscure former military figures of the Pol Pot regime; a section of First Indochina War veterans who lived much of the post-Geneva period in Vietnam and escaped purge on return to Cambodia in 1970; and a few new recruits who had been too young or apolitical under Sihanouk and Lon Nol.

Pre-Independence

Some of the key questions about the formation of the party in the 1940s and 1950s are slowly being answered. The Pol Pot–led leadership tried to obscure the Vietnamese role in the creation of the PKK.[2] The Vietnamese themselves let out only what served their interest in the fight with Cambodia. Internal documents show that the party long regarded 1951 as the date of its origin. A key party history, written for its anniversary in 1973, explains that "the international communist movement and the Vietnamese communists . . . injected proletarian class Marxism-Leninism into our revolutionary movement." The document traces the background of Cambodian communism to the "Indochinese Communist Party, about 40 men in 1951; in the French Communist Party, 10 men in 1951; and in the Thai Com-

[2] Vietnamese Vice Foreign Minister Nguyen Co Thach gave the first public confirmation of the Vietnamese role in creating a Communist party in Cambodia during the formation of the Lao Dong Party in Vietnam after the formal dissolution of the old Indochinese Communist Party. See his remarks after reading a Vietnamese peace proposal of February 5, 1978 (FBIS IV, February 6, 1978:K5). Cambodian efforts to denigrate the Vietnamese role and accuse Vietnam of subverting the PKK are best conveyed in the *Black Paper* published by the Ministry of Foreign Affairs of Democratic Kampuchea (Democratic Kampuchea 1978a). The PKK itself formally, if implicitly, recognized the break with Vietnam at its September 30, 1976, founding anniversary when it changed the year of founding from 1951 to 1960: "the Party decided to arrange a clean and pure history according to the stand of independence and self-reliance" (*Revolutionary Flags*, September–October 1976c:4). The 1951 creation provisionally existed to draw up a line for a true party organization.

munist Party, 3–4 men in 1951" (Democratic Kampuchea 1973:7). After the party publicly emerged in 1977, claiming a 1960 date for its formal establishment, the Khmer ambassador to North Korea nevertheless told a Pyongyang banquet that the party had a 1951 founding (FBIS IV, October 4, 1977).

The original creation, the Revolutionary Cambodian People's Party, was probably not a true Marxist-Leninist organization. A captured contemporary Vietnamese telegram orders Chinese and Vietnamese communists living in Cambodia to join the Vietnamese Lao Dong Party, also an offshoot of the dissolved Indochinese Communist Party, instead of the new Khmer grouping. The cable explained that the Khmer party was a sort of united front and "is not the vanguard of the working class (American Mission Saigon. No. 598. Translation of Telegram No. 749 S.D.C.S)."

The Revolutionary Cambodian People's Party grew out of the wing of the anti-French "Khmer Issarak" independence movement that had come under Vietnamese control. The steps along the way included the foundation of a National Central Executive Committee (the Moutkeaha) in 1950. This body had followed on the emergence in 1949 of a "Khmer National Liberation Committee." That creation had a certain resistance captain, Dap Chuon, as Vietnamese-backed leader, but he rallied to Sihanouk in October 1949 (to betray the prince and suffer death ten years later). The earliest Khmer ties to Vietnamese communism date to at least 1945 when Prime Minister Son Ngoc Thanh entertained Viet Minh contacts who sought to coordinate resistance to the returning French. After Thanh's arrest, his economic minister, Pach Chhoeun, the same Cambodian resistance leader who had sparked the 1942 creation of the Khmer Issarak in Bangkok, subsequently tried for Vietminh support, but the French crushed his budding effort in the ethnic Khmer areas of the Mekong delta in April 1946.[3]

The 1951 party did not have enough time to grow. Prince Sihanouk's Royal Crusade for Independence began in 1952 and caused massive defections from both the Thai-oriented and the Vietminh-dominated Khmer independence ranks. Finally, the 1954 Geneva Conference closed the door on the Cambodian communist movement as communist powers bowed to Royal Cambodian insistence that the Khmer radicals be excluded. Two thousand or more Khmer, pretending to be Vietminh fighters, went to North Vietnam by ship under the terms of the Geneva accords. A small number stayed in Cambodia to continue activities both legal and clandestine.

---

[3] Much of this background can be found in Khmer Peace Committee, 1952:12 and Reddi 1970:159–54, 162, 176–81. See Democratic Kampuchea 1978a:12, 22, 25, 30 and Kiernan 1981b:163–174.

Era of Political Struggle

1950s: CONFUSION AND BETRAYAL

Secretary Pol Pot's September 1977 party history depicts the 1950s as a time when poorly organized intellectuals cast about for issues to mobilize the people. The party tried to tackle Sihanouk's Cambodia on three fronts, with a legal political organization, a leftist press, and clandestine struggle.

The legal challenge to Sihanouk was totally rebuffed as the PKK's creature, the political party known as the "Pracheachon Group," went down to defeat in the 1955 and 1958 national elections. They could not, nor could any political grouping, compete with the mass organization, the Sangkum Reastr Niyum (People's Socialist Community), which King Sihanouk abdicated to build in 1955. A few years later, the Pracheachon leadership went underground, citing suppression in a later account of their motives. The leftist press flourished for a number of years before the 1959 murder of the editor of one procommunist daily.

The clandestine party itself suffered from lack of a "political line," slight resources, poor quality cadre, and major problems in its national leadership, divided between an in-country wing and an expatriate wing in North Vietnam. After 1954, a "temporary central committee of Sieu Heng, Secretary; Tou Samuth; Ng.M.; S.V.; and N.T.Nh." launched into a political struggle. This initial body foundered on unspecified urban activities. A renewed central committee of 1956 split rural and urban committees between Sieu Heng and Tou Samuth, repectively, as chairmen (Democratic Kampuchea 1973:12–14).

Unfortunately for the nascent movement, Sieu Heng betrayed the party by working for Lon Nol. His betrayal began as early as 1956, and he formally defected to the Royal Government in 1959.[4] Phnom Penh security services must have known just exactly who the enemy was. Party Secretary Pol Pot had admitted that "in 1959 about 90% of our revolutionary forces in rural areas [Sieu Heng's committee] were destroyed (FBIS IV, October 4, 1977:H8)."

RENAISSANCE IN 1960

The restructuring of the party began with a major national congress on September 30, 1960. Tou Samuth became secretary and the party changed its name, eventually to become the Communist Party of Kampuchea.[5] Sa-

---

[4] An American Embassy officer interviewed Sieu Heng in Battambang in early 1972. Sieu Heng disingenuously replied to a question about his 1954–1959 activities by saying he returned from Hanoi to do some farming and then "worked for" General Lon Nol.

[5] The 1960 name change was to the "Workers' Party" (Khmer Republic Military Intelligence 1972.) The document claims the PKK changed its name to Communist Party of Kampuchea in 1966, as does the "Short Guide to Party Statutes," translated as part of the documents in Carney 1977.

loth Sar, a teacher now called Pol Pot, one of the first French-trained younger elements in the party during the early 1950s, took the deputy secretary position. The assembly approved a political line, and formed "the Marxist-Leninist Party in Cambodia (Democratic Kampuchea 1973:18)."

The rejuvenated party quickly came to official attention. Prince Sihanouk criticized the legal manifestation of the party, the Pracheachon Group, by name in January 1962, calling it a communist party directed from abroad. On July 20, 1962 the "enemy" kidnapped the party secretary and presumably murdered him. Leadership passed to the man we know as Pol Pot (Democratic Kampuchea 1973:18 and Democratic Kampuchea March 1978a:22).[6]

CLANDESTINE STRUGGLE

The suppression of the Pracheachon Group and the antileftist campaign throughout 1962 convinced party leaders that they should disappear. Then acting secretary Pol Pot headed for the bush in 1963 along with Ieng Sary and Son Sen, both subsequently revealed as members of the Standing Committee of the Central Committee of the PKK. In April 1976, the three became premier, deputy premier charged with foreign affairs, and deputy premier charged with national defense, respectively, in the national government of newly renamed "Democratic Kampuchea."

Other figures stayed in Phnom Penh, notably party theoretician Khieu Samphan, who eventually became head of state in April 1976. In the early 1960s he joined Sihanouk's political movement, became a National Assembly deputy, and served in the August 1962 cabinet for two months. Only in 1967, when Sihanouk threatened military court for Khieu Samphan and two other prominent leftist deputies in connection with a peasant uprising at Samlaut in western Cambodia, did that trio join the maquis. A number of other teachers and intellectuals had trickled into the bush in the intervening years to become cadre for an armed struggle.

At the same time, a wing of the party existed in Vietnam, biding its time. Old line leaders like Son Ngoc Minh and Chan Samay, active in the First Indochina War, led the Vietnam branch. They apparently had little or no say about activities in Cambodia. Sometime after the 1970 coup, Ieng Sary himself moved to Hanoi. He did so doubtlessly as much to watch the external wing of the PKK as to establish liaison with the Vietnamese party.

Difficulties with the Vietnamese arose early over both theory and practice. The Pol Pot group claimed that Hanoi ridiculed their class analysis, arguing that, like Laos, Kampuchea had not developed into a class society. The Vietnamese themselves have recently suggested that they had opposed the PKK's political line of both armed and political struggle (Chanda 1978).

[6] For information on the supression of the Pracheachon Group, refer to Leifer 1962a:11–15 and 1962b:20–24. The Mission du Front Uni National du Kampuchea (1972) gives reasons for the Pracheachon's decision to dissolve.

They did so, according to the PKK, to assure their troops' sanctuaries in Cambodia and their access to supplies funneled through Sihanouk's bureaucracy (Democratic Kampuchea 1978a:31–36).

Armed Struggle Begins

REVOLT

A peasant uprising in Samlaut District of Battambang Province in early 1967 provided the spark for armed struggle. The revolt evidently surprised the party as much as it did both Sihanouk, who was on a cure in France, and his government in Phnom Penh (Kiernan 1976). Pol Pot has said that the party had to dampen the Samlaut rebellion because it was premature and would have been crushed. The government could have massed forces against such an isolated movement (Pol Pot 1977:17–18). Indeed, central authorities reacted in Samlaut with fire and sword.

Real action got underway January 17, 1968, when newly created party forces hit a government post at Bay Damram near Battambang City. The PKK dates the founding of the Revolutionary Army of Kampuchea to that attack, when party "secret defense units" were formed into guerilla units.[7] This two-year era of civil war, as Pol Pot described the 1968–1970 fighting, showed the party leadership's ability to capitalize on genuine peasant grievances. Peasants particularly reacted against government efforts to enforce low official paddy prices while traders were paying top dollar to buy rice for resale to PAVN and Viet Cong troops in the sanctuaries (Kiernan 1976 II:20).

Despite two years of sporadic armed dissidence, by the time of Sihanouk's overthrow in 1970, insurgent forces had neither the strength nor the armament to stand up against even the 30,000-strong ceremonial and civic action force the government fielded. Pol Pot publicly claimed that party forces had 4,000 regular troops and 50,000 guerrillas. Party documents, however, admit that regular forces were organized into companies.[8] Such a small-scale organization suggests that forces were scattered and probably not nearly as numerous as 4,000 regulars.

COERCION

The question of coercion in this early armed struggle is so far incompletely answered. The initial phase of dissidence in early 1968 in western

[7] The date and history are in then acting Prime Minister Nuon Chea's January 16, 1977, speech to a Phnom Penh rally celebrating the army's anniversary (FBIS IV, January 19, 1977, and Kiernan 1976 II:5).

[8] The claim for the number of regulars is in his speech (Pol Pot 1977:H22). The organizational stage is given in *Revolutionary Flags*, 1975:43, 45. The article stated it was a speech by the chairman of the party Military Committee, subsequently revealed to be Pol Pot himself, delivered to a July 22, 1975 meeting for 3,000 military unit representatives. I have sent copies of this and other unique source material to the Echols Collection at Cornell University Olin Library.

and southwestern Cambodia drew some 10,000 villagers at least temporarily into the maquis (Kiernan 1976 II:18). How many villagers left voluntarily and how many left under pressure cannot be known. Party-ordered violence against civilians appeared as early as January 27, 1968, when insurgents executed the chief of a village defense committee. During coordinated attacks in seven provinces, beginning February 27, rebels kidnapped local officials in Kirirom and publicly executed seven village chiefs and some deputy chiefs. The government put down the party's challenge in 1968 by taking a large base camp in Battambang. But dissidence continued and so did the use of terror. In June 1969, rebels executed centrally appointed officials in five villages around the nation.

VIETNAMESE SUPPORT

The North Vietnamese tactical concern in Cambodia lay in assuring supplies, transit of men and material, and sanctuary for their war to conquer South Vietnam. Major help to the local communist movement was not part of their aims. They had some strategic assets, however, especially the several thousand Cambodians who had been in North Vietnam since 1954. In a March 1968 speech, Prince Sihanouk claimed that six of Khieu Samphan's agents recently captured included some trained as cadres in Hanoi and one ethnic Vietnamese sapper (Kiernan 1976 II:22–23). He ordered the agents shot without trial, however, which makes this contention difficult to prove.

Other information argues that the prince was not merely trying to undercut potential popular support for the rebellion by tarring it with the Vietnamese brush and bringing into play the centuries of hostility between the two peoples. A defector from the North Vietnamese central office for South Vietnam's research section reported in 1973 that seven years earlier, in 1966, the Vietnamese had organized a unit designated "P–36" to support the PKK. The unit reported directly to Politburo member, Le Duc Tho. It aimed to help develop PKK cadre, exploit propaganda themes, and give other assistance to the Cambodian party. Before Sihanouk's overthrow, P–36 trained Khmer or ethnic Vietnamese born in Cambodia. Most returned to Cambodia in 1970 at PKK request as advisors.

This unit may have been a direct response to PKK demands for greater assistance in the mid-1960s. Pol Pot and other PKK leaders visited Hanoi in 1965. Vietnamese party central committeeman and political director of the party daily, *Nhan Dan*, Mr. Hoang Tung, has said that the Khmer spent a few months in Hanoi on that visit before going on to China (Chanda 1978). The timing suggests that Pol Pot was able to get a modest increase in clandestine Vietnamese support for the PKK even at a time when the Vietnamese were negotiating formally with the Sihanouk's government to recognize Cambodia's frontiers.

In 1968 Sihanouk also cited Vietnamese aid, especially through the heavily Vietnamese-influenced Lao communists, the Pathet Lao, to hill tribes in revolt in Ratanakiri Province. Hill tribe grievances against central officials and a desire for greater autonomy, if not independence, figured prominently in that dissidence. Early on, the Vietnamese party probably provided aid in an effort to exploit the conflict and assure the security of their base areas by crippling Phnom Penh's administrative hand in the highland areas.[9]

The War

The PKK fought the war on two fronts: an in-country armed struggle with the party leading the NUFK and a Beijing-based diplomatic effort led by the prince as chief of the Royal Government of National Union of Kampuchea. In this effort to isolate the Khmer Republic, Sihanouk came under the watchful party eye of Ieng Sary, who arrived in Beijing in August 1971 from liason duties in Hanoi (*Far Eastern Economic Review* 1972). Ieng Sary held the title "Special Representative from the Interior." He finally returned to Cambodia in 1974, by which time Sihanouk had proved his good faith in supporting the alliance he made with Cambodian radicals immediately after the coup.

During the war, the party continued to try to keep its existence and role secret. Ordinary members of the NUFK were unaware of the extent of ever-expanding party control. Sihanouk's repeated efforts to equate communism with treason during the 1950s and 1960s meant that the party could not show itself without endangering the appeal of the NUFK. Moreover, the PKK itself had too few cadres to show without exposing them to anticommunist elements in the NUFK or to attack by infiltrators from the Republic. In addition, open domination by the PKK might have weakened the NUFK and Royal Government's case internationally, especially among the nonaligned states.

The party maintained public secrecy until late 1977, when four days of celebration, September 27–30, brought its existence and control to the world's eye. Refugees, however, had observed that the party began to emerge internally in parts of Battambang in the spring of 1977. Despite this public assumption of leadership, reporters for the Yugoslav press visiting Cambodia as late as March 1978 wrote that PKK membership was still secret in rural areas (Mihovilovic 1978).

[9] For an exposition on the situation in the highlands, see Kirk 1971:108–10 and Whitaker et al. 1973:72. A different view is given in Pomonti and Thion 1971:118–22. The two French authors emphasize local grievances and dismiss the Vietnamese role. For some indigenous documents, including a conversation on this subject between then Lt. General Lon Nol and the ambassadors of the Democratic Republic of Vietnam and the National Liberation Front, see *Le Sangkum* (1969), as reprinted in Khmer Republic 1970:12–15.

INITIAL FOREIGN SUPPORT

The Vietnamese communists moved faster to support their Khmer allies than the United States did to aid the men who deposed Sihanouk. A White House spokesman said the U.S. approved a shipment of captured AK–47 assault rifles to Phnom Penh from South Vietnamese stocks on April 15, 1970, nearly a month after the prince's March 18 deposition (U.S. Congress 1974). The PAVN, however, got the war in Cambodia underway in less than two weeks. Lon Nol's information ministry dated the beginning of hostilities to March 29, two days after Vietnamese communist diplomats left Phnom Penh in the wake of a breakdown in talks on the withdrawal of their troops from Cambodia.[10]

Propaganda formed the initial pro-Sihanouk effort. On March 26 the Vietnamese distributed leaflets and broadcast Sihanouk's appeals from sound trucks in rubber plantations near the Vietnamese border (Kirk 1971:112–13). On April 3, American journalist Donald Kirk and a Canadian television team bumped into a Vietnamese unit in a village about seventy miles southeast of Phnom Penh. The village suported Sihanouk's army and displayed a letter in Khmer reporting Sihanouk's Beijing broadcasts and promising a new government for Phnom Penh "under the multinational front and the Cambodian Liberation Front."

BUILDING INSTITUTIONS

The Vietnamese were beginning to build the base of a revolutionary administration. A young Cambodian who escaped from one such village described the process (*New York Times*, July 20, 1970).[11] A twenty-man Vietnamese unit in mufti but fully armed arrived at the village of Prek Ambel about March 28. This "armed propoganda team" claimed to be fighting for Prince Sihanouk. They forced the village chief to sign a pledge of support for them and burned village records. After a brief interlude when Cambodian government troops made a last appearance in the village, the Vietnamese returned and their ranks swelled, eventually reaching about four hundred men with twenty Khmer sympathizers. They taxed rice and sawmill owners in cash and requisitioned food. An interpreter translated pro-

---

[10] Much of this story is in *Documents on Vietcong and North Vietnamese Aggression against Cambodia* (Khmer Republic 1970); particular attention should be given to the Introduction and the subsequent report on the March 16, 1970, Cambodian Government–Vietnamese Embassy meeting to negotiate the withdrawal of Vietnamese communist troops. The report notes that the Vietnamese had accepted Khmer official regret over the sacking of the North Vietnamese and Provisional Revolutionary Government of South Vietnam embassies in Phnom Penh and were working with the Khmer in an ad hoc commission to settle damages. The cause of their withdrawal from Cambodia was therefore rather a matter of changed policy than anger at the March 11 sacking of their missions.

[11] See U.S. Department of State 1971 for a description of the activities and shortcomings of this effort to build a revolutionary administration in Cambodia from the Vietnamese communist viewpoint, as revealed in captured documents.

Sihanouk propaganda and lectured on three occasions. Leaflets called for Cambodia's liberation from the Americans. Six men were murdered: five as alleged government agents and one for fighting with a Cambodian sympathizer. Vietnamese troops recruited five youths of Sino-Vietnamese extraction. Sharp restrictions on movement and travel came into effect.

If this young man had stayed a little longer he would have seen the Vietnamese pick members of the village to serve on hamlet committees of the NUFK. In 1970, the Vietnamese, not the PKK, selected members of most hamlet, village, district, and even sector (province-level) committees. This "confusing" situation prevailed until mid-1971. Naturally, those the Vietnamese drafted to serve "lacked deep political education generally."[12] Many of these new leaders were apparently misfits, perhaps opportunistically motivated to serve the Vietnamese.

Not all institution-building was Vietnamese. In areas near long-implanted Khmer communist groups, Cambodian cadre representing the NUFK conducted elections for hamlet and village chairman by secret ballot. One such election took place in late May 1970 in Kampong Trach district of Kampot province. The village chief then selected his staff (Quinn 1974 and 1976).

The Vietnamese also began the expanded military organization for the NUFK. In a typical case, one defector from Democratic Kampuchea's Revolutionary Army said in 1977 that when the PAVN took over his home district in Preah Vihear Province in June 1970, they selected him as a member of the village guerrilla unit. In January 1971, he transferred to the district militia and later in the year rose to squad leader. In August 1972, following a pattern described by other defectors during the war, he joined the Alliance of Communist Youth of Kampuchea. Thus, by late 1972, he made a transition from Vietnamese-sponsored to PKK-controlled organizations.

TRANSFER OF POWER

Transferring political and military authority from the Vietnamese to Cambodian control took about two years. PKK history complicated this crucial shift because the several thousand Khmer under training in Vietnam had their own chain of command.

CONTROL BY THE IN-COUNTRY FACTION

Pol Pot's group prevailed as the Vietnamese-oriented wing of the political party apparently lost out by mid-1971. In late 1970, several thousand Khmers from the group that had been sixteen years in Vietnam left for the

---

[12] A defector wrote this after rallying to the government in early 1973. Published as Ith Sarin, *Sranaoh Pralung Khmer* (Regrets of a Khmer soul), Phnom Penh, 1973, translated in Carney 1977:54. The Khmer Republic Military Intelligence (1972) also noted the poor quality of many such leaders and consequent political damage they caused.

battlefield in Cambodia. Senior party activist Son Ngoc Minh told these cadres that the party in Cambodia would give them assignments on arrival. He did not accompany them and, according to a defecting member of the group who had joined the PKK in 1957, a number of other senior Khmer officials in Vietnam had broken with Son Ngoc Minh because he was too close to the Vietnamese.[13]

This long association with Vietnam had seriously undermined all the "Hanoi-Khmer" in the eyes of the indigenous movement. Moreover, once the trained troops and cadre left Vietnam and scattered throughout the insurgency in Cambodia, the Vietnam-based chain of command lost its control. These cadres, however, were still regarded as the thin edge of the Vietnamese wedge, and began to be purged starting in late 1973. Pol Pot's government charged in 1978 that Vietnam tried to overthrow the PKK leadership, implying that the Hanoi-Khmer were the traitors.[14] Vietnam retorted that Cambodia murdered the very Khmer whom the PKK had asked Hanoi to train.

Chinese views and their actions form another likely element in the ascendancy of the Pol Pot group. Having welcomed Sihanouk and his Royal Government after the coup, China assumed a direct role in funding and arming the Khmer insurgency. The Chinese would have been intensely atttuned to the possibilities of expanding their own brand of communism to Cambodia and, at the same time, of assuring their geopolitical aim of limiting Vietnamese influence in Southeast Asia. Throwing Chinese weight on the side of the in-country Khmer leadership would have served those objectives. Besides, the Chinese had already met the Pol Pot faction when he visited China in 1965.[15] The Chinese would also have known Phnom Penh–based Khmer radicals from their activities in the Sino-Cambodian Friendship Association, founded in the capital in 1964. Khieu Samphan, for example, was a member of the association's press and periodicals subcommittee.

An institutionalization of the in-country leadership's ascendancy took place in the summer of 1971 with Ieng Sary's transfer to Beijing. He no

[13] *Realites Cambodgiennes* (1971) carry stories on the press conferences held by these two ralliers, Ieng Lim and Keoum Kun. Some of the information comes from conversations U.S. Embassy officers had with the two.

[14] For further discussion of the violent struggle between Khmer and Vietnamese communists, see Chapter 2 by Karl Jackson and Chapter 6 by Kenneth Quinn.—ED.

[15] China in 1965 was in competition with the U.S.S.R. for influence in liberation movements and followed an interventionist policy in party-to-party relations that would not necessarily affect the good state-to-state relations then existing with Sihanouk's Cambodia. The visit would have been kept secret to protect those ties. Teng Hsiao-ping (Deng Xiaoping) and Liu Shao-chi then held appropriate party jobs to have received the Khmer party delegation. No evidence so far links the Cambodian party with China's radicals in the period 1965–1971. I am grateful to my former colleague Galen Fox for much of the above Chinese background. (For more material on possible links between the Khmer Rouge leadership and Maoist radical thought, see Chapter 8 by Kenneth Quinn and Chapter 9 by Karl Jackson.)—ED.

longer needed to monitor activities of the Vietnam-oriented wing of the party in Hanoi. Sihanouk's activities had become far more important to the in-country faction.

OPERATIONAL MILITARY CONTROL

By the end of 1972, the conflict in Cambodia had evolved into full-scale civil war. Foreigners provided the logistics and heavy firepower. NUFK troops emerged from behind the Vietnamese wing in 1972 and by early 1973 operated with minimal Vietnamese support, primarily in heavy weapons units and advisory teams.

The developments contributing to the early emergence of an increasingly independent communist-led army included a major setback to the Republic's forces at PAVN hands. In late October 1971, near Kompong Thom City, PAVN troops hit an overly ambitious Republican military operation from the flanks.[16] By December 1, government forces were falling back in panic with massive casualties and losses of supplies. The defeat crushed the offensive spirit of the Republic's army and demonstrated the military incompetence of then Prime Minister Lon Nol, who actually gave orders for battalion-sized maneuvers during the operation from his residence in Phnom Penh.

In addition, Vietnamese priorities shifted to battlefields at home, forcing their Cambodian proteges to go it alone. In April 1972, PAVN launched the Easter Offensive in South Vietnam. An important effect of the attack in Cambodia was the cutting of Route 1, west of Svay Rieng. That provincial border capital was, therefore, isolated for the rest of the war. In addition, Route 2 through Takeo into Vietnam was definitively severed later in the year, eliminating any chance for road resupply of Repubic forces from stocks in South Vietnam.

MILITARY STRATEGY AND ORGANIZATION

As the PKK military apparatus developed its own strategy, much of the subsequent military history of the war centered on the effort to strangle Phnom Penh. That effort finally succeeded in February 1975 when efforts to push a vital convoy up the Mekong River gauntlet failed, and the United States was forced into a politically and financially expensive airlift of food and munitions to the capital.

Achieving that stranglehold took three years of growth, with the insurgent forces essentially on their own. Expanding in size, the PKK-led army matched the growth with increasingly sophisticated organization and with innovative tactics, especially night operations. Very tough discipline, unknown to most of the Republic's army, and promotion by merit created the

[16] *Nhan Dan* editor Hoang Tung specifically told Chanda (1978) that Vietnamese communist troops defeated this operation and confirmed the extent of the Vietnamese role early in the war.

core of a solid fighting force. By the end of 1970, according to the Khmer Republic's intelligence service, NUFK main forces numbered twelve to fifteen thousand men. They increased to eighteen to twenty-five thousand in November 1971 and to thirty-five to forty thousand by May 1972, at the time they assumed an independent role. From company-level organization before the coup, the army formed into battalions in late 1970 and by May 1972 had reached regimental level. Most of the forty-two confirmed main-force battalions operated independently. However, by late 1971, a "Joint Command Committee" grouped three or four battalions for operational purposes. In May of 1972 regiments were formed with three battalions.

Despite heavy losses from air attacks, 1973 was also a year of growth. Former Khmer Rouge military sources claim that brigades came into existence in 1973, each with fifteen to seventeen battalions. By February 1974, more than 175 battlions existed. The four to six existing brigades unsuccessfully atttacked Phnom Penh in early 1974 before turning their attention to lines of communication and isolating the capital by all but air or river convoys.

When the war ended in April 1975, the army had 230 battalions, including thirty-five to forty regiments and twelve to fourteen brigades. Their units were invariably understrength, especially due to the heavy casualties of the 1974 and 1975 campaigns, but their main forces numbered about fifty-five to sixty thousand troops, including some women's battalions. They showed greater command skills in 1975 by throwing one hundred battalions into the successful assault on Phnom Penh, as against the seventy-five battalions dedicated to the failed affort in the 1973–1974 dry season.[17]

A General Staff existed on paper, with Son Sen as its chief, but a "General Committee of the Battlefield" actually did the operational planning. We can expect that Son Sen had a role in this committee and that Pol Pot, as chairman of the party military committee, also participated. At this point, most troops remained under control of the region. Regional brigades were not given to the party central committee to control until after victory (*Revolutionary Flags* 1975:44).

SUPPLIES

The success of their arms also depended directly on the organization of the population and on a supply of food and weapons. Most of their arms

[17] This discussion is a distillation of the Khmer Republic's Military Intelligence report (1972) previously cited and the "End of Tour Report" of Brigadier General John Cleland, February 1974, and that of then Brigadier General William Palmer, April 1975. The two officers headed the American Military Equipment Delivery Team Cambodia. Their reports were released under the Freedom of Information Act in 1977. In addition, the Party Military Committee Chairman's (Pol Pot's) remarks in *Revolutionary Flags* (1975:50) highlight force structure development into brigades. I have also drawn on the memory of a former regimental political commissar to correct the mistaken American belief that the PKK forces had formed and used the term "division" before the war ended (Carney 1980).

came via the massive Vietnamese logistical network: AK–47 rifles, 12.7mm machine guns, 82mm mortars, Soviet 122mm rockets, and Chinese 107mm rockets. However, in 1973, the PKK troops captured about two dozen American-made 105mm howitzers and many small arms.

Of considerable additional importance to the war effort were the contraband dealings in food, medicine, and gasoline with government regional military administrations, especially the Battambang region, which was spared the war until mid-late 1974 because of its key logistical role as a source of insurgent supplies. Worse, some government officers sold ammunition to the insurgents: a notable case involved mortar rounds sold from Kompong Cham in 1973 shortly before the August 1973 attack that destroyed the town and saw most of its population carried off before relief arrived. Such illegal trade with "Liberated Zones" received impetus from the example of "legal" trade. The Republican government, for example, encouraged rubber trade with insurgent zones in exchange for fuel and other necessities. The rubber gave the Republic its chief source of foreign exchange, apart from foreign donations into a special "Exchange Support Fund."

POPULATION CONTROL

Organizing the population had three aims: to create a base for recruiting troops; to assure food production; and to supply a pool of new party members and cadre. Most information on population organization begins in 1972, when reports began to describe special groups incorporating men, women, youth, and school children. These organizations evolved within the framework of the NUFK. Party associations remained clandestine. The ostensible aim of these mass organizations was the same as that of the NUFK: to return Sihanouk to power, although this shifted beginning in 1973 with increased open denigration of the prince's role. A 1972 description of the organization of recently captured hamlets in Svay Rieng province noted that separate associations grouped children aged 6–14; young single males 14–30; young women; married women; married men; and old people. Each group had specific assigned duties: the old cared for very young children; children joined work brigades. That this structure was prescribed for newly captured hamlets suggests it had been tested in areas longer under PKK control.

During the war, clandestine radio would regularly cite "patriotic associations" whose members served the goals of the NUFK. A complete list appeared in the broadcast reporting the holding of the front's "First National Congress" in July 1973 (FBIS IV, July 24, 1973):

Patriotic Monks of Kampuchea
Patriotic Women of Kampuchea
Patriotic Youth of Kampuchea

Farmers Association of Kampuchea
Workers Union of Kampuchea
Patriotic Intellectuals of Kampuchea
Patriotic Merchants
Patriotic Monks and People from Phnom Penh

To a certain extent this was for external consumption to show the outside world the breadth of support for the revolution. It also served the same purpose internally, but reflected in part the reality of the organization of the hamlets.

For party purposes, members joined "Democratic" rather than patriotic associations. Democratic associations existed for women and peasants, and the Youth Alliance grouped male and female young people (Carney 1977:56). The party controlled these associations and drew their candidate membership from patriotic organizations at hamlet level. The party associations expanded throughout the war. In late 1972, only squad leaders in the army were usually Youth Alliance members. By 1973, defectors or captured noncomissioned officers were invariably in the youth movement. A proper class background became increasingly important for membership in the party organizations. A defector who said he joined the Youth Alliance in 1972, explained that he was dismissed from it two years later when the party reclassified his parents from poor to middle peasants.

The need for supplies and for population control suggests why the July 1973 National Congress included representatives of Patriotic Merchants. Much to the unhappiness of party historians, traders played a key role in the war up until mid-1973. Merchants were allowed to rent out land confiscated from pro-Republican traitors. In addition, traders handled the smuggling from peasants who had not entered the then voluntary collectives. The revolutionary administration permitted traders to profit from the traffic with Republican zones after paying taxes. Rice, cloth, salt, fuel, and machinery were in traders' hands, with the result that "our state was their satellite" (*Revolutionary Flags* 1975:8–9).

COLLECTIVIZATION AND CONTROL

By mid-1973, the party prepared to change this state of affairs with a sweeping restructuring of agricultural and economic activities. Discipline and control over the population had begun to increase beginning in late 1971 when the Khmer negotiated administrative control from the Vietnamese. Kampot, Kandal, and Kompong Thom provinces reported greater restrictions on trade in 1971, including a tax system on trade with outside areas and a pass system controlling freedom of movement. Although private land ownership continued, peasants were encouraged to join cooperatives. As late as the end of 1972, peasants in Kompong Speu could withdraw from cooperatives.

In 1973, however, the party abolished land ownership in the primary liberated areas, ended the traders' role, and enforced complete collectivization. They slowly demonetized the economy with a return to barter, thus strangling traders. The party laid the foundation of the system which would prevail in Pol Pot's Cambodia from 1973–1979.[18]

These decisions had their own logic in terms of both internal and external developments. Increasing party control over the military and civil sides of the NUFK, major changes in the war in Vietnam resulting from the Paris accords, and the realization that the Congressionally mandated end to U.S. Air Force bombing would open up military opportunities, all encouraged the party to press its ultimate political aims.

Moreover, Sihanouk's spring 1973 visit to parts of liberated Cambodia must have brought the party leadership to realize that the prince still had wide popularity. They pushed efforts to denigrate him even harder, with the aim of undercutting his possible future competition with the party. A symbolic reduction in Sihanouk's role occurred in November 1973 with his announcement that all of the Royal Government ministries would be formally transferred from Beijing to Cambodia. The PKK's Chinese allies demonstrated their acceptance of this line by their singular treatment of then army Commander-in-Chief and Deputy Premier Khieu Samphan when he visited Beijing as part of a mission abroad in early 1974.

Vietnamese maneuverings also sparked the PKK to toughen its political line. The party says it rejected Vietnamese advice to negotiate and denied the possibility that the January 27, 1973 Paris accords might apply to Cambodia. After meeting with in-country leaders in Hanoi at Tet in February 1973, Prince Sihanouk reversed his tentative public talk of peace and returned to a harder line. Cambodian party leaders may have feared that the Vietnamese would betray them as part of a resolution of the war in Vietnam. The PKK feared the Vietnamese because in 1954 at Geneva, the Vietnamese agreed to drop the Khmer communist movement. Pol Pot has bitterly recalled this event, noting that the "revolutionary struggle of our people and the war booty that was subsequently captured vanished into thin air through the 1954 Geneva agreement." (Pol Pot 1977:H7).

POPULAR RESPONSE

A Cambodian politician once observed that his people had an infinite capacity to endure misrule. He was speaking about the Khmer Republican regime, but the remark suits PKK rule as well. A source of wonder to

---

[18] On postrevolutionary economic organization see Chapter 2 by Karl Jackson and Chapter 4 by Charles Twining.—ED.

observers of the revolution was the lack of popular reaction to the party's brutal restructuring of Khmer society and remaking of individual personality.

From 1973 onward, life in the liberated zones became increasingly harsh and rigid. Efforts to level the population included confiscation of goods, relocation of villages to new areas, dormitory living in some areas, enforced changes of hairstyle for Moslem women, requirements that all wear black clothing with no jewelry. The PKK instituted a rigid work schedule beginning with early morning rising on command and a hard work regime throughout the day. Deprivation of food rations, arrest, and jail or execution greeted critics of party policy (Quinn 1974).

Given the opportunity, many inhabitants of the PKK zones fled. Some moved into South Vietnam. A major influx entered the Khmer Republic's control at Kompong Thom city beginning late January 1974. By late February, more than thirty thousand refugees had crossed to the government side. They did not come to escape bombing, for American bombing ended August 15, 1973, and the small Khmer Republican Air Force hardly operated in the area. Instead, party forces had left a vacuum in Kompong Thom as they joined other units to attack Phnom Penh. Aggressive Republican patrolling chased off the remaining forces and provided the opportunity for the voluntary flight of refugees. The Western press interviewed these refugees in detail throughout February and March.

Even admitting the difficulty of either flight or resistance by the population of the PKK areas, the question remains: why did the inhabitants of government zones fail to heed the refugees' lessons? Many Western observers in Phnom Penh believed that what was happening under the PKK was due to the "exigencies of war," and that Khmer "common sense" would eventually reassert itself after victory (Woollacott 1977 and Ponchaud 1978). Many Khmer, including most of the prominent Phnom Penh families, had relatives on the other side with Sihanouk, whom they believed would protect them. Others, including senior figures, were intriguing with the party. Overall, a sense of war weariness was obvious to all observers in Phnom Penh. It blinded nearly everyone to the logical extention into peace of PKK policies and actions.

Enthusiasm in Phnom Penh was high when Sihanouk was deposed in 1970, at least partly because this gave Cambodia an opportunity to fight the Vietnamese. The leadership of the March 18 coup included then Premier, Lt. General Lon Nol; acting Head of State Cheng Heng, acting National Assembly head In Tam; and First Deputy Premier, Lt. General Sisowath Sirik Matak. Perhaps their earliest error was to permit a pogrom against Vietnamese residents of Cambodia. Thousands of innocent Vietnamese died before the new leaders brought the troops under control.

It is not surprising that lack of competent leadership was the newly created Republic's fatal flaw. Sihanouk had reserved decision making to himself for more than fifteen years. Anyone who exercised an independent mind threatened the prince and was persecuted or, if powerful enough, sent abroad as an ambassador, as was Sirik Matak. Many were content with a ceremonial role and opportunity to make money through association with Chinese or Vietnamese compradores.

No one would have picked Lon Nol to lead a modern state. He was a traditionalist of considerable prestige in the military and affection popularly. But he could not lead an armed force that increased from a lightly armed ceremonial and civic action body of some thirty thousand men to as many as three hundred thousand nominal soldiers. Unlike the communists, Lon Nol did not understand the need for greater discipline and control of corruption. He and others remained convinced that peasant attachment to Buddhism would defeat communism.

The Phnom Penh leadership also grievously misread the intentions of the United States. They lacked the experience to evaluate international affairs in terms of interests and assumed that an ideologically anticommunist America would support them as a matter of course. They had no idea at first about the need to inform opinion in the United States: Lon Nol's first ambassador to Washington was a kindly, elderly traditionalist who spoke only French. He was not replaced until the spring of 1973 when a bright, tougher, American-educated professional fought an unsuccessful rearguard action against the powerful American antiwar movement.

FOREIGN SUPPORT

The Cambodian war could not be separated from the war in Vietnam. President Richard M. Nixon dispatched American troops in an "incursion" into Cambodia to help "Vietnamization." Lon Nol and his peers embarked on an anti-Vietnamese crusade after they came to power partly because it matched the desires of their people and partly in anticipation of American approbation and assistance.

During the 1970–1975 war in Cambodia, the United States supplied to the Khmer Republic $1.18 billion in military materiel and an additional $503 million in assistance administered by the Agency for International Development. American diplomatic support bolstered the Khmer Republic's international position. The staff of the U.S. Mission in Phnom Penh was limited by Congress to a maximum of two hundred. Forbidden from giving tactical military advice, the U.S. Mission made proposals on structure and organization of government forces.

In direct military activity, U.S. forces began operations over Cambodia on March 18, 1969, with clandestine B–52 strikes under what became code named as "Operation Menu."[19] American tactical and strategic aircraft patrolled and fought in Cambodia until the Congress ordered a bombing halt effective August 15, 1973. American ground troops fought in Cambodia from May 1 to June 30, 1970, in a limited attack against PAVN sanctuaries along the border with Vietnam. Other nations, including Thailand and Indonesia, helped train government forces and, along with their neighbors, Japan, and a number of European states, contributed to the Khmer Republic's economic stability by providing foreign exchange to the Exchange Support Fund.

On the communist side, the U.S.S.R. maintained an embassy in Phnom Penh until October 1973 when they withdrew all but a caretaker staff and tried to open a channel to Sihanouk in Beijing. The 1975 victors, however, kept the Soviet Union frozen out of Cambodia despite occasional moderately friendly exchanges of national day greetings. The Soviet Union hailed the fall of Phnom Penh to the anti–Pol Pot front in 1979.

China had a major role in Cambodia from 1975 to 1979 and was a pillar of foreign support during the war. The People's Republic of China played host to Sihanouk and the Royal Government, furnished money to run its diplomatic apparatus, and provided weapons and ammunition, as did North Korea and Cuba to a much lesser extent (*Far Eastern Economic Review*, December 25, 1971). Vietnam's crucial role has been detailed above.

Norodom Sihanouk's personal ties to leaders of countries in the Non-Aligned Movement greatly facilitated the effort to isolate the Khmer Republic diplomatically. One unsuccessful effort to wrest the U.N. seat from the Republic failed at the U.N. General Assembly in 1973 by the device of deferring the question until the next session. At the 1974 session, the Republic's supporters narrowly managed to preserve its seat and pass a Resolution involving the United Nations in a search for peace in Cambodia. Throughout the war, however, an increasing number of nations formally recognized the Royal Government, as a result of PKK success on the battlefield, Sihanouk's position as titular leader of the insurgency, and partially as a gesture to the Chinese as a potential source of aid. The prince gave the struggle legitimacy in many areas of the world or at least caused the revolution to receive equal consideration with Lon Nol's administration.

Post-Victory

The PKK offensive launched on New Year's Day 1975 succeeded 112 days later in forcing the United States Mission to evacuate the Khmer Republic. What U.S. Ambassador John Gunther Dean had feared, an "uncontrolled solution," was at hand. Five days after the evacuation, on April 17, the

---

[19] For a discussion of the secret bombing of Cambodia, see Shawcross 1976b. The U.S. Administration's view of the bombing is briefly discussed in Nixon 1978:380–82, 384 and Kissinger 1979.

Communist Party of Kampuchea inaugurated a regime that controlled Cambodia until January 7, 1979, when PAVN, the spearhead of a "Solidarity Front for the Salvation of the Kampuchea Nation," seized Phnom Penh.

What happened in Cambodia from 1975 to 1979 beggared the grimmest wartime predictions of opponents of Khmer communism, dismayed socialist sympathizers of the Cambodian revolution, and discredited early apologists for the regime.[20] The brutal implemetation of party policies for changing Cambodian society and personality resulted in hundreds of thousands of deaths through mass executions, disease, malnutrition, privation, or ambush during attempts to flee.

Immediately after they entered the capital, the new authorities ordered the evacuation of Phnom Penh and the other enclaves.[21] They have said they did so to take food-poor urban dwellers to an allegedly food-rich countryside and put war-generated refugees back into food production. Another publicly expressed aim was to neutralize espionage networks. In internal publications the party adds an ideological note. The cities were emptied to ensure victory over the "concept of private property," a concept that had disappeared in the collectivized liberated zones (*Revolutionary Flags* 1975:8–9). At bottom, the party could not tolerate urban centers because it did not have the sophisticated cadre needed to control the towns. In addition, it needed to restore the agriculturally based, war-devastated economy and decided to make everyone a farmer rather than merely let the refugee peasantry return to the land.[22]

The twin dividends of the population policy were the liquidation of potentially dissident former civil and military figures and the dismantling of the Sangha, the Buddist monkhood, the only remaining institution that might have challenged the party by representing the traditional Cambodia.[23] The other pillar of ancient Kampuchea, the monarchy, was discred-

[20] Some representative points of view on the Pol Pot regime would include, on the critical side, Shawcross 1976a and 1978a and Lacouture 1977a, 1977b, and 1978. Sympathetic treatment is in Porter and Hildebrand 1976 and Summers 1975 and 1976. Also of interest is Chomsky and Herman 1977. Works by authors with greater background or better judgment in Cambodian affairs include Ponchaud 1976 and 1978 and Chandler 1977. Since 1979, in any case, few have remained sympathetic to the Democratic Kampuchea regime, as incontrovertible evidence has detailed its brutality, dwarfing even Stalin's excesses.

[21] This was no ad hoc decision, as is shown by the fact that heads of families on the march were required to fill out a preprinted, mimeographed half sheet of paper with data on their home village and members in their party. The form bore the legend "Exodus Reception Committee" (Kenapak tetuol pracheachon chumleas). The refugee who provided a copy of his form after trekking from Phnom Penh to Thailand in a forty-two-day odyssey received the document at a checkpoint on the Prek Kdam ferry point, Route 6, Kompong Cham Province. Pol Pot has said that the decision to evacuate the city was taken in February 1975 (FBIS I, October 3, 1977:A23). Commanders received word of the evacuation about ten days in advance of the fall of Phnom Penh (Carney 1980).

[22] For similar interpretations of the decision to depopulate the cities, see Chapter 2 by Karl Jackson, Chapter 5 by François Ponchaud, and Chapter 6 by Kenneth Quinn.—ED.

[23] Minister of Culture, Information, and Propaganda Mme Yun Yat told visiting Yugoslav journalists in 1978 that "Buddhism is incompatible with the revolution" because it was an

ited first by the Khmer Republic and then by the PKK, who from 1973 increasingly denigrated their ally Sihanouk in political instructions for cadre and to the populace at large. Sihanouk returned to Cambodia in September 1975. After traveling to the U.N. General Assembly that year, he visited friendly nations and arrived back in Phnom Penh in December for what seemed like the rest of his life. In early April 1976, he "retired" to the seclusion of what amounted to house arrest. He dramatically reentered the world scene in early January 1979 with a flight from Phnom Penh to Beijing and on to New York to denounce Vietnamese aggression before the U.N. Security Council.

THE NEWEST CAMBODIA

The Vietnamese-oriented wing of Cambodian communism reentered Cambodian history in 1979. According to their official biographies, some of the leaders of the "Solidarity Front for the Salvation of the Kampuchea Nation" (created December 2, 1978, in Vietnam) joined the revolution in the early 1950s.[24] This timing suggests affiliation with the Vietminh-oriented wing of the Khmer independence movement. Little known to students of Indochina, these men were in junior positions throughout the 1970–1975 war. Some stayed in Vietnam. The old-line leaders have gone: Son Ngoc Minh, according to the Vietnamese, died around 1972 (Chanda 1978).

At this writing in 1988, the question is not completely settled, as troops of the Pol Pot regime fight on, having first retreated to guerrilla base headquarters and then joined an anti-Vietnamese front with Prince Sihanouk and another noncommunist resistance leader. The Vietnamese have tried to protect and nurture the Phnom Penh regime without igniting the traditional Khmer hatred of things Vietnamese, due to their large presence and obvious control over the new authorities. These new authorities owe a tremendous debt to Vietnam for making their accession to power possible.

Conclusion

The leadership of the Communist Party of Kampuchea left the city for the maquis in the 1960s with no possible expectation of early victory. In 1975, they brought an armed peasantry into the cities and moved the urban population to the countryside to begin a restructuring of Cambodian per-

---

instrument of exploitation and that, in any case, Buddhism was dead. See Stanic 1978. Stanic notes later in the article that one former monk disagreed with Yun Yat, saying that Buddhism and communisn had the same humane goals and no great antagonism existed between them.

[24] Brief biographies of nearly all of the Heng Samrin leadership appeared on electoral posters for the May 1, 1981, National Assembly elections. About half of the 148 candidates date to the First Indochina War. Only about two dozen claim early training and residence in Vietnam. Fewer than one hundred of the old Hanoi-Khmer are left, claims one senior figure (Heder, 1981: interview with Hem Samin).

sonality and society according to the PKK's version of communism. A small and active movement, but not a match for government troops in the late 1960s, the PKK radicals needed the massive upheaval of war. The deposition of Sihanouk and the threat to Vietnamese sanctuaries in Cambodia gave them war. The coup ended the repression of the party's powerful nemesis, Norodom Sihanouk. He was not merely neutralized, but came onto their side, where his name served as a major drawing card to expand military strength. The North Vietnamese army gave protection to the fragile but growing Khmer insurgent organization.

The party could not reveal itself during the war. Sihanouk had made communism anathema to the ordinary Khmer. Only in September 1977, after the party had extended its authority over Cambodia did the PKK publicly emerge, partially in response to the tactical requirements of the struggle with Vietnam.

The original party leadership, established under Vietnamese communist aegis, gave way to a mixed group, including many French-trained, highly nationalistic and much younger men and women. They took control of the party by mid-1971 and by 1977 had carried out successive purges, first of Vietnamese-trained cadre and then of putative "traitors" in their ranks. However, the PKK policy of complete independence from Vietnam, as expressed by military initiatives along the border, in the end provoked Vietnam to take drastic actions. The Vietnamese swept the PKK leadership out of Phnom Penh and installed a group of more junior members of the Communist Party of Kampuchea.

Party discipline, military innovation, and competent leadership enabled the PKK to beat a larger but less-motivated and often poorly led army of the Khmer Republic. Refugee tales of harshness in the liberated areas were discounted as exaggerated or written off to expediency. Corruption and incompetence helped generate war weariness in Phnom Penh. Family ties to the insurgents fostered a general belief in the reasonableness of the other side and sapped the popular will to resist the revolution.

The leaders of the Khmer Republic did not understand that American weariness and opposition to the war in Vietnam would limit assistance to them. Neither they nor anyone else could have anticipated that Watergate would cripple the U.S. Administration's ability to deal with Congress in general.

Even in the final weeks of the war, some Cambodians in Phnom Penh expected that the United States would rescue their cause. By then the unrealistic and incompetent Khmer Republican leadership, unable to profit from the bravery of its troops and incapable of instilling a sense of purpose and discipline in its people, had lost the war as surely as the superior discipline and performance of communist troops and cadre had won it. The population of the Republican zone welcomed surrender when April 17, 1975, came.

2. The Ideology of Total Revolution

by Karl D. Jackson

On April 17, 1975 the Khmer Rouge army captured Phnom Penh from the faltering forces of Lon Nol's Khmer Republic. Forty-four months later, the victors were swept from their capital by a Vietnamese invasion force. The intervening period may have witnessed the greatest per capita loss of life in a single nation in the twentieth century. After an initial period in which the facts of the tragedy were denied (Porter and Hildebrand 1976; Dudman 1976; Chomsky and Herman 1979), most of the world loudly condemned those responsible for the unrelieved carnage accompanying the Kampuchean revolution. The entirely justified international revulsion led to a search for the guilty. The post-1975 atrocities were blamed on American policy makers, especially Nixon and Kissinger (Shawcross 1979), or the Kampuchean revolution was denounced as the work of a few homicidal maniacs, particularly Pol Pot, Khieu Samphan, and Ieng Sary.

Unfortunately, neither of these exercises in moral outrage sheds much light on the dynamics of the Kampuchean revolution. Although the massive American bombardment that fell on the Kampuchean people between 1969 and 1973 supplied the insurgents with a potent hate-object and undoubtedly delivered to the revolution thousands of recruits and sympathizers, the American bombing and support of Lon Nol's Khmer Republic do not explain why, after the fighting had ended, the revolutionaries chose to direct the fire of war against their own people, singling out for eradication army officers, bureaucratic functionaries, royalty, Western-educated professionals, landowners, skilled laborers, Buddhist monks, and the Cham and Vietnamese-Khmer ethnic minorities. The bombing and civil strife may partially account for the amount of rage present in Kampuchea in 1975, but they cannot explain the internal objects of this rage or why the purge's inclusiveness increased rather than decreased as post-liberation Democratic Kampuchea became farther removed in time from the civil and international hostilities of the early 1970s. Although revolutions and civil wars have often produced initial waves of vengefulness, the killings in Kampuchea were a systematic program that rose in amplitude throughout the four-year reign of Democratic Kampuchea. (On the killings, see Quinn 1976; Ponchaud 1978; U.S. Department of State 1978; U.K. Government 1978; Per-

AT VARIOUS stages I benefited from the suggestions of several colleagues. Special thanks are due to Gerard Maré, Kenneth Jowitt, Don Van Atta, Aarpn Wildavsky, and David P. Chandler.

37

manent Mission of Canada 1978; Barron and Paul 1977; Boun Sokha 1979: 208–10; and Chapter 6 by Kenneth Quinn.)

Similarly, increased understanding does not result from dismissing the revolution as an insane aberration from an otherwise gentle Khmer culture. First, insanity usually refers to the absence of stable and rational behavior, the inability to connect means with ends over a long period of time. The Khmer revolutionaries, however, who cut their political eyeteeth among the radical Parisian left of the 1950s, explained many of their goals with logic and clarity in their Ph.D. dissertations and sought to make these goals a reality, albeit via extreme means, twenty years later in Kampuchea. Second, the insanity of homicidal maniacs is often visible to the naked eye, and yet none of the observers allowed into Pol Pot's Kampuchea depicted any of its prominent leaders as raving, dishevelled lunatics. In fact, Pol Pot, Khieu Samphan, and Ieng Sary convinced observers that they were serious, thoughtful, and intelligent revolutionaries (see Brown and Kline 1979; Becker 1978a; Dudman 1979; Sihanouk 1980). Third, as we shall see, the goals sought by the Khmer Rouge were far from unique. In fact, these goals mirror the thinking of the radicals surrounding Mao Zedong during the Great Leap Forward and the Cultural Revolution. Finally, the hypothesis that the Khmer revolution resulted from the mental illness of a few individuals is further undermined by the fact that world history is not replete with examples of revolutions organized and carried through on a national scale by certified madmen. Dismissing Hitler or Stalin as mad does not amplify our understanding of the political systems of the Third Reich or Stalinist Russia; understanding Democratic Kampuchea requires close scrutiny of the goals and motives of the revolution. Even though we must deduce these goals from imperfect sources (official broadcasts, speeches, and refugee reports), understanding the political phenomenon of Democratic Kampuchea requires moving beyond moral condemnation to an attempt to envision the kind of Kampuchea that the Khmer Rouge leadership was trying to create. It is only by understanding their ideology and comprehending how these totalitarian goals actually found expression in the context of revolutionary upheaval that we can arrive at a balanced evaluation of one of history's most grisly events. To understand the carnage of Kampuchea one must attempt, albeit tentatively, to discover causes as well as immediate effects.

Having rejected the propositions that explain Kampuchean events as mere by-products of either American foreign policy or the madness of a few Khmer leaders, it is critically important to try to understand Democratic Kampuchea on its own terms by analyzing the goals of its leadership.[1] In

---

[1] For heuristic purposes I have chosen to ignore differences within the Khmer Rouge elite, treating them as fairly homogeneous even though there were obviously substantial discrepancies between Hu Nim and Hon Yuon on one side and Pol Pot on the other. My point here is

essence, the revolution's ideology was dominated by four interrelated themes: (1) total independence and self-reliance; (2) preservation of the dictatorship of the proletariat; (3) total and immediate economic revolution; and (4) complete transformation of Khmer social values. Each theme can be found in both official statements and actual policies during the 1975–1979 period. For the most part, I will not consider whether the Khmer Rouge analysis of the ills of Cambodian society was correct in an empirical sense; after all, the important thing is that this small elite of French-educated intellectuals acted as if their analysis were correct and shaped policies accordingly.

Total Sovereignty and Self-Reliance

Virtually every revolutionary movement emphasizes nationalism. The theme of national sovereignty and self-reliance, however, was raised to extraordinary prominence by the Khmer Rouge, who identified this goal as the number one priority of the Khmer revolution. In his three-hour address on September 27, 1977, Pol Pot stated that correcting Cambodia's relations with the outside world by expelling the imperialists and their economic and cultural influences was the fundamental priority of the party from its inception in 1960. Speaking of the first congress of the Cambodian Communist Party, Pol Pot stated that imperialism was not just a matter of military dominance and government by outsiders. Instead, he perceived even the post-1954 era as a period of foreign cultural and econmic dominance in which Kampuchea was ruthlessly exploited. The nation would only become truly independent when it had cast off all foreign influences and assumed total control of all of its own affairs.

At the time [1960], Cambodia was a satellite of imperialism, of U.S. imperialism in particular. This means that *Cambodia was not independent*, did not enjoy freedom, was in the state of being *half slave and half satellite of imperialism*. . . . Economically, culturally, socially, and even politically speaking, Cambodia was not independent. . . . Thus, though in form it was independent and neutral, in essence it was not, since its economy was under the blanket of U.S. imperialism. . . . a semicolonial country . . . Cambodia was a victim of foreign aggression in the economic, cultural, social, and political and military fields. . . . Imperialism did not commit armed aggression against us, but it launched economic, cultural, social, and military aggression by taking control of everything. (1977:H10, emphasis added)

In reviewing the weaknesses of Kampuchean progressive movements, Pol Pot emphasized the need for indigenous goals and methods. Interestingly, this injunction itself is an echo of the Maoist doctrine of people's war.

---

to establish central tendencies rather than to break the elite into its constituent parts. See Kiernan and Boua 1982:227–317 for an alternative approach.

Now that we have established that we need a line, what kind of a line is it? *A line copied from other people will do no good.* This line should be based on the principles of independence, initiative, self-determination, and self-reliance, which means that we must rely primarily on our own people, our own army, our own revolution and on the actual revolutionary movement of the masses in our own country. (1977: H22, emphasis added)

The Khmer Rouge elite propagated a myth that victory in the civil war was an example of the virtue of near-total self-reliance. Even though Lon Nol's best fighting units were destroyed between 1970 and 1972 in battles with North Vietnamese regulars, official Kampuchean accounts refuse to acknowledge Vietnamese assistance and insist that international assistance was "only supplementary." (See Pol Pot 1977:H22, H27; Sihanouk 1980:25–27.) After the victory, Kampuchean leaders articulated Maoist precepts about the triumph of revolutionary morale over modern materiel.

We must understand the true nature and results of our revolution. When we won the victory over the U.S. imperialists, did we have any planes? . . . We were victorious over the U.S. imperialists . . . leaders of imperialists in the world. Did we have any planes then? No, and we had neither naval vessels nor armored vehicles. . . . This army had no planes, tanks, or artillery pieces and was short of ammunition; however, our fight was crowned with success. (FBIS IV, January 19, 1977:H4)

The concern for complete independence and sovereignty is a theme directed at virtually any state having contact with Kampuchea. Visiting foreign delegations from fraternal countries were always treated to protestations that the people of Democratic Kampuchea wanted only

to live peacefully in their own territory and to entertain friendly relations with all countries in the world, near and far, in conformity with the principles of equality and mutual respect for each other's independence, sovereignty, territorial integrity, noninterference in each other's affairs, nonaggression, and mutual proft. However, our Cambodian people and Cambodian Revolutionary Army will not allow any country to commit acts of violation and aggression or interfere in their internal affairs. (FBIS IV, January 24, 1977:H2)

According to Sihanouk, Khmer Rouge leaders repeatedly expressed anti-Vietnamese racial animosity (Sihanouk 1980:10, 17–18), and this is hardly surprising given the record of Vietnamese encroachment on Cambodian sovereignty. When the French protectorate was declared in 1863, Cambodia was on the verge of being partitioned by Thailand and Vietnam. The southern portion of Vietnam, including the area around Ho Chi Minh City, had been Cambodian territory until it was lost to expanding Vietnamese power during the eighteenth century. More recently, one of the most important reasons for Sihanouk's ouster in March 1970 was his policy of appeasing the Vietnamese communists, allowing them to dominate eastern Cambodia and giving them access to the port of Kompong Som. By 1970, important elements of the Khmer elite felt that this policy had failed and that national sovereignty had been abridged. Furthermore, Vietnamese troops resisted attempts both by Lon Nol and Khmer Rouge troops to reassert sovereignty in eastern Cambodia prior to 1975. Finally, the Khmer Rouge leadership felt betrayed by the Vietnamese as a result of the Paris peace accords of 1973 as well as by Vietnamese attempts to control the flow of Chinese military supplies reaching the Khmer revolutionaries between 1973 and 1975. The Khmer Rouge leadership feared that Cambodia would be colonized by Vietnam after the United States had been expelled from Indochina, and this is why ideological pronouncements placed so much emphasis on sovereignty and complete self-reliance. Their fear of Vietnamese designs led them to reject outright "the special relationship" sought by Vietnam because this would probably have included the right to station Vietnamese troops on Kampuchean soil as well as substantial influence, at the very least, over Kampuchean foreign policy (see FBIS IV, January 3, 1978:H8–10). Hanoi repeatedly stated that it desired the same relationship with Phnom Penh that it had established with Vientiane after 1975 (see FBIS IV, January 9, 1978:H4, K1, 5–6).

Self-reliance and complete independence meant no formal alliances with any outside power. Even the relationship with China received relatively muted reference in Kapmuchean public statements, and nothing analogous to the November 1978 treaty between Vietnam and the Soviet Union was ever signed between Democratic Kampuchea and the People's Republic of China. Immediately after capturing Phnom Penh in 1975, the new leaders publicly disavowed any willingness to permit the kind of military cooperation that Vietnam probably viewed as essential to its national security. Radio Phnom Penh publicly indicated the new regime's divergence from the appeasement policies of Sihanouk's Cambodia by declaring,

The long-standing strategic position of our Cambodia is to firmly pursue the policy of independence, peace, neutrality, and nonalignment. Our people absolutely *will not allow any country to establish military bases in Cambodia* and are firmly and irrevocably opposed to all forms of foreign interference in Cambodia's internal affairs. . . . (FBIS IV, May 6, 1975:H2, emphasis added)

Furthermore, Khmer spokesmen emphasized their divergence from Vietnam's foreign policy by publicly rejecting the concept that the United States should pay war reparations to the new government.

The United States attacked our Cambodia, ravaged and ruined it and plunged our people into the most awful suffering and calamities. But we Cambodians . . . believe that the blood freely shed by our people . . . is priceless and should not be "reimbursed" in dollars or other material "indemnities." . . . Taking everything into account, we prefer to dress our wounds ourselves, however serious they may be. (FBIS IV, May 14, 1975:H5–6)

Fundamentally, the Kampuchean communist elite believed that most, if not all, of Kampuchea's problems stemmed from its subordinate position in an international system controlled by others. They feared not only established enemies such as the United States, Vietnam, and Thailand but also more amorphous kinds of dependency resulting from international economic and cultural relations. The most thorough exposition of Kampuchean concern about the negative impact of international economic integration is found in the doctoral dissertation of Khieu Samphan, who may have been the regime's chief ideologue.

According to Khieu Samphan's thesis, submitted in 1959 for a doctorate in economics at the University of Paris, "international integration . . . is the root cause of underdevelopment of the Khmer economy" (Khieu Samphan 1979:44). The intrusion of the international economy into an essentially precapitalistic Khmer economy in the late nineteenth and early twentieth centuries "diverted development onto its current semicolonial and semifeudal path" (Khieu Samphan 1979:34). This resulted in the wholesale destruction of Cambodian "national crafts" such as silk and cotton weaving because mass-produced foreign goods selling at cheaper prices cut traditional textiles completely out of the market. This destruction of Cambodia's nascent industrial sector forced unemployed laborers back into subsistence agriculture, thereby reinforcing precapitalistic tendencies in the countryside. In addition, the modern urban areas populated by civil servants, military personnel, and commercial traders were an "unproductive investment" because they failed to contribute meaningfully to economic development (Khieu Samphan 1979:42). He dismissed most of the emerging modern economic sector by stating that it was either involved in the production of luxury goods or constituted artificial modernization stimulated by international imports and demands rather than domestic ones. Under this characterization he included water and electricity production, tobacco, rice and alcohol distilleries, breweries, soft drink firms, ice houses, and all commercial firms, transport companies, garages, banks, housing firms, cafes and restaurants (Khieu Samphan 1979:25–29). Virtually the entire urban sector was labeled as unproductive because it was perceived as serving a small minority, the compradore bourgeoisie, and its way of life was being paid for with agricultural exports produced by peasant laborers. Foreign investments in plants that assemble goods with foreign materials or according to foreign designs lived off the artificially created demands of the commercial trading and governmental classes. Prices rose domestically, but none of this resulted in genuine industrialization using local materials and selling to a local mass market.

Each separate component [of Khmer industry] is, rather, part of an ensemble centered abroad. Thus, industrial development is wholly dependent upon outside circumstances over which the Khmer firm has very little control. This is not a situation of interdependence among several autonomous economic ensembles, but one of clear unilateral dependence of components of the Khmer economy upon the ensemble represented by industries from advanced capitalist countries. (Khieu Samphan 1979:28)

Under the circumstances, not even the overseas Chinese became genuinely modern capitalists; instead, they were only the agents of foreign international undertakings (Khieu Samphan 1979:55). American foreign aid, and any foreign aid that encourages commercial development, was labeled as useless. In the words of Khieu Samphan, "It seems clear to us that it is the international integration of the economy which is ultimately responsible for the overdevelopment of 'tertiary' and other unproductive activities. Only the limiting of international integration would allow a genuine reconversion movement to take effect" (1979:55). He alluded to the developmental benefits to be gained from a policy of limited autarky: "No country can industrialize, however, within a system of free trade. The only periods of serious industrialization in underdeveloped countries arose during periods of world war, a time when forced autarky reduced foreign competition and cut off foreign capital" (Khieu Samphan 1979:76). In spite of this statement, Khieu Samphan specifically rejected complete autarky and called for monopolistic state control over exportation of the major commodity crops. He predicted that as a result the state would attain control of "80 percent of all foreign exchange." Importation of consumer goods would be substantially reduced, and the hard currency saved would be shifted to importing capital goods to spur industrialization in a development plan favoring the public sector (Khieu Samphan 1979:80).

If we turn from Khieu Samphan's dissertation to Radio Phnom Penh, similar attitudes are expressed, although in more extreme form. While Khieu Samphan had spoken of largely unintended consequences of international integration leading to Cambodian economic weakness, Radio Phnom Penh asserted,

For centuries, both the imperialists of old and new colonialists tried to keep Cambodia weak and backward. Without the oppression and aggression of the imperialists and old and new colonialists, Cambodia would not have remained an underdeveloped agricultural country but would have changed through a natural historical trend. (FBIS IV, June 11, 1975:H1)

Furthermore, the necessity of economic self-reliance was stressed with regard to international aid. Radio Phnom Penh repeatedly excoriated the Khmer Republic of Lon Nol (and later the Socialist Republic of Vietnam) for accepting public charity, as helpless beggars in the international system.

No one can be as contemptible as the Lon Nol clique . . . which ignominiously lived by begging. . . . Each year it produced nothing. In 1974 alone, the clique had to spend more than 70 billion riel. However, it did not have one cent of its own and depended entirely upon U.S. imperialist aid. Each month the clique begged for everything, including rice, salt, wheat flour, and even firewood. . . .

Entirely different from the traitorous republic, *the new Cambodia is now capable of providing everything for itself.* (FBIS IV, July 1, 1975:H1, emphasis added)

The Khmer Rouge elite felt with extreme sharpness the pangs of cultural imperialism. Referring to the initial period of Cambodian independence after 1954, an official announcement in April 1977 stated:

In this period, *we lost all sense of national soul and identity.* We were completely enslaved by the reactionary, corrupt, and hooligan way of thinking, by the laws, customs, traditions, political, economic, cultural, and social ways and lifestyle, and by the clothing and other behavioral patterns of imperialism, colonialism, and the oppressor classes. (FBIS IV, April 28, 1977:H1, emphasis added)

Just how complete was the Khmer Rouge elite's sense of cultural alienation from the Western accoutrements of the Phnom Penh lifetstyle is indicated by the following official description of what they found when they captured Phnom Penh on April 17, 1975.[2] (In Chapter 5, François Ponchaud identifies alienation from all that was urban and Western as one of the motivational wellsprings driving the Khmer Rouge.)

Upon entering Phnom Penh and other cities, the brother and sister combatants of the revolutionary army . . . sons and daughters of our workers and peasants . . . were taken aback by *the overwhelming unspeakable sight of long-haired men and youngsters wearing bizarre clothes making themselves undistinguishable from the fair sex.* . . . Our traditional mentality, mores, traditions, literature, and arts and culture and tradition were totally destroyed by U.S. imperialism and its stooges. Social entertaining, the tempo and rhythm of music and so forth were all based on U.S. imperialistic patterns. Our people's traditionally clean, sound characteristics and essence were completely absent and abandoned, replaced by *imperialistic pornographic, shameless, perverted, and fanatic traits.* (FBIS IV, May 15, 1975:H4, emphasis added)

There is nothing extraordinary about the Khmer Rouge rhetoric of sovereignty, independence, and self-reliance in political, economic, and cultural affairs. The set of principles integrating dependency theory with Marxism has become fairly standard among aspiring radical elites in the Third World. (For example, see Amin 1974, 1976, 1977.) The truly extraordinary aspect of the Khmer revolution is the doctrinaire literalism with which they applied these abstract principles without regard for the awesome costs to Cambodia in terms of diplomatic isolation, economic devastation, and massive human suffering. Other elites have talked long and loud on these subjects while out of power but have implemented their rhetoric very selectively

---

[2] In Chapter 5, François Ponchaud identifies alienation from all that was urban and Western as one of the motivational wellsprings driving the Khmer Rouge.

once sobered by the responsibilities of power. The scope and extreme literalism with which the Khmer Rouge elite pursued the ends of complete sovereignty and self-reliance are what make them virtually unique.

The outside world after April 17, 1975, reacted with a combination of shock and incredulity when the revolutionary elite emptied its cities, destroyed Western consumer goods, burned books and libraries, partially liquidated its Westernized elite, severed most of its diplomatic relations, abolished money, markets, and foreign exchange, established state control over all foreign and domestic trade, and cut almost all trade links with the outside world. Yet most of these deplorable acts can be understood, at least in part, if one assumes that the Khmer revolutionaries were trying to establish total sovereignty and self-reliance in the cultural, economic, and political realms.

In international affairs, application of the doctrine of self-reliance led the revolutionaries to seal Cambodia off from all but a very few close allies, primarily the People's Republic of China and the People's Republic of North Korea. With the exception of a few other socialist countries, all embassies were closed and their personnel unceremoniously trucked out of the country (see Ponchaud 1978). Even those countries allowed to establish embassies found their diplomatic personnel virtual prisoners, with no informal contacts permitted with surrounding Cambodians.

Diplomatic observers, both East and West, wondered in 1977 whether Kampuchean foreign affairs were being run by rational individuals, because Kampuchean military units were involved in serious border skirmishes with Laos, Thailand, and Vietnam. Although in late 1975 Kampuchea, with approximately seven million inhabitants, could hardly hope to win a major engagement with Vietnam, it adopted a position of intransigence vis-à-vis any form of an Indochina Federation, sent its troops on vengeance missions into Vietnam whenever it perceived its borders had been violated or threatened, and facilitated nightly raids against Thai villages. Furthermore, since 1973 the Khmer Rouge had sought to liquidate Khmer communist cadres trained by the Vietnamese and expel or liquidate individuals of Vietnamese ethnic background regardless of their locations in Kampuchea (see Sihanouk 1980 and Quinn 1976). Sihanouk, in his position as a Khmer Rouge ally, was privy to this process.

After I left the liberated zone [April 1973] and returned to Peking, the Khmer Rouge decided to make the Viets feel much less at home. They arbitrarily regrouped the Vietnamese population of each *khum* [commune], each *srok* [district] into cooperatives that quickly turned into concentration camps. . . .

That is how, starting in 1973, the Khmer Rouge emptied out Tonle Sap (Great Lake), our lakes, and our rivers of their Vietnamese inhabitants. . . . In 1969 there were more than 400,000 ethnic Vietnamese in Kampuchea. After their coup, Lon Nol and his supporters eliminated or banished to South Vietnam at least half of these Yuons [a derogatory word in the Khmer language for referring to Vietnamese]. The Khmer Rouge finished the job between 1973 and 1975, as I had it from Khieu Samphan. (Sihanouk 1980:21–22)

The number one priority of the regime was to guard jealously its territorial integrity. When this priority is combined with traditional hatred of all Vietnamese[3] and fear of being colonized by the Vietnamese communists, the only logical element lacking is some sense of how seven million Khmers were to defeat forty-eight million well-armed Vietnamese.

The policy of the aggressive reaction or overreaction to Vietnamese provocations has been described as "the small bristly dog gambit" (Pike 1978:3,4), in which the much weaker power protests itself by punishing even small infractions with extreme reactions.[4] This strategy militates against any compromise and almost certainly leads to escalation if the stronger military power persists in its goals. The Khmer Rouge leadership actually seems to have believed that they had defeated the United States and Lon Nol without significant external assistance. This belief, when combined with adherence to the Maoist belief in the ultimate superiority of ardor over armament, led to the Khmer Rouge boldness in the face of Vietnamese designs (see Sihanouk 1980:85, 92). Sihanouk's testimony as an inside observer convinced him that the Khmer Rouge actually believed that Kampuchea could defeat Vietnam in a direct conflict.

Son Sen, Vice Prime Minister in Charge of National Defense, claimed his glorious "revolutionary army of Kampuchea" felt it could make quick work of General Giap's army, not to mention Kukrit Promoj and Kriangsak Chamanond's much less imposing Thai Army. [Sihanouk 1980:38] In a late 1978 press conference, Pol Pot mentioned in all seriousness the "probability" that Czechoslovakian, Hungarian, Bulgarian, and East German troops would be sent to the rescue of the Vietnamese, Soviet, and Cuban regiments Kampuchea had "put to flight." Pol Pot unblinkingly stated that the Vietnamese were too weak to stand up to the Kampuchean Revolutionary Army "all by themselves." (Sihanouk 1980:51)

The forced evacuation of Phnom Penh and the other major cities immediately after the victory of April 17, 1975, was for the outside world the single most inexplicable event of the Cambodian revolution. Understanding this policy requires reference to the paramount goals of political, economic, and cultural self-reliance. For the Khmer Rouge, the cities were centers of foreign domination.[5] Before the civil war swelled the urban populations

---

[3] On anti-Vietnamese attitudes, see Chapter 5, pp. 153–54, by François Ponchaud.

[4] The small bristly dog gambit may also have been seen as Cambodia's only alternative. The leadership in Hanoi since the 1930s had sought to control all of Indochina. The Khmer leaders may have reasoned that immediate, high-level military confrontation was preferable to slow stangulation by a powerful and persistent Vietnam. Also, the Khmer Rouge may have calculated that Vietnam did not want direct control badly enough to become involved in open, large-scale warfare; the Khmer strategy of raising the ante from mere subversion to open war may have been meant to deter Vietnam from seeking its long-term goals at least for the time being.

[5] On Khmer Rouge resentment of foreign dominated urban areas, see Chapter 5 by François Ponchaud.

with Khmer refugees, the cities were dominated by very large Vietnamese-Khmer and Sino-Khmer bureaucratic and commercial populations (see Chapter 5 by François Ponchaud). Furthermore the cities were dominated by the institutions that had opposed the revolution: the monarchy, the army, the foreign embassies, the compradore bourgeoisie. Finally, the cities, and especially Phnom Penh, were the seat of the "decadent, perverted social culture" that had been inflicted upon Cambodian youth and the masses in general by "U.S. imperialism and the Lon Nol clique" (FBIS IV, July 21, 1975:H2).

Given the fear of continued foreign subversion, the most direct way to disorganize the potential opposition was to drive the city population into the countryside where it could be reorganized into more readily controlled units. In one fell swoop, this policy nationalized the property of the foreign minorities that had previously dominated Khmer urban life. It also gave the Vietnamese-Khmer a powerful incentive to flee to Vietnam, which they did by the tens of thousands. Pol Pot's own description of the decision to evacuate the cities designates national security in the face of "spy rings," "imperialist plots," "land grabbing," and "enemies of all stripes" as the sole explanation.[6]

One of the important factors for Cambodia's success after April 1975 is the evacuation of the city residents to the countryside. This was decided before victory was won, that is, in February 1975, *because we knew that before smashing all sorts of enemy spy organizations, our strength was not strong enough to defend the revolutionary regime.* Judging from the struggles waged from 1976 and 1977, the enemy's secret agent network lying low in our country was very massive and complicated. But when we crushed them, it was difficult for them to stage a comeback. Their forces were scattered in various cooperatives which are in our own grip. . . . In spite of a number of border clashes, it is impossible for them to attack and occupy Cambodia from outside. (FBIS IV, October 4, 1977:A23, emphasis added)

In addition to neutralizing externally influenced populations, evacuating the cities dealt an immediate coup de grace to Cambodian involvement in the system of international commerce that Khieu Samphan had identified as the root cause of Cambodia's underdevelopment. This initial policy of autarky (1975–1976) was expected to encourage the rebirth of the crafts and nascent industrial establishments that had been put out of business by foreign manufactured goods. Self-reliance was expected to stimulate long-dormant sectors of the economy. In addition, the manufacturing plants that existed in prerevolutionary Cambodia were to be transformed into enterprises using local raw materials to manufacture simple plows and other farm

[6] Of course, the Vietnamese reaction to seeing their Cambodian allies liquidated and Vietnamese residents driven from Cambodia was to engage in anti–Pol Pot subversive activity. The Vietnamese from 1973 onward actively sought to dislodge the virulently anti-Vietnamese leadership of the Khmer Rouge (see Sihanouk 1980:22–23; Boun Sokha 1979; and Chapter 6 by Kenneth Quinn).

implements (FBIS IV, April 20, 1977:H4–6). Finally, the pursuit of economic self-reliance dictated a forced-draft effort in rice production and irrigation. "If we have rice we can have everything" was the major economic slogan of the regime, and evacuating the cities provided the regime with the man-power believed necessary for the rapid expansion of land under cultivation and for the vast irrigation projects begun throughout the country after the victory of 1975.[7]

The Khmer Rouge publicly spurned foreign aid even though they surrep-titiously accepted Chinese aid and a number of Chinese advisors. The goal of complete national self-reliance was applied in rejecting all offers of non-communist aid regardless of the immediate tragic consequences for the Cambodian population. All foreign medical supplies ceased being imported in 1975, and a planeload of French medical supplies standing by in Bangkok in late April 1975 was not permitted to fly to Phnom Penh (Ponchaud 1978:35). The new government instead promoted, in Maoist fashion, the use of medicinal compounds produced from local herbs and other sub-stances. The raging epidemics of 1975 and 1976 stand in mute testimony to the ineffectiveness of this aspect of self-reliance. In November 1976, in one of its first international trading transactions, the Kampuchean government was forced by dire circumstances to purchase $450,000 worth of DDT for its anti-malarial campaign.

In the same way that local medicines were supposed to take care of mas-sive medical problems without outside help, immediate self-reliance was applied to rice production. Although the civil war was not concluded until halfway through the year and although the rice shortage was thought (es-pecially by outsiders) to be one of the main reasons for evacuating Phnom Penh, the government is not known to have imported rice, and the Kam-puchean ambassador to Beijing explicitly refused a Canadian offer of wheat that would have alleviated famine conditions.[8] Because of its doctrinaire application of the concept of self-reliance, very substantial numbers of its people perished from lack of food. Acceptance of international assistance, especially from the West, would have been an admission of Lon Nol-like weakness, and this was an unacceptable ideological price for the Kampu-chean elite to pay. What follows is a Khmer Rouge official's explanation of the reluctance to accept food aid in spite of the internal starvation.

[7] The Cultural Revolution in China was also characterized by the massive transfer of popu-lation from the city to the countryside to stimulate rural development and remove troublesome elements from the cities. During this period a total of thirty million people had been sent from the cities of China (see Hinton 1973:71). Absent from the Cultural Revolution, however, was the blanket moral rejection of all individuals who had contact with urban life.

[8] Charles Twining in Chapter 4, pp. 115–16, concludes that sufficient rice stocks existed in Phnom Penh to feed the city for at least several weeks and that international food aid was available from multiple sources.

Angkar does not want to hear anything about foreign help since our fundamental principle consists in being masters of our destiny and to rely on our own strengths, on our own resources. If we liberated our country, it is precisely because it had not been independent for centuries. And why have we lost our independence and dignity? It is because we have been accustomed to relying only on others. You have to know that foreigners never give something for nothing. *Being for once truly independent, we are not going to barter our freedom for continued aid.* There are countries who are eternally dependent on giveaways. As for Cambodia, it has chosen its path. We have fixed for ourselves as a primary task to reach food self-sufficiency in three years. But we have gone ahead of the plan. *Starting from this year [1977], people no longer die of hunger.* And, several years from now we shall attain abundance. (Quoted by Boun Sokha 1979:198, emphasis added)

In the area of culture, refusal to acknowledge dependence upon the outside world, and especially the West, was striking. The central bank, symbolizing Cambodia's link with the international economic system, was intentionally demolished with explosives and the bank notes were allowed to flutter through the deserted streets of the capital city. The Roman Catholic cathedral in Phnom Penh was not blown apart like the national bank; it was disassembled stone by stone until no trace whatever remained of the most prominent Western religious edifice in the country.[9] (See Chapter 7 by David Hawk for a photograph of the entirely empty cathedral site.) Although the top of the revolutionary elite accepted many of the most radical Maoist nostrums, fear of dependency or, at least the appearance of dependency, on any imported ideology may have been the reason why the announcement of the Kampuchean Communist Party's existence was delayed until September 1977.

In Cambodia, the first years of peace must have been almost indistinguishable from war, a living hell in which millions were driven from the cities, large numbers were executed, and famine stalked the land. Yet, Pol Pot characterized this period of suffering as the greatest period in the last two thousand years simply because Kampuchea had achieved total independence and self-reliance: ". . . This is as great as it is unprecedented in our country's two-thousand-year history. We are independent politically, economically, militarily, culturally, in literature and art and other fields. This is the best part of our independence and sovereignty." (1977:H27).

Preservation of the Dictatorship of the Proletariat

The development of the Khmer Rouge between 1970 and 1979 falls into two distinct stages: the national front stage, from March 1970 to the capture of Phnom Penh in April 1975, and the stage of power consolidation, from

[9] The driving motivation here may have been the hatred of the Vietnamese, because most Roman Catholics in Cambodia were Vietnamese (Steinberg 1959:59).

April 1975 to the fall of Phnom Penh to the Vietnamese in January 1979. When the Khmer Rouge were mobilizing their forces to oust the Lon Nol government they divided Cambodian society "into five distinct classes: the working class, the peasant class, the bourgeoisie, the capitalist class, and the feudal class" (Pol Pot 1977:H11). They concentrated their attack "against imperialism and the feudal landowner class" and sought to win over all other groups including "the workers, peasants, bourgeoisie, intellectuals, students, national capitalists, Buddhist monks and patriotic and progressive personalities" (Pol Pot 1977:H11). The revolution, during its drive on Phnom Penh, addressed direct appeals to Lon Nol's soldiers, bureaucratic functionaries, and the Buddhists' hierarchy, among others. Even though the Khmer Rouge were liquidating pro-Sihanouk and pro-Vietnamese within their own ranks, publicly they sought to ride into power on a wave of national unity and reconciliation.

Under the most favorable circumstances of the Cambodian revolution which has reached its final stage of victory, the Cambodian nation and people, the NUFC, RGNUC and CPNLAF have *decided to pardon low- or high-ranking fraternal government employees from all the services, all categories of officers, servicemen, politicians, and personalities, and all small or high-level members of all agencies of the traitors' regime.* Only the seven traitorous chieftains are to be punished by our Cambodian nation and people, our NUFC, RGNUC and CPNLAF for their extremely antinational, archfascist and archdecadent crimes. (FBIS IV, March 7, 1975:H4, emphasis added)

Internally, we hold the great unity of the entire people irrespective of social classes, political tendencies, religious beliefs and regardless of their past . . . except for the seven traitors Lon Nol, Sirik Matak, Son Ngoc Thanh, Cheng Heng, In Tam, Lon Boret, and Sosthene Fernandez. (FBIS IV, March 12, 1975:H3)

As Pol Pot himself later admitted, these alliances were tactical, and after the capture of Phnom Penh in April 1975, the Khmer Rouge immediately adopted a very exclusive definition of what constituted a loyal Cambodian, that is, a Cambodian whose past activities entitled him to full-fledged participation in the new Cambodia. Within days of the capture of the capital, many who were supposed to have been amnestied were rounded up for execution, and by the time of the first anniversary in April 1976, "the people" in Khieu Samphan's speech included only "workers and peasants and the revolutionary army" (FBIS IV, April 16, 1976: H1–8; see also, Hu Nim's speech for a similar exclusive formulation, FBIS IV April 16, 1976:H8–10). Roughly a year later, Pol Pot's monumental history of the Kampuchean communist movement was addressed exclusively to "representatives of the collective peasants," "representatives of all branches of our Revolutionary Army," "representatives of all government ministries and departments," and "all our masses of collective workers" (Pol Pot 1977:H1).[10]

[10] From Carney's analysis it is clear that the party's definition of what constituted an ac-

This alteration of verbal formula had more than linguistic implications. Revolutions are violent sociopolitical processes in which an existing order is overthrown, and in some cases utterly destroyed and displaced by a new social, economic, and political order. What occurred between 1970 and 1975 was the seizure of state power by an armed minority of not more than sixty thousand combatants who immediately launched a total revolution utterly despoiling the old elite and reserving for themselves the paramount positions of power in the transformed social, economic, and political system. What is distinctive about the Khmer Rouge is not that they reserved positions of power for themselves and decreased the power of the former elite; what is distinctive is that they entered Phnom Penh with a plan for forthrightly exterminating entire social categories and destroying all of the institutions of pre-1970 Cambodian society. The decision to evacuate all cities was made at the national party congress in February 1975. Outside of each city the evacuees were sorted into class categories that determined relative harshness of individual treatment (see note 21 of Chapter 1 by Timothy Carney; Ponchaud 1978; Barron and Paul 1977; U.S. Department of State 1978; Swain 1976).

Rather than running the state with existing personnel for at least a transition period (as Lenin had done), the Khmer Rouge immediately applied massive doses of terror to atomize or eliminate all potential competitors and institute a nonbureaucratic, decentralized, radically Maoist state controlled by a small army and party for the benefit of the lowest status members of the old society, namely the poor peasants. The Khmer Rouge sought to change entirely the pattern of Kampuchean history that had previously been dominated by clique-ridden, semibureaucratic states, an amalgam of the Indianized kingdoms of the first millenium and the colonial state of the late nineteenth and early twentieth centuries. Terror was the chief instrument of the dictatorship of the proletariat which sought, as quickly as possible, to liquidate: all officers, as well as most noncommissioned officers, and many enlisted men in Lon Nol's army; many bureaucrats of the ancien régime; all royalty (with the exception of Sihanouk); large and medium size landowners; those engaged in commerical enterprise (primarily the Vietnamese-Khmers and Sino-Khmers); skilled laborers who had worked in factories in the Lon Nol area; many Western-educated professionals; all Khmer Moslems (Chams); and many Buddhist monks.[11] In several of these instances, the intent and practice seems to have been to eliminate

---

ceptable social background varied with the party's external circumstances. United Front tactics were utilized before the April 17, 1975, victory as well as after they were expelled from Phnom Penh by the Vietnamese. The most restrictive definitions of acceptability were in the 1975–early 1978 period when they felt most free to reject all who did not have unblemished lower-class backgrounds. See Chapter 3 by Timothy Carney.

[11] In Chapter 5, pp. 164–65, François Ponchaud mentions the degree to which guilt by family association is a prerevolutionary pattern of traditional Cambodia.

whole social categories, whereas in others exceptions were made. For instance, although the top of the Buddhist hierarchy was marked for immediate extinction, *bonzes* (Buddhist monks) who were willing to forsake their traditional roles and return to the work force found a place in the new society.

All revolutions elevate certain groups at the expense of others. To the extent that millions of persons lost their positions, their land, their homes, and their lives, this allowed relative upward mobility for a substantial segment of the remaining population. Although conditions varied according to region, the population of Democratic Kampuchea was divided into three categories, depending upon class background and political past: individuals with full rights (*penh sith*), those who were candidates for full rights (*triem*), and those who had no rights whatever (*bannheu*) (Heder 1980:1–4; see Chapter 3 by Timothy Carney for a more extensive discussion of class distinctions). The new privileged group received full food rations and were allowed to join any organization, including the party and the army. Almost all of the *penh sith* had joined the revolution at an early stage and came from the poorest, most uneducated segments of the rural population. Those with candidate status (*triem*) were second in line for rice rations and were allowed to hold minor political offices. Most of these were drawn from the rural population, but as time went on some of the poor who had been forced from the cities in April 1975 were promoted to candidate status. The lowest category, the *bannheu* or depositees, had no rights whatever, not even the right to food. These were former landowners, army officers, bureaucrats, teachers, merchants, and urban residents (Heder 1980a). Most individuals targeted for liquidation in Democratic Kampuchea fell into this category. Those not immediatley executed received a near-starvation diet and were expected to work to the point of exhaustion. The urban poor were an initial target of Khmer Rouge hostility because they had been "contaminated" by the cities and many had fled to the cities rather than rallying to the revolution during the civil war; therefore, in Khmer Rouge eyes they deserved to be "quarantined" until they had proven their loyalty to the revolution (Boun Sokha 1979:199–200; see also, François Ponchaud's description of Khmer Rouge antagonism toward the urban population in Chapter 5).

It would be impossible to estimate with any assurance the sizes of these three status categories, but it is probable that the vast majority of the population were either candidates or depositees and that those with full rights must have constituted a small portion, undoubtedly less than 15 percent of the total population.[12]

[12] The only statistical estimates are of unknown validity. Three quarters of the million urbanites may have died from execution, starvation, or disease during the first year of the regime. By 1977, according to this source, there were 1.9 million revolutionary peasants, a half million former urbanites undergoing purification, and 1.4 million nonrevolutionary peasants

What remains equally unclear is just how much transfer of wealth actually occurred. Most of the wealth of Cambodia was in the cities that the regime evacuated; conspicuous consumption and private property were forbidden; and in a society cut off from the outside world and beset by endemic shortages and raging epidemics, it is difficult to conceive of a monetary meaning for economic mobility. However, the regime itself over radio Phnom Penh talked specifically about rewarding

our poor farmers [who] sent their beloved sons and daughters to the revolutionary organization.

In our present revolutionary era *their children are respected*, cared for, and educated politically, morally, and organizationally. Now their children have been *educated, given a role to play*, have *all sorts of job opportunities* in this revolutionary society, and are respected as people. Some of them are in the army, [word indistinct], in transport units and production teams, and some of them function as economic cadres and so forth. This is quite a change for our rice farmers who were oppressed and scorned during the preliberation period. For this reason they are grateful to the revolutionary organization and will continue to follow the revolution forever. (FBIS IV, June 9, 1975:H4, emphasis added)

Given the relatively meager supply of material inducements available in Cambodia at the end of the fighting, most of the benefits collected by the winners of the civil war were probably in the form of higher social and political status and good economic prospects for the future after Cambodia had achieved its revolutionary breakthrough by becoming a modern agricultural and industrial country.

Regarding political privileges, an official announcement made it clear that candidates for the People's Assembly elections in March 1976 had to "have a good record of revolutionary struggle for national and people's liberation" (FBIS IV, March 18, 1976:H1). This probably meant that only veterans of the armed struggle could stand for election. Antigovernment guerrillas operating inside Cambodia at the time reported that individuals who had been living in Lon Nol areas at the end of the revolution, the so-called new people, were not allowed to vote (see FBIS IV, April 30, 1976:H3). Running for high office and other privileges were reserved for "the male and female combatants," "the sons and daughters of the poor peasants," the veterans of the revolution that Radio Phnom Penh constantly lauded. The core of this group were members of the regular armed forces. The army was the premier organization of the new society at least until the existence of the communist party was revealed in September 1977.[13] Having destroyed the

---

who had been deported from the cities (see Boun Sokha 1979:208–10). This leaves a population of only four million by 1977, which seems low.

[13] Civil servants of the new regime were almost never mentioned by Radio Phnom Penh, whereas the activities of male and female combatants were described frequently, and those of

old army as well as the bureaucracy, the revolutionary army was required to serve a double function—protecting national security and supervising economic recovery, reorganization, and growth. (See Chapter 3 by Timothy Carney for a detailed analysis of the organizational structure of Democratic Kampuchea.)

As Radio Phnom Penh stated,

From our revolutionary army's bloody sacrifice and great revolutionary heroism over the past five years of struggle was born the historic, brand new Cambodia. It has been three months since our people and revolutionary army completely liberated Phnom Penh and the rest of the country. In that time our revolutionary army has launched a ceaseless offensive to defend the beloved fatherland's independence, peace, neutrality, sovereignty, democracy, and territorial integrity on the one hand and on the other to repair communications lines, clean up cities, restore factories, revive the economy, resolve the water conservancy problem, increase production, and grow the rainy season rice crop with soaring enthusiasm.

Our revolutionary fighters on every front are engaged in a seething, unsparing drive to fulfill their revolutionary duties without even resting from the struggle to liberate the capital. The combatants and cadres have swept and cleaned carcasses left behind by U.S. imperialism and the Lon Nol clique. They have helped to gradually return factories to their normal operation. They have repaired wharves and ports, railway stations and railroads. . . .

Most of the combatants and cadres of both sexes are now enthusiastically taking part in the drive to build dams and grow rice. (FBIS IV, July 22, 1975:H4)

At the local level, because the Khmer Rouge possessed guns, this gave them the power of life and death over individuals who had been their social, economic, and political superiors before the revolution. The possession of absolute power, especially over the depositees, in and of itself was probably perceived by some as a very substantial, albeit nonmaterial, reward for serving Angkar (the Revolutionary Organization). Khmer Rouge soldiers ordered about and terrorized individuals who had formerly been respected because of age, wealth, office, Western learning, or adherence to the way of Buddha, and this new-found power must have been intoxicating for many Khmer Rouge who had been poor, illiterate villagers before the revolution and remained scarcely more than children in age even as they wielded absolute power over their elders.

Although power and privilege may explain why rank and file Khmer Rouge at the local level carried out their orders and in so doing made the revolution, what remains unexplained is why the Khmer Rouge elite thought it advisable to institute such draconian measures against their own people. The most important motive for the elite was a sincere desire to create a new type of egalitarian revolution the likes of which the world had

---

cadres less frequently. This is because there were relatively few civil servants, as indicated by the fact that foreign visitors to Phnom Penh found the ministries empty or nearly empty.

never witnessed, one that would raise up the poor to positions of genuine prominence rather than merely elevate the middle class representatives of the poor and thereby create a "new class." "The essence of our revolution is to crush the oppressor classes. . . . The party should serve and represent the true interest of the poor classes" (Pol Pot 1977:H5).

The passionate desire to increase the stature of the downtrodden probably stemmed less from inequality at the village level, where land was still relatively plentiful[14] and more from the experience of Khmer Rouge leaders with the gross inequities of urban life, especially in Phnom Penh. The sense of outrage concerning urban inequality and corruption is particularly evident in the Khmer Rouge portrait of the final days of the Lon Nol regime.

. . . the enemy-held areas, such as Phnom Penh, were turned into havens of crime where the most perverse, corrupt practices abounded to an extent never experienced before in Cambodian society. While the poor people, men and women, the young and old alike, were dying from hunger or from assassination, detention, and the most savage tortures, the bigshot traitors and their henchmen indulged themselves in the most arrogantly luxurious life. . . . the people were left to live and die in the mud and mire in sickness and misery. By contrast, the restaurants, dancing halls, bars and night clubs—the most corrupt places—boomed and were teeming with prostitutes, CIA agents and the human liver-eating "Mike Force" soldiers. (FBIS IV, June 25, 1975:H2)

The Khmer Rouge sought to eliminate inequalities in a permanent fashion by exterminating individuals who possessed middle or high status under the old regime by dint of wealth, education, occupation, or lineage. Emptying the cities, eliminating many depositees, abolishing money and markets, and adhering to a doctrine of permanent class struggle between the *penh sith* and *bannheu* allowed the Khmer Rouge leadership to create almost overnight their vision of an egalitarian society.

The new Cambodian society is a community in which man is no longer exploited by man. It is a community without oppressed or oppressors. It is an equal society where there are no rich or poor and all are equal and harmoniously united in the common effort to increase production, defend, and build their beloved fatherland. (FBIS IV, July 21, 1975:H3)

At present, all of us are equal. There are no rich nor poor classes. Everybody works, either in the fields or in the factories. It is thus evident that total equality exists in

[14] Although Pol Pot (1977) contends that the peasants were exploited and oppressed to an inordinate degree, the average size of landholdings and the availability of new land indicate a relatively prosperous Cambodian peasantry, at least before 1970, when compared with rural Java or the Mekong Delta before the land-to-the-tiller program (see Jackson 1980:46–52 and Callison 1981). On landholding and the absence of sharply felt distinctions in Cambodia before 1970, see Steinberg 1959:90–94; Ebihara 1964:100–104; Lacoutre 1978; Amin 1977:148; and Hou Yuoh 1955). For a contrasting interpretation of landholding and peasant welfare, see Kiernan and Boua 1982.

our equal, equitable and democratic Cambodian society which is endowed with harmony and happiness.[15] (FBIS IV, January 6, 1976:H7)

A second motive articulated by the revolutionaries was their moral revulsion toward the old ruling elite and its institutions. Those who had supported Sihanouk (before 1970) and Lon Nol (1970–1975) were *not* perceived as fellow countrymen who had made mistakes and could be remolded to perform useful functions in the new society. Instead, the new elite portrayed its opponents as counterrevolutionaries who were unfit to live in Cambodia: "These counterrevolutionary elements which betray and try to sabotage the revolution *are not to be regarded as being our people.* They are to be regarded as enemies of Democratic Cambodia, of the Cambodian revolution, and of the Cambodian people" (Pol Pot 1977:H28, emphasis added). Essentially the social, economic, and political elite of precommunist Phnom Penh was perceived as totally corrupt and debauched beyond redemption. Hence, "the oppressive, blood-sucking and bone-gnawing regime of the traitorous Lon Nol clique" (FBIS IV, May 23, 1975:H3) had to be destroyed utterly in order for a new revolutionary Cambodia to be born. Official announcements openly admitted that the leaders of the Lon Nol government and an unspecified number of supporters had been eliminated: "As for the archcorrupt, archfascist regime and the seven traitors, as well as the handful of their insignificant hencemen, they were forever thrown into the trashcan of history by our people and revolutionary army. *None of them can any longer raise his head*" (FBIS IV, January 7, 1976:H1, emphasis added).

The goal of establishing a state ruled by and for its poorest elements is by no means unique. Likewise, moral revulsion toward defeated foes is commonplace in history. What is unusual in the Cambodian instance is the scope and duration of the violence. To explain this we must look beyond ideology, that is, beyond the goals of the revolutionaries, to their perception of the immediate revolutionary situation and the ways in which circumstances at the advent of their power shaped the policy of eradicating all potential foes. It is the combination of the sectarian drive to establish a perfect dictatorship of the proletarit and the preception that the revolution's grip was constantly threatened from within and without that led to the adoption of a strategy of revolution by eradication. Not only were the goals of the revolutionaries extreme, given the Cambodian stage of social and economic development, but in addition the revolutionaries lived in constant fear that

---

[15] This vision of equality obviously viewed the world through a lens that distorted reality to a substantial degree. First, the depositees did not even have the right to food. Second, refugees reported with bitter irony that working villagers were given a bare minimum of food, whereas the Khmer Rouge supervisors were given much more food. Reports also indicate that the Khmer Rouge combantants and cadres married whomever they chose. They explained that "everyone is in the Organization" but they were "the sons of the Organization" and therefore had complete freedom (see also Ponchaud 1978:100–125).

their revolution would either be coopted by the former ruling classes or crushed from without by traditional enemies such as Vietnam and Thailand. The necessity of permanently eliminating all potential counterrevolutionary elites derived from a pervasive fear that revolutions are often betrayed, usually by their leaders who tend to be corrupted by the system they are abolishing, thereby becoming a new class of exploiters. (See my comments in the Introduction concerning fear of betrayal as a typical characteristic of radical sectarian movements such as the Khmer Rouge.)

According to Pol Pot, past attempts to throw off exploitation in Cambodia had always been crippled by leaders who deserted the masses after successful rebellions and joined the feudal class, "those peasants who defeated the feudal landowners always proclaimed themselves part of the feudal landowner and warlord class and became in turn the oppressors of the peasant class" (1977:H5).

This fear of betrayal required eliminating not just individual enemies but entire classes that had served as the social and economic magnets for previous rulers of Cambodia. As Pol Pot stated: "The feudal landowner's oppressive system, not the individuals, was to be attacked" (1977:H12).

Repeated references were made during the entire period to the necessity of maintaining the gains of the revolution. Maintaining the domination of a worker-peasant administration was often paired with the number one priority of the regime, preserving national sovereignty and independence (FBIS IV, April 18, 1977:H2). In Khieu Samphan's speech celebrating the third anniversary of the revolution he emphasized these themes:

> . . . we must carry on the task of defending our Democratic Cambodia, *protecting our worker-peasant administration and preserving the fruits of our Cambodian revolution by resolutely supressing all categories of enemies . . . We must wipe out the enemy in our capacity as masters of the situation . . .* Everything must be done neatly and thoroughly.
>
> We must not become absentminded, careless, or forgetful because of past victories. On the contrary, we must further steel ourselves, remain alert, constantly maintain the spirit of revolutionary vigilance and continue to fight and *suppress all stripes of enemy at all times.* (FBIS IV, April 18, 1977:H3–4, emphasis added)

This vision of a revolution in constant jeopardy was not entirely fanciful (see Boun Sokha 1979:218–19; Lacouture 1978; Paul 1977). Not only were the Vietnamese an ever-present threat, but the Khmer Rouge at the moment of victory in 1975 were probably too small and too weak to dominate the country unless they immediately reorganized it and destroyed or paralyzed the old elite and its supporters. The Khmer Rouge in 1975 were a relatively small communist movement directing a military establishment of approximately sixty thousand largely illiterate peasants. The failure of the Khmer Rouge to penetrate the administrative organs of Phnom Penh before victory, when combined with the illiteracy of their own cadres, made it virtually impossible for them to control the old administration by merely supervising it from above. From this perspective, the educated bureaucratic elite of Phnom Penh were not only superfluous but dangerous to the peasant-dominated society the revolutionaries endeavored to create. With only sixty thousand operatives, the victors could not hope, in the long run, to dominate the sophisticated elements of Phnom Penh and the other major cities. As Pol Pot himself admitted in Beijing, "our strength was not strong enough to defend the revolutionary regime" (FBIS I, October 4, 1977:A23), especially in the context of a capital city swollen to several million persons, including thousands who had fought for Lon Nol. Hence, the ferocity of the purges conducted in the name of preserving the dictatorship of the proletariat were related both to the weakness of the movement itself and to its ideological goal of creating a revolution genuinely controlled by workers and peasants. Because of the difficulties inherent in such a goal, Pol Pot and his confederates followed a policy of permanent purge that "strove to create a society with no past [and] no alternatives" (Sihanouk 1980:120).

Total and Immediate Social and Economic Revolution

It is superficial to describe the Khmer Rouge as intent on returning to the pastoral simplicity of the Angkor era of Cambodian greatness between the ninth and fourteenth centuries. According to this interpretation, the Khmer Rouge emptied the cities because they rejected modern, city-based civilization and sought to transform Cambodia into the kind of largely rural society that predated both colonialism and capitalism. This interpretation misrepresents the aims of the Khmer Rouge elite. The Cambodian revolutionaries despoiled cities populated by their archenemies, the Westernized commercial and governing elites, but they also, almost immediately, began a limited program of repopulation, bringing "the sons and daughters of poor peasants" to run the existing factories and other modern establishments. Likewise, although they abhorred capitalist forms of modernization, the Khmer Rouge were, if anything, radical proponents of forced-draft industrial and agricultural modernization.[16]

[16] See Chapter 4, pp. 132–36, by Charles Twining for a complete description of Khmer Rouge industrial and agriculture policies. That the Khmer Rouge sought industrialization as well as agricultural modernization is reflected by the national coat of arms specified in Chapter XII of the constitution. It contains a network of field embankments and irrigation canals, "which are the symbol of advanced agriculture," and "factories, which are the symbol of industry" (FBIS IV, January 5, 1976:H4).

Furthermore, frequent references are made to exporting, indicating that autarky was a temporary rather than a long-term policy. This fits perfectly with Khieu Samphan's dissertation, which proposes stringent control by the state over Cambodia's international trade but not total withdrawal from international commerce. (FBIS IV, July 3, 1975:H3; July 16, 1975:H2; and July 25, 1975:H1–2).

In the agricultural field *we are sure* that we can achieve new progress *by leaps and bounds*. Regarding our future outlook, we should *quickly change* our beloved motherland from an underdeveloped agricultural country into a modern one and from a modern agricultural country into an industrial country, thus finally achieving the goal of a modern agricultural and industrial country. (FBIS IV, June 18, 1975:H2, emphasis added)

The Khmer Rouge sought not to turn back the pages of time to an earlier era of Khmer greatness but to rush forward at a dizzying pace regardless of the consequences. By combining the idealism and heroic virtue extolled by Maoism with a Fanonist or Stalinist reliance on wholesale terror, the Khmer Rouge sought to stimulate the Khmer people to participate in a forced march toward a vision of communist modernity.[17] In the same way that Mao, during the Great Leap Forward, sought to move ahead simultaneously to greatly increase rice production, irrigation, and backyard steel production, the Khmer Rouge vision of modernization emphasized extreme haste, the critical importance of rice, and the simultaneous pursuit of industrial advancement, especially through cottage industries located in self-sufficient communes. Immediately after the liberation of Phnom Penh, an official radio commentary reflected revolutionary optimism. With the total mobilization of the nation's labor resources they expected to achieve diverse developmental ends simultaneously and immediately.

For the present we will all immediately launch the offensive in raising the level of dam water in order to *double or even triple the harvest* of the rainy season rice crop compared with that harvest during the revolutionary war. *At the same time*, we will strive to enhance and develop domestic weaving and all other handicrafts. Regarding industry, we have a fundamental industrial base which we are gradually developing. We will *preserve, maintain, save, create, and develop everything both quantitatively and qualitatively* and will defend and preserve the property of our nation and people with a spirit of great responsibility. (FBIS IV, May 5, 1975:4, emphasis added)

The army was the critical institution for energizing this drive to modernization at the local level.[18] It exemplified all the revolutionary virtues that were intended to serve as models for the rest of the society. The army's victory in the revolution against the United States was perceived as a model of the triumph of man's heroism over the sophistication of weaponry, the potency of correct ideology over material obstacles. The army was depicted as doing everything, everywhere, with great haste and optimism, and it is clear that Radio Phnom Penh hoped that the army's revolutionary enthusiasm would be emulated by all nonmilitary personnel.

---

[17] For a discussion of the relationship of the Khmer Rouge to Maoism, Fanonism, and Stalinism, see Chapter 9 by Karl Jackson.

[18] See Chapter 3 by Timothy Carney, which emphasizes the importance of the party as a decision-making institution. The army, in contrast, executed decisions rendered by the party's central authorities.

At the same time, the Cambodian revolutionary army is plunging into an extremely active drive to build the country. In various cities, at all construction sites, along diverse communication lines throughout the country, our revolutionary army, whose clothes still smell of gunpowder, is launching a construction offensive with ardor and revolutionary optimism. The brothers are repairing old bridges and highways which were savagely destroyed by U.S. imperialism during the war. They are building new highways and bridges to enhance transportation, increase production, and improve the people's livelihood. They are cleaning up cities, restoring ports, repairing airfields, building dams, digging ditches, tilling ricefields, tending saltworks, raising livestock, fishing, and carrying out transportation work. (FBIS IV, May 14, 1975:H6)

During the Great Leap Forward, Mao Zedong said, "with grain and steel, everything becomes possible" (Guillermaz 1976:229). Likewise, rice was the critical commodity for Kampuchean modernizers.

Rice is the basic crop of our people as well as the basis of new Cambodia's economy. If we have plenty of rice, we have plenty of everything. (FBIS IV, July 16, 1975:H1) *If we have rice, we have everything;* our people can eat their fill and we can export it for hard currency. The more rice we produce the greater potential we have for export. The more we export, the better we can afford to buy equipment, machines, and other instruments necessary for building our industry and communications lines and for rapidly changing our agriculture. (FBIS IV, July 25, 1975:H3, emphasis added)

The means for rapidly increasing rice production were almost identical to those advocated in China during the Great Leap Forward. By reorganizing farmers into large communes, vast labor surpluses were to be created to substitute for nonexistent capital, thereby facilitating rapid production increases. The aim was to transform all Cambodian farmers from the traditional single crop of rice per year to two crops per year (FBIS IV, May 23, 1975:H2–3). Even swidden agriculturalists were moved from the highlands to the lowlands and inserted into new organizations for wet rice cultivation (FBIS IV, July 2, 1975:H5). Moving to two crops per year necessitated a very substantial increase in the irrigation facilities available during the dry season. For this reason, construction brigades, sometimes numbering tens of thousands of workers, were set in motion all over the country to build new water storage facilities and dams.[19] The LANDSAT photographs of Cambodia after liberation bear out regime claims that vast numbers of irrigation projects had been constructed.

Some of our revolutionary sayings go like this: "If you have rice, you have strength," and "you need water to plant rice just as you need rice to wage war . . ." (FBIS IV, May 2, 1975:H3)

[19] See Chapter 4 by Charles Twining for a full description of efforts to expand irrigation and the human costs involved.

We should follow our revolutionary saying: "We plant rice relying on our own force, not the skies." (FBIS IV, May 2, 1975:H3)

When we master irrigation we will be able to grow rice at least twice a year. Our goal is to have three crops a year (FBIS IV, July 14, 1975:H2)

The cardinal assumption was that rice growing consumed only 120–130 working days per year under the traditional single-crop system. The remaining days theoretically could be utilized by organizing young persons into roving work armies for building infrastructure and irrigation. Also, in each commune food was available only in the communal mess halls, and child care was provided by specialists, usually those too old to work. Reorganizing the family by abolishing nutritional and child care functions of the individual household was expected to free most women for full-time labor in the fields. Thus, by adopting lifeways similar to those advocated in China during the Great Leap Forward and Cultural Revolution, the Khmer Rouge leadership expected to increase vastly the labor available for modernizing the country. Finally, this substantial labor force was augmented by surviving ex-city dwellers: the bureaucrats, soldiers, merchants, and persons in tertiary manufacturing who had been labeled as economically "unproductive" by Khieu Samphan (see Khieu Samphan 1979).[20]

In addition to creating labor through reorganization, the commune structure was designed to elevate the poorest part of the social structure, eliminate private property, end all exploitation, and replace individual interest with devotion to communal or national goals. These social changes, in turn, were expected to lead to a spontaneous outburst of productive activity.

The long-repressed production potential of the people—poor peasants and middle-lower-class peasants, once morally and politically harnessed and organized into solidarity teams for increasing production—has become a concrete power and resulted in the construction of dams, lakes, and ponds throughout Cambodia's liberated zone. What used to be dry now has water and what used to be arid, cracked land has become green ricefields. (FBIS IV, May 21, 1975:H1, emphasis added; see also, Pol Pot 1977:H30)

Solidarity teams for increasing production, set up in all villages and communes throughout our country, are the backbone and driving force of the greatest movement for increasing production ever known in Cambodia's history. . . . our countryside is greatly developed and is in a position to feed our seven million people sufficiently and even abundantly. (FBIS IV, May 12, 1975:H7; see also, Pol Pot 1977:H30)

As well as spurring rice production, the new economic policies were intended to resuscitate the national crafts, which, according to Khieu Samphan, had been throttled by competition from cheap foreign imports. The

[20] See Chapter 4 by Charles Twining for details on the Khmer Rouge attempt to revolutionize the rural economy and with it the country.

suspension of foreign trade, the elimination of money, and the limitation of trade to barter between communes provided just the conditions of self-reliance and limited autarky that the Khmer Rouge theorists expected to stimulate the rebirth of local crafts and small industries (FBIS IV, May 12, 1975:H7; June 10, 1975:H6; April 8, 1977:H1; April 20, 1977:H4–6).[21] Not unlike the self-reliant commune industrialization projects of Mao's China, Kampuchean communes were required to develop handicraft and other forms of local production.

This year . . . while tilling and harrowing the land in the campaign to grow the rainy season rice crop, our brothers have also grown corn, bananas, sweet potatoes, and other crops and cleared several hundred hectares of land to grow cotton and mulberry trees to feed their silkworms for the development of the textile industry. To develop the textile industry, our brothers *in every village*, district, and production group have built mechanical and manual looms. In some places they have built semiautomatic looms. In other places there are paper mills, rubber shoe, soap, fish sauce powder, and bean noodle factories. *At the same time*, our brothers have made their own farming tools, knives, axes, jars, dishes, pots and pans, kettles, spoons, and so on. These tools have been produced thanks to the activities and initiative and the inexhaustible craftsmanship of our poor farmers who are the real masters of the governing power, the masters of the revolution, and the owners of their own destiny in the new Cambodian society. (FBIS IV, May 7, 1975:H2, emphasis added)

Revolutionary haste was the order of the day. Within a matter of weeks after the capture of Phnom Penh, the cities had been emptied, a large portion of the old elite had been executed, villages that had not joined the revolution early enough had been forced to migrate to another part of the country, and the country's entire economy had been completely transformed. Rice production was expected to treble in a single year if only enough enthusiasm and heroism could be mobilized to overcome the material obstacles (FBIS IV, June 10, 1975:H5). Over the entire period, official statements are peppered with the language of Mao's Great Leap Forward. Economic tasks were depicted as military offensives and battlefronts, and it was expected that Democratic Kampuchea would leap forward.

Our male and female *combatants* and people will surely succeed in their determined *offensive* to build our beloved fatherland by leaps and bounds and make it prosperous. (FBIS IV, May 9, 1975:H3, emphasis added)

Our workers are engaged in an unceasing offensive *aimed at a very spectacular great leap forward*. Our peasants are waging a continuous offensive to achieve *a very spectacular great leap forward*. Our revolutionary troops are also waging a permanent offensive aimed at achieving *a very spectacular great leap forward*. . . . The people in every district and every establishment all over the country are waging an offensive, doing their duty for the sake of *a very spectacular great leap forward*.

[21] On the barter system, see Chapter 4, pp. 120–22, by Charles Twining.

All are waging the offensive and thereby achieving *the very spectacular victory of the great leap forward.* (Radio Phnom Penh, April 11, 1976, quoted by Ponchaud 1978:109–10, emphasis added)

In the new year we pledge to continue to intensify the struggle ten- or twenty-fold in order to make our Democratic Cambodia *leap forward with successive great victories* . . . (FBIS IV April 20, 1977:H6, emphasis added; see also, FBIS IV April 20, 1977:H1 and October 11, 1977:H25)

The small elite of Democratic Kampuchea was distinguished by its nearly unlimited hubris. It made no secret of the contempt felt for the Soviet and Vietnamese models of modernization. In addition, the elite set out to achieve its goals at "a great leap forward pace" in spite of the catastrophic failure of the Great Leap Forward in China itself. Direct warnings from experienced Chinese communist leaders did not deter the Khmer Rouge from setting out immediately to achieve pure communism. The presumptuous nature of the Khmer Rouge elite is depicted in Sihanouk's description of a discussion he attended between Khieu Samphan, Madame Ieng Sary (Ieng Thirith), and Zhou Enlai.

In Peking in 1975, we visited Zhou Enlai—already seriously ill—in his hospital room. I heard him advise Khieu Samphan and Ieng Thirith (Mme Ieng Sary) not to try to achieve total communism in one giant step. The wise and perspicacious veteran of the Chinese revolution stressed the need to move "step by step" toward socialism. This would take several years of patient work. Then and only then should they advance toward a communist society. Premier Zhou Enlai reiterated that China itself had experienced disastrous setbacks in the fairly recent past by trying to make a giant leap forward and move full speed ahead into pure communism. The great Chinese statesman counseled the Khmer Rouge leaders: "Don't follow the bad example of our 'great leap forward'. Take things slowly: that is the best way to guide Kampuchea and its people to growth, prosperity and happiness." By way of response to this splendid and moving piece of almost fatherly advice, Khieu Samphan and Ieng Thirith just smiled an incredulous and superior smile.

Not long after we got back to Phnom Penh, Khieu Samphan and Son Sen told me their Kampuchea was going to show the world that pure communism could indeed be achieved at one fell swoop. This was no doubt their indirect reply to Zhou Enlai. "Our country's place in history will be assured," they said. "We will be the first nation to create a completely communist society without wasting time on intermediate steps." (Sihanouk 1980:86)

Haste was derived from the regime's revolutionary optimism, and in turn, the flurry of activity at building sites all over Cambodia reinforced the sense of false optimism in an ascending spiral of rhetoric that may have shackled the Khmer Rouge elite with manacles created by its own words. As in the Great Leap Forward in China, massive amounts of labor were subtracted from rice cultivation for opening new land, increasing irrigation, and reopening factories, and this policy was pursued in the face of the self-evident severe food shortages found throughout the land, especially in 1975–1976. And yet, because of the steadfast nature of its beliefs in the potency of its new organizational forms, the regime constantly overstated its achievements and refused to retrench even when early expectations were obviously confounded and the country became desperately short of grain. An example of the extravagant claims is provided by the following statement over Radio Phnom Penh less than a month after the fighting had stopped: "In our country there is no problem with famine, budgetary deficit, or the so-called deficit in the balance of payments. All of our seven million people have rice to eat and are joining our valiant revolutionary army to build a new Cambodia which is independent, democratic, nonaligned, gloriously flourishing—a Cambodia that is not a satellite of any country" (FBIS IV, May 12, 1975:H7).

Indeed there could be neither a budget deficit nor a shortage in hard currency for international trade because both had been abolished by fiat; however, the very real nature of the food shortages was attested to by refugees throughout the four-year reign of the Khmer Rouge. The elite actually seems to have believed that the self-sufficient communes had defeated the Americans and would provide an economic panacea in peacetime. In the words of Pol Pot,

The movement of cooperatives—which are collective mass organizations—has gone from strength to strength throughout the country from 1973 to date. *These cooperatives have enabled us to win victory over U.S. imperialism* and to successfully increase production for the support of the front and for the improvement of the people's livelihood during the most devastating war. Since liberation *they have enabled us to defend the country and feed our nearly 8 million people well, relying on* the highest principles of independence, sovereignty and self-reliance. In fact, this has been made possible thanks entirely to the collective forces of these cooperatives. (1977:H28, emphasis added)

At present, our cooperatives constitute a collective corps [*angapheap samuhapheap*] that is fairly strong in political, ideological, and organizational matters throughout our countryside—a corps which has well fulfilled all revolutionary tasks and has transformed the arid, impoverished Cambodian countryside of old into an increasingly beautiful countryside equipped with extensive networks of reservoirs, trenches, and canals, blossoming in verdant farmland. (1977:H30)

The myth of economic invincibility may have resulted in part from the cushioning effect of the American food aid in Cambodia. To the extent that the communes were unable to feed the entire population in liberated areas during the last two years of the war, these people fled to Phnom Penh and other cities where, as refugees, they eked out an existence based on foreign food inputs. This artificial backup mechanism ceased to exist when the Americans withdrew and the Khmer Rouge refused to countenance external aid. Postwar optimism about food production may also have resulted from misinformation being fed to the leadership by Khmer Rouge cadres who, as citizens with full rights, had first call on all food. Traditionally, Southeast Asian administrators have not been wont to speak truth to power. Adding chaos and permanent purge to the tradition of not communicating unpleasant news upward may have resulted in completely misleading reports reaching the leadership in Phnom Penh. The dearth of accurate statistics is indicated by the fact that the country's total population in some official pronouncements is set at seven million, whereas in other statements the population is listed as nearly eight million. The Khmer Rouge claimed to have solved the food problem and begun exporting rice to Vietnam before the 1975 victory (see Simon 1975:221). Further, they declared themselves ready to export rice in 1977 (FBIS IV, April 20, 1977:H4), and the regime at times claimed the Cambodian people were very well fed, with 312 kilograms per annum available for each person (see FBIS IV, April 18, 1977:H5). Although these claims are partly the dissimulation of a failing regime, it is probable that misinformation and revolutionary optimism together produced this hoax of plenty in the presence of famine.

Haste, revolutionary optimism, and the rhetoric of simultaneous agricultural and industrial modernization were the symbols of total revolution. At the local level, every life was affected. Traditional leaders were eliminated and the bottom of society rose to the top of the revolutionary structure. In addition, Khmer Rouge policies were designed to abolish the concept of personal interest as a prime mover in human affairs. In doing so, the revolutionaries adopted a prominent goal of Mao Zedong's proletarian revolutionary line, but characteristically extended it to extreme never conscienced by the Chinese radicals themselves. The radicals of the Cultural Revolution depicted "from each according to his work" as a bourgeois rather than socialist principle and sought to replace it with "to each according to his needs" (Dittmer 1980:373). Although the Maoist radicals perceived monetary exchange and commodity trade as inevitable generators of inequality and elitism within socialist society, they balked at eliminating these fundamental social institutions. The Khmer Rouge, in contrast, showed no such restraint and followed the critique of the Chinese radicals to its logical, if extreme, conclusion by abolishing money, markets, most commodity exchange, and virtually all private property. In place of these, the state set the rice ration and supervised the very limited amount of commodity exchange between self-reliant communes. "Surplus" rice was collected and stored in central warehouses controlled by the Khmer Rouge rather than by the villagers. With the exception of Khmer military cadres who received a disproportionate share, "to each according to his needs" became standard and was enforced by making the commune dining hall the only source of food in the village.

The immiserization of the peasantry produced by the utopian revolutionary reorientation of the Khmer economy has been chronicled by the emaciated bodies of those who lived long enough to flee to Thailand and Vietnam. In the search for "pure communism" the Khmer Rouge reduced a war-torn, but traditionally resilient, economy to one almost without prospect of spontaneous regeneration. Not only did they fail to achieve rapid modernization, but by any modern standards the economy had ceased to function by the time the Vietnamese army put a stop to the experiment. The most vital ingredient in economic modernization, be it capitalist or communist, is skilled manpower, and Khmer Rouge policies in this area alone probably set back Cambodia's march to any form of modernity by at least half a century. Plainly, a great gap existed between the equal and prosperous society they sought and the social catastrophe they wrought. Even those who originally supported their triumph were eventually disillusioned by the severe disjunction between lofty ideals and despicable means, between long-term goals and the reality of autogenocide.[22]

The Revolution in Social Values

True revolutions alter international relations, elevate new groups to power, and change important elements of economic life. In addition, the Khmer revolution altered completely and immediately the most basic aspects of Cambodian social life such as language, religion, family life, and work habits.[23] To an extraordinary degree the Khmer Rouge sought to replace the slack ways of traditional Cambodia with iron discipline, corruption in high places with unswerving devotion to the interests of the lowly, a hierarchical society with an egalitarian one, and a remote bureaucratic regime with an intrusive, omnipresent but antibureaucratic revolutionary organization. To accomplish a permanent revolution they instituted a new moral code, disestablished Buddhism, romanticized revolutionary struggle and violence, and emphasized ideological militancy and heroic labor as crucial values for Cambodia. In doing so, the revolutionaries sought to alter fundamentally the Khmer value system and way of life.

Extreme moralists accentuate the negative, and the Khmer Rouge were not exceptions. Particular emphasis was placed upon purifying the cities and the whole society in both a physical and moral sense. "Cleaning up" the cities and the society referred not only to removing the clutter of war but, in addition, was undoubtedly a euphemism for purging the cities of oppositional and depraved elements:

. . . Immediately after the liberation of Battambang on 17 April 1975, our revolutionary army which took over the city took up the task of *cleaning up* and *eliminating the filth of the rotten old society left behind by the traitorous clique.* Our male

[22] See Chapter 4 by Charles Twining for a more complete exposition of the revolutionary economy.

[23] On language, family life, and religion, see Chapter 5 by François Ponchaud. On altering class patterns, see Chapter 3 by Timothy Carney.

and female combatants and cadres *cleaned up* the streets and various buildings, closed down the gambling dens, drinking lairs, and prostitutes' brothels, shut up the black markets where the traitorous clique used to steal and pilfer from our people, and repaired buildings damaged by the enemy, thus returning the whole city to a clean image in a very short time. (FBIS IV, May 14, 1975:H7, emphasis added)[24]

During the very period when the cities were being emptied and the officers and officials of the old regime executed, Radio Phnom Penh spoke repeatedly of efforts to clean up the filth left behind by the old regime:[25]

A *clean* social system is flourishing throughout new Cambodia. Since 17 April, Cambodia has been totally and permanently emancipated. The sound, clean social system formerly prevailing in the liberated zone has now been expanded to Phnom Penh, a number of provincial capitals and throughout the country. [Emphasis added]

This new social system is sound, *clean*, free of corruption, hooliganism, graft, embezzlement, gambling, prostitution, alcoholism, or any kind of hazardous games. (FBIS IV, May 9, 1975:H1, emphasis added)

Radio Phnom Penh lauded villagers for similar activities after the April 17 victory "They have rid the area of all vestiges of the old regime, *cleaning up* the village, wiping out old habits, and taking up the new revolutionary morals" (FBIS IV, July 9, 1975:H2, emphasis added).

Revolutionary morality was enshrined in the twelve-point moral code of the army (see Ponchaud 1978:117–18 and FBIS IV, June 3, 1975:H1–2). Four of the principles emphasized the need to "love," "honor," and "serve" the people, that is, the "laborers and peasants." One principle enjoined the soldiers to "continually join the people's production and love thy work." Three injunctions warn of the evils of corruption, intoning that cadres should not "steal so much as one pepper," "touch the people's money," or "put out thy hand to touch so much as one tin of rice or pill of medicine belonging to the collective goods of the state or the ministry." Gambling, drinking, and any "improper [behavior] respecting women" are expressly forbidden. The final command intones, "Against any foe and against every obstacle thou shalt *struggle* with determination and courage, *ready to make every sacrifice*, including thy life, for the people, the laborers, and peasants, for the revolution, and for angkar, *without hesitation or respite*" (Radio Phnom Penh, January 31, 1976, quoted by Ponchaud 1978:118, emphasis added).

These are truly revolutionary precepts when viewed from the perspective of the prerevolutionary society whose leaders looked down upon peasants

---

[24] For a detailed description of the "clean-up" operation that actually took place, see Ponchaud on the evacuation of Battambang and the immediate execution of its commercial, military, and bureaucratic elite (Ponchaud 1978:41–45).

[25] FBIS IV, May 5, 1975:H3–4; May 7, 1975:H1; May 9, 1975:H1; May 12, 1975:H5; May 13, 1975:H1; May 14, 1975:H7; May 20, 1975:H6, 8; May 21, 1975:H6; May 22, 1975:H8; May 23, 1975:H5; May 27, 1975:H4; June 2, 1975:H5–6; June 3, 1975:H2; June 9, 1975:H1–3; June 13, 1975:H1; June 19, 1975:H1; June 24, 1975:H2; June 25, 1975:H2.

and laborers, engaged in age-old practices of appropriating to themselves the "people's money," practiced conspicuous consumption, and flaunted sexual potency as a trademark of the powerful (Anderson 1972). Before war and revolution came to Cambodia most marriages were arranged by parents with the consent of both parties. Substantial play was given to sexual banter in village festivals (see Steinberg 1959:82–85). Premarital sex was frowned upon, and this prohibition was enforced by social disapproval. With the advent of the new revolutionary morality, husbands were separated from wives for long periods, permission to marry was only granted by Angkar, and premarital sex became subject to extreme punishment, sometimes even the death penalty (see Paringaux 1977; Wise 1977; U.S. Department of State 1978).

Drinking and gambling had been very prevalent practices in Cambodia before the revolution; both were explicitly prohibited by Angkar. These prohibitions bear the personal stamp of Khieu Samphan, the unmarried intellectual whose dissertation railed against rice alcohol distilleries as "poisoning . . . the population" (Khieu Samphan 1979:28).[26] Soon after assuming power, Khieu Samphan declared all these vices had been eliminated: "There are no thieves, drunkards, hooligans, or prostitutes in our country; none" (FBIS IV, January 6, 1976:H5).

Before the Khmer Rouge took power, Cambodia was considered to be the most Buddhist country in Southeast Asia.[27] To be Khmer meant being Buddhist. The countryside was dotted with more than 2,500 temples, and most men became monks at some point in life. The monkhood represented an oasis from mundane concerns such as earning a living, maintaining a family, and living up to one's station in society. Buddhism's impact on entire generations can be assumed from the fact that most males spent an average of two years as monks (Ebihara 1964:104).

Immediately after victory the Khmer Rouge moved swiftly to expunge all vestiges of Buddhism from daily life because its doctrines and practices contradicted vital aspects of the revolutionary doctrine.[28] The most fundamental aspects of Therevada Buddhism are associated with the pursuit of the ultimate goal of nirvana and the more proximate end of attaining a more favorable reincarnation by accumulating karma or merit (see Steinberg

[26] That Khieu Samphan never married violates several mores of prerevolutionary society. Males either married or became monks; those reamining unmarried outside the monkhood were the subject of social disapproval (Steinberg 1959:83).

[27] I am indebted to the insights of Roger Welty, a former monk, for several of these comments on Buddhism.

[28] As François Ponchaud has shown, in Chapter 5, pp. 170–76, the distinction between Buddhism and communism can be overdrawn. For instance, both the Khmer Rouge and the monk renounce personal interest and practice self-abnegation, albeit for quite different reasons. The communist cadre renounces private property in the name of a classless society but remains nonetheless a materialist. The monk (as distinct from the Buddhist layman) renounces personal interest and private property as part of his general withdrawal from worldly concerns.

1959:59–73; Spiro 1970; deBary 1958 and 1969). The basic teachings of the Buddha, as summarized in the Four Noble Truths (*Ariya Sacca*), advocate withdrawal from the world as the only permanent means of alleviating suffering: all life is inevitably sorrowful; sorrow is due to craving for sensation, satisfaction, and permanence; sorrow can only be stopped through the extinction of craving; this can be achieved only through the progressive abandonment of individuality attained by carefully disciplined moral conduct culminating in the life of concentration and meditation of a monk. (See deBary 1958:99.) This profoundly pessimistic view of the human condition and man's incapacity for improving his lot in any enduring way is graphically illustrated by the Buddhist affirmation, "Life is a curable disease." Ultimate release from the suffering imposed by the continual cycle of rebirth and death can best be sought by abandoning worldly concerns and becoming a monk, "a wanderer from home into homelessness." Becoming a monk means becoming a mendicant, begging for one's food, and thereby allowing others to gain karma through the act of giving. Monks must abstain from labor in the fields, lest they harm any living being, even insects, which might be crushed underfoot. Furthermore, laboring mightily is merely another example of how the futility of craving is made doubly painful by the obvious impermanence of all such achievements; according to Buddhist thought, setting out to change the world by transforming society submerges individuals in the hopeless quest for the same illusory permanence. The road to nirvana entails the abandonment of all materialism, even the concept of the self, and opens up the distant possibility of escaping from the distinctly unsatisfactory nature of human existence.

Obviously, Khmer Rouge plans for immediate social and economic revolution and their emphasis on mobilizing the entire population for a "great leap forward" into modernity contradict the concept of monkhood and the very essence of the search for nirvana.

The Buddhist religion is the cause of our country's weakness.

The *bonzes* are bloodsuckers, they oppress the people, they are imperialists.

Begging for charity like the *bonzes* do is an offense to the eye and it also maintains the workers in a downtrodden condition.

It is forbidden to give anything to those shaven-asses, it would be pure waste.

If any worker secretly takes rice to the *bonzes*, we shall set him to planting cabbages. If the cabbages are not full grown in three days, he will dig his own grave. (Khmer Rouge propaganda quoted by Ponchaud 1978:130–31)

Whereas the search for nirvana deprecates desire to assert control over life (Steinberg 1959:63), the revolution called for herculean efforts to control the water, plant rice, and industrialize the country through "all-out physical and moral efforts" (FBIS IV, April 21, 1976:H1). Struggle and hard manual labor in and of themselves were positive moral values for the Khmer Rouge, whereas the life of the monk on his road to nirvana depreciates such concerns as transitory and ultimately meaningless. Further, the concept of raising up the downtrodden connotes a sense of collectivism and social responsibility that is foreign to Therevada Buddhism. A monk is not his brother's keeper; he does not come any closer to nirvana by shepherding his flock along the same path. Therevada Buddhism emphasizes detachment, whereas revolutions extol involvement. According to Therevada Buddhism, what happens to me is of no concern to you or to me; it is inescapable because of things past. The principle of *upekkha*, equanimity, enjoins the individual to ask three questions about any given social situation. First, does it concern me? Second, can I do anything helpful? Third, will I do anything about it? If the answer to any one of these questions is negative, the best thing to do is nothing at all, and there is and should be no guilt whatever associated with disinterested detachment.

Buddhism has always stood for doctrinal tolerance in both religion and social life. Buddha said, "Come wander with me, if it is right for you," and "A show-er of the way, am I." Each individual must find his own truth, his own road to nirvana. In contrast to Christianity, in the history of Buddhism there are no long theological debates where groups of believers are branded as heretics and subjected to persecution because of their beliefs. Individual behaviors, rather than strict adherence to particular beliefs, are central to Buddhism. In contrast, the Khmer Rouge were radical sectarians who were completely intolerant of nonrevolutionary beliefs and behaviors: "Our brothers and sisters are determined to fight all moral and material nonrevolutionary concepts, including those of private property, personality, vanity and other nonrevolutionary concepts" (FBIS IV, January 28, 1976:H2). Under the rule of Angkar, capital punishment fell swiftly on all who demurred from revolutionary beliefs. Whereas a Buddhist monk would never even point out the moral shortcomings of another monk, the Khmer Rouge enforced revolutionary intolerance by initiating the *chhlop* system of spies charged with rooting out unorthodox beliefs at the local level.

The pursuit of nirvana is an impossibly distant goal for most Buddhists, especially those outside the monastery. For most Buddhists the pursuit of karma has more immediate importance than approaching far-off nirvana. Most Buddhists seek to do good in their present lives in order to accumulate merit that will elevate them in future lives. Whatever your present status or fortune and whatever befalls you in the present, they were determined by your behavior in past lives (Spiro 1970).

The doctrine of *karma* is antithetical to the completely equal society sought by the Khmer Rouge. According to Buddha, the karma of each person is different from birth onward (see deBary 1969:25). The poor are not poor because of exploitation by the rich but because in their previous lives they failed to do good and give generously, and they have, therefore, been accorded a justly diminished status. Although the doctrine of karma allows for upward social mobility and in fact encourages worldly pursuits for lay persons,[29] it supplies moral legitimacy for any inequalities that exist in a particular society (see Spiro 1970:446). Because karma provided a powerful doctrinal justification for the social and economic inequalities the Khmer Rouge sought to eradicate, Buddhism became an immediate and primary target for annihilation.

Giving to monks and monasteries provided the most obvious means to accumulate merit in prerevolutionary Cambodia. Donating a building to a monastery, sponsoring a novice monk, feeding a group of monks, or feeding a single monk were all considered to be more meritorious than other forms of charity. Although no figures are available for Cambodia, 10–30 percent of cash income at the village level was probably devoted to Buddhist ceremonial activities and merit making.[30] The pursuit of karma through giving probably constituted a considerable drain upon economic expansion in prerevolutionary Cambodia and this tendency to stifle capital formation may have been what the Khmer Rouge meant when they denounced the *bonzes* as "bloodsuckers."

The Khmer Rouge were willing to liquidate the traditional ruling class, empty the cities, abolish markets, money, and private property all in the names of egalitarian collectivism, rapid economic development, and the dictatorship of the proletariat; the same goals led them to execute the chief *bonzes*, defrock ordinary monks, forbid the accumulation of merit through giving, and profane Buddhist temples throughout the country.

That the Khmer Rouge resorted to violence very frequently throughout their four-year rule has become an acknowledged fact. Although the scale of the bloodbath under the Khmer Rouge was unprecented, violence itself was no stranger to Cambodian society before 1970. The murder rate in rural areas was sufficiently high to warrant government suppression of the homicide statistics (Meyer 1971:37). During the aftermath of the coup against

[29] Through economic success an individual proves that his karma is good, and he also accumulates the wherewithal to give more generously, thereby insuring further accumulation of karma. Although wealth alone does not compensate for evil deeds, the good man who is rich has comparative advantage over the good man who is poor in the matter of karma accumulation. This means that Max Weber's interpretation of the influence of Buddhism on economic development was partially incorrect. Most Buddhists do not remain monks for their entire lifetime, and merit making encourages economic accumulation by the laity. The real problem, however, is that this accumulation from quite worldly activities is expended disproportionately on Buddhism rather than being saved and reinvested in productive enterprise (see Spiro 1970).

[30] This estimate is derived from the intensive fieldwork of Manning Nash and Melford Spiro in upper Burma; my assumption is that the proportion of income devoted to Buddhist activities in prerevolutionary Cambodia would have been within the same range (see Nash 1965 and Spiro 1970).

Sihanouk in 1970, thousands of Vietnamese residents were slaughtered, and Khmer officials were surprised at the international outcry provoked by films of these executions. During 1970 in Kampong Cham two members of parliament were killed by an angry pro-Sihanouk crowd. They were flayed into pieces and their livers were grilled and eaten by the crowd (Meyer 1971:38). The civil war from 1970–1975 was notable for the lack of compassion among combatants; neither side took many prisoners and consumption of human liver took place on both sides.[31]

The fact that massive amounts of blood were shed by the Khmer Rouge diverged from the Khmer norms in scope rather than in kind. In addition, the Khmer Rouge publicly glorified revolutionary violence and blood sacrifice and celebrated them in the country's most important official documents. The blood sacrifices of the revolution became a sanctifying symbol attached to the constitution, the National Assembly, and the national anthem. Virtually every line of the national anthem mentions bloodshed. It is as if the revolutionaries sought to harness the darker, more violent side of Khmer national character by giving violence a new cultural and political legitimacy.

> *National Anthem of Democratic Kampuchea*
> The red, red blood splatters the cities and plains of the Cambodian fatherland,
> The sublime blood of the workers and peasants,
> The blood of revolutionary combatants of both sexes.
> The blood spills out into great indignation and a resolute urge to fight.
> 17 April, that day under the revolutionary flag
> The blood certainly liberates us from slavery.

In ceremonies surrounding the adoption of the new constitution, Information Minister Hu Nim stated, "This constitution, is the path cleared by the fresh blood of the Cambodian workers, farmers, revolutionary army, nation, and people" (FBIS IV, Janury 6, 1976:H1). Hu Nim reiterated the theme in marking the first anniversary of the April 17, 1975, victory.

The *red blood* of our brothers and sisters and comrades in arms has flown into brooks and streams all over the sacred territory of beloved Cambodia, our fatherland; this is the *blood* of our brothers and sisters and comrades in arms—great heroes, valiant and wonderful sons and daughters of Cambodia, cadres, male and female combatants and Cambodian people, workers, peasants, and laborers. (FBIS IV, April 15, 1976:H1, emphasis added)

Blood symbolism is again apparent when Khieu Samphan speaks before the first elected representative assembly:

[31] For additional examples of prerevolutionary traditions of violence, see Chapter 5, pp. 165 and 174–75, by François Ponchaud.

Our assembly is certainly born from the flesh and *blood* shed so profusely by our people, workers and peasants during thousands of years of their protracted struggle.

The Constitution of our Democratic Cambodia is the soul of our country, the basic foundation for both the domestic and foreign policies established at the cost of much *blood* shed by millions of our Cambodian sons and daughters since time immemorial. (FBIS IV, April 16, 1976:H12, emphasis added)

This concern for blood symbolism and violence as "the essence" of the Cambodian revolution reached a crescendo with the following statement by Pol Pot in the context of his September 27, 1977, speech:

Our national anthem clearly shows *the essence of our* people's struggle. As you know, our national anthem was not composed by a poet. *Its essence is the blood* of our entire people, of those who fell for centuries past. *This blood call* has been incorporated into the national anthem. Each sentence, each word shows the nature of our people's struggle. *This blood* has been turned into class and national indignation. *This blood* led us to the great victory of 17 April 1975 and still calls for us to defend the people's state power, protect the fatherland, and build a prosperous and glorious Cambodia *at a great leap forward pace*. (1977:H25, emphasis added)

One can only speculate about the meaning of this blood symbolism, but several possible interpretations come to mind. First, at a manifest level the Cambodian civil war from 1970 to 1975 had indeed been very bloody, and the sacrifices were worthy of commemoration by the victors. This does not explain, however, why the blood symbolism is tied to the national anthem, the constitution, and the representative assembly. Second, at the time of these announcements, bloodshed was occurring throughout Cambodia as the old elite was progressively hunted down, and sweeping purges were being carried out within the Khmer Rouge itself. Perhaps the symbolism was meant to provide a public rationale for the killings by linking them with the new institutions; when tens of thousands of men, women, and children were being killed, perhaps cadre guilt needed to be assuaged by connecting bloody deeds with more lofty and seemingly permanent institutional changes.[32] Third, the blood symbolism seems to glorify revolutionary violence for its own sake; only through bloodshed can true independence and liberation be achieved. In a sense, the French-educated Khmer Rouge elite echo Franz Fanon's thesis that true liberation cannot come without violence and that the only true revolutionaries are those who participate directly in the shedding of blood (see Fanon 1963 and Chapter 9 by Karl Jackson). As Pol Pot himself stated, participation in revolutionary violence was superior to education or propaganda for mobilizing the rural masses for armed struggle: "Our people were awakened not by education or propaganda; they

---

[32] Under the Third Reich, blood symbolism may have served a similar function in preparing SS officers for the morally trying circumstances in which they, like their Khmer Rouge counterparts, would be expected to violate basic societal and humanitarian norms in the pursuit of ultimate revolutionary goals.

gained awareness through the movement of struggle, through class anger and through class conflict, which they decided to resolve through revolutionary violence" (1977:H13).

The ideological pronouncements of the Khmer revolution mirror radical Maoism with regard to the primacy of human willpower over weapons and machines, the superiority of the wisdom of the common people over academic learning, and the power of heroic labor to overcome all natural and material obstacles. The Khmer Rouge, like their Chinese counterparts, felt they could replace machines and technical solutions with political militancy and thereby transcend normal development obstacles. In a speech on April 15, 1977, Khieu Samphan claimed the production targets for 1977 would be fulfilled by May 1977 and asked the rhetorical question, "Have these achievements been made possible by machines? *No, we have no machines. We do everything by mainly relying on the strength of our people. We work completely self-reliantly. This shows *the overwhelming heroism* of our people. This also shows the great force of our people. *Though barehanded, they can do everything*" (FBIS IV, April 18, 1977:H5, emphasis added).

Radio Phnom Penh's portrait of the armed struggle against Lon Nol emphasizes this same belief in the ability of heroism alone to triumph over technologically superior forces (FBIS IV, April 28, 1977:H3–4 and Ponchaud 1978:105, 108):[33] "The great victory of the Cambodian revolution, based as it is on the stand of political conscience and revolutionary morals, is irrefutable *proof that the human factor is the key and that the material factor is only secondary*" (FBIS IV, June 3, 1975:H2, emphasis added).

The Khmer Rouge echoed the Maoist idea that technical and theoretical education divorced from the common people, from political struggle, and from the work situation itself was a throwback to imperialism, to the European educational system that hampered Asian progress. According to Khieu Samphan,

In the old regime, did the school children, college students, and university graduates know anything about the true natural sciences? Could they tell the difference between an early rice crop and a sixth month rice crop? Did they know when and where rice was to be sown and transplanted? No, they did not. Therefore, we can say that they were separated from reality. Consequently, they could do nothing truly substantial. They relied completely on foreigners, expecting foreign equipment and even foreign experts to do the jobs for them. Everything was done according to foreign books and foreign standards. Therefore, it was useless and could not serve the needs of our people, nor could it be of any help in building our nation.

By contrast, our children in the rural areas have always had very useful knowledge. They can tell you which cow is tame and which is skittish. They can mount a

[33] Pol Pot describes the Chinese revolution in an almost identical manner (FBIS IV, September 20, 1976:H4).

buffalo from both sides. They are masters of the herd. They have practically mastered nature. They know the different strains of rice like they know their own pockets. . . . They really know and understand. Only this should be called natural science because this type of knowledge is closely connected with the reality of the nation, with the ideas of nationalism, production, national construction, and national defense. (FBIS IV, April 18, 1977:H6–7)

Anti-intellectual tendencies were reflected in the vision of the Cambodian past presented by the group of French-trained intellectuals forming the core of the Khmer Rouge. They blamed the peasant reluctance to join the revolution on teachers as well as the ruling classes. Monks and teachers in the old educational system prevented the exploited classes from becoming aware of the fact of their own exploitation. In the words of Pol Pot,

This conflict was, however, contained—hidden—because the landowner class, the ruling functionaries, and *the teachers at the pay of the oppressor classes*, forced them [the peasant masses] and duped them into burying this conflict. Such lies as the belief in a former life and the influence of the stars and past deeds were also instrumental in misleading the peasants about the conflict. (1977:H12, emphasis added).

Students trained under the old regime were depicted as "brainwashed," as spurning "all kinds of productive labor," and as "wantonly" spoiling and cheapening "the good name of the fraternal workers and peasants" (FBIS IV, September 25, 1975:H3). In public speeches the revolutionary leadership belittled scholars and intellectuals in spite of the fact that men of learning had occupied a position of very high status before the revolution. In describing the constitution, Khieu Samphan said,

No scholar or historian drafted or wrote this constitution with a view *to deceive our working classes*, peasants, and revolutionary army. Those who wrote this constitution, determined its meaning, and put it together were the people, workers, and revolutionary army who sacrificed their sweat, blood, bones, and flesh to the struggle to overthrow the old and colonialism and other oppressive regimes in order to build a new regime—that of the workers, peasants, and the revolutionary army. (FBIS IV, April 16, 1976:H3, emphasis added; see also FBIS IV, January 6, 1976:H2–H9)

In line with the antimanagerial proclivities of the Great Leap Forward and the Cultural Revolution, the Khmer Rouge insisted that in reorganized, revolutionized Cambodia everyone was a worker or peasant, and managerial positions were eliminated because they did not contribute directly to production: "Everywhere throughout the country our workers completely control all the factories. Moreover, at every site no one remains idle in offices just sending out circulars. Everybody works in the fields . . ." (FBIS IV, January 6, 1976:H7).

The methods chosen to rectify these social defects were similar to ones adopted in the People's Republic during the Cultural Revolution. Initial depopulation of the urban centers in Cambodia forced all urban residents not previously involved in manual labor to "learn from the people," that is, to become peasants. In the fashion of the Cultural Revolution, the "brainwashed" students and other products of the old educational system were reeducated through hard labor.[34] Under the new regime, the educational models to be emulated were neither university graduates nor monks but revolutionary peasants.

. . . the fraternal youths and students have reconciled themselves *to humbly learn from and emulate the workers and peasants, from the poor and lower-middle peasants in particular.*
Through productive labor assumed in order to gradually provide for their own need, the fraternal youths and students have gained a greater grasp of reality. They have become increasingly aware that *only this collective productive labor can restore* their faith in themselves, return *their love and affection for the fatherland, nation and people, workers and peasants, as well as give them back a sense of judgment.* (FBIS IV, September 29, 1975:H3–4, emphasis added)

Taking yet another cue from the Cultural Revolution, schooling was not to be separated from working because educational specialization would eventually breed elitism and lead to impractical, theoretical solutions to real work problems.

Our goal is to keep schooling close to production work . . . we learn technological skills and implement them while working. (FBIS IV, April 18, 1977:H7)

You should learn while working. The more you work, the more you learn and the more competent you become. (FBIS IV, October 4, 1977:H26)

Theory should be learned at the same time it is being applied to actual work. Our people study and at the same time directly serve the production movement. To implement this, schools are located mainly in the cooperatives and factories. (FBIS IV, October 4, 1977:H34)

Even in medicine, on-the-job training was the order of the day, and operations were performed by untrained personnel (FBIS IV, May 13, 1975:H6; October 4, 1977:H35). Although surgery by novices provides an extreme case, the logic is that through seizing political power people gain control over technology and thus become expert. All technical problems become relatively simple operations when they are actually carried out, and the Khmer Rouge believed that liberating persons politically and placing them in a new role would lead automatically to the acquisition of the requisite skills. In the words of Khieu Samphan,

[34] In reality, being identified as an intellectual often meant not redemption through labor but death by execution or prolonged hard labor on starvation rations. Refugees indicate that identifying yourself as a person of education was equivalent to signing your own death warrant. (See Schanberg 1980:39–44.) The subtleties of the revolutionary theoreticians were apparently applied rather crudely by local operatives who tended to execute anyone with more than a grade school education.

In the past, here in Phnom Penh, did you ever see any Cambodian operate a lathe? Very rarely. No Cambodian would touch anything that had to do with machinery. Only foreigners were mechanics. Look now! Cambodian children are everywhere. They can do it. We are pleased with this new trend.

This, therefore, is a new stage in the building of our nation's technical ranks. *Our worker-peasant class, under the leadership of our revolutionary organization, immediately grasped technical expertise after it seized political power.*

Our ports are much more efficient, better maintained, and more smoothly run than ever before. In efficiency they are not far behind many of the world's larger ports. . . . This shows that *technical skill is not the determining factor. The determining factor is in fact the political and ideological stand of our fraternal dock workers.* Their stand is lofty, their revolutionary ideology firm, their sense of responsibility high, their patriotism unquestionable. *All this more than compensates for any lack of technical skills.* (FBIS IV, April 18, 1977:H7–8, emphasis added)

In another parallel with the Great Leap Forward and the Cultural Revolution, the Khmer Rouge assumed that heroic labor could substitute for capital, technology, and foreign assistance. Huge work teams were often assembled for major irrigation projects. Everyone not incapacitated by either old age or childbirth was expected to labor mightily in the fields twelve to fourteen hours per day, seven days a week (FBIS IV, April 2, 1976:H6). The relatively languid pace of preliberation rural life was replaced by long, hard days of manual labor usually unassisted by anything but the simplest tools. There can be no doubt that the Khmer Rouge instituted a new work ethic, the likes of which had never been seen before in Cambodia. They forced peasants to work harder, reorganized them into mobile labor brigades, and praised continual exertion as a model to be emulated.[35]

Each solidarity team has devoted a proper proportion of its labor force to building its own irrigation system. The fraternal people have now matured to the point where they can strive independently to resolve their water problems in their drive to increase production, triumphing over natural calamities in all circumstances. *Our brothers are happy to work day and night.* (FBIS IV, June 9, 1975:H3, emphasis added)[36]

In their efforts to defend and build the country, our brothers and sisters of all categories, including workers, peasants, soldiers, and revolutionary cadres, have worked *around the clock with soaring enthusiasm, paying no attention to the time or to their fatigue;* they have worked in a cheerful atmosphere of revolutionary optimism; . . . (FBIS IV, April 2, 1976:H6, emphasis added)

Viewed in retrospect, the value changes sought by the Khmer Rouge are remarkable in both scope and method. Seldom has any regime sought so much change so quickly, from so many. Furthermore, the revolutionaries relied disproportionately on raw physical coercion rather than on party or-

---

[35] See Chapter 4 by Charles Twining for a detail description of labor organization and the new work ethic of Pol Pot's Cambodia.

[36] See also FBIS IV, May 21, 1975:H5; May 22, 1975:H8; May 27, 1975:H4.

ganization, reeducation, or the mass media to accomplish their ends. In sharp contrast with their Vietnamese communist contemporaries, the Khmer Rouge ruled almost exclusively with the sword rather than the pen, the loudspeaker, or the school. Although there were political indoctrination meetings, these were fairly infrequent and played a much less vital role in sociopolitical transformation than in Vietnam. According to refugees, whenever the Khmer Rouge were faced with lack of comprehension or passive resistance, they chose to exterminate rather than reeducate. Formal schools were closed immediately after liberation, newspapers were nearly nonexistent, and radio listening was restricted largely to Khmer Rouge cadres. The special camps for former officials and army personnel who had not been immediately executed, resembled death camps rather than institutions in which hard labor and intensive study might hold the prospect of enlightenment and eventual reintegration into Cambodian society.

3. The Organization of Power

by Timothy Carney

In mid-1977 a U.S. Congressman asked a State Department witness in hearings on human rights violations in Cambodia whether he could explain who was in charge there, what was the "shadowy organization," and "how the organization establishes its authority throughout the country" (U.S. Congress 1977a:17). The witness briefly outlined the limited knowledge of the time. Five years later, a Cambodian trained in public administration both in Phnom Penh and Paris marveled that in the period they held power, the Khmer Rouge issued no decrees and passed no laws beyond their January 1976 constitution. They seemed deliberately to ignore the administrative and legal frameworks that make up most states, even those of such disparate systems as socialism, communism, and theocratism. All have recognized some set of principles at least as their formal operating guides and acknowledged a written or unwritten constitution as their basis.

Among the relatively few archives of Democratic Kampuchea available, laws, government decrees, or an official journal are conspicuous by their absence. The only laws the Khmer Rouge regime seems to have cited were those of dialectical materialism (*Revolutionary Flags*, September–October 1976b:88). The only statutes appear to be those of the Communist Party of Kampuchea (Carney 1977:56–61). The only justice was administrative, despite the nominal appointment of a judicial committee in the April 1976 government of Democratic Kampuchea.

The Congressman's questions remain, although enough evidence is now available to identify the leadership and describe the organization and how it established itself throughout the country. What has become clear is that the party, the government, and the army leadership were synonymous, with the party leadership dominating all activities within the fledgling state.

Building the Party

Because of the diverse sources of its recruits during the war, one of the main problems of the PKK was to identify and train potential party members for both the military and the civilian sides of the administration. The clandestine nature of the party exacerbated the difficulty of selection. In liberated areas the secrecy was not perfect, however, and the party organization, Angkar, came to mean the government. Party members were instructed to be on the lookout for hard-working people with the right "spirit." Backgrounds were not so important early on. The "base class" was always the

79

NORTH REGION

NORTHEAST REGION

NORTHWEST REGION

CENTRAL REGION

KRATIE SECTOR

WEST REGION

EAST REGION

SOUTHWEST REGION

KOMPONG SOM SECTOR

DEMOCRATIC KAMPUCHEA
Regional Divisions

— — International boundary
—·—·Regional boundary

0   50 KILOMETERS

0   50 MILES

AEM

"poor and lower-middle peasant," but in the early years of the war, recruits for mass organizations from rural areas also came from the middle class, defined to mean those cultivators who had enough land to enjoy a small surplus after the harvest. After the war, class background became much more important and reexamination of biographies resulted in cases of dismissal from party organizations.

After victory in April 1975 the party went about building itself more cautiously. United-front tactics gave way to purity of class background as a criterion for advancement. An early 1978 document states that for "a number of years" the party has "closed the door" on new membership and even reduced the number of members of "bad composition" (*Revolutionary Flags* 1978:38). In the Western Region, a ranking party representative said in July 1977 that the previous six months had seen fair numbers of traitors and dangerous party members "wiped out" (*ja'n jhli*).[1] Recruitment resumed in July 1977 and membership expanded "rather well." Internal publications paid considerable attention to cadre formation, and after the party emerged from clandestinity in September 1977, the national radio regularly broadcast items on the need to train, improve, and build cadre (FBIS IV, December 29, 1977). The anti-intellectual bias of the PKK comes through in the emphasis that higher education earns no extra consideration. "Training depends essentially on practical work." A more fundamental broadcast in April 1978 set forth the formal structure of party building (FBIS IV, April 27, 1978). Citing a party directive of July 1977, Radio Phnom Penh emphasized the enhanced role of the party since the war against Lon Nol, especially in management. New members needed good class qualifications, experience in revolutionary movements and a good personal history that could be fully verified.

Building the party first meant selecting the "progressive masses in the base class." Once identified, such progressives were to be given minor responsibilities in the cooperative, to build experience and as a test. This broad mass of progressives served as the pool from which to draw "core" (*snol*) or "non-party cadre of the cooperative." The core took the leadership role in more important jobs. The core organization then served as the pool for potential party members. Spotty evidence suggests that extensive purges after the 1975 victory so thinned ranks that the PKK later decided it needed more cadre to meet the Vietnamese threat. Limited hostilities had taken place along the border in April 1977.

[1] This early euphemism covers a massive purge of party people in the Northern Region and the Northwestern Region, with other areas shortly to follow. Useful material on this and related wider-scale purges of the general population, including base people, is in Summers's paper on the cooperatives (1982:23–24, n29) and Heder's introduction to the situation in 1979 (1980b). 'The Last Plan,' a contemporary document believed to have been written by Pon, head of the Tuol Sleng state security interrogation center, depicts the alleged plots against Democratic Kampuchea (see Appendix D).

The Radio Phnom Penh description above draws almost word for word from a July 1977 speech of a high-ranking party cadre visiting the Western Region. His remarks, reprinted in the party monthly, *Revolutionary Flags* of August 1977,[2] noted a series of purges throughout the Western Region and cautioned of the dangers in trying to build party membership from such "infected" localities. He emphasized that identifying and expanding the base of progressive masses was the fastest way to build clean cadre. The first place to look for progressives is within the "base class" of poor and lower-middle peasants, second is among middle peasants. The target for the Western Region over the following six months was three hundred new party members.

Class Organization

The PKK set up an elaborate class hierarchy, perhaps more elaborate than the Cambodian situation required, partly in order to confound Vietnamese assertions that class formation in Cambodia and Laos was undeveloped. Published sources of class definition date to the mid-1960s, when Hu Nim divided up rural society into poor, middle, and rich peasants on the basis of landholdings.

At the clandestine 1960 congress of the PKK, the party reportedly defined five distinct classes: the working class, the peasantry, the petite bourgeoisie, the bourgeoisie, and the feudalists. By 1977, however, the analysis had expanded to ten principal classes and class categories. (See Table 1 at the end of this chapter.)

The ordinary peasant fleeing from Cambodia in 1979 did not have this scheme down pat. But those who fled from the food-short and disease-ridden Democratic Kampuchea zones on the Thai–Khmer border knew exactly where they fit. Aside from the cadre and troop commanders (who would know as a matter of course since they were usually party members), the people in these areas were mostly "base persons," those who had been under Khmer Rouge control before the 1975 victory. Asked how many hectares of land their parents tilled, they replied and often volunteered their class.

In theory, class background determined the leadership of the cooperatives. Although May 20, 1973, is the founding date of the Khmer Rouge

---

[2] The August 1977 issue of *Revolutionary Flags* devotes the entire issue to remarks by the party representative. An earlier view of the stages to full party membership is in "A Short Guide to Implementation of Party Statutes" (Carney 1977:56–61. The word "cell" should be retranslated as "core" throughout that source. The term "core" [*snol*] first appears in Ith Sarin's writings [Carney 1977:43, 44], where it often seems to be used more generally as well as to mean the core organization. An early use in party documents is in 1976 [*Revolutionary Flags* 1976a:59]. Party documents also use the word in its general sense. For a later exposition of the steps to membership, see *Revolutionary Flags* 1978:39–40).

effort to create a nationwide system of cooperatives (FBIS IV, May 24, 1977), the actual transformation even in the already "liberated" areas took considerable time. In Sector 25, Saang-Koh Thom (Kandal Province), the effort to organize cooperatives began in June or July 1973. The goal was to put Khmer in charge of all aspects of the society, from culture to economic production to military affairs, including food production (for the troops) and agricultural modernization. The sector chairman, Non Suon (called Chey), said that poor peasants and 60 percent of the middle peasants should hold all positions in the cooperatives. In Sector 25, the party analyzed class makeup as 40 percent poor and lower-middle peasant and 60 percent middle peasant or rich (Heder 1980c, Interview No. 14). Only after 1975 was membership in the cooperative compulsory. In many other sectors, the proportion of poor and middle peasants could have been higher, because Sector 25 is located between the Bassac and Mekong Rivers, giving it well-watered, fertile soil suitable for high-value truck gardening.

In fact, after 1975 the party formally defined only two classes: the workers and the peasants plus the "revolutionary ranks." The last included the party, the core organization, and the troops (*Revolutionary Flags* 1976b:52–53). The analysis recognized that the farmers included "old," that is, former, peasants but from higher class backgrounds who thus had a potential for struggle in the new situation. "New" peasants included many of the old petit bourgeois who had not joined the revolution before April 1975. "Life and death struggle" for "new" peasants resulted because, as former rich peasants, capitalists, and feudalists, they were perceived to be beyond the possibility of being reformed. By early 1978 this view had softened. A description of class policy classified capitalists, petit bourgeois, and small landholders as a third force—after poor, lower-middle, and middle peasants. Even various stripes of "reactionaries" could be drawn into the revolution, except for the few in the most fierce category.[3]

The post-victory period put the party in complete control but with an inadequate number of cadre. The three or four million people coming from Khmer Republic–controlled zones included numbers of "class enemies" as well as potential workers and poor and lower-middle refugee peasants. When the urban populations arrived in the countryside, they filled out bi-

---

[3] The change in tone between the September–October 1976 and March 1978 issues of *Revolutionary Flags* is striking. By 1978 the Khmer people had undergone severe trial in many areas, with large numbers of deaths from execution and privation. More were to come with the revolt and purge in the Eastern Region two months later and a subsequent nationwide campaign against the few remaining Vietnamese, their spouses, or ethnic Khmer born in Vietnam (Khmer Krom). Serious work needs to be done on DK policies of 1978, since some sources (Heder 1980c:Interview No. 4) claim that a party directive proclaimed a nationwide amnesty in August 1978. Other information suggests Democratic Kampuchea was opening up to the rest of the world and possibly even softening toward talks with Vietnam. The questions are whether these moves really took place, whether they were tactical or fundamental, and whether Vietnam understood them but attacked anyway.

ographies. Security officials and cadre judged them for class determination. In the Northeast Region,[4] Sector 505, "new people" deemed "poor" immediately joined the cooperative that included all of the base people. Those regarded as middle class were formed into work groups. Arrests depended to a degree on local leaders: in some areas authorities picked up only ex-soldiers and high-ranking civil servants. Elsewhere, even students disappeared. Not all died. A few were returned after jail terms. In 1976, work groups in Sector 505 joined the cooperative. Half the new people were given "full rights" (*ben siddhi*) as cooperative members; the other half were called "deposited" or "sent" (*phnoe*) because they were put with the base people to use their example and "forge" themselves anew. In between was a category of "probationary" (*triem*) membership for those advancing toward full rights.

The genesis of these categories has yet to be determined. The full rights and candidate status may go back to the 1973 founding of cooperatives. After 1975 most of the urban people were depositees, but some base people apparently merited reduction to this status (Heder 1980a:6). Full-rights members ate much better than depositees in several areas, including Sector 505 in the Northeast in 1975–1976. More important than food in the long term, however, was that full-rights members of a cooperative could, with "education," become "progressives" and then be built into the core, at the bottom rung of the party's organizations (*Revolutionary Flags* 1978:45; Carney 1977:58).

Civil Organization and Party Control

The cooperative was the organizational foundation of Cambodia from 1975 to 1978.[5] The party seems to have been aware that it lacked sufficient members to run the cooperatives along proper lines. The effort to purify (*samrit samramng*) cooperatives directly related to efforts to purify the party because the cooperatives were to be the source of new party members, tested through stages by being given ever-more-challenging duties. The PKK, according to Vietnamese figures, had only fourteen thousand members in 1975 (Kiernan personal communication). This figure probably included

[4] Northeast Region interviews are rare and this source, whom I talked with in a transit camp in September 1980 gave a complete description of the membership categories and the situation of his zone. I am not aware of any open publication of the terms dividing cooperative membership before the Heng Samrin regime set it forth (FBIS IV, 15 May 1979). See a full explanation in Heder (Heder 1980:6-7). Nor did my colleagues uncover this scheme from refugee interviews before 1979.

[5] For additional information on organization of the economy, see Chapter 4, by Charles Twining.—ED.

full and candidate party members. Controlling the population after victory must have seemed impossible.

The cooperatives moved into the scale of hundreds of families after the 1975 decision to expand their size to encompass villages (*ghum*), as the process of transformation into the higher-level stage of agricultural production cooperatives began. Village committees of the wartime years dissolved as cooperative committees formed. By mid-1976, refugees confirmed this new structure. Two refugees said that up to four hundred families were then in such village-scale cooperatives (U.S. Department of State [1978] Airgram from Embassy Bangkok, September 21, 1976). Plans called for district-level cooperatives as the next stage, abolishing district committees and leaving organizational lines to run from the cooperative to the sector, then to the region, and finally to the center.[6] A former regimental committee leader said that the fifth (PKK) congress in August 1978 announced the goal of eliminating district committees in the near future "to lessen the burden on the people of the district apparatus" (Heder 1980c:Interview Nos. 24, 25). District committeemen would return to live among the people. Later, regions would be abolished, he added, leaving only the cooperative, sector, and central committees.

For the ordinary Cambodian, the cooperative itself was organized on military lines. He dealt with the chief of his group (*krom*) of ten families or platoon (*kong*) of three *krom*. Military terminology continued through the thousand-family civilian equivalent of regiments and on up to divisions. At a minimum, each group had a three-member leadership. Thus, visible power in a thousand-family cooperative would be about thirty people. In fact, the party organization chart for a thousand-family cooperative, based on a nationwide party decision discussed at a February 1977 meeting in the Western Region, specified thirty party members, fifty core organization members, and fifty progressives on the average (*Revolutionary Flags* 1977:4). The party members probably were the senior members of each of the committees. Core and progressives would presumably have led various efforts in the fields and served as staff for the committees.

In late 1972, the party did not even control all the subdistrict committees, much less village committees (Carney 1977:8). Less than five years later, their vastly expanded population required even more cadre. The contradiction arose in trying to recruit cadre while simultaneously purging the party. After the July 1977 decision to expand party membership, the purges in the

---

[6] By September–October 1976, the party monthly, *Revolutionary Flags*, was claiming that hamlet (*phum*) committees had dissolved into the cooperatives, adding that a "fair number" of sub-districts (*khum*) had become cooperatives and that *khum* committeemen had become members or cadre of cooperatives. District committees remained intact, but members were urged to live and work in cooperatives to learn and build themselves.

Northwest Region accelerated, having gotten underway in the spring.[7] The purges were known as "sweeps." First came the Northern Region sweep, or "First Battlefield," of 1976, then the Northwestern Region sweep, or "Second Battlefield," of 1977, followed by the Eastern Region sweep of 1977–1978. The last saw a heavy toll among villagers too.[8] The resumption of recruitment in July 1977 may have been a popular manifestation of the easing of "class enemy" categories that became noticeable at the theoretical level by March 1978.

The leadership positions at mid and lower levels throughout the country after 1975 went largely to demobilized soldiers. This process had begun in 1973 when wounded and disabled soldiers entered some village organizations (Carney 1980). Refugees repeatedly confirmed that the committee chairmen in cooperatives or at higher levels were ex-soldiers. One such official served until victory as political commissar of the sixteenth regiment, first brigade, of the Soutwest Region. In July 1975 he became chairman of Sector 37 (Kompong Seila), from which he moved to Kompong Som as chairman of the state fisheries office. Radio Phnom Penh publicly identified him at Kompong Som after the election of March 1976 and during the visit of Deng Ying Chao, Zhou Enlai's widow, in February 1978. This heavy use of ex-military should be expected after a war that required mass mobilization. Ex-troopers would have gotten many of the key jobs as a matter of course.

Nonmilitary party cadre also had a share of the administration. So apparently did some new people of highly dubious class background. In the Western Region, a party representative told a regional conference in July 1977 that "enemies and various classes" other than poor and lower-middle peasants held a "fair number" of cooperatives, Sector 32, for example. District 18 (southern Kompong Tralach) even had ex-Lon Nol military as leaders of cooperatives, and, in Sector 37, former Sino-Khmer businessmen, "thau ke," actually chaired some cooperative ten- and even thirty-family *krom* and *kong*, respectively (*Revolutionary Flags* 1977:24, 31). This was "no way to build Socialism." These people were viewed as beyond reform and unsuitable to work for the revolution.

[7] The Heng Samrin authorities compiled at least three separate lists of people purged at the Tuol Sleng center. Two form part of the Tribunal documents for the trial *in absentia* of Pol Pot and Ieng Sary and cite purged party people. The third is a Khmer listing of murdered civil servants, teachers, engineers, and former Lon Nol military personnel from corporal on up. See Barry Kramer's *Wall Street Journal* article, October 19, 1977 for an account of the purge of party people in the Northwest Region.

[8] Life in general in the Eastern Region was *relatively* better than many other areas. One scholar who pioneered study of the area argues that the leadership there was more in the tradition of early Khmer communism (Kiernan 1981a and 1981b). Others argue that estimates of deaths in the Democratic Kampuchea period were overstated due to ignorance or political expediency (Vickery 1981, 1984). The question warrants a careful, nonpartisan study.

Cadre Education under Party Instruction

Educating and constructing cadre required regular meetings, criticism and self-criticism sessions, and formal schooling. During the war years the leadership put heavy emphasis on training for "Front" cadre and on clandestine training for the party members. After April 1975 the party's Central Political School under Deputy Secretary Nuon Chea moved to the old Soviet Technical Institute. Each separate ministry in Phnom Penh had its own school as well (Heder 1980c:Interview No. 17).

Refugees generally described cooperative meetings as devoted to planning agricultural tasks or harping on themes related to security or the improved situation over the old society. But, by early 1978 the party emphasized that technical matters alone were not sufficient (*Revolutionary Flags* 1978:45). A more systematic approach aimed for meetings every month. Class, class struggle, enemy goals formed the themes. Meetings, the radio, short documents from the region and sector committees, and word of mouth disseminated the line. At the cooperative level, full-rights and candidate members might spend one full day in school every three months, and even depositees might study with them, or, better, just with the candidates, to draw "correct lessons." The party youth organization, the Communist Youth League (Yuv KK), enjoyed a special status as a leading core organization in line with the PKK view of youth as the cutting edge of the Cambodian revolution. The Yuv KK had its own monthly publication, *Revolutionary Young Men and Women*.

Party members themselves underwent continuing ideological and practical training. Cadre had to be models in every field they led. Besides the party schools, the party monthly magazine, *Revolutionary Flags*,[9] widely disseminated policy lines and changes, ideological and theoretical views, and technical points on the raising of dikes and dams and steps to produce three tons of rice per hectare. It circulated only among party members. In addition, regular region-level congresses discussed themes that subsequently appeared in *Revolutionary Flags* for party-wide dissemination and then on Radio Phnom Penh for national edification.

Promotion for these cadres was doubtless more by merit during the war than during the 1975–1978 period. After purges began in 1976, we might expect that loyalty was more important. A clean background became a prerequisite, and in July 1977 the party center's representative told a Western Region meeting that increasing party strength first of all depended on re-

[9] This internal party monthly carried five flags on its cover, presumably, one for each of the original five regions. In 1977 the cover changed to one flag between the August issue and the special issue of October–November. The party had publicly emerged at the end of September, and the change may have symbolically marked full central committee control.

viewing biographies to separate the good from the bad (*Revolutionary Flags* 1977:20). He noted that because confusion had obtained then, earlier biographies were undependable guides to building new party members. Everyone was included, the regions, the sectors, the ministries and offices, and the army.

The Armed Forces

The armed forces, the "most loyal tool of the dictatorship of the Revolutionary Organization" (FBIS IV, August 23, 1977), or "the proletarian dictatorial instrument of the party" (*Revolutionary Flags* 1976c:55), was assigned two roles after victory. First, it was to help build agriculture; second, and increasingly important, it served to pressure the Vietnamese and Thai borders and then defend against the Vietnamese response. Part of these security duties also included internal security against traitorous elements.

The post-victory change in role began with the first sweeping alterations in Khmer national institutions. On July 22, 1975, Pol Pot, in his capacity as chairman of the party high military committee, presided over a ceremony of organization for the Revolutionary Army of the party Central Committee (*Revolutionary Flags* 1975:24). During the war years, the armed forces were, by 1973, structured as brigades of sixteen to seventeen battalions. Regional party committees controlled the brigades and the center used them through a "General Committee of the Battlefield" that ran operations from 1973 to 1975, before creation of a real General Staff.[10] Even in 1975, the regions apparently did not hand over all of their troops to the central committee. Only at the beginning of 1976 were a number of East Region and Southwest Region brigades placed under Defense Minister and Chief of the General Staff Son Sen. The senior Eastern Region brigade commander, Chan Chakrey, then a member of the party committee for the region, moved to Phnom Penh as deputy secretary of the General Staff only to be purged following what may have been his failed attempt to mount a coup in May 1976. The well-known General Staff membership during the 1975–1978 period follows. Parentheses indicate dates of purge (Carney 1980 and FBIS IV, August 1976).

General Staff of the Revolutionary Armed Forces of Kampuchea
POL POT: Chairman
SON SEN alias KHIEU: Chief of the General Staff

---

[10] A General Staff existed on paper, at least, as early as January 1972, when clandestine radio broadcast names of the military "High Command," which included Son Sen as chief of the General Staff. Interviews of PKK cadre (Heder 1980c:Interview Nos. 17, 25) suggest that the General Staff did not really operate until 1975–1976. A major difficulty sorting out the military structure has been faulty translation of terms for units. See Chapter 1 for a fuller explanation.

CHAN CHAKREY (19/5/76): Deputy Secretary of the General Staff; Political Commissar of Brigade 170

SEAT CHHE or SAT CHHE or CHHEAT CHHE alias TUM (29/4/77): Member of the General Staff; former party Secretary of Sector 22; member of the party Central Committee

TITH NAT alias NAT alias SOEUNG IM: Member of the General Staff; he became a Foreign Ministry cadre and was arrested there

Nat is known to have been in the Southwest Region where Vorn Vet had sent him in 1967 (Democratic Kampuchea 1978c). He was commander of Sector 33 in the Southwestern Region in 1974, according to Khmer Republic intelligence. Tum was a senior figure from the Eastern Region. Chan Chakrey was a military figure whose unit came from the Eastern Region. The General Staff probably formed under the leadership of the party military committee. Its members may have represented each of the regions, and the party center.

The deteriorating relationship with Vietnam and massive military purges from 1976 to 1978 spurred creation of additional brigades at the end of 1977. In 1979 the military reorganized, with the formation of divisions of three regiments each. A number of brigades were redesignated; for example, the 164th became the 3rd Division. Other brigades kept their designation but changed to the slimmed-down structure. The scanty information available on commanders after the purges and the Vietnamese attacks of 1977–1978 suggested that a number of recently demobilized officers returned to the ranks from their party government jobs.

Recruitment for the army apparently had only a brief hiatus after April 1975. At a regional congress reported in June 1976, a party representative noted that clear understanding of plans and policies would make cooperative members satisfied to let their children join the army and mobile work brigades (*Revolutionary Flags* 1976:23). As of September 1976, refugees agreed that the army was recruiting and training. Recruits came from "long-held" villages. Fifteen-year-olds from "trustworthy" families were recruited in Battambang, where training took place at the center in Sisophon used during the Lon Nol era (U.S. Department of State [1978] Airgram from Embassy Bangkok, September 21, 1976). One young peasant recruited in mid-1975 described two-week basic training in Oddar Meanchey that included reconnaissance and guerrilla fighting (U.S. Department of State [1978] Airgram from Embassy Bangkok, October 6, 1976). Political education apparently advanced more quickly for soldiers than for civilians after 1975. The recruit learned that principles of socialism and communism, along with nationalism and true democracy, formed the basis of government. Marxism-Leninism and Maoism were also subjects in the political curriculum.

Command and control functioned through a three-member committee at each level of military organization. Most important was the political commissar. He headed the command committee. Next came the military commander and finally the deputy military commander. A defector described his rise through district and provincial military commands from 1968 to 1971, when he moved to a regional battalion as political commissar. In 1973 he became political commissar of a regiment. Among his duties was building the youth league apparatus in the military.

The Government

The January 1976 constitution ordained an Assembly of the Representatives of the People of Kampuchea as the supreme national foreign and domestic policy-making body. The People's Representative Assembly (PRA) selected: a State Presidium of three members to function as head of state; a government to implement laws and policies; and a judiciary to defend the people's rights and punish lawbreakers.

After the March 1976 national elections and the selection of the PRA Standing Committee headed by Nuon Chea, the Assembly dropped into obscurity. The election itself did take place in a number of localities nationwide. Some refugees actually and correctly remembered the names of their deputies. All 250 deputies, as nearly as can be determined, did exist. They were members of sector committees, central government offices, or brigade command committees. For example, military representative Ket Oeun, purged in 1977, was a member of a Northern Region brigade committee; representative of fishing workers, Chap Lonh, was a member of the Kompong Som City party committee.

The first, and only, plenary session of the PRA lasted from April 11 to 13, 1976. Rather than issuing laws and decrees, the body sent out a press release (Democratic Kampuchea 1976). The Assembly approved the March 20 elections and set forth its method of functioning and organization. Members were to remain at work with the people and continue as workers, farmers in cooperatives, or combatants. Between annual plenary sessions, the functions of the Assembly would be carried out by a Standing Committee of the Assembly of the Representatives of the People of Kampuchea. The Assembly also approved Prince Sihanouk's request to retire, according him a retirement pension of "8,000 dollars." Then the body named the members of the State Presidium, the government, the judiciary, and the Assembly's Standing Committee and noted the creation of six committees attached to the vice-chairman of the Council of Ministers for Economic Affairs: agriculture; industry, commerce, communications, energy, and rubber plantations. Each committee chairman was given ministerial rank.

The press communique also listed "Directives" of the Assembly on foreign and domestic policy. The constitution was to be correctly implemented. The "great union" of the nation and people was to be consolidated, further developed, and defended. Production, especially in agriculture, was the target of renewed offensives. Solidarity and friendship was to be further developed with revolutionary movements and all peace and justice lovers everywhere, "including progressive American youth," to fight against imperialism, colonialism, and neocolonialism, and all reactionary forces.

The ministries and the committees, especially those in the office of the deputy prime minister for economy, had real substance. Grouped broadly under members of the Standing Committee of the party Central Committee, the organization consolidated foreign affairs under Ieng Sary and defense affairs under Pol Pot, as head of the party military committee, and Son Sen for day-to-day action as chief of the General Staff. Son Sen may also have supervised internal security matters.[11] Member of the party Standing Committee Vorn Vet (Sok Thouk), as deputy prime minister for economy, ran the six committees related to economic affairs. Nuon Chea, the party first deputy secretary, supervised key aspects of party building, the political school and the youth league. Thus a structure of ministries existed, but in reality they were more like party functional units[12] (qanab-hab).[13]

Party Leadership

In reality, the party formed not only the leadership core, but, to very nearly the lowest level, the only real organizational structure in the country. From the organization of ten-family groups to the Central Committee, in each platoon and brigade, at each ministry and office, a party committee sought full control. At the top, the Central Committee, as of August 1978, had about thirty members (Heder 1980c:Interview No. 25), counting full and candidate members (see Table 3 at the conclusion of this chapter). Most were regional and sector secretaries and deputy secretaries or, presumably, senior commanders.

The Central Committee was expanded at the third party congress in 1971, probably to meet expanded leadership needs of the wartime situation. Among new members of the Central Committee in July 1971, according to Vorn Vet (Democratic Kampuchea 1978c:32), were a mixture of political/military figures. Included were Men San (Ya), the Northeastern Region

[11] Heder (1980c:Interview No. 4) notes that a document relating to Tuol Sleng operations carried Son Sen's alias, Khieu. This evidence is not conclusive.

[12] These units worked and ate together and were supposed to be nearly autonomous. When DK villagers and cadre stumbled into Thailand in May 1979 and again in September and October, they indicated that unit structure and autonomy often remained. Anyone without a unit went hungry, as he had no organization to depend on.

[13] The list of key officers of the PRA, the State Presidium, and the government (as of April 1976) can be found at the end of this chapter. The accompanying date in parentheses usually means date of arrest; some mean date of execution. Sources include the various Tuol Sleng documents noted above and interviews, especially the Heder series (1980c).

party secretary; Chou Chet (Sy), the man who became Western Region secretary when it split from the Southwestern Region; Se (better known as Kang Chap), an important Southwestern Region cadre who became Northern Region secretary after Koy Thuon was assigned to head the state Commerce Commission; Sua Va Sy (Doeun), Koy Thuon's deputy in the Commerce Commission who replaced him after his purge in 1976; and Um Neng (Vy), deputy commander of the Northeastern Region, a long-time revolutionary. All of these men had died by late 1978 in a variety of purges.

Central Committee offices carried on daily business. The Central Committee itself met at intervals or in response to crises, such as a meeting in October 1978, presumably convened to discuss the battlefield situation. Khieu Sampan had taken over the central office of the Central Committee in 1977, an indication of his important but secondary role. Other offices of the Central Committee included the notorious S–21, the state security office that conducted the party purges and ran the ghastly torture and interrogation center at Tuol Sleng in Phnom Penh.

The primary body of the Central Committee was its Standing Committee. In August 1978 the Standing Committee included:[14]

POL POT: Secretary
NUON CHEA: First Deputy Secretary
TA MOK: Second Deputy Secretary
IENG SARY: Member
VORN VET: Member
SON SEN: Candidate Member
TA KEU: Candidate Member

So Phim, who was purged when the Eastern Region rebellion was crushed in May 1978, had been third deputy secretary general. According to Vorn Vet's December, 1978, confession, So Phim had been a member of the Standing Committee since mid-1966. Vorn Vet himself was arrested in November 1978 and presumably killed in December. He had joined the party Central Committee in 1963. Ta Keu is said to have been purged as well. Vorn Vet noted that he met Ta Keu in Phnom Penh in 1961, where Ta Keu was especially active in youth work. Ta Keu subsequently rose to be deputy of the Phnom Penh city committee under Vorn Vet in 1963. In 1965, Vorn Vet sent him to the Northwestern Region, where he appears in Khmer Republic military intelligence charts of 1974 as Ta Koeu, miltary commander.

[14] Thion's chronology (Thion and Kiernan 1981:288) cites a document from the genocide trial of Pol Pot–Ieng Sary listing the Standing Committee as of mid-1977: Pol, Muon, Phim, Mok, Won, Van, Nhim, Ken, Khieu. Thion correctly matched Pol to Pol Pot; Muon is probably an error for Nuon, Nuon Chea; Phim is So Phim; Won is Von, Vorn Vet; Van is known to be Ieng Sary; Nhim is surely Nhim Ros, alias Muol Sambat; Ken is not Son Sen, but may be a typographical error for Keu; Khieu is not Khieu Samphan, but is the alias for Son Sen.

Unconfirmed reports now identify Son Sen as a full member of the Standing Committee. Khieu Samphan and Ke Pauk (alias Ker Vin, alias Pok, former Northern Region chief of staff who became secretary of the Central Region and was in 1983 undersecretary of the General Staff) were selected in 1983 as candidate members to maintain the Standing Committee size at seven members.

By 1978 the party had divided the country into East, Northeast, North, Central, Northwest, West, and Southwest Regions. In addition, Kratie and Kompong Som were autonomous entities. Party leadership overlapped government and miltary structures. Many of the names came out when senior Chinese officials, including Zhou Enlai's widow, Deng Ying Chao, traveled in the Cambodian countryside in late 1977 and early 1978. Most names were seen again only on the execution lists from the state security office's Tuol Sleng interrogation center. No nonparty individuals were ever mentioned as part of the 1975–1978 leadership, except possibly Dr. Thioun Thoeun, whose actual membership is likely but not confirmed. (Table 4 at the end of this chapter lists the purges in the Northwestern Region.)

No satisfactory explanation exists for the all-consuming series of purges. Every region suffered, although the Eastern Region may have lost the largest number of people. This occurred in response to central party orders following the May 1978 attack on that region by troops of Central Region party secretary Ke Pauk (Pok) and Central Committee troop commanders Nha and Van. The documents from the counterespionage service suggest that the party, at a very high level, believed that it was the target of a bizzare series of plots involving Soviet, Nationalist Chinese, American, East German, and Vietnamese intelligence services. The isolation of the regions, the existence of dissent over the harsh line after 1975, the consequent antiparty activity, and the real activity of various foreign powers, particularly the Vietnamese, doubtless fueled this counterespionage paranoia. A lasting effect has been mistrust of the Southwestern Region cadre who replaced the purged officials of other regions.

Few of the senior region leaders appear to have survived. The Central Region secretary, Ke Pauk (Pok) and his deputy, An, survived. Ke Pauk, as of late 1983, retained his post as the undersecretary general of the Khmer Rouge General Staff. Northwestern Region Committee member Kantol survived as Heng Samrin's trade union official under his alias Heng Teav. The secretary of the Kompong Som city committee, Ta Muth, in 1983 held his position as Khmer Rouge military commander on the northern border, and his one-time deputy, Krin, remained a member of the Coordination Committee for Cultural Affairs of the coalition government of Democratic Kampuchea under his real name, Thuch Rin. In 1988 he defected to Prince Sihanouk. In the Southwestern Region, Ta Mok had taken over control of three other regions by the end of 1978: West, East, and North. His deputy,

Bith, probably ran day-to-day operations in the Southwest. Bith himself became a member of the State Presidium in the wake of purges.

The party figures were the actual leaders of Cambodia. No real separation of the party, the government, and the army existed. In the region and sector committees, the deputy secretary was the military chairman as well. He could order the troops out. Both the secretary and the deputy had authority over civil and military affairs. Sector chairmen of party committees and political commissars of brigades sat as members of the region committee, ensuring, in theory, smooth transmission of policy down and information up. Region committees had important authority over the mobilization of labor. If a sector wished to use labor forces greater than a thousand men to raise a dam or dike, they required regional approval. Such a large force demanded that the region ensure logistics of both materiel and food (Carney 1980).

The discussion of key policy lines took place at a still higher level. The party congress acted to bring new members into the Central Committee and to discuss the vital issues and directions the Standing Committee had elaborated. The Communist Party of Kampuchea had held perhaps five congresses by the end of 1978 (Heder 1980c:Interview No. 26).[15] The first took place September 30, 1960, to rebuild the party after Sieu Heng's 1959 betrayal. The second took place in 1963 when Pol Pot became secretary, again after a period of repression. The third, according to Vorn Vet's confession (Democratic Kampuchea 1978:32), took place after a nationwide "study" session in July 1971 at party headquarters in the forests of the Northern Region. The fourth took place just after victory in June or July 1975 to set Cambodia on the path of the socialist revolution and the building of socialism. The last took place in August 1978 when about sixty people, including Central Committee members and some additional sector and military chairmen met in Phnom Penh. Pol Pot, Nuon Chea, and Ta Mok presided. Discussion centered on the Vietnamese situation, internal problems, and steps to move further toward communism.

That August 1978 meeting elaborated on policies that the Standing Committee had created. The full congress discussed the direction for the next four years. Fighting Vietnam took priority. Steps to futher communize Cambodia by dissolving intermediate organizational structures were discussed. Actually implementing that direction was left to the Central Committee. Operational decisions went to the regions as Central Committee directives (sarajar). One such directive in 1973 ordained the establishment of cooperatives. A directive of July 1977 ordered the renewed expansion of

[15] Heng Samrin's regime does not recognize any congresses held during the Pol Pot era and claims that its May 1981 meeting was the fourth party congress. It is possible that Heder's source exaggerated an ordinary Central Committee plenum into a party congress, but this seems somewhat unlikely.

party membership. One refugee claimed that a directive of August 1978 ordered a nationwide amnesty (Heder 1980c:Interview No. 4), presumably to cope with the Vietnamese threat by ending the reign of terror.

Conclusions

By their 1975 victory, leaders of the Communist Party of Kampuchea presided over a disparate cadre. Senior and mid levels drew from the anti-French dissidence that the Vietminh had nourished. Others had joined the movement during the Sihanouk years, some reacting to the prince's personal rule and corruption of Khmer society or to individual injustices. Others were educated in leftist ideology by teachers or close relatives. After 1970, an influx of peasants and even of pro-Sihanouk city dwellers entered the party's united-front structure. Those who entered the military gained promotion through merit and entered party organizations as education awakened their political consciousness. Coercion played a major role, silencing those who did not agree with party goals. Combined with the superior organization of the PKK, discipline gave the party an enormous advantage over other, much more loosely structured, Khmer institutions.

Fundamental to the success of the party was an obsession with secrecy. Perhaps born of the trauma of betrayal by a party secretary in 1959, this secrecy ensured control by the party center. Regions were kept isolated from each other to the point that nationwide study meetings were a rare, noteworthy occurrence. In part, difficulties of communication enforced this secrecy and encouraged development of a system of couriers.

By 1975, the party had greatly expanded from its precoup strength of four thousand, in 1970, to fourteen thousand full and candidate members. Many thousands more formed the core organization, which functioned as a pool for eventual selection of candidate party members. But full party control over the millions of people forced into cooperatives was not possible. Nor, despite a state security apparatus down to at least district level (Heder 1980c:Interview Nos. 19, 25, 26, 28), did the center apparently have full and timely information on the variations of party policy at local levels. Instead of continuing to expand to cope with the increased administrative needs, the party paused and purified its ranks. The "new" people were themselves riddled with "class enemies" who were hiding their backgrounds. And the leadership apparently came to believe that even its own ranks included enemy agents. Moreover, with victory, the ideologists presumably could afford the leisure to reexamine cadre biographies to demote or purge those of unacceptable class background.

The party apparently keenly felt its lack of control over the administrative structure. In October 1978, Ieng Sary told intellectuals and former diplomats held in the special concentration camp in Phnom Penh that the Central Committee only "grasped" 45 percent of the nation's cooperatives. This was two years after a party representative had complained that former Lon Nol troops and even Sino-Khmer businessmen had become members of co-operative committees in some sectors. Considering the extent of interven-ing purges to "purify" the party, Ieng Sary was probably accurate.

In 1977 and 1978 worldwide attention was called to the massive deaths among the Cambodian population: they were executed for a variety of causes, starved, worked to death, or felled by untreated disease. Since the Vietnamese conquest of Cambodia, revelations as wide-ranging as Stalin's terror have brought out continuing purges, arrests, and executions within the PKK itself, accompanied by torture and forced confession. The regime clearly believed in an external threat to its existence. In a sense, this is bred into Khmer bones, menaced through centuries, first by aggressive neigh-bors, the Thai and the Vietnamese, then by a French protectorate whose real intentions came to be viewed with suspicion and whose Sûreté jailed many of the leading nationalist and communist advocates of independence. A sense of national danger was firmly instilled. Differences in approach be-tween French-educated and some of the indigenously trained leaders who had ties to the Vietminh doubtless fueled this insecurity. Fears of Vietnam-ese intentions were reinforced by repeated expressions from Hanoi that a "special relationship" existed between Cambodia and Vietnam, despite re-iterations of Cambodian antipathy toward any regional grouping. Ieng Sary denied any such interest in Bangkok in October 1975, and Radio Phnom Penh repeatedly broadcast rejection of this Vietnamese initiative.

In analyzing the party's response to fear of traitors, the only conclusion is that the regime gave itself over to counterespionage paranoia. The bizarre interpretations of agent networks and multiple, antagonistic intelligence af-filiations that the party interrogators accepted suggests an indulgence in fantasy that gave rein to the nightmares of the state security branch. In fact, Democratic Kampuchea did not even trust its Chinese advisors who were spied upon and had their work double-checked where possible. At the same time, party leaders seem to have been increasingly unwilling to brook any opposition; disagreement with policy became tantamount to treason. In the rural areas, the tendency was to keep one's head down. Surviving party figures say that they were initially unsure when informed that some leaders had betrayed the revolution. However, even so seemingly knowl-edgeable a leader as Vorn Vet, a deputy secretary of the Standing Commit-tee of the Central Committee, joined in the purging. Others went along until it was too late for them. Even after the party resumed the recruitment of new members, arrests and executions continued. An amnesty said to have been proclaimed in August 1978 would have been too little and too late.

Although the party stopped recruiting after victory, the army continued.

For the military, the lessons of the 1970–1975 war showed the requirements of a new fighting force. Troops had to be young, both to be amenable to discipline and to ensure that only bachelors made up the ranks. A traditional weakness of Khmer military organizations was that families accompanied the troops and, in danger, soldiers looked after their families first, rather than staying on the line. Recruiters ensured the class background of recruits. At training areas, recruits were taught a smattering of communist theory, probably to serve as a base if their intelligence and job performance merited their selection for the core organization, the first step to eventual party candidacy.

The government of Democratic Kampuchea seemed to relate more to the outside world than to the administration of the nation itself. The Standing Committee of the People's Representative Assembly regularly sent congratulatory messages abroad, but never discussed any laws. Senior government figures spoke on the radio in hortatory roles. The State Presidium received the credentials of the handful of ambassadors accredited to Democratic Kampuchea.

The structure of power in Cambodia from 1975–1978 was that of the Communist Party of Kampuchea. The party had entered the 1970–1975 war with a small military wing under full party authority. It took care to maintain that control during the war. Its theory demanded full control of the population down to the lowest cooperative. Party directives were the nation's laws, and party committees supervised their implementation. The party regarded itself as all-knowing. Its prescriptions were all-embracing. The party leadership insisted, as Ith Sarin had described in 1973 (Carney 1977), that failure was an individual fault, not an error of policy or command.

With information coming only from its security apparatus, the party fell under the spell of the counterespionage myth, consuming itself as it had nearly consumed the people of Cambodia over three years of social experimentation. No traditional institutions remained to check party authority: no Sangha to act as a moral counterweight, no feudal leadership factions to balance each other off. The political style had changed from reduction of opposition by seduction and surgical violence, to threat, terror, and coercion. The new style crushed opponents in the name of policy and spirit, unity and obedience to orders.

The Vietnamese push of December 1978 showed how fragile the party, army, and government structure had become. Repeated purges had broken the links of command between officers and men and shattered morale both in the army and in the party. Those targeted as traitors who knew they were not, hardly knew what to do: die in the name of the party like Koestler's hero, or flee to Vietnam to fight the party center. The Cambodian people themselves had long since had enough of the PKK. They welcomed the Vietnamese army, with its plating of anti–Pol Pot Khmer, with applause. The Vietnamese reached their Mekong River target quickly, and then invoked contingency plans to move across most of the rest of Cambodia, driving the remains of the PKK into guerrilla resistance.

Table 1. Kampuchea's Class Structure: The CPK View

Class	Members / Definitions	% Total Population
Feudal		5
Royalists	Members of the royal family	
"Feudalists"	Former ministers or provincial governors; high-ranking military officers	
Capitalist		
Compradore	Those with foreign trading connections; defeated in the war	
Patriotic	NUFK supporters during the war; eliminated in 1975 abolition of private trading	
Petite Bourgeoisie		5
Upper level	High civil servants; holders of licences, higher degrees	
Middle level	Teachers, coiffeurs, tailors, artisans, or self-employed small businessmen	
Lower level	Low ranking civil servants, employees, clerics	
Peasants		85
Rich peasants	Landowners employing hired labor and modern equipment for all work	10
Middle peasants		5
Upper level	Landowners employing hired labor to work 60% or more of their land	
Middle level	Landowners employing hired laborers to work 20%–60% of their land	
Lower level	Small holders who work their own land and who have enough to eat the year round	
Poor peasants		
Upper level	Peasants lacking one or more	70
Middle level	means of production who are	
Lower level	obliged to work the land of others and who have insufficient food to eat for varying lengths of time each year. Criteria for levels varied from region to region	
Workers		5
Independent laborers	Carpenters, handymen, *cyclopousse* (pedicab) drivers	
Industrial workers	Factory workers, rubber plantation workers, dock workers	

Table 1. Kampuchea's Class Structure: The CPK View (*cont.*)

Class	Members / Definitions	% Total Population
Party workers	Workers in mobile youth brigades attached to the Central Committee; cadres in the administration and the army	
Special Class		
Revolutionary intellectuals (overseas NUFK supporters); reactionary intellectuals (overseas nonsupporters of NUFK)	Members of the Special Class or the "Class Apart" were Kampucheans outside Kampuchea as of April 17, 1975, and selected residual elements from the old regime	
Military, police, and high officials of the old regime		
Buddhist monks (treated as petit bourgeois)		

SOURCES: Pol Pot, *Les grandioses victoires de la révolution du Kampuchéa sous la direction juste et clairvoyante du parti communiste du Kampuchéa* (Phnom Penh: Le Ministère des Affaires Etrangères du Kampucnea Démocratique, 1978), pp. 44, 84, 87, 91, 94, 96; François Ponchaud, "Vietnam-Cambodge: Une Solidarité Militante Fragile," Paris: Exchange-Asie, Dossier no. 43 (March 1979), pp. 11–12, and refugee sources.

Table 2. Parliamentary, State, and Government Officers, 1976

Standing Committee of the People's Representative Assembly (PRA)

Nuon Chea	Chairman and First Deputy Secretary, PKK
Nguon Kang ?alias Ta Mok	First Vice Chairman and Second Deputy Secretary; PRA representative of Southwestern Region peasants; Party Secretary, Southwestern Region; probably member, Party Military Committee
Peou Sou alias Khek Pen (mid-1977)	Second Vice Chairman; PRA representative of Northwestern Region peasants; Deputy Party Secretary, Northwestern Region
Ros Nim (F)	Member; PRA representative of Eastern Region peasants
Sor Sean alias Sa Sien alias Tep Sean ?alias Nup Sa Khum (1/3/77)	Member; PRA Representative of Kratie Sector Peasants; Commander, Sector 102, Kratie (1974); possibly Deputy Party Secretary, Sector 106 (1977)
Mey Chham alias Mey Chhan alias Mey Son (17/2/77)	Member: PRA representative of overland and water transport workers
Kheng Sok	Member; PRA representative of Southwestern Region peasants
May Ly	Member; joined Heng Samrin regime
Thang Si alias Sy alias Chou Chet (26/3/78)	Member; Party Secretary, Western Region
Ros Preap alias Ruos Preap (purged)	Member; PRA representative of Northern Region peasants

Table 2.   Parliamentary, State, and Government Officers, 1976 (*cont.*)

State Presidium

Khieu Samphan	Chairman; member, Party Central Committee and head of its Central Office (1977)
So Phim alias So Vanna alias Yann alias Samnang (5/78)	First Vice Chairman; member, Party Standing Committee (by mid-1960s); Party Secretary, Eastern Region
Nhim Ros alias Muol Sambat alias Ta Kong alias Ta Kao (11/6/78)	Second Vice Chairman; Party Secretary, Northwestern Region

Government

Pol Pot alias Salot Sar	Prime Minister; PRA representative of rubber plantation workers; Secretary, Party Standing Committee; Chairman, Party Military Committee
Ieng Sary alias Van	Deputy Prime Minister, Foreign Affairs; member, Party Standing Committee
Vorn Vet alias Von Vet alias Sok Thouk alias Sok alias Penh Thuok (2/11/78)	Deputy Prime Minister, Economy; member, Party Standing Committee
Son Sen alias Khieu	Deputy Prime Minister, National Defense; Chief of General Staff; candidate member, Party Standing Committee
Hu Nim alias Phoas (10/4/77)	Minister of Information and Propaganda; Party Secretary for Information Ministry; PRA representative of Phnom Penh factory workers
Thioun Thoeun alias Pen	Minister of Health
Ieng Thirith (Mrs. Ieng Sary)	Minister of Social Affairs; PRA representative of Phnom Penh factory workers
Toch Phoeun alias Phin	Minister of Public Works; PRA representative of Phnom Penh factory workers
Yun Yat (Mrs. Son Sen)	Minister of Culture, Education, and Instruction; PRA representative of Phnom Penh factory workers

Judiciary Committee

Kang Chap alias Chan Sum alias Se (2/8/78)	Chairman; Secretary, Northern Region; member, Party Central Committee; formerly Party Secretary, Sector 35, Southwestern Region

Committee Chairmen under Deputy Prime Minister for Economy (The chairmen of these bodies held the rank of minister. They changed with regular purges from 1976 on.)

Agriculture	Chey Suon also called Non Suon (1/11/76); replaced by Vice Chairman Sai Neng alias Duong Thuon (3/77); in 1983 Savat
Industry	Cheng An (Fall 1978)
Commerce	Koy Thuon alias Khuon (25/1/77); Chhoeur Doeun alias Sua Va Sy (12/2/77); Prom Nhem alias Tit Sun (25/11/76); in 1983 Van Rith, former Vice Chairman
Communications	Mey Prang (?late 1978), once Secretary of Railway Workers Party Committee

Table 2.   Parliamentary, State, and Government Officers, 1976 (*cont.*)

Energy	Chairman reportedly never named
Vice Chairman	Eng Me Heang alias Chhun, Deputy Party Secretary of Ministry for Energy Service (26/1/77)
Rubber Plantation	Phuong (6/6/78)

NOTE: The dates in parentheses are usually those of arrest. Order of dates is day/month/year.

Table 3.   Party Standing Committee and Central Committee, 1978

Standing Committee (Rank is not certain after the first three.)

Pol Pot alias Salot Sar	Secretary; Chairman, Party Military Committee; Prime Minister; PRA representative of rubber plantation workers
Nuon Chea alias Nuon	Deputy Secretary; Chairman, Standing Committee of PRA
Ta Mok ?alias Nguon Kang alias Thieun Chhith alias Chhith Chhoeun alias Ta Dapram alias Eng Ek	Second Deputy Secretary; Party Secretary, Southwestern Region; First Deputy Chairman, Standing Committee of PRA
So Phim alias So Vanna alias Yann (5/78)	Member; Secretary, Eastern Region Party Committee; First Vice Chairman of State Presidium
Ieng Sary alias Van	Member; Deputy Prime Minister, Foreign Affairs
Vorn Vet alias Von alias Sok Thuok alias Sok alias Penh Thuok (12/78)	Member; Deputy Prime Minister, Economy
Son Sen alias Khieu	Candidate member; Minister of Defense; Chief of General Staff
Ta Keu or Koeu (1978)	Candidate member; former Military Commander, Northwestern Region

Central Committee (As cited by Vorn Vet[*] or assumed due to important positions either listed on Radio Phnom Penh[**] or from Tuol Sleng documents and interviews.)

NORTHEASTERN REGION

*Men San alias Ya alias Ney Sarann (20/9/76)	Member; regional Party Secretary
*Vy alias Um Neng (1978)	Member; regional Deputy Party Secretary; Deputy Commander of region (1974)
Tim alias Chhean Chuon (10/4/78)	Member; member, regional Party Committee
Bun Than alias Chan (31/2/77)	Member; member, regional Party Committee

NORTHERN REGION

*Se alias **Kang Chap alias Chan Sum (2/8/78)	Member; regional Party Secretary; former regional Party Secretary, Sector 35
**Sok	Member; regional Deputy Party Secretary; former regional Party Secretary, Sector 33 until 1976; fled to Vietnam in 1978 after transfer to Eastern Region
Sreng alias Chor Chhan (18/2/77)	Member; regional Deputy Party Secretary; (The Last Plan [Appendix D] calls him Deputy Party Secretary of Central Region, arrested 17/2/77)

Table 3. Party Standing Committee and Central Committee, 1978 (*cont.*)

CENTRAL REGION

**Pok alias Ke Pauk alias Ker Vin — Member; regional Party Secretary; former regional Military Commander; in 1983 candidate member of Standing Committee and Undersecretary General of General Staff of National Army of Democratic Kampuchea

**An (purged) — Member; regional Deputy Secretary

Sreng alias Chor Chhan (17/2/77) — Member; regional Deputy Party Secretary; (two Tuol Sleng lists carry him as Deputy Secretary of Northern Region, arrested 18/2/77)

NORTHWESTERN REGION

**Nhim Ros alias Nhim alias Moul Sambat (11/6/78) — Member; regional Party Secretary; Second Vice Chairman of State Presidium

**Peou Sou alias Khek Pen — Member; regional Deputy Party Secretary; Second Vice Chairman, Standing Committee of PRA; Deputy Party Secretary, Sector 4; liaison officer with the Thai at Poipet

Sarun ?alias Saroun — Member; regional Party Secretary (1978); former Party Secretary, Sector 7; former member, Western Region Party Committee and Secretary, Sector 31

**Neou Rin (purged) — Candidate member; member, regional Party Committee; former Deputy Secretary, Sector 35

Say alias Ros Mau (6/77) — Member; member, regional Party Committee

**Kantol alias Heng Teav — Member; member, regional Party Committee; in 1983 Heng Samrin regime trade union official

WESTERN REGION

*Chou Chet alias Sy alias **Thang Si (26/3/78) — Member; regional Party Secretary; member, Standing Committee of PRA

**Saroun ?alias Sarun — Member; member, regional Standing Committee; possibly transferred to Northwestern Region (q.v.)

**Ran — Member; member, regional Party Committee

SOUTHWESTERN REGION

**Bith alias Ranh Bith — Member; regional Deputy Party Secretary; became member of State Presidium after 1978

**Chong alias Prasith (1974) — Member; regional Deputy Party Secretary; an ethnic Thai in charge of Sector 11

EASTERN REGION

**Chan (purged) — Member; regional Deputy Party Secretary

**Phuong (6/6/78) — Member; member, regional Party Committee; Chairman, Rubber-Planting Committee, Office of Deputy Prime Minister for Economy

Lin alias Sokh Khnar (5/6/78) — Member; member, regional Party Committee; chairman of regional office

KOMPONG SOM PORT

**Mouth alias Ta Muth — Member; Secretary, Kompong Som Port Party Committee; Political Commissar, Navy Brigade 164; in 1983 a division commander; son-in-law of Ta Mok

Table 3.   Party Standing Committee and Central Committee, 1978 (*cont.*)

Saom alias Phi Som alias Chhun Sok Nguon alias Sun Sok Nguon	Member; Chairman or Deputy Chairman, Kompong Som Port; PRA representative of dock workers
**Krin alias Thuch Rin	Member; Deputy Secretary, Kompong Som City Party Committee; PRA representative of dock workers; member for Social and Cultural Affairs, regional Party Committee and Political Commissar, Sector 32 (1974); in 1982 joined the coalition government; defected to Sihanouk in 1987
**Lonh alias Sok Sim alias Chap Lonh	Candidate (?) member; member, Kompong Som City Party Committee; PRA representative of fishermen; formerly regional Deputy Secretary, Sector 37; formerly regional Political Commissar, sixteenth Regiment, First Brigade
PHNOM PENH Khieu Samphan alias Hem	Member; head of Central Office of Central Committee from 1977; Chairman of State Presidium
**Pang (purged)	Member; Chief of Protocol of Central Committee; deputy head of Central Office
Koy Thuon alias Thuch alias Khuon (3/76)	Member; Party Secretary and Chairman, Commerce Committee; Party Secretary, Northern Region until 1975
*Doeun alias Sua Va Sy alias **Chhoeur Doeun	Member; Party Secretary, Commerce Committee; until 1977, head of Central Office of Central Committee
Non Suon alias Chey alias **Chey Suon (1/11/76)	Member; Party Secretary and Chairman, Agricultural Committee; former regional Party Secretary, Sector 25
**Mei Prang	Member; Chairman, Communication Committee; PRA representative of railway workers
Toch Phoeun alias Phin (26/1/77)	Member; Party Secretary for Communications and Transport; Minister of Public Works
**Cheng An alias An (late 1978)	Member; Party Secretary and Chairman, Industry Committee; former Party Secretary, Sector 15, Special Region (1971); former member, Phnom Penh City Party Committee (1963)
Hu Nim alias Phoas (10/4/77)	Member; Party Secretary of Propaganda Ministry; Minister of Information
Phok Chhay alias Toch (14/3/77)	Member; cadre in Service "870," cover designation for Central Committee; former Political Commissar of Southwestern Region forces (1974)
Hou Youn (1975 or 1976)	Member; Minister of Interior (1974); possibly chief of Central Office of Central Committee (1974)
Tum alias **Chheat Chhe alias Seat Chhe	Member; member of General Staff; regional Party Secretary, Sector 24
Chan Chankrey alias Mean (19/5/76)	Member; Deputy Secretary of General Staff; Political Commissar, Brigade 170

Table 4. Northwestern Region Leadership Purges, 1977–1978

Name / Alias	Position	Arrest / Death
Party Administration		
Nhim Ros / Moul Sambath / Ta Kong / Ta Kao	Party Secretary	11 Jun 78
Peou Sou / Khek Bin / So	Deputy Secretary and Deputy Chairman of PRA; representative of Northwestern Region peasants in PRA (position listed only as Deputy Secretary, Northwestern Region, Sector 4)	23 Jun 77 or 22 Jul 77 /
Neou Rin	Member, Standing Committee	reportedly purged
Ruas Mau / Thon / Say	Member, Standing Committee; chief of Northwestern Region Office or regional Party Chief of Staff	26 Jun 77
Kan Tol / Teav / Heng Teav	Member, Northwestern Region Committee; in 1983 member of PRK's Council of State and member of the PRK Parliament from Battambang; head of PRK trade union	
Douc Pheach / Nup / Men Nup	Member, Sector 1 Party Committee; PRA representative of Northwestern Region peasants	12 Sep 77 /
Chea Huon / Vanh	Member, Sector 1 Committee	12 Sep 77 /
Um Sam Uon / Sawe Ret (*sic*)	Member, Sector 2 Committee	4 Aug 77 /
Hom Chhal / Vang	Member, Sector 2 Committee	4 Aug 77 /
Sray Iem or Srey Oeum / Ven	Secretary, Sector 2 Committee	28 Mar or 23 Aug 1977 / execution date unknown
Phok Sary / Tum	Secretary, Sector 3 Committee	30 June 78 / 22 Sep 78
Vom Chet or Von Chet / Cu	Deputy Secretary, Sector 3 Committee	12 Aug or 18 Dec 1977 / execution date unknown
Lek Soet / Vong	Secretary, Sector 4 Committee	27 Jun 78 (*sic*) / 16 Apr 78
Thin Tham / Hieng (possibly also Min Tha My / Hieng)	Secretary, Sector 4 Committee	18 Dec 77 / 26 Jul 78
Sun Kun / Sui (also Sun Korn / Suy)	Deputy Secretary, Sector 4; in 1974, Commander and Political Commissar, Sector 4	23 Jun or 22 Jul 1977 / execution date unknown
Toch Much	Member, Sector 4 Committee	5 Aug 77 /
Men Chun or Men Thun / Hung	Secretary, Sector 5 Committee	20 Aug 77 /

Table 4. Northwestern Region Leadership Purges, 1977–1978 (*cont.*)

Name / Alias	Position	Arrest / Death
Heng Rin / Mei	Secretary, Sector 5 Committee	16 Nov 78 / 15 Dec 78 (*sic*, probably should be 1977)
Sieng Ngan / Thun	Former member, Sector 5 Committee	2 Sep 77 /
Kung Len / Le	Member, Sector 5 Committee	2 Sep 77 /
Um Chhuon / May	Former member, Sector 6 Committee	23 Jun 77 /
Oum Tuoi	Secretary, Sector 7 Committee	28 Jun 77 /
Ke Kim Huot / Sot / Man	Secretary, Sector 7 Committee	12 or 13 Jul 77 / 10 May 78
Regional Offices		
So Neu or So Nau	Member, regional staff or regional General Staff	13 Jun 77 /
Muon Mau	Chief, regional Agricultural Service	30 Jul 77 /
Van Nhup	Chief, regional Agricultural Service	23 Oct 77 /
Vai Huon	Chief, regional Agricultural Service	18 Dec 77 /
Sin Eng / Suon	Chairman, regional Commerce Committee	30 Aug 77 /
Ke Can or Keo Can / Doeun	Assistant, responsible for regional commercial matters	3 Aug 77 /
Tea Dam	Chief, regional Commerce Committee, stationed at Phnom Penh	30 Jul 77 /
Se Sann or So Sanh / Yean	Director, regional supply depot	16 Jul 77 /
Hypot Keo	Deputy Director, regional supply depot	16 Jul 77 /
Chheach Chu / Puch	Director, regional rice milling service	3 Aug 77 /
Nup Soeun	Director, rice milling service	1 Jun 77 /
Yun Chan	Director, commercial rice mill	1 Jul 77 /
So Pham / Chet	Director, regional textile mill	28 Jun 77 /
Hy Sary	Chairman, regional Construction Committee	10 Aug 77 /
Keo Sam On or Kao Sam On / Saravyth	Director, regional packing factory	2 Sep 77 /
Som Hang	Chairman, regional coffee farm	25 Sep 77 /
Neang Nau / Se	Member, regional Coffee Farm Committee	25 Sep 77 /
Kao Sa Nat / Rit	Vice Chairman, regional Cotton Farm Committee	16 Oct 77 /
Military		
Sa Run or Sa Rum / San / Nong Sarim	Political Commissar, Northwestern Region Brigade	20 Jun 77 /

Table 4.   Northwestern Region Leadership Purges, 1977–1978 (*cont.*)

Name / Alias	Position	Arrest / Death
Ly Mi Suon / Khleng	Deputy Political Commissar, Second Brigade	18 Jun 77 or 18 Dec 77 / execution date unknown
Uch Suong / Son	Member, Northwestern Brigade staff	22 Jun 77 /
Sum Then or Xun Then / Khoi	Member, Second Brigade Committee	21 Sep 77 /
Neou	Member, Northwestern Brigade Committee	?
Em Nut / Sung	Deputy Chief, Northwestern Region (Military) Security Service	16 Jan 78 /

4. The Economy

by Charles H. Twining

There exists no pattern for the revolutionary experiment of the Khmer. We want to implement something which so far never existed in history. There exist no models for doing this, neither the Chinese model nor the Vietnamese can be applied to us. We are reorganizing the country on the basis of agriculture. With the yields of agriculture we will build an industry which will have to serve agriculture. The Khmer people have centuries of experience in planting rice, so that we must start out from rice cultivation.—Ieng Sary quoted in *Der Spiegel*, May 9, 1977

After liberation, under the clear-sighted guidance of the correct Cambodian revolutionary organization, this region profoundly changed, and the people live in a joyful atmosphere. Now, our people have become the full masters of the water, land and rice fields. For that reason, our brothers are striving to plunge into the battle to increase production with soaring enthusiasm in order to contribute toward restoring the economy of new Cambodia.—Radio Phnom Penh, July 26, 1975, discussion of the scene from Battambang to the Thai border

Regardless of whatever twisted meaning the word "joyful" might have had in Phnom Penh, there is no doubt that the Democratic Kampucheans were fully intent upon developing the economy of their country on an agricultural base. "Work" was the watchword from the fall of the Khmer Republic until Vietnamese troops extinguished their regime in January 1979. The country's leadership had studied in France, during which time its members inquired seriously into the merits of Marxism, then returned to a Cambodia whose economy was floundering and whose society was highly stratified and corrupt. Afterwards, they went into the forests for long years, during which there was time to both think and study. The result of all this was a very firm commitment to economic change and development and equally firm ideas as to how to go about it.

Undergirding their conclusions was, one strongly suspects, the Cambodian fear, developed with the fall of the old Khmer Kingdom of Angkor many centuries earlier, that their country's survival was chancy at best, situated as it was between two expanding giants—Vietnam and Thailand— on its eastern and western frontiers. Prince Sihanouk and his royal ancestors had had their own varied ways of assuring their—and their people's— survival. The Cambodian communists undoubtedly saw their best means over the long term in the strength that comes through development—economic, social, and political—even if initially it would have to be forced upon the people. Because no other country could be trusted to act in a purely

109

selfless way toward Cambodia, their theory of development stressed complete self-reliance.[1] A human tragedy of almost unprecedented proportions occurred because political theoreticians carried out their grand design on the unsuspecting Khmer people.

Economic Goals

The Democratic Kampuchean (hereafter DK) leadership wanted genuinely to create a country totally independent from every point of view. To achieve this state, Cambodia must be self-contained and self-reliant to the point of autarky. Essentially, it must pull itself up by its own bootstraps to achieve a greatness exceeding that even of Angkor, in which everyone would benefit equally and from which Cambodia could deal with the outside world from a position of strength. This would be a difficult process, requiring military vigilance and, admittedly, tremendous sacrifice on the part of the people, but the end product would surely be worth the costs, the leaders believed. They saw only total revolution as assuring a break from the constraints of the past and propelling the country on to that nirvana. These were very attractive ideas. The leadership's goals had political, economic, and social aspects that together constituted an indivisible whole.

A strong economy in which everyone contributed skills and labor toward its advancement was vital in this context. The emphasis was on production. Easily the most important statement to emerge from Cambodia during the entire period was that of party secretary Pol Pot on the seventeenth anniversary of the party on September 27, 1977. In it he set forward his economic intentions:

We take agriculture as the basic factor and use the fruits of agriculture to systematically build industry in order to advance toward rapidly transforming a Cambodia marked by a backward agriculture into a Cambodia marked by a modernized agriculture. We also intend to rapidly transform the backward agricultural Cambodia into an industrialized Cambodia by firmly adhering to the fundamental principles of independence, sovereignty and self-reliance.

He went on to note that, in agriculture, the party was concentrating upon water storage so as to maximize rice production. Listing accomplishments in water projects, he declared, "All of this has been built by our workers and peasants who completely rely on their own efforts." Rice production served two purposes: as food for the people and as an export "in order to accumulate capital to finance our national defense and reconstruction efforts." Turning to industry, he observed that special attention was given to factories "which serve agriculture and the people's livelihood." Factories

[1] For an elaboration of self-reliance as an important Khmer Rouge theme, see Chapter 2 by Karl Jackson.—ED.

using imported raw materials were converted over to use local materials (Pol Pot 1977:H34).

The emphasis on simultaneous agricultural and industrial modernization within a self-sufficient commune structure, the stress on irrigation, the desire to send unproductive urban elements to work in the fields, and the necessity for revolutionary haste all smack of Mao's Great Leap Forward and Cultural Revolution despite Ieng Sary's denial of the relevance of all outside models.[2]

The Rationale

The question of what motivated the DK leadership to do what they did has been an extremely difficult one for outsiders and—more importantly—for Cambodians themselves to answer. To refugees who succeeded in reaching Thailand after April 1975, their experience under DK rule was a nightmare—bewildering, incomprehensible, un-Khmer. They often sought the facile explanation: the Vietnamese or the Chinese were behind it; we Cambodians don't act that way. To other observers, however, it seemed obvious that the leadership was too proud, too xenophobic, to allow anyone, including the Chinese and especially the Vietnamese, to dictate how to run the country.

IDEOLOGICAL

When the future DK leaders took their turns studying in France, those about whom we know fell into Marxist groups. Like most students, they were undoubtedly disgruntled over the inequities back home. Among this handful of people, intense men like Khieu Samphan surely gave considerable thought to what could be done to ameliorate the situation. Yet, if one reads through the two accessible dissertations, those of Khieu Samphan and Hu Nim, they do not strike you today as terribly radical (their tone and content possibly were softened so that their authors could live in Sihanouk's Cambodia), but some similarities with what subsequently transpired are recognizable.

Khieu Samphan recommends in his 1959 work a rather complete revamping of his country's economic structure so as to promote a more equitable and Cambodia-oriented development and allow his country to deal from a position of economic strength with the rest of the world. He observes that most of Cambodia's agriculture is precapitalistic (subsistence agriculture) or feudal (used for personal consumption or to pay land rents and debts), except for rubber production, which is almost wholly for export and brings

---

[2] For similar conclusions, see Chapters 2 and 9 by Karl Jackson and Chapter 8 by Kenneth Quinn.—ED.

little benefit at home. In his eyes, Cambodia's weak industry exists primarily to serve the outside world, through production for export or through the repatriation of profits. The owners of the capital are located outside Cambodia, pulling the strings and thinking only of their personal interests. Any earnings that may remain inside the country are used for the purchase of imported goods, benefitting only the swollen, nonproductive commercial sector and leaving the poor farmer entrenched more than ever in a rut. His analysis of his country's situation is interesting but probably fairly typical of fashionable French intellectual thinking of the time.

Khieu Samphan's solution is for "autonomous development." "Inducements" or "persuasion" could turn the landowners away from exploitation of the poor and transform them into energetic agricultural or industrial capitalistic entrepreneurs. "Severe measures" were reserved for use against the outside world so that Cambodia could gain control of its own foreign trade. He opts for directing and restricting international trade and capital so that domestic agriculture and industry, and consequently trade, can be restructured by encouraging cooperatives where possible and by creating a stronger government sector. His appeal for industrialization is particularly strong. Khieu Samphan terminates his thesis with a call for all sectors of the society to exert leadership to bring about this rebalancing; in doing so he sought a leadership allied with true democracy and drawing its strength from the support of the people. The latter was, perhaps, the forerunner of the vague kind of phrase the DK leadership was to employ all too often during their years of power.

Except for the controls advocated over what moves in and out of the country, Khieu Samphan's approach toward the people is not particularly dictatorial. Instead, it is the rather dreamy one of, "If they understand clearly enough, they will naturally lend their support enthusiastically." At first blush, the manner in which Democratic Kampuchea cut itself off economically from the outside world in 1975 might be viewed as an extension of Khieu Samphan's thinking, but he *never* suggested the complete kind of autarky and isolation that his government adopted. Finally, one can probably see a connection between his desire for mutual development of agriculture and industry to serve one another and the DK leadership's focus on that connection.[3]

Hu Nim's emphases in his 1965 dissertation were in broad agreement with Khieu Samphan's: an economy badly structured and dependent upon the outside world that limits Cambodia's development; the need to control foreign trade and finance; recognition of the importance of the link between agriculture and industry; and the desirability of creating agricultural coop-

[3] For further material on Khieu Samphan's dissertation, see Chapter 2 by Karl Jackson.— ED.

eratives. The goal was the same, too: increased and more equitable development serving the Cambodian people. Hu Nim was very keen about the planning mechanism and creating specialized state economic organizations to lead and assist in development. He wanted the state to control and direct private trade but not take it over; brusque nationalization would simply make a mess of things. He saw industry not as an end in itself but serving agricultural development and producing consumer items to reduce imports. Industry would be best if concentrated in state and mixed sectors of the economy or if run as cooperatives rather than operating purely privately, although Hu Nim was not suggesting that the latter should be removed completely.

In economic development, Hu Nim's most important element was a state economy serving exclusively the workers. Hu Nim (who would later become minister of information and propaganda prior to his execution July 6, 1977) examined in his thesis the Chinese, North Korean, and North Vietnamese models of development and was obviously an admirer of them all (see Becker 1981b). He noted the stages through which the development of cooperatives had passed in those countries. He admired the fact that the North Koreans succeeded in the space of five years in moving from no cooperatives at all to having one large one per district, emphasizing self-reliance in their approach to development. In China, he described how the resulting communes were larger than cooperatives, developed a diversified economy of their own, and were at the same time the basic administrative unit. He observed that since 1960 the Chinese had decided that industry must serve agriculture. He noted that in North Vietnam agricultural cooperatives had succeeded due to the enthusiasm of the peasantry and the energy of its new cadres.

Examining Cambodia, Hu Nim used 1962 figures showing his country's land distribution. He reported that 30.7 percent of all farming families had less than 1 hectare of land, equal to 5.18 percent of the total land owned. On the other hand, 4 percent of the population held 4 hectares or more, for a total of 21.45 percent of land owned. He concludes that the proportion of the farming population with little or no land was greater than 50 percent. Although the Cambodian land tenure situation appears to have been no worse than that existing throughout Southeast Asia (and probably better than the average), Hu Nim saw nevertheless a great need for agrarian reform in his country, with the final goal being mutual help and cooperative groups, "the only way of escaping the individual poverty cycle." He warned of one thing, however, that the Cambodian peasant is very attached to his plot of land and his right to it must be respected! Only by persuading—not by ordering—peasants to exchange land could progress be made toward that goal. Participation in cooperatives must be voluntary, and democracy must be the golden rule within them. Each member of an agricultural cooperative should keep his own property title. Hu Nim felt that once the advantages of cooperation were explained to the peasantry, it would catch on like wildfire (Hu Nim 1965:296).

In all, Hu Nim appeared to be very much a middle-of-the-roader. He wanted change, but change developed on the basis of planning, enlightenment, and understanding, not harsh coercion. Like Khieu Samphan, and like many idealistic young intellectuals the world over, he wanted mass participation to serve as the guiding force for all this but left rather vague any plans for how to achieve it. The DK leadership was similarly imprecise, of course. Hu Him presented some well conceived ideas in this thesis, which was perhaps more throughly researched, more pragmatic, and less "ideologically driven" than Khieu Samphan's. Hu Nim himself came across as such a moderate, an apostle of voluntary change, that one often wonders what his true feelings were about all that subsequently occurred.

The economic views of Khieu Samphan and Hu Nim had obvious relevance to policies adopted in Cambodia after the DK leadership actually assumed power. The dissertations are probably fairly good indicators of the kinds of Marxist formulations prevalent among Khmer revolutionary leaders in general. One person who joined the communist side in 1973 said that everyone in his camp in Stung Treng district of northern Kompong Cham province devoted some of the day to studying and some to working in the fields. Even high-ranking leaders like Hou Yuon would spend a symbolic period daily performing manual labor and, even though he was preoccupied with trying to run a war, Hou Youn also spent a brief period each day in study. Lesser adherents to the revolutionary side spent several hours a day in study. It would have been fascinating to see what they were mulling over, to overhear their discussions. Presumably the sessions dealt with theory, translated into what would best suit Cambodia, and the practice of manual labor was meant to link these theories with reality. (One cannot help but recall the Chinese practice during the Great Leap Forward and the Cultural Revolution of sending intellectuals down to work in the rice fields in order to give them a new sense of "reality".) The overall perspective propounded by Khieu Samphan and Hu Nim was quite impressive as a system, particularly if all important DK leaders actually participated in studying it. Ideology is obviously an important component of the reason why Democratic Kampuchea developed as it did.

DIRE NECESSITY

Did the sudden collapse of the Khmer Republic catch the DK leadership unprepared, with the economy in such bad straits that they had to take ill-considered actions just to cope? I would submit that they coped just as they had decided they would do. An extraordinary party congress held in February 1975, reportedly presided over by Khieu Samphan, is generally thought to have made the decision to evacuate the cities and abolish all currency after the takeover. The fact that the cities were all emptied within several days of their fall, with the people knowingly directed to spots in the countryside where they camped at least temporarily, does not give the impression of a sudden, jerky action. This had all been organized beforehand.[4]

Until Pol Pot made his famous statement in September 1977 declaring that the cities had been emptied for security reasons to break up and disperse any hostile groups, the usual line had been that the inhabitants went into the countryside because food was in scarce supply. What was the food situation at the time of the takeover? Cambodia's latest rice harvest was in December 1974–January 1975. In the country's rice bowl, the northwest, the harvest had been good. Because little could be exported or even moved around the country easily, merchants in the area were reportedly "stuck" with a surplus. In the southeast (Prey Veng, Svay Rieng), the harvest was also said to be good. In the communist-controlled area of Kompong Thom, there was apparently a good rice crop. In other communist-controlled areas, we do not have adequate information, but one could surmise that the country had produced a good crop in the zones of both sides, except where the war and accompanying population movements had seriously disrupted cultivation. There is disagreement as to whether Phnom Penh, swollen with almost half of the country's total population, had thirty or sixty days' rice supply remaining, but it would not have been difficult to locate it. The warehouse manager of a major voluntary organization engaged in feeding people right up to the end estimated a sixty-day supply. This is far from a negligible amount.

At the time of the final takeover, the victorious side could perhaps have moved supplies about the country. This, however, is asking a great deal at the outset of a new situation, requiring the taking of inventories, the organization of transport, and persuading local commanders unsure of the new situation in which they found themselves to give up precious stocks. Still, if Phnom Penh had several weeks' worth of rice in the city, something other than the brusque movement of people could have been arranged. Instead, one had the impression that the decisions had already been taken and were merely being implemented in the post–April 17 period without regard for the realities of the food situation. The inhabitants of the city were the "enemy" and required harsh discipline before they could be allowed to assume a place in the new revolutionary order.

There was another option: international aid. We do not know for sure what the possibilities were, being especially ignorant of aid opportunities

---

[4] Timothy Carney in Chapter 1 provides further information on the premeditated nature of moves taken to restructure the country immediately following April 17, 1975.—ED.

available from the allied communist side. A number of refugees reported seeing rice in the summer of 1975 in bags from the People's Republic of China, so presumably that country was able to and did provide emergency food supplies. Could and would it have done more, if asked? The Soviets and their Eastern European friends were eager to make amends for their lack of contact with the eventual victors during Lon Nol days and could presumably have been tapped for assistance, but the Cambodians never really forgave them and had nothing to do with them. Vietnam, needless to say, was fully occupied with its own victory. With regard to the rest of the world, the DK leaders were completely untrusting. Both the French and the Japanese genuinely wanted relations that could well have translated quickly into aid, but rather than accepting these offers the Cambodians branded the two countries as enemies instead. One leading private voluntary organization, the Save the Children Foundation, made constant offers of assistance, and the International Committee of the Red Cross made known on various occasions its desire to help, but without success. Three different national Red Cross / Red Crescent organizations from nonaligned countries sent medicines to Thailand to be transported into Cambodia just after the takeover, and these were rejected by the new government.

The communists were fiercely independent; they were going to link up with no one, being persuaded in their seeming paranoia that any such moves would result in their resubjugation by outside forces. If there was a key phrase used in lectures given the people at night from 1975 until the collapse of Democratic Kampuchea, it was "national independence." At the beginning, only the Chinese, who had somehow "proven themselves" during the war years, were "allowed" to furnish assistance, and even this, I would submit, was taken at arm's length. Thus, the aid option was rejected from almost all parties so far as Democratic Kampuchea was concerned.

The result was that 1975 was a year of hunger. Except for that relatively minor amount of food allowed to enter Democratic Kampuchea from outside the country, Cambodians were limited to consuming what was at hand until the next uncertain harvest at the end of the year. While those villagers who were not uprooted held on to what personal stocks they could, the new authorities quickly assumed control of rice and other food stored in warehouses unevenly distributed around the country. They were very conservative in doling it out, surely realizing how valuable it was and how long it needed to last. They gave priority for its consumption to cadres and soldiers, with the large percentage of the population that had been recently turned out of the cities and considered to be unfriendly and even meriting punishment receiving relatively little. The starvation caused by the disruptions of 1975 (warfare, change of ruling officials, massive population movements) was to be repeated for virtually the same reasons in 1979.

ECONOMIC EFFICIENCY

Had the Cambodian communist experience in the liberated zones prior to 1975 shown that the best way to develop the economy was through rapid collectivization? One suspects that although this, coupled with terrible violence, may have been a good method for controlling people, it was not necessarily the most economically productive method, at least not in the short or medium term. Like other agricultural peoples, Cambodians are attached to their land; it is an integral part of their being. Since the areas taken over prior to April 1975 were almost all rural, there would have been a great deal of resistance to giving up one's land. A cooperative attitude is one that must be nourished and encouraged. Instead, the communists forced it upon the population with the expectation that after a generation or so, the people would come to see agricultural cooperatives as the best method.

Refugees who fled from the liberated zones prior to April 1975 did so because of the violence, the forced labor, and the lack of food. In Siem Reap province, for example, the communists brought to the area an excess of violence, massacring people for reason or no reason, breaking children's heads open, showing that they were the masters. After a while they calmed down, and the population was thoroughly terrified.[5] The emphasis then was work, work, and more work, all in groups. The rice produced in Siem Reap in 1974 for the most part went to supply the war effort, so that the people themselves received relatively little. The same description can be given for practices instituted in the area along the Vietnamese border (see Quinn 1974). How efficient this method was (compared to any other method of control and production) may not have entered the minds of the "liberators" who, fighting against fairly desperate odds, probably believed passionately that anyone not with them was against them. There was a war on, after all, and everything had to be done to support it. The only persons who could have changed the policy—and obviously did not—were those at the top; the others—the young "have nots" or others on the communist side, the doers rather than the thinkers—were simply carrying out orders, often in an uncomprehending but unquestioning way, at least during the war. When these people began questioning the methods or their continued separation from their families after 1975, they were purged.

In any case, it was natural for the victors to organize the population newly taken over in April 1975 in the same way they had organized their liberated zones earlier. Because the people in areas held by Lon Nol until near the end were considered to be the real enemy, why should they be treated more gently?

[5] See Chapter 6 by Kenneth Quinn for additional material on violence.—ED.

GENERAL

The lines the communists followed in the economic organization of Cambodia in 1975 evolved from the early thinking of the Cambodian intellectuals in France and were more sharply defined during the long years in the forests from 1963 and 1967 onwards. The appeal—wonderfully exciting in the abstract—was for a purification that, somehow returning to the idealized ways of yesteryear, would succeed in making a new Cambodia, one that could stand by itself.[6] Perhaps they saw it as the only way the country could survive with threatening neighbors and a hostile world.

Three factors may have combined to produce the perception that only a radical departure from all past organizational forms could restore Cambodia's vigor and independence.[7] First, their isolation in the forest may have made the threat to their country and to Khmer culture seem even more immediate.[8] In addition, the simplicity of rural life may have made them think that all economic ties regarding property, money, and markets could be readily transformed by returning to a more simplistic state of nature. Second, the on-going political situation presented them with a whole series of opponents bent upon their utter destruction, including: Sihanouk, who persecuted them prior to his overthrow; Lon Nol, who likewise sought to destroy them; and the Vietnamese (communist and noncommunist), who invaded and occupied their country. This may have convinced the DK elite that safety could only be achieved by eliminating all of their opponents, pro-Sihanouk; pro–Lon Nol; and pro-Vietnamese alike. Third, the DK elite, like all political actors, had a natural desire for power, and their lack of substantial support within the Phnom Penh elite may have contributed to their radicalism. Their vision of the Cambodian future required completely transforming the society, its property ties, its economic base, and its political structure. They thought they were closer to the people than those characters living off the fat of the land in Phnom Penh under Sihanouk and Lon Nol, but in their own way the Khmer Rouge leaders were living in their own peculiar dream world, in which the human element was virtually forgotten. What they saw as a rational economic organization may have made sense only in the isolation of the forest. As an operative policy, it was cruel and unrealistic. One suspects that their difficulties made this small group of idealists dig in their heels all the more, translating opposition as a threat to

[6] I know of no better description of the glorified Cambodian communist domain than Chapter 14 of Sihanouk's *My War with the CIA* (Sihanouk and Burchett 1973). Excellent propaganda at the time, the communists' respect for private property and mutual aid in work are among its themes.

[7] For additional material on the possible motivations of the revolutionaries, see Chapters 2 and 9 by Karl Jackson, Chapter 5 by François Ponchaud, and Chapter 6 by Kenneth Quinn.— ED.

[8] For additional comments on the Khmer Rouge as the "forest people," see Chapter 5 by François Ponchaud.—ED.

their dreams and to their own survival. One may choose to describe most of the DK leaders as intellectuals, but if so, they were rather ignorant of, or rejected for theoretical reasons, the nature of the interdependent, modern world of the twentieth century. Their distrust of it, their failure to skillfully use what the world had to offer, had tragic consequences that continue to be felt in Southeast Asia.

Organization of the Economy

GOVERNMENTAL

What glue held the economy together and gave it direction? Refugees would know at best only the lowest level of the country's political, social, and economic organization. The key agents appear to have been those persons responsible for economic matters from the village up through the central level. At the center, that person would have been Vorn Vet, deputy prime minister for economic affairs, who was purged in 1978.[9] Such important policy decisions as from whom to accept aid and the pace at which to expand cooperatives were, so far as we know, taken collegially by the Politburo or the larger Central Committee. Vorn Vet would have been responsible for overseeing everything of an economic nature on a continuing basis. How many people he had working with him at the central level is a matter of conjecture. All we know from the reports of visitors to Phnom Penh during this period is that the number of officials in ministries appeared to be small.

Six committees emerged in the new government created in 1976: agriculture, commerce, communications, energy, industry, and rubber plantations. If one accepts that these had an important substantive role in making the economy work, presumably under Vorn Vet's general supervision, then they can be seen to provide an umbrella apparatus at the top serving as action offices for the various aspects of the economy.

In a completely state-operated economy, the central element of coordination and direction is all important. Yet we assume, for lack of contradictory evidence, that most of the higher level economic administrators were inexperienced in running the new socialist economy, which was completely different from anything Cambodia had ever experienced. The absence of administrators trained to run a centrally planned economy meant the simplest way to run the economy was to place everyone in the same basic agricultural organization. The only citizens not relegated to these self-sufficient agricultural units were civilian officials, the military, and other specialized occupations. It is doubtful that local conditions were allowed to influence the uniform application of revolutionary policies. According to

[9] See Chapter 3, p. 92, by Timothy Carney for confirmation.—ED.

numerous refugees, for example, rice was planted on soil whether it was good or not; each administrative entity had to undertake a specified amount of irrigation work, whatever the need.

Since the local level received the emphasis in Democratic Kampuchea and provided the input that made the country what it was, it would seem important to have had experts go out from the central or other levels to inspect and advise people on what to do. Did this occur? We do know that central-level personnel went on inspection tours. However, one wonders whether this practice was restricted to special projects. No refugee whom I ever interviewed had heard of a visit from a central government official to his local area. (A person such as Ieng Sary, accompanying a group of visitors to the Angkor ruins and stopping off at a cooperative, would have been an exception, of course, but he could hardly have provided any real expertise). No ordinary worker in a cooperative had seen regional officials either. The highest level with which people ever really came into contact was the district, whose few officials and cadres made occasional visits to the local cooperatives. The emphasis at such times was to give orders to officials or to encourage the people to work harder, produce more, and dig faster. Educationally, these district officials covered the entire scale from illiterate to literate. Probably with few exceptions, expertise from on high was simply not available.

A portrait of a district adviser might be gleaned from the following example. A person of some authority in an enclave of Democratic Kampuchea along the Thai–Cambodia border in 1980 was a man who described himself as a primary school teacher in Battambang Province in the prerevolutionary period. Afterwards, he stated he worked on the district level as a cadre advising on agricultural methods until the beginning of 1979. Asked from whence he obtained his particular expertise, he replied that he just tried to do the best he could as a person who had some education. Obviously, technical education and administrative experience were not important job qualifications for a district administrator in Democratic Kampuchea.

BARTER AND LOCAL ECONOMY

One feature that distinguished Democratic Kampuchea from the rest of the world was the absence of money. In April 1975, stories of Cambodian riels blowing in streets or being used in fires, with nothing to replace them, stirred the imagination. Now, with the downfall of that regime, we know that it had apparently planned to introduce its own currency—bills minted at that time were found after the Heng Samrin takeover—but the leadership changed its mind at the February 1975 party congress.

Self-sufficiency was the principle throughout the land. Rice was grown for consumption by the populace and for export outside the local area. Each cooperative had one rice pounder to remove the husks from the kernels of rice. Foods such as manioc and cabbage were grown for local consumption; chickens and pigs were raised similarly. Normally, all would be done communally for the cooperative, but visitors to Cambodia during the DK years reported seeing small gardens or a few chickens around individual homes. Such cows and buffalo as existed were communal property. The idea in each cooperative was that there would be blacksmiths, carpenters, and weavers who would contribute their services in lieu of at least some fieldwork. Blacksmithing was probably the most important skill, to repair and even manufacture the hoes, axes, or plowshares necessary for agriculture. The extent to which a cooperative had people skilled in all these functions by 1979 is debatable, but the DK leaders were trying. (It was interesting to observe in a DK civilian border settlement in 1980 one small, crude but operable, forge. People said they had no use for it at present but that it was important to have, nevertheless. The symbolism of that forge among a group of people who were obviously "believers" in the system was reminiscent of the backyard furnaces in Maoist China's Great Leap Forward.)

An individual was allowed to have two basic possessions of his own: a bowl and a spoon. City people who suddenly found themselves in rural Cambodia in 1975 with just the barest of personal belongings often had to fashion these somehow out of pieces of wood. Once regular shoes wore out, footwear consisted of "Ho Chi Minh sandals" improvised from pieces of rubber tires. (The villagers who considered themselves fortunate were those who had a supply of old tires). Some people had more goods, of course, and became very adept at hiding a watch, a little gold, or a radio. Once any of these items was discovered, communist soldiers would seize them or demand them if small favors (for example, some additional rice to eat) were to be accorded. Often, the "new people" (those liberated in 1975) looked with envy at the "old people" who, by dint of joining the Khmer Rouge earlier, may have remained in their old villages and were allowed to keep a number of their original material goods. Once these goods were used up or wore out, however, not even the "old people" were allowed to replace them.

Since no entity can be entirely self-sufficient in most circumstances, even in revolutionary Cambodia there had to be some movement of goods within the country. Not everyone had a supply of old tires or had cloth and garment makers. Salt had to be brought inland from the coast. When rice was scarce or nonexistent in an area, some would be transported from an outside storage point. Who controlled all this? It was certainly "up the line," but the focus of power remains unclear.

Along the Thai border just inside Cambodia, DK villages composed partly of base people (a concept to be explained shortly) were established after the fall of the DK regime. They often move supplies to DK troops in the field as well as to other areas where persons with continued loyalty to the former government reside, a role similar to that which the transport corps played prior to 1975. During the 1975–1978 period, the corps assured the movement of supplies throughout Cambodia.

The activities of our transport workers since liberation have increased many fold because of the greater need for supplies throughout the country. Among the goods handled by transport units are fuel oil, dishes, pots, pans, production tools, rice, salt, and fish paste. These products are being transported from one sector to another in growing quantities to help solve the needs of the brothers who are striving to boost production in the fields. (FBIS IV, March 17, 1976:H2)

The corps' operations during that time must have been a rather vital element in keeping the economy functioning.

Some refugees suggest that sectors or provinces might best be viewed as persons, each forced to trade with others for those items he or she lacked. I found an example once of a village in which some people raised silkworms, gathered the silk, and wove it, sending it to destinations well outside the immediate area in exchange for foodstuffs. The rule of thumb in Democratic Kampuchea seems to have been one set of new clothing per person per year. Clothing not made in cottage industry or taken off persons who were executed[10] came presumably from the operating textile factories. For those textile workers unable to produce all of their own food needs, food from clothing-deficient areas could perhaps be regarded as their "compensation." One assumes that economic organization developed as a complex barter arrangement, something akin to discovering and fitting pieces into a puzzle, without the aid of currency market exchange mechanisms. It must be granted that there was a certain rhythm to it by the time a couple of years had passed.

THE FOOD SUPPLY

Cambodia has always been about rice, a crop that received increased emphasis under the DK leadership. It was a symbol of independence, evidence that one was standing on one's own feet. The entire work schedule of a cooperative was based upon the rice crop(s). At harvest time, everyone—young, old, and sick, as well as specialists who might be engaged in, say, silk weaving at all other times—would be out in the fields, often until late in the evening, working by torchlight. Other activity, such as planting manioc or digging an irrigation ditch, would take place after duties connected with the rice cycle were completed. One might say that this would be normal, but in Democratic Kampuchea there was rigidity and uniformity in the organization of labor to such a degree that it was often seen by the people as ridiculous. The word of when to plant, when to weed, when to harvest, was often transmitted from on high. An entire region might begin planting all on the same day, although the water conditions over such a large expanse

10 In some places this was a deliberate policy.

could hardly be expected to be uniform. The lectures the people received perhaps several evenings a week were not usually the negative, accusing kind occurring in neighboring Vietnam. They frequently had a single focus: the need to work harder and, specifically, to grow more rice.

Producing rice was a rather thankless job, since one's only compensation was just enough rice, if that, to ensure survival. During and after the harvest people might enjoy a heartier portion of rice. Otherwise, a person did not benefit throughout the year from his hard work. There was little incentive in that propertyless society; you worked to avoid being killed. Even in death, one's body might be used as fertilizer. Hence, a phrase developed for those executed: "to be turned into a coconut."

In Democratic Kampuchea, the rice harvest was distributed as follows. Most villagers had no idea how much rice they had produced, for it was taken away by oxcart or truck at the end of each day or two during the harvest season to an area depot. Rice would be brought back to villages during the year in the minimal quantity needed to sustain life. In some villages, however, rice was stored in former *wats* (temples) or other places and doled out during the year. There were circumstances where people were able to have a fairly good idea how much rice they retained and how much was hauled away; estimates averaged roughly 50 percent in each category. (See, for instance, Andelman 1977:A14; Department of State 1978: Twining airgram, March 31, 1976:10.)

The state benefited from the system, but it would have been a longer time than Democratic Kampuchea lasted before the farmer would have benefited to a very significant degree. The amount of rice produced but not returned to the farmers would have been available for export and for feeding non-self-sufficient segments of the population (officials, soldiers, factory workers, salt workers, railroad personnel, and the like). Relatively speaking, this number would have represented quite a small percentage of the total population, *at most* several percent. Half of the military force raised its own rice. These mainforce units and trainees were located on permanent sites away from villages and were required to be fairly self-sufficient. Although it is a fallacy that all the soldiers ate well, many had it easy and lived well in return for exerting little effort.

AGRICULTURE

There were two major themes that emerged over and over again in Democratic Kampuchea: national independence and the development of the agricultural base. No phrase typifies these themes better than the oft heard, "With rifles in one hand and hoes in the other, our workers, peasants, and revolutionary armed forces are striving grandly to build Democratic Kampuchea." Village propaganda sessions would push "the need to work

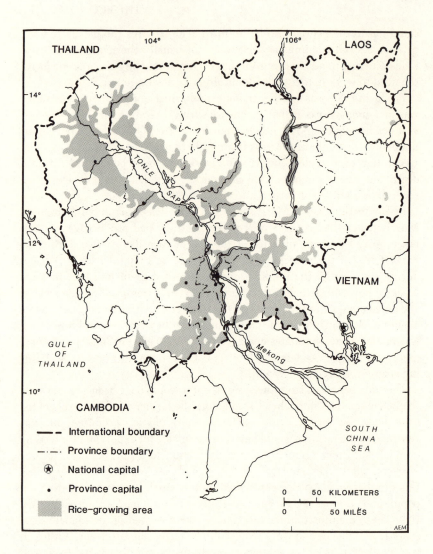

THAILAND

LAOS

104°

106°

14°

TONLE SAP

12°

VIETNAM

GULF
OF
THAILAND

10°

CAMBODIA

Mekong

SOUTH
CHINA
SEA

— — International boundary

—·—· Province boundary

⊛ National capital

· Province capital

   Rice-growing area

0   50   KILOMETERS

0   50 MILES

AEM

harder," "the need to produce more," "independence," and "the revolution."

It is natural, in a country where approximately 85 percent of the people worked traditionally in agriculture, for a government to acknowledge the importance of this sector. But the DK leadership manifested a special view that attached almost a Jean Jacques Rousseau romantic quality to agricultural labor, a feeling that it was possible to turn back the clock to something pure and authentic. This was to take place amidst a complete social reorganization. People were to lose their individual identities and work together in large numbers for the common good; this was supposed to occur in a country where, despite efforts to get them going, cooperatives in the Western sense of the word had had little success over the years. One should recall that in traditional Cambodia, as in neighboring Thailand, there were frequent exchanges of labor. For example, one family might help one or more other families to harvest rice and the others would then be obligated to repay the first family in like labor when it was time for its own rice to be harvested. Other institutions, such as tenant farming, existed, but all were quite different from the obligatory system that in DK parlance became known as the "cooperative."

The roughly 30 percent of the people under communist control prior to the final takeover in 1975 were those who had survived the often brutal seizure of their villages and had been producing rice and supplying manpower to meet the needs of the military. Often, but certainly not always, they were redistributed throughout a fairly large "liberated" area or moved just a short distance to sever property ties and to prevent them from fleeing.[11] One Cambodian who returned to his native village in Chhuk district of Kampot Province in 1975 found, for instance, that all the inhabitants had been moved one or two kilometers shortly after the village had been taken over in 1970. In the pre-1975 period, two patterns of agricultural organization existed in such areas: (a) mutual aid teams and (b) solidarity groups for increasing production. Quinn, who monitored conditions in the provinces bordering Vietnam's Mekong Delta (from Kampot to Svay Rieng) during 1970–1974, described the first system, where families retained individual responsibility for doing everything on their land except harvesting, which was done communally. The communists controlled all rice harvested. Some of it was returned to the population and the remainder sent elsewhere to support the war effort. The second system consisted of communal land ownership by interfamily groups, communal labor, and rice distribution along the same lines as in the first system. Individuals were still allowed to own chickens, ducks, pigs, cattle, and other livestock. The smaller animals

---

[11] For a dramatic description of forced movement severing all property ties, see Chapters 6 and 8 by Kenneth Quinn.—ED.

could be slaughtered and sold without permission and the larger with permission of the district. Bands of local militia enforced the rules. (See Quinn 1974:29–30).

The mutual aid teams, representing a rather free system, appear to have constituted the original method the revolutionaries of the 1960s used for organizing people collectively. According to Pol Pot, the second system dated from 1973 and consisted of cooperatives (which he termed collective mass organizations) and trade based on barter (Pol Pot 1977:H28 and Chapter 1 by Timothy Carney, p. 27). These were instituted gradually in the areas having mutual aid teams, the true *mulethaan* or base areas. In addition, the second, more communal, pattern of the solidarity groups was used in areas subsequently "liberated." In newly liberated areas the second system constituted a more abrupt break with the past and undoubtedly required greater force to achieve. In it, ten to twelve families were grouped together for work purposes, laboring on communally controlled land. A man from Prey Veng said this was the system that his village was forced to adopt when taken over in 1974, spreading to a commune-wide base the following year. It was also the system reportedly in effect in northwestern Cambodia in areas "liberated" in 1974–1975.

With the takeover in April 1975, all remaining private ownership of land throughout the country was abolished immediately. The "new" people, constituting the major portion of the population, were formed into solidarity groups within a matter of days in existing or new villages. Short of troops, the authorities generally had to rely upon the "base" people (that is, supporters of the Khmer Rouge or persons under their control prior to 1975) to supervise them. The "new" people (including the 50 percent of the total population living in the cities at the time of the takeover) were particularly suspect in the eyes of the poorly educated or illiterate farmboys who comprised the victorious army. Everyone was put out on the land. Those from outside Phnom Penh were moved around and around, working to clear fields, dig canals, build roads, or build settlements. Often there were no tools available whatsoever. Those from Phnom Penh, as is well known, were put out on fields in all directions from the city. Then, several months later, these same people were the objects of a second mass movement, particularly to the northwest, but also to other parts of the country, including even the sparsely populated northeast.

The trauma descending on the new people being so rapidly integrated into a radically different system must have been tremendous. Placed in unfamiliar surroundings, they were treated roughly and forced to work in a new group structure by fellow countrymen who seemed alien and hostile.

Within the space of less than a year, the entire population, with the exception of persons in specialized work, learned that it was now divided into something called cooperatives. (One simply did not hear the word before the end of 1975 or beginning of 1976. The base people had presumably heard it before, but these were not the ones usually fleeing into Thailand). Cooperatives began small, varying in size anywhere from fifty to five hundred persons. In 1977 they became larger and more uniform in size, often joining the inhabitants of several villages to incorporate an entire commune.[12] By late 1977, Pol Pot reported that 20 percent of Cambodia's cooperatives consisted of seven hundred to one thousand households, 30 percent had four hundred to six hundred households, and 20 percent were made up of one hundred to three hundred households. Most cooperatives, he said, had already evolved from village cooperatives to commune-level cooperatives (Pol Pot 1977:H30). The cooperative was attaining the fullest extent of its expansion and development. This remained the pattern at the end of 1978. A reasonable estimate of a typical cooperative's population is about two thousand persons.[13]

For work purposes, people were either *kemlang ping* (full strength = adults) or *kemlang ksaoy* (weak strength = small children and the elderly). Those who were full strength were divided into two groups. The first, *kemlang 1*, consisted of young, able-bodied, single people who comprised mobile work teams (*kong chhlat*). It was organized into (a) groups of children (from ages 7–8 or 10 to 14 or 15) who lived apart from their families, outside the village, sometimes at a single location in a district, separated by sex, and doing fairly hard and steady work, and (b) the young adults from ages 14–16 until marriage. The latter group did the really strenuous work of digging irrigation reservoirs and canals, building large dikes, logging, and land clearing, from sunrise to sundown, and often at night. The mobile work, teams varied in composition according to administrative level. At the regional and sector levels, work teams consisted of youths from long-time base areas (*mulethaan*). At the district level and in the communes, work teams were comprised of the offspring of poor farmers and other disadvantaged classes, whereas in villages teams consisted of the offspring of the "advantaged" classes that came under DK control only in 1975. The young people in the regional and sector work teams were better fed and housed than those on the lower three levels who, for the hard work they did, received only a few mouthfuls of rice and lots of bindweed in return. Work teams often slept for very long periods at the work sites, which Ponchaud considers to have often been in the category of "state farms" (Ponchaud 1978:91).

[12] Carney provides a good, succinct description of the evolution of cooperatives in Carney 1977:18–20.

[13] The word "cooperative" applied exclusively to agricultural groupings (including, whenever possible, persons with blacksmithing, weaving, and other skills to make the unit self-sufficient). Persons working in factories and fishing or in rubber or salt production were not in cooperatives; they were known only as factory workers and so forth, or as a group or unit of factory or rubber workers. There were no fishing or salt cooperatives.

The second "full strength" group, *kemlang* 2, was comprised of married, able-bodied men and women who were divided by sex but generally worked closer to the village. Many persons in this category usually slept in the village, but there were certainly exceptions to this policy, particularly among the men, who were sometimes sent considerable distances to work for extended periods. The *kemlang* 2 people worked in the rice fields of the cooperative, constructed and maintained its irrigation systems, and did local wood cutting. At harvest time, the women did the reaping and the men the threshing. Perhaps fifteen women would be assigned to reap one hectare in a day, while each man had to beat three hundred, four hundred, or reportedly even five hundred bundles in a day. Alternatively, both men and women reaped and threshed; everything depended upon the local assignments. Typical work hours varied. The day could begin as early as 4:30 A.M., moving to the fields at 5:00, lunch and a break from 11:00 to 12:30 P.M., then working again until 5:00 P.M. When there was moonlight, and as required, one might work again from 6 to 9 P.M. or even later for those who had not fulfilled their work quota. In other instances, the working day was from 6 A.M. to 6 P.M., with a noon break.

Finally, the "weak strength" group, *kemlang* 3, did the "small" work. The group comprised the elderly as well as the very young. Mothers returned to the fields when their children were three months old and elderly grandmothers would assume responsibility for the infants. (One heard some sad stories of how the infants could not have their need for milk met during the daytime, and cried plaintively throughout the day.) Small children (from a few years old to the age of entering a mobile work team or else going to the fields with their parents) were organized by sex; especially pliant ones showing promise were chosen as president of their group. The boys' group had an adult male leader, the girls, an adult female. The children worked from 6 to 11 A.M. each day, picking up cow dung and weeding, while staying close to the village. The elderly also worked around the village, raising chickens, keeping small garden plots, building small dams or dikes or caring for the orchards. Every Khmer had his or her place in the economy; no one was idle.

Everyone with a *kemlang* (therefore, even the children with their "presidents") was organized in units along military and strict sexual lines:

Three *krom* (groups or squads of 10 to 11 persons each, further divided into units or *pouk* of 3 persons each, 1 leader and 2 followers) equaled one *kong toic* (platoon);
Three *kong toic*, totaling 100 persons including the leader, equaled one *kong thom* (company);
Three *kong thom*, each with 100 persons, equaled one *kong vorea toic* (battalion);

Three *kong vorea toic*, of 300 persons each, equaled one *kong vorea thom* (regiment).

An experienced agricultural worker was desired to serve as the head of each *krom*. Above this level, almost without exception, leadership was provided by a *mulethaan* (base) person long associated with the DK leadership. As one rose higher in the structure, these leaders were often former DK soldiers. By 1977, the president of the commune committee was responsible for overseeing the cooperative(s) in the local commune, although their actual administration, including giving daily marching orders to the work force, was left in the hands of the economic member of the commune or village committee. There would be frequent reorganization of the elements of the work force depending upon the work to be done.

One had the feeling that, as the state is theoretically to wither away under Marxism, so, too, was the lower-level administrative apparatus to have disappeared eventually under the Khmer brand of communism. Perhaps in time, the village and commune levels were to have disappeared, to be replaced solely by the leadership of the relatively self-sufficient cooperative. By 1977, for instance, there were presidents of cooperatives who were equally presidents of village committees. It was an interesting evolution that was in process.

Despite the absence of expertise from above at the local level, perhaps the solidarity groups and cooperatives would have succeeded if they had utilized the skilled manpower available in their midst. Although there was some propaganda to the contrary, one did not hear of any instance in which someone with agricultural skills was actually given a say in how or when to undertake rice planting, canal building, or anything else. In cases where people said they tried to speak up, they were quickly made to understand that advice or expertise was not desired and, indeed, their action often placed them under a cloud of suspicion. A local communist leader might decide, for instance, where a rice field should be located, although experienced farmers knew that the land was too poor or too long untilled to provide much of a harvest as compared to other land in the area. One did not contradict such decisions. Pity the poor DK agricultural or hydraulics official at the regional or central level who was responsible for seeing that things were done correctly over a huge area; this was an impossible job with no one to rely upon but oneself.

Irrigation is a field where the new regime went through a particularly long period of trial and error. Apart from some special, large projects around the country, there seemed to be general guidelines requiring that each administrative unit dig so many meters of canal or build so many meters of dam, whether the conditions of the area called for it or not. Local leadership would usually follow this by rote rather than by exercising flexibility. Ordinary citizens would have no say in where a canal or dam was to be located.

In debriefing refugees during the DK period, an interviewer learned quickly what an important component of their work was preparing irrigation canals and the like. Numerous horror stories were recounted. Elderly monks who had not done manual labor for decades were forced to do particularly punishing work digging for very long hours. People—including pregnant women—stood in water sometimes up to their necks all day in the cold or rainy seasons, working on canals, with legs and feet swelling up and bleeding. Leeches would attach themselves without the worker knowing perhaps until a considerable time afterward; large leeches might even enter the anus, sometimes never to reemerge. Some of the worst stories one heard were connected with irrigation work. If a person pleaded illness while working under such conditions, the individual may or may not have been permitted to stop working, but if the worker did stop and then dared to eat food with everyone else at mealtime, that person would be in real trouble for "playing at being sick" (as the masters described it), their wisdom being that a sick person could not be hungry.

Apart from the horror stories, the subject of irrigation also provided a great source of merriment. Two men living in Kandal Province's Kien Svay district in mid-1975 spoke of the miles of irrigation canal they had to dig in the earth with dirt sides at ninety-degree angles to the base; the entire system collapsed during the rainy season. Two farmboys who became DK soldiers in early 1977 and fled to Thailand in April of that year broke into laughter in a Thai provincial jail as they described the new canal system created in their home areas west of the Tonle Sap. When the monsoon flooding occurred in mid-1976, not one canal held up. In the period 1975–1978, Cambodia became a land of reservoirs and irrigation canals. As time passed, it was apparent that the new regime was slowly increasing its expertise in the field of hydraulics. Once again, though, the inflexibility of the system seemed to be an important impediment.

The performance required in carrying out work tasks is worth examining for a moment, for it says a great deal about the system. Essentially, whoever was in charge of a group of workers (for instance, one of the cooperative's team chiefs or the head of the village committee) determined how much work had to be performed in a day or, alternately, the hours to be worked. Where tasking specified a particular amount, the requirement would be levied by individual or by group: so many meters of irrigation canal to be dug or rice field to be cultivated. Typical work requirements were (a) one person must build two square meters of a dam, (b) a *kong toic* platoon of thirty people must transplant two hectares of rice seedlings, (c) a group of eight people must harvest one hectare (10,000 square meters) of rice in a day, or (d) everyone must thresh thirty bundles of rice at night.

Frequently—and this is worth noting—the work requirements were not particularly onerous by traditional Khmer peasant standards. An important difference was that under the DK rulers, one worked every day, at least until the beginning of 1977, when the leadership took the "generous" step of permitting work to halt once every ten days. Cambodians often said, "We had no strength to keep ourselves going, only heart." In traditional times, there were periods of hard work, of course, but, in that gentle land which produced food almost by itself, these were liberally interspersed with periods of relaxation or mild work. Finally, it must be admitted that the city people were simply not as accustomed to that kind of life as were lifelong peasants.

Under the DK leadership's quantitative work system, workers knew that if they finished their own portion by 2 P.M., they were free to stop and go home. Needless to say, no one worked more than to fulfill the daily requirement, and the urge to get away was overwhelming. One might be working in the hot sun in an open field. When you were given your hour off for lunch and rest, chances are that you would remain in the same field, often unable to escape the hot sun. If while you were working you had to go to the bathroom, a too-lengthy amount of time away would be noticed by the team chief, who would probably remark on it at the next nightly meeting of the village. The informal rule was, of course, that repeated criticism led to execution. There was absolutely no reward for working more than your allotted share, hardly the way to get a dedicated work force.

On the other hand, a person might be assigned an unrealistic amount of work to be done in a day. It had to be done, even if it meant that you worked until midnight. There was no shirking; an allotment was an allotment. One young person who worked in Cambodia until fleeing in early 1979 described an occasion when each person on her team had to transplant 900 square meters of rice seedlings (almost one tenth of a hectare) per day. She worked late into the night to meet her assignment, often unable to see even what she was doing and sometimes running into the person working next to her. It did not matter what kind of job she did; all that mattered was that she did what she had been ordered to do. The basic point is that there was extraordinary rigidity in this system that allowed no variation. Some work assignments were too onerous, others too light, but modification was simply not permissible. In this forced labor system you did just what you had been told to do.

Finally, an important feature of the DK agricultural system was its emphasis on programming work. While after April 1975 this was done initially with considerable wasted effort, it soon became more of a science, but with a rhythm nevertheless artificial to any farmer, due to its "not a moment to be wasted" nature. Basically, life was a continuous process of working in the rice fields during part of the year and on the irrigation system during the remainder of it, with no respite in between. Vegetable or other crops would be planted in succession as well, then left basically alone until ready for harvesting. In one village in Siem Reap province, for instance, everyone was in the fields planting cauliflower just before the rice harvest. When it was time for the latter, everyone moved over into the rice fields. In their "spare time," people were making farm implements, fishing poles, bamboo dishes, or vessels for carrying water, all of which the DK leadership referred to as handicrafts. "Tempus fugit" seemed to be the watchword.

INDUSTRY

While agriculture was of primary importance, the DK elite did not neglect the industrial side, or so it seemed, particularly in the difficult, early period after takeover when the new government was publicizing every achievement it could find. It was in this way that the world learned of a number of factory reopenings. Whether one believed every word of Radio Phnom Penh or not, it was clear that Cambodia was trying to make its factories operational again. What the radio broadcasts neglected to add was that this was occurring often as a result of Chinese (and possibly North Korean) technical assistance. (Interestingly, DK cadres encountered in 1980 were very reluctant either to confirm or deny this aid.) Broadcasts did sometimes give credit to workers who remained on the job—when they were permitted to do so—despite the change of government and evacuation of the cities. One can hypothesize that problems in resuming factory operations must have stemmed from the lack of maintenance during the interim period or the lack of experienced workers, since there were few reports of damage to factories at the time of the takeover.

In Phnom Penh, the government announced after almost five months that some seventy factories in the city were again operating (FBIS IV, Sept. 9, 1975:H3). One began hearing of the appearance of locally made cigarettes from Cambodian tobacco, of textiles, tools, and batteries for flashlights and the radios of the cadres and soldiers. The DK embassy in Hanoi began serving Cambodian cigarettes and liqueur to its visitors. One factory manager who was sent out to the countryside in 1975 and returned to Phnom Penh to manage a cigarette factory in 1979 estimated that 80 percent of the existing factories were from the pre-1975 period, with the remaining 20 percent newly erected by the DK leadership. A plant that did appear to be new in DK days was frequently featured in the regime's publicity: a very modern-looking factory full of new lathes and other equipment, producing pumps and other steel products. The equipment was not always new, but was often reconstituted old equipment from factories no longer in existence. As an example, the factory manager cited his own cigarette factory, which had been one of three in 1975. With no former workers remaining, the DK leaders had kept only one of these operating ("M.A.C.," which started up with

French and English capital in 1954, making cigarettes using tobacco from Kompong Cham, the U.S., and Brazil, and which had built up large stocks at the time of the 1975 takeover). Presumably, this was done by cannibalizing machinery from the other two factories.[14]

Elsewhere in the country, the large cement plant in Kampot resumed production. Within six months, Battambang's industrial sector was operational: the sugar mill (reopened with Chinese help), the jute bag plant, the yarn and textile mill, the brick-making facility, and the rice-milling plants. One heard stories of the workers at the sugar cane and bag factories being replaced as new, presumably more "acceptable," workers began mastering their training. Some of the old ones were sent to the fields, others just disappeared. The managers of the sugar mill and textile plant, as well as the two deputies at the latter, were reportedly executed.

A curious development about 1976 centered on the important town of Mongkol Borey. One heard reports that buildings were being dismantled in Battambang, with at least some of the lumber hauled to Mongkol Borey. At the same time, large purchases of tractor parts worth hundreds of thousands of dollars were being made in the Thai border town of Aranyaprathet, the financing reportedly coming from a People's Republic of China (PRC) account held in one of the Bangkok banks. Soon there was evidence of a tractor assembly plant located in and around a part of the *lycée* at Mongkol Borey. Indeed, there were rumors that the DK leadership wanted to make the area one large industrial site. In 1977, new tractors began appearing all over at least northwestern Cambodia. Refugees coming from locations quite removed from one another uniformly called them North Korean tractors. It was never clear how it all fit together, but stories did indeed seem to converge.

On the other hand, no Cambodian government ever seemed to have very good luck with the refinery at Kompong Som. Commencing production in 1969, it suffered damage soon after the war began to spread in 1970. This was followed by communist rocketing and partial takeover in April–June 1974, with the damage from the rockets ending any future refining prospects. The bombings associated with the Mayaguez incident, a serious fire in late 1975 or early 1976, and finally a reported dispute between the Chinese and DK officials whereby the Chinese would repair it only if the Cambodians would agree to use the waxy Chinese petroleum (which the DK rulers did not want), all lead to considerable doubt that the facility ever became productive.

What kinds of people operated the factories during the DK regime? One person, who said he was in charge of factories in Phnom Penh throughout

---

[14] The Vietnamese came in early 1979 and hauled most of the equipment to Vietnam. In the second half of that year, the PRK began trying to restore all three factories to operating status.

that time, had studied electronics at the University of Phnom Penh for two years. He never completed his studies, forsaking them for the revolutionary cause in which he believed. In any case, he brought *some* expertise to his job, as well as the right "credentials." He claimed with some pride that the DK government really had the factories "humming." Another, who was more vague about what work he did in the supervision of a Phnom Penh factory in 1975–1978, had been studying fine arts in Phnom Penh in 1970, after which he went back and forth between there and the liberated zones until takeover. When seen in 1980, he was almost certainly a political cadre; perhaps he had performed a political oversight role in the factories. As far as can be determined, the workers themselves were selected on the basis of the correct socioeconomic background. Preferably, they were from the base areas and, hence, more trustworthy.

It may be instructive to recount the story of a Phnom Penh factory worker. A fairly simple fellow in his late twenties, he said he had a farming background. In 1975 he went to Phnom Penh and entered a training course. When a blanket factory opened in an old movie theater in 1976, he worked there until the Vietnamese takeover. Some equipment was made locally to produce 20–25 blankets per day and large machines were imported, capable of producing 225–250 blankets daily. These targets had to be met. Several Chinese and North Korean technicians were present to demonstrate how to operate the equipment. The sixty Cambodian workers were divided into four groups (*krom*) of fifteen persons, each. Men and women worked together but had to separate by sex after hours. Anyone who was "intimate" disappeared, but marriage was possible. At night, one either continued to work or engaged in political study. All workers were housed around the factory. They could walk around Phnom Penh, "but there was nothing to do." Unless you were the one "big shot" out of a typical one hundred persons resident in the city, you could not obtain a pass to leave the city. If you were ill, there was good Chinese medicine available (it began entering the country soon after the DK takeover), and Chinese physicians were stationed about the city. Food was adequate. Obviously, factory workers lived fairly regimented, dull lives but, so long as they made their work targets and did not "fool around," they constituted a relatively preferred class of the population.

Several industries other than manufacturing should be touched upon. First is salt, in which Cambodia has always been self-sufficient. Some of the terrible stories one heard of suffering in mid to late 1975 were attributed to the near or complete absence of salt in much of the country. One person told of not having a taste of salt for nineteen days, for example. Indeed, it was this period in which considerable quantities—truckload after truckload—of salt were "smuggled" openly across the Thai border into Poipet. By the end of 1975, however, the new government seemed to have restored its production in the Kampot area and established a distribution system (including by bicycle) around the country. Complaints of lack of salt generally ended, although there would still be periods in one area or another when salt would be in severe, if temporary, shortage.

Next is rubber. One of the staples of the country's peacetime economy, there was considerable destruction to the trees in eastern Cambodia during the war years. Some production continued there, however, and was shipped intermittently down the Mekong. In addition, large rubber plantations near Kompong Som were said to have been in excellent condition throughout the first half of the 1970s. Judging from announcements on the radio and from the rubber that began to be shipped out of Cambodia in 1976, rubber was a priority sector, and realistically so. In the prewar period, rubber had been the second most important export, and there was no contradiction in the communists continuing this emphasis if only private ownership were dissolved. Already on October 18, 1975, Radio Phnom Penh reported on the activities at the Chup plantation, the country's largest. It noted that even during the heavy U.S. bombing in 1973, the workers remained at their tasks and that, after takeover, they continued working "to produce more and better rubber to contribute to the efforts to make the country strong and stable and have it progress by leaps and bounds."

An important part of the managerial and labor force in the eastern Cambodian rubber plantations had always been Vietnamese. What happened to them during the roundups and subsequent expulsion of all Vietnamese in the summer and fall of 1975 is unknown, but one imagines that the loss of their expertise had significant implications for the Cambodian rubber industry although, as elsewhere, this would not have been an important consideration for the "liberators." In any case, Cambodian workers stayed on the job. Cambodian rubber began appearing in Aranyaprathet in 1976, generally a dirty, inferior product. No one knew from what part of Cambodia it came or whether it had been produced years earlier or was newly produced. The consensus was that it was old. Later in 1976 there were reports of rubber being exported in greater quantities through Kompong Som. A Cambodian rubber worker who labored for years in the Mimot area before taking refuge in Thailand in 1980 reported that the DK regime maintained the rubber plantations relatively well. Ironically, it was the Vietnamese whom he faulted when, in the period after the 1979 takeover, they made no effort whatsoever at upkeep.

A third industry was fishing. Of particular importance traditionally was fresh-water fishing in Cambodia's large central lake, the Tonle Sap, carried out especially by Vietnamese and Cambodian ethnic Muslims, the Chams. Fish and fish products from there were well liked throughout Cambodia, as well as in Thailand. Even during the 1970–1975 period, elephant fish from the Great Lake were shipped as far away as Hong Kong. Many of the Vietnamese living near the lake left willingly or forcibly from 1970 onward, and it is likely that any who remained after the 1975 takeover soon found themselves on their way to southern Vietnam. What happened to the Chams of the area is uncertain. The Chams constituted a problem for the new rulers because the communists scorned religion in general and Islam in particular. Many Chams died, and others were probably dispersed. We know that the DK leaders tried to keep local Khmers fishing there, and it was clear that fishing was continuing. Dried fish, fish sauce, and fish paste were already being bartered in Aranyaprathet by the summer of 1975, and it was universally agreed that the source had to be the Tonle Sap.

The DK regime devoted some attention to the marine fisheries sector of the economy. Apart from Thai fishermen from north of Koh Kong Province who braved considerable danger by fishing Cambodian waters either clandestinely or with the agreement of local DK authorities to whom they delivered a quantity of gasoline or other products in exchange, the only marine fishing done after 1975 was from settlements under DK direction scattered along the coast. A resident of one of these settlements arrived in his small fishing boat in Khlong Yai, Trat (Thailand), from Somlong Koo, Koh Kong Province in March 1977. His story is worth recounting. After the town of Koh Kong was emptied in 1975, he was moved three times until he was placed in a settlement of four hundred persons on the Gulf of Thailand. Everyone was there to fish. The man's family was 200 kilometers inland. In two years he had been allowed to visit twice, for two days each time. Five men—known literally as fishing laborers—would be joined by a communist civilian in a motorboat and they usually fished at night. Typically, fuel would be available for a couple of days, then supplies would be exhausted for 2–3 days. The catch was placed on an uninhabited island, to be bartered with the Thai for products needed in the Koh Kong area. When there was no fishing due to lack of fuel, everyone would plant manioc and vegetables, work in rice fields, or care for the ducks. As elsewhere in Cambodia, food was not plentiful except at harvest time. One can probably assume that our source's experience was fairly typical of persons in fishing settlements.

The last specialized industry meriting attention is lumber. A considerable amount of logging has always been done in Cambodia, and there were perhaps as many as five hundred small sawmills. It is safe to assume that many of these became operational again after 1975.

After a couple of years, as the situation became relatively more "settled" in Cambodia, it was obvious that more forward thinking was being done within the central government about the economy. In 1978, Pol Pot expressed his view of his country's future industrialization. He said the target for the next fifteen to twenty years was the establishment of light industry, food-grain processing, an iron industry, machine building, and fuel, power, and chemical industries. He observed that a steel mill capable of supplying one-fourth of Cambodia's requirements was already under construction. There was, of course, no chance to realize this dream. How reasonable it was cannot be appraised without more details on the proposal, but on its face Pol Pot's program appeared to be a relatively moderate program of light and heavy industry.

INFRASTRUCTURE

In modern limited warfare, the side with the financial resources builds good airports and ports or improves existing ones. Surface transportation systems may or may not have resources poured into them, but what is built up may easily be blown up, with what remains being patchy, at best. In Cambodia, however, what remained in April 1975 was not particularly impressive.

Aviation Facilities. With the collapse of the Lon Nol government, the country's two dozen airports were not in good condition, although they had served remarkably well under difficult conditions. At the big one, Pochentong outside Phnom Penh, the main runway and parking areas were full of holes from 107-mm rockets. The holes in the runway were merely filled in when convenient, but not even this was done for holes blasted in the aprons. Considerable debris was lying around. The new authorities made at least a modicum of repairs to Pochentong within the first six months of takeover; the airport became an important center for aircraft repair and maintenance for captured UH–1 "Huey" helicopters as well as C–47 aircraft and any others that could be made to fly. Furthermore, Pochentong airport became a sizeable base of operations for a reported four hundred Chinese aircraft workers and for DK trainee pilots and workmen. Adequate repairs were required to handle the Chinese Civil Aviation Company Boeing 707s that began serving Phnom Penh in the summer of 1975 on an irregular, and then a regular, basis. Also, the regular—if fairly empty—Vietnamese service ran for a little over a year in 1976–1977.

At the other two airports of which one heard, Battambang and Siem Reap, minor work may have been done, but these airports served little purpose, at least until the Cambodians began flying in visitors to Angkor via Siem Reap in 1976. In the first six months after April 1975, the major effort at those two airports seems to have been made by what refugees believed were North Koreans, who tried to make T–47 and any other abandoned aircraft flyable again. Siem Reap gained a certain notoriety because a major mass burial ground was located at the end of the runway. Besides Siem Reap, the other supposedly international and military airport, at Ream near Kompong Som, was bombed during the Mayaguez affair. For a long time, there was no indication that it was repaired. Interestingly, the PRC constructed a large military airport for the DK regime to the west of the town of Kompong Chhnang prior to the Vietnamese takeover.

The regime placed little importance on aviation, generally. Refugees often mentioned how quiet the skies were, as if Cambodia were somehow removed from the modern world. When Lt. Pech Lim Kuon, a DK pilot, fled in April 1976, there were no other fully trained DK pilots, although some were undergoing training in both the PRC and at Pochentong. Important leaders flew around the country by helicopter; otherwise, there was little air activity. Aviation gasoline was never plentiful. There were often rumors that the Chinese flew aviation gasoline into Pochentong, which must have been terribly expensive, rather than shipping it inland through Kompong Som.

Ports and Waterways. The commercial port Kompong Som (Sihanoukville) was in relatively decent condition in April 1975. During the Lon Nol period it was the connection between the port and the capital city rather than the port itself that had presented problems. The U.S. bombing during Mayaguez was serious at Kompong Som and the naval base at Ream. If refugee reports in mid-1975 were accurate, naval activity never really stopped at Ream, however. The small craft at Ream were augmented later in the year by new coastal patrol vessels from the People's Republic of China. Whatever damage was caused at Kompong Som just could not have been too serious, because ocean-going vessels, primarily from the Chinese, began calling there late in 1975.

Presumably, the inland port of Phnom Penh was of fairly marginal value during most of the DK period, since all but local, relatively small vessels would have had to pass through increasingly hostile Vietnam to reach the sea. One refugee who traversed Phnom Penh in September 1975 said he saw no boats at all. Still, there were several reports in 1975 and early 1976 of Vietnamese barges moving up the Bassac River, and perhaps the Mekong River as well, hauling petroleum or rice. These soon ended, however.

As in Thailand, inland waterways have always been important in much of Cambodia, and reports of Khmer boats engaged in distributing rice or collecting rice from settlements along rivers and other waterways in 1975–1978 were undoubtedly accurate. In addition, large numbers of former residents of Phnom Penh were moved by the old ferry boats from southeastern Cambodia to Kompong Chhnang or to Kompong Thom in 1975. For instance, five thousand persons destined for Preah Vihear province traveled by water to Kompong Thom, then walked the remainder of the way. As time went on, the paucity of reports about water transport probably resulted from the on-going scarcity of petroleum.

Roads. There is no question that many roads had been badly battered during the war years or were in poor condition due to lack of maintenance.

Frequently, Cambodian refugees recounted filling in holes in roads or constructing roads in newly cleared areas. Road work occurred when the rice-growing season had ended. Bridges must have been in terrible shape, and government information releases sometimes showed new or makeshift bridges under construction.

A couple of highways were of particular importance. One was Route 4 from Kompong Som to Phnom Penh, which the Khmer Republic tried to keep open in 1970–1975 with only sporadic success. As much as the DK regime had a "lifeline" afterwards, Route 4 was it. The highway seems to have been repaired quickly, because months would be required to reopen the corresponding rail link. Soon, goods arriving at Kompong Som were trucked to Phnom Penh. Throughout 1975, this was done a bit gingerly, as resistance elements sometimes attacked trucks as they moved in convoy or dug trenches across the road. By approximately the spring of 1976, this menace was gone and there were more stories of trucks operating on the highway both day and night, indicating that there was security and that the road was in reasonably good condition.

During the months following the takeover, repairs were also made to Route 5 (the southern route linking Phnom Penh and Battambang) and most likely to the other major thoroughfares: Route 7 joining Phnom Penh and Kompong Cham, Route 6 to the north of the Tonle Sap, and Route 1 between Phnom Penh and the Vietnamese border opposite Saigon. The rule of thumb seemed to be that existing roads were to be repaired and new ones built only to the extent that this permitted transport—by truck, oxcart, or bicycle—to take place adequately.

Railroads. The railroads were evidently of a particularly high priority for the DK government. Scarce soldiers guarded the rails (as well as key highway junctions). Scarce resources were spent on upkeep and improvement of the lines. There was always enough diesel fuel kept on hand for the engines (a statement not easy to make about any other commodity in Democratic Kampuchea). Indeed, the DK government constructed a two-million-liter tank in the Battambang area to store the diesel fuel.

On the oldest portion of the railroad—from Phnom Penh through Battambang to Poipet—only the Battambang to Poipet leg was intact after 1972, and it operated right up until the takeover. Indeed, when several hundred Khmer Republic army and air force officers and enlisted men who had been training in Thailand decided to return home in May 1975, the communists transported them by rail as far as Phnom Thipedey (south of Battambang) before the men disembarked, went to work in the fields, and gradually "disappeared." Elsewhere on that line there was considerable damage, and repair work began within one or two months after April 1975. Thus, when the DK leadership began moving hundreds of thousands of former Phnom Penh residents to the northwest in late summer, they were able to proceed by rail—packed into freight cars—only on the Pursat to Sisophon portion of the route. The entire link from Phnom Penh to Poipet was open by the end of 1975.

The repair of the Kompong Som to Phnom Penh portion, cut since 1970, was a greater undertaking for the DK regime. Until 1975, the communists had been taking the railroad ties to use in dam construction or were burning them. In that year, the Chinese shipped oak ties of poor quality to Cambodia. DK soldiers with no technical expertise whatsoever were responsible for the reconstruction. They used as laborers veteran railroad workers, but did deign to ask them for advice. Dividing up the entire portion into sixteen-kilometer sections, there were twenty workers assigned per section. Emphasis was on speed: the communists told the laborers that if the Lon Nol government could repair a section in three months, they would do it in one. Reconstruction was completed in the first half of 1976. Then, an incident occurred that forced the communists to do the work over again. A twelve-car train carrying petroleum to Phnom Penh simply fell off the tracks one day. The train was a total loss. The decision was taken to replace all the ties—this time with ties sawed from the local wood used traditionally—and work began in mid-1976. By August 1976, there was at least one train operating in each direction between the port and the capital.

Once operations became normalized on the railroad, a pattern emerged. Unlike the post-DK era, when the Vietnamese used the railroad to move troops, there was no regular passenger traffic. The railroad existed only to move vital freight. This meant transporting fuel oil, cement, and salt to as far as Battambang and taking rice from that rice bowl at least as far as Phnom Penh. Materials such as iron for bridge construction or for use in some of the major dam projects were hauled by rail, as were tractors and rice-harvesting equipment. The importance of the railroad during the DK period should not be underestimated.

Indicative of the desire of the Cambodian communists to have an operating railroad is the fact that they, like the Vietnamese after them, encouraged the railroad workers to remain at their jobs after takeover. Thus, while the city of Battambang was being evacuated, railroad employees located at their nearby cantonment (some two thousand persons, including families) were not turned out into the countryside. One management-level employee told how all personnel at that location became "workers" in 1975. During the following year, the number of employees and family members doubled to some 4,600. All railroad workers and their families were divided into cantons and were required to be self-sufficient in food, each unit having five hectares set aside for growing its own rice and other foodstuffs. As a symbol of their special status, railroad workers were permitted to read the DK weekly newspaper and monthly magazine in the one information office established per canton. (In a village, on the other hand, only soldiers or cadres and members of the village committee would have had the same privilege.) Workers received two outfits of clothing yearly, double the normal ration in the countryside. Nevertheless, during DK rule, some two hundred railway workers and family members "went away to study." These just happened to be the people who would not work hard or complained or were not considered to be "in the movement."

Beginning in 1976, approximately 50 percent of the workers were new, including former communist soldiers whose guns were shipped back to Phnom Penh. They also included a large number of youngsters aged seven years and above (children of DK military and civilian officials and long-time railway workers) who stood around, listened to what was being said and done, studied for two hours a day, and spent the rest of their time working in the rice fields and planting vegetables. Later, they began to work on the railroad. Clearly, this was the "new" generation being trained to take over from the "old" at some point.

Running the Battambang regional operation was a revolutionary with the assumed name of Sinong Ker who had joined the movement in 1955. Not only was he a regular party member but he was also a member of the Central Committee and a member of the committee approving new members of the party youth movement. Sinong Ker was not very well educated, being able only to read Cambodian, but he had the political credentials, demonstrating again the importance the communists placed on the railroad. In reality, he leaned on the long-time railroad workers to operate the railroad. They in turn would give the appropriate orders to the younger workers, and the DK overseers would watch. Sinong Ker was executed in August 1977 and replaced by someone "even dumber," Ta Mom, a middle-aged peasant and old revolutionary.

Refugees reported a number of sightings of Chinese near railroad repair projects or on trains. Yet, the source for much of the Battambang information maintains that there were neither Chinese involved with the Battambang operation nor with the repairwork being done to the Kompong Som–Phnom Penh portion. Trains were driven by long-time workers and new DK trainees, he maintained. In the same way, there were reports of new engines from the People's Republic of China appearing in April 1976. Yet, the Battambang source said that the eight engines working in and out of that main yard were all old French five hundred or eight hundred to one thousand ton engines.

Finally, it is not generally known that the DK rulers were working on a completely new line to replace the one running from Kompong Som to Phnom Penh, with 1.4-meter gauge compared to the existing 1-meter width. By late 1978 all the bridges for the new route were completed (one twelve meters wide), but the ballast, ties, and rails had not yet been laid.

The work was being supervised not by an engineer but by an old railway worker. All was to have been completed by 1980.

Other. If there was any telephone or postal system in operation throughout the DK era, one never heard of it. Those things were just not considered necessary. A military radio system linking key centers seems to have been important, and there was reportedly a system of couriers. Whether the intercity radio-telephone system survived after 1975 is unknown. The central government maintained the sole telecommunications link with the outside world, to Beijing.

The final elements in the infrastructure must have seemed unimportant to the DK leadership: water and electrical systems. Both were city-oriented systems in that anti-urban environment. Phnom Penh had an old colonial water system that worked during the Khmer Republic period under Lon Nol, albeit frequently with little pressure. Visitors to Phnom Penh during the DK period often mentioned having to use buckets of water, although there was evidence of much improvement by late 1978.

Toward the end of the Khmer Republic period, Phnom Penh's electrical power operated sporadically, particularly in the last months when it was off in the afternoons and throughout the nights. This was said to be due to lack of fuel for the thermal stations. Visitors from 1976 onward reported seeing a number of lights, for example, in the area around the stadium where important generals of the previous regime once lived. Lighting of at least parts of a sparsely populated city was presumably maintained for reasons of security or prestige. One irony is that, because electricity had been so spotty before the communist takeover, there were many generators in Phnom Penh, but many of these were broken up by the communist soldiers in the early days of victory.

Outside Phnom Penh, the large Prek Thnaot dam project in Kompong Speu province was left unfinished in 1975. Its construction had been supported by the Japanese, and others, to provide hydroelectricity and water for irrigation. The DK leaders claimed that they completed it without foreign assistance in 1978 and that it was intended for irrigation purposes.

WHAT DOES all this tell us? That for the DK government, it was the surface infrastructure—roads, and particularly the railroad—that really counted. Important resources were devoted to railroad maintenance, operation, and construction. Large numbers of peasant farmers and, probably frequently, troops as well, were dispatched to repair roads—usually by hand—or build new ones, so that the road network became usable, if of poor quality. The leadership may have wanted the cooperatives to be as self-sufficient as possible, but this was only part of the picture. Obviously, it recognized the importance of transporting agricultural production as well as heavy industrial and other goods if the country's economy was to develop rather than stagnate. Kompong Som port also occupied a key position in the scheme. The emphasis was quite a modern one.

Regime Performance

What did Democratic Kampuchea have to show for itself in early 1979 after almost four years of control throughout the country and much longer periods in large areas? Frankly, it is very difficult to evaluate the performance. Its reconstruction to crude but usable levels of roads, bridges, and railroads inevitably required considerable effort before progress could be made in economic development. New zones of cultivation were created out of forest and other land, necessitating more road building. The amount of work done was enormous, even if individual efforts were often mechanical or less than logically directed. Slowly, progress was being made of a sort, but at an unacceptable human price. One must question very seriously whether the means being used could have endured, unchanging, sufficiently long enough to have brought about real development.

RICE DEVELOPMENT

One may describe the main rice crops harvested annually in December–January as follows:

Late 1975 to Early 1976. After terrible hunger during the summer and fall months, considerable disease, the forced migrations of hundreds of thousands of persons across the country, and the relocation of people at least several times around more confined areas, the rice harvest, while understandably not large, appeared to be somewhat better than outside observers had expected, all things considered. At least the starvation during the late summer and fall of 1975 was alleviated until late spring, generally. The new government gave three thousand tons of rice after harvest to the newly communized Lao as a goodwill gift, probably more an act of solidarity rather than evidence of a large harvest.

Late 1976 to Early 1977. At least half of the population was in a very weak condition, especially those persons "liberated" only in March–April 1975. Nevertheless, with a stabilized population, the rice harvest was particularly good in the southern and southwestern portions of the country, which had good rainfall; however, results were very uneven in the northwestern rice bowl. A number of refugees from the northwest described the amount of land tilled as only 50 percent that of the previous year, due to the general weakness of the people. In Koh Kong, in contrast, more land was reportedly tilled than in 1975, and in Kampot Province the amount cultivated was about the same as before. The government's claim that production was adequate to feed everyone and still have a surplus for export of 150,000 tons was examined by one scholar, who estimated that this meant a theoretical four hundred grams per inhabitant per day (Jackson 1978a:88), an amount that a great many people did not enjoy. If one estimates a population of six million, with everyone regardless of age eating four hundred grams per day (a total of 876,000 metric tons per year), and add to it the claimed export surplus, the total is 1,025,000 metric tons per year. This is a figure well below half that of earlier crop years in the 1960s and early 1970s.[15] Although Cambodia's population was undoubtedly larger in those earlier years, the proportion of persons engaged in agriculture in Democratic Kampuchea was much larger by dint of the virtual abolition of cities. Rice production was off by 50 percent in spite of the devotion of virtually all national resources to its production. Judged on the basis of either absolute production or production per capita, the DK results were very disappointing.

Late 1977 to Early 1978. After late rains and terrible flooding, which often overtaxed the irrigation systems, the rice harvest in much of the country was better than anticipated but still unsatisfactory. Besides exporting the so-called surplus, the government claimed that everyone was entitled to 312 kilograms of rice annually: almost one kilo per day. Refugee accounts flatly contradict this statement. One has the feeling that people adapted to their diet and the work regimen and that a "survival of the fittest" climate was prevailing.

Late 1978 to 1979. What was described as the "worst drought in 70 years," with the loss of 10 percent of the crop necessitating late replanting (Becker 1978b:A10), resulted in a crop that was hardly satisfactory in any case, but warfare, change in government, and chaos during the harvest period led to a ruined, wasted, even stolen harvest, whose aftermath—famine—was of disastrous proportions.

With contributions from Chinese agricultural expertise and the excellent, heavy hoe blades China furnished Cambodia in great quantity as part of the Chinese aid program, the DK regime did take steps to encourage rice production. For the year ending April 17, 1977, Radio Phnom Penh noted: "The brothers have focused on preparing and using natural fertilizer, selecting and screening good rice strains, compounding and using agricultural remedies, and experimenting with various planting techniques in order to further increase our rice production" (FBIS IV, April 20, 1977:H4). It is true that great efforts were made to collect human and animal wastes for fertilizer and to find faster-growing varieties. Amazingly, however, a number of

---

[15] See the figures cited in Department of the Army 1973:267.

farmers from the northwest, where floating rice has been traditionally important in areas subject to severe inundations, reported that the DK officials told them not to bother to cultivate it, that that kind of rice was only for cows. Cadres and soldiers told people that the aim was to have three crops per year. Sometimes the effort was made in areas with an inadequate year-round water supply, with hardly surprising results. Some locations did see two rice crops grown in a year (presumably one shorter-growing and one longer-growing), back to back. And there were places in the northwest, Kampot, and probably elsewhere, that did achieve three full plantings in succession in a year by 1977 or 1978, as opposed to one regular planting in the same areas in 1975. One Cambodian described his cooperative's success in growing three crops thus: "One day we'd be harvesting and the next planting new rice," he said with amazement, some pride, and a general attitude that things were moving faster in the fields than a human could comprehend.

Annual plans frequently mentioned the goal of producing three tons of rice per hectare for each rice crop. Because rice was generally being hauled away to local or district depots even as it was being harvested, it is unrealistic to expect refugees to be able to estimate the amount of rice produced per hectare. Simon, perusing Radio Phnom Penh, found in mid-1978 one rationalization for the failure to meet that goal: "Enemy running dogs of all colors planted within our cooperatives sabotaged the 3-ton-per-hectare target."[16] This is obviously far easier than to admit to widespread failure to achieve any real degree of self-sufficiency or even to achieve the levels produced, say, prior to World War II under colonialism.

IRRIGATION

The Cambodians went through a harsh trial and error period with their irrigation works beginning in 1975. A number of people died in the process of digging. The communists had set their usual, inflexible goals: visitors reported in August 1978 that every region had more than one irrigation reservoir holding 100–200 million cubic meters and dozens of canals, each over twenty miles long; every province had medium-size reservoirs each holding 50–60 million cubic meters of water; and every district had small reservoirs. The visitors said that, in all, a third of the country was then under irrigation. Similarly, a refugee from Kampot observed in his area that each sector had a large dam, each district a medium-size one, and each village a small one. Pol Pot's own claim that one-third of all agricultural land had been brought under irrigation is an interesting statistic but cannot be

---

[16] Simon 1978:25. He also cited the Yugoslavs observation in 1978 that they saw full rice graneries in the countryside, but the authorities were unable to move the rice to other areas due to poor roads and a lack of transport. Unquestionably, the DK government had real problems (Simon 1978:26).

evaluated very satisfactorily, since there are no comparable figures of any reliability for a previous period.

How well did the irrigation system work? Stories were legion in 1975 of people being instructed to dig ditches insufficiently deep to hold the water, or with sides so high that the water could not be brought out into the fields easily, and the like. Emphasis was always on speed, as if either a quota had to be met or a leader was out to impress his superiors. By 1978, however, visitors to Cambodia—Japanese, Yugoslavs, journalists—were agreeing that the water system seemed to be working. Even before, there were the reports from such places as Battambang and southern Oddar Meanchey provinces of some successful double and even triple cropping, attributed to continual work and successful water management. It should be recognized that triple cropping had only been done experimentally in the Battambang area in pre-communist days. In propaganda, small pumps were often shown being used in connection with irrigation.

Attempts to evaluate the DK success in irrigation seem to come to rest on one extreme side or another. One side is expressed in the boast of Social Action Minister Ieng Thirith to a Lao women's group that, thanks to irrigation, "Our people have been able to solve their food problem and produce sufficient rice for their own needs. Our people's living conditions have been greatly improved" (FBIS IV, April 26, 1977:H4). Another side, often cited since the 1979 takeover by the Vietnamese, is that the irrigation works were often poorly conceived and built, at times contributing to erosion and disturbing natural drainage more than increasing productivity.

There is probably some truth in both views. Visitors to Cambodia during the rainy season in 1979 often referred to the muddiness of rivers as proof that the irrigation works constructed at such high human costs were crumbling. Thus, it is interesting to note that ordinary Cambodian farm folk who heard this statement as they came to the Thai border for rice in 1980 disagreed vehemently. Not without pride in their accomplishment in building the massive works, they claimed that construction was solid enough and had withstood the 1979 rains reasonably well. If rivers were muddy, it was because the land was not being cared for, people agreed. Farmers said the works would continue to function in future years, assuming they were maintained. Indeed, one heard of areas of the country where, beginning in late 1979, the Vietnamese began to encourage the villagers to go out in their "solidarity teams" and repair and maintain the dikes, canals, and dams. It was a recognition that what had been built was of value, and this commentary is more valuable than any propaganda to the contrary.

EXPORT-IMPORT TRADE

At the outset, Cambodia looked as if it were hermetically sealing itself off from the rest of the world. Except for aid going in very quietly from China and North Korea, and for the rampant smuggling at Aranyaprathet and some at Trat-Koh Kong in the west and the Cambodian–Vietnamese border in the vicinity of Route 1 in the east, nothing was happening. There was talk of legal trade with Thailand, then and subsequently, without result due to DK indecision. In 1976, Cambodia did begin making some purchases of medicines and U.S. DDT (for which waivers were granted by Washington). A Cambodian trading corporation, the Ren Fung Company, established an office in Hong Kong, apparently financed by the Chinese, and became the country's principal purchasing agent in the West. Purchases through Hong Kong increased with time. Exploratory feelers between Cambodia and Japan resulted in the export of farm machinery commencing in 1977.

Cambodia's foreign trade really began in mid-1975 and increased incrementally in subsequent years. The country was obtaining salt, rice, jute bags, some mosquito nets, spare parts for machinery, medicine, and petroleum at Aranyaprathet, resulting in a boom for that small border town. It paid for these products with cash, sometimes in handfuls of brand new $100 bills (said to have been "found" in a bank in Phnom Penh or Battambang). The Cambodians also offered in payment dried fish, fish sauce, and fish paste, some works of art rifled from *wats*, and even watches, the fate of whose previous owners one could only guess. Even with the cash and the produce, the Cambodians were generally in deep deficit to the Thai, and it would be interesting to know if the deficit was ever erased. Poipet served as the transfer and storage area. As time went on, the range of products being traded changed. Jute bags and salt were no longer needed from outside, whereas more machine parts were. Fish products continued to be exported, and rubber joined the list. As relations between the two countries worsened, particularly with the Cambodian attacks on Thai border villages in early 1977, the trade halted, but never for very long, as clandestine ways were found to conduct it. All in all, the Aranyaprathet area was serving the vital trade function it had in previous times and as it continued to do after the Vietnamese founded the Peoples Republic of Kampuchea (PRK) in 1979.

Elsewhere, in the Trat–Koh Kong waters, trade was proceeding in various ways, thanks to the fishing boats in the area. The fisherman cited earlier noted that catches from his group's boats were placed on a particular island, along with pepper, which southwestern Cambodia specializes in growing. The Cambodian authorities would make known their desires for goods to the Thai, who would then leave the petroleum or whatever at the appointed spot in exchange. The source said the transactions usually proceeded surprisingly well.

Along the Vietnamese border with Svay Rieng Province, the Vietnamese apparently had a sort of market situation similar to that of Aranyaprathet–Poipet in operation at least in 1975. Refugees from the area described the barter that occurred relatively freely, but one did not hear of it a year later.

It was rumored that the dirty rubber beginning to appear at Aranyaprathet in 1976 was destined for Singapore. This perhaps paved the way for the expansion of trade that occurred between Singapore and Cambodia in subsequent years through the port of Kompong Som. A Singaporean trade mission visited Cambodia in 1978.

Unless DK records are discovered, it would be difficult to know with any accuracy the details of Cambodia's more far-flung trade, particularly with its communist allies, including the terms by which it was conducted. Yugoslavia and Romania furnished some aid in later years, but there is no firm evidence that they had any trade with Cambodia. One official told a journalist that 35,000 tons of rubber were being shipped to Singapore, China, and North Korea; kapok was going to Japan; and rice was underway to Madagascar and elsewhere in Africa (Becker 1978b:A10).

The U.S. Central Intelligence Agency described Cambodia's trade in calendar year 1978 as follows: exports were probably less than $1 million and consisted of natural rubber, rice, pepper, and wood, with China the leading client. Imports were listed as food, fuel, and machinery, all worth probably less than $20 million, coming particularly from China and North Korea (CIA 1979:104–5). Compare these figures with the country's trade in, say, 1968: exports $81 million (40 percent rice, 21 percent rubber), imports $90 million (chemicals 16.5 percent, machinery 15.7 percent). There is a very significant difference in volume of trade. It is an interesting commentary that the autarkic DK regime allowed its trade balance to be so much more in deficit (apparently) than the more freewheeling royal government of 1968.

It should not be thought, however, that Democratic Kampuchea exported and imported in a random manner. Once the initial takeover and reconstruction/construction periods were over, the trade that occurred was conducted in the way that theoretician Khieu Samphan in his university days would have approved (and perhaps did). Pol Pot stated openly what was happening: his country began "exporting tens of thousands of tons of rice in 1977 in order to accumulate capital to finance our national defense and reconstruction efforts" (Pol Pot 1977:H34). DK leaders along the Thai border confirmed in separate interviews that government policy required considerable amounts of rice to be sent abroad in order "to pay for machinery to build the country," such as tractors. They added that new industrial equipment in Phnom Penh was paid for in the same hard way. Presumably, in their own minds, they would have added military hardware to the list as well. Obviously, Cambodia was pulling itself up mostly by its own bootstraps (albeit with important help from its Chinese friends), but at what a price!

WHAT THEY DID NOT DO

There were some important features of the pre-1975 economy that the communists chose for one reason or another not to continue. One that stands out particularly is their failure to continue the important gem mining for which the Pailin area has traditionally been known. The gem miners were all turned out into the countryside at takeover, and a number of them subsequently fled to Thailand's Chanthaburi Province. Early on, refugees said the DK leaders explained that there was no time then for gem mining. A reporter was told in late 1978 that sapphire mining "would require too much manpower" (Becker 1978b:A10). It is ironic that the only persons who benefited from the Cambodian government's gem embargo were Cambodian resistance forces along the Thai border; they went into Pailin and brought out gems hidden by a Sino-Khmer businessman, with a consequent division of the spoils.

Another field not pursued was livestock raising on a large scale. Pakistanis resident in Cambodia for a generation or more had provided the expertise to manage these herds located in Siem Reap, Oddar Meanchey, and Battambang provinces. Some of their production during the war years went all the way to Saigon. There seemed to be no effort to persuade these Pakistanis—who were more Cambodian than anything else—to stay on and continue their money-making work. They were distrusted as foreigners, their religion was scorned, and their endeavors simply did not fit into the new system.

Perhaps a third area is coffee growing. Refugees fleeing to Thailand told how a coffee plantation in the Pailin area was ripped up to create rice fields. The destruction of this highly productive economic asset probably occurred because some DK functionary knew that his instructions were to plant rice, and so he did. Some coffee may have been grown in the country later in the period.

Finally, there has frequently been speculation that oil existed offshore in the Gulf of Thailand. Exploration had occurred without results, and there were sometimes rumors that the DK leadership would give the green light to a Western firm to continue exploration, with obvious benefits to Cambodia should oil be discovered. This never occurred, however. It is likely that the suspicion of foreigners "spying" from their drilling platforms was the overriding factor, which this leadership never quite overcame.

NUTRITION

This is one of those particularly difficult areas to discuss on the basis of the limited information available. Conditions around the country varied, and whether it was the harvest season or those several difficult months prior to the next harvest, made an important difference for food intake. Before it became common to eat communally in 1977, there were some people who would receive a can of rice per day (half that amount for children). A Carnation milk can filled with milled American rice weighs 400 grams. That would have been a reasonable, if minimal, amount to consume. (Many Asians eat more than one kilogram of rice per day.) SORAPA (the government's Société pour le Ramassage de Produits Agricoles) estimated in 1974–1975 that persons living in the countryside in Battambang province were indeed consuming that amount daily.[17] Similar verification of human needs has come from the noted nutritionist, Jean Mayer, who suggests that a kilogram of food per day will feed approximately two people (Mayer 1979:4).

I would suggest that, on the basis of my own interviews of refugees in 1975–1977, very few people could have been obtaining even that minimal amount of 400–450 grams, and many were receiving 250 grams or less. A milk tin of larger-grained Cambodian rice actually weighs only about 250 grams. Sometimes there would be one can per family; sometimes five adults would share that quantity for the day. Often in the months of greatest hunger, people would receive just rice soup, containing only a few kernels of rice or only the husks, with water. With the institution of communal dining, it was difficult to know the quantity of rice being given, since one did not prepare it oneself, but there was great variation: one meal of thin rice soup, another of a plate of rice; both meals consisting of gruel; sometimes only one meal. There are people who will tell you that they ate nothing but rice gruel during the first two years, after which gruel alternated with rice.

In addition to the basic staple, some leafy vegetable like spinach, occasionally some fish, and very occasionally a piece of meat, might be included. One particular kind of weed, bindweed, was frequently added, and there are many refugees who never want to hear of that plant again. People would try to add whatever they could find themselves: a piece of the stem of a banana tree, manioc, heart of palm, leaves from trees, or an occasional dead bird. This is hardly a balanced diet, and refugees were often quite anemic. The supply of salt fluctuated greatly.

Once the first nine months of hunger under the communists had passed and a full rice harvest was in, it would be fair to estimate that the "new" Cambodians consumed on the average two hundred to three hundred grams a day. According to reports, the more settled "base" people probably had a more abundant diet, although there were certainly exceptions. By early 1976, starvation as a cause of death was largely reduced, although scarcity and real periods of hunger never disappeared. Those Cambodians who were surviving were often thin and dark, wiry even, not enjoying full strength, but they were at least alive.

One demographic study of Cambodia concludes that Cambodia's population—perhaps 7.4 million in 1975—may have fallen to an estimated 5.8 million by the time the Vietnamese toppled the DK government (CIA 1980:4). Although the study does not attempt to speculate on the number of deaths from starvation alone, the figures can only lead one to conclude that the political, economic, and social system of Democratic Kampuchea was, in reality, an absolute disaster for the people of Cambodia.

[17] I am indebted to my friend Warren Hoffecker, previously with the Catholic Relief Service in Cambodia, for this useful information.

5. Social Change in the Vortex of Revolution

by François Ponchaud

"A radical revolution, more radical, and destined to push further, that that of China or the USSR." Following upon the information gathered between 1975 and 1978, that filtering abroad in the wake of the foreign invasion of January 1979 only confirms this judgment, which was aired by Karj Bork, Swedish ambassador to China, after a brief visit to Kampuchea in March 1976. Not only the cities, but also a good number of villages were emptied of their inhabitants, the latter being regrouped into cooperatives; Buddhism, which, in symbiosis with agrarian cults, had shaped the Khmer soul and molded the nation's social structures, was systematically eradicated; traditional values regulating social relationships within the family and the larger society gave way to other values, giving rise to a different language and ethic. An entirely new world was what the Cambodian revolutionaries sought to fashion, in socioeconomic terms as well as culturally. If all revolutions are inherently totalistic and endeavor to transform all facets of life, never before has one gone so far so fast in the realization of its goals.

At first sight, this revolution seems to be in complete breach with the history and culture of the Khmer. What enabled the revolutionaries to transform the tradition of their people with such apparent ease? Marxist ideology, revised and viewed through the prism of the Chinese Cultural Revolution, pushed to its extreme, was able to provide the small nucleus of leaders who imposed their views on the population at large both an instrument of struggle and a tool for the exercise of dictatorial power. Nevertheless, this ideology cannot in itself account for the variations among the multiple revolutions that it has inspired. The personality of the leaders of the Cambodian revolution, as well as their own life histories, could have informed certain decisions, inasmuch as it is a fact of history that individuals themselves play a considerable part in its unfurling. These leaders, however, were the products of a certain type of society, of a particular civilization, through which they reinterpreted the Marxist teachings imported from abroad. Furthermore, they could not have imposed a revolution without there being some connivance on the part of the people, some convergence of deep yearnings.

Did the Khmer culture predispose itself to the excesses of the revolution? Were the Khmer people indeed more malleable than any other? Certainly, there are no simple explanations. Rather, various strands of explanations present themselves as a cluster of partial and converging insights serving to

151

shed light upon the underlying mechanisms of this radical revolution. To look for certain conspiring associations between the revolution and the cultural context in which it unfolded cannot explain everything, since revolution above all is a political phenomenon in which various groups confront each other. Furthermore, a revolution does not follow a logical course; it is an explosion of collective violence, in certain ways akin to a passion: while the leaders might seek to justify their acts through a theory in which nonindigenous French, Soviet, and Chinese inputs play a large part, both they and the people more often act out according to unconscious reflexes welling up from the depths of a secular tradition. In conjunction with investigations of more important variables, however, research into the underlying cultural factors will perhaps allow us to put in context and better weigh the relative significance of the revolutionary choices made—disconcerting choices to those viewing them from the standpoint of another culture.

Without in any way seeking to justify the excesses of Pol Pot, it appears that this revolution bears the stamp of the Khmer culture: it is the revolt of the hinterland indigenous peoples against the foreigners; it is the rising up of the youth against the elders and the ancesters. Even though Angkar, the Khmer Rouge core organization, obliterated Buddhism from the Khmer landscape, ironically, some (but by no means all) Buddhist beliefs facilitated the rise and dominance of the Khmer Rouge. Furthermore, the absence of effective intermediary structures between the people and their successive leaders predisposed the society to the unrestrained exercise of power. As Marxists, the leaders of the Cambodian revolution analyzed the mechanisms of the society they sought to transform and endeavored to make use of those mechanisms—indeed, to supersede the fundamental structures of the society—in order to better buttress their power.

Revolt of the Chenla Peasants

The decision on the part of the victorious revolutionaries that most intensely scandalized the West was without a doubt that to expel all inhabitants from Cambodia's cities. The sacrilege of destroying the symbols of a consumer society—air conditioners, stereo systems, cars, various gadgets—and of abolishing the use of currency only added to the scandal. It exemplified a radical challenge against a mold of society considered by the West to be a hallmark of progress. Even from an orthodox Marxist perspective, which views industrial development as an indispensable avenue of social progress, it was, to say the least, unexpected. We must look beyond possible economic and strategic rationales positing among other things the need for a redeployment of the urban population to facilitate the development of the country's agricultural resources, and examine this decision in the Khmer context.

The typical urban-rural opposition found in many developing countries was itself reinforced by local generators of tension in Kampuchea. Different in composition at the start, the population of the cities and that of the countryside evolved in widely divergent cultural contexts. Through the institution of its administration and schools, the French protectorate served to deepen the urban-rural dichotomy that became even more pronounced after independence. Foreign bred, the cities were akin to cankerous growths that the revolutionaries held as their duty to expunge in order to regain ancestral purity. Originally small market towns, Cambodia's cities owed their rapid development to the French protectorate, whose policy it was to center its administration, build schools, and promote commercial growth therein. In part integrated to home-country markets, the growing Cambodian trade required the presence of an increasing number of Vietnamese and Chinese compradores who served as intermediaries between the peasants and their French protectors. They marketed agricultural produce, thereby providing the peasants with currency for tax purposes, and sold them manufactured goods from overseas.

Furthermore, the French administration had enticed to the cities a good number of Vietnamese civil servants, artisans, and service personnel. In 1921, the Chinese and Vietnamese constituted 32.2 percent and 25.9 percent of the total population of Phnom Penh relative to 8.1 percent and 6.6 percent, respectively, for the country as a whole (Forest 1980:82, 446, 472). The tendency for Cambodian cities to be settled by foreigners slowed substantially during the century and, according to the census of 1962, 18 percent of the capital's residents were Chinese and 14 percent were Vietnamese by ethnic origin, with the remaining 69 percent being Khmer (Migozzi 1973:240). In addition, one finds a marked swelling of the cities in comparison with the total Cambodian population: in 1962 Phnom Penh by itself had a population of 390,000, 6.9 percent of the total national population, nearly half of which were Chinese or Vietnamese (30 percent Chinese and 28 percent Vietnamese, according to Fisher 1964:570).

Moreover, most of the members of the new administrative class were either Sino-Khmer, Vietnamese-Khmer, or Kampuchea Krom Khmer who, toward the late 1960s, held a sizable proportion of the top leadership positions both in the government and in the army (Meyer 1971:83). Hence, it is little wonder that Cambodian peasants perceived the centers of wealth and power as being dominated disproportionately by foreigners against whom they already held longstanding feelings of racial animosity.[1]

---

[1] As Willmott and Forest aptly demonstrated, the relationship between Khmer and Chinese was rarely fraught with tension, but came to be founded on a certain pattern of division of labor within Cambodian society (Willmot 1967; Forest 1980). Nevertheless, onto this ethnic differentiation that hitherto had survived free of violent conflict, the revolutionaries superimposed a Marxist analysis of class antagonism. For the first time, a foreign observer on April 18,

With the development of an administrative and state enforcement system modeled on the West, town and countryside—already separated by differences in populations—grew further apart as each evolved in separate cultural contexts. Schools played a decisive role in this regard. Whereas the Khmer peasant continually strove to win over to his side the spirits of the earth, as well as those of the ancestors, in order to guarantee the fertility of his rice fields and the regularity of rainfall, his urban counterpart gradually uprooted himself from this religious environment that was felt to be no longer pertinent as a source of protection.

To the peasant, and for traditional Khmer society that revolved exclusively around agriculture, knowledge consisted above all in mastering a moral ethic, judged to be indispensable to the collective well-being of the community. It was in being able to separate truth from falsehood (*khos-treuv*), merit-incurring action from its opposite (*bon-bap*), that the peasant could win over the influence of the invisible beings holding sway over the destiny of men. In this society, it was not to the literate that veneration was due, but rather to the "saintly": to the hermits, central characters in Cambodian folktales, to the monks and the ex-monks who were "knowing" (*bandet*), the *achars* (laymen in charge of the pagodas), and, more generally, to the "old ripe ones" (*chas-toum*) who were held to be rich in human and spiritual experience. Veneration was even granted to the crafty types, who had savoir faire and who, in the folktales, would swindle the rich and fool the literate.

For the urban dweller on the other hand, it was diplomas that counted, opening the doors to administrative careers, in conjunction with technical

1975, could hear from the mouth of a cadre, "It's the Chinese who is an enemy of the Khmer people," an expression that heretofore had been directed only at the Vietnamese. Under the Khmer Rouge regime, however, the Chinese do not appear to have been subjected to any particular discrimination due to their race but, rather, like other citizens, only out of considerations for their status in society.

As for the conflictual ties between Khmers and Vietnamese, they were a constant throughout all regimes: such reflex responses of a defeated people directed at their subjugators is a legacy of three centuries of incessant struggle. Khmers of all social backgrounds and political stripe make frequent use of such sayings as *"Kom poup tè Ong,"* "don't knock over the gentleman's tea," recalling the cruelties that the satraps of Ming Mang inflicted on the Khmers, burying them alive and allowing only their heads to show to be used as a stand for their braziers. It is not accidental that the most venomous ant is referred to as a "Vietnamese ant." "The Vietnamese never forsake their deceitful ways," and so on. All these expressions and idioms are manifestations of a collective unconscious, generating violence. This latent antagonism can easily degenerate into racial violence, as occurred—among other instances—during the anti-Vietnamese pogroms instituted by Lon Nol in March–April 1970 in which more than four thousand Vietnamese were murdered. Beyond informing the political analyses in terms of which the Khmer revolutionaries gauged the vulnerability of their people in the face of a looming and conquering Vietnam, these atavisms played a role in the various purges of pro-Vietnamese Khmer cadres that took place in 1971 and 1973, as well as in the explusion of the Vietnamese minority in 1973 and again in 1975. In 1978, Cambodians who had Vietnamese features, or who simply were too pale, became as much the victims of this racist hatred as of the political will to eliminate a fifth column.

expertise, which allows one to master the world in the way of the West. Moral ethics no longer comprised a first order of concern and could even be relegated to oblivion should daily necessity warrant it. But moral perversion and prostitution, which hardly existed in the countryside for both economic and religious reasons, tended to spread in this moral climate that denied the omnipotence of the invisible world, and where neighborhood ties also could no longer play a regulatory role with regard to morality. On this score, the 1970–1975 period, which witnessed a massive inflow of millions of uprooted peasants into the cities, notably into Phnom Penh, was particularly significant: cut off from their ethical and religious moorings, the refugees from the countryside encamped in the cities lost their moral bearings and were contaminated by the debilitating influence of city life.

By introducing schools, primarily in the cities, the French protectorate—and later Prince Sihanouk's regime—brought in elements that had a corrosive influence on traditional society. Whereas in the countryside the pagodas served to initiate the young to prevailing ethics, a primary objective of the school system under the French protectorate was to provide the country with a corps of officials to further the administration of the country along Western lines. Whereas previously official posts were bought by shrewd individuals who, while perhaps ignorant, knew how to amass wealth, the French protectorate gave access to officialdom only to those holding diplomas. Under the protectorate as well as under Sihanouk, becoming educated and obtaining a diploma meant having the opportunity to join the ranks of the elite, with the sole view to take part in the administration. Diplomas came to be objects of true fascination among the young, since they provided the only channel for social mobility and opened the doors to all ambitions. Given, however, that the relentless opening up of new official posts could not keep apace indefinitely with the inconsiderate expansion of the Western styled educational system during Sihanouk's reign, a crisis was bound to erupt (see Pomonti and Thion 1971:77). "Semi-intellectuals" who had received several years of secondary education would not stoop to work in the fields yet could not obtain gainful employment in the administration. They were pushed to the margins, unable to take part in the country's developmental tasks.

By fostering such different paths to knowledge and administration, schools furthermore served to deeply alter the social relationships tying the cities to the countryside. Before the French protectorate, various official posts were bought by the rich, who managed to recover their outlays by further extracting from the peasantry. Generally from the same area as their administrative subjects, their appetite for gain was checked by a type of inherent self-regulatory mechanism: because of kinship ties, the mandarin had to maintain a certain decency, and could not cross certain limits without worrying about possible revolt. Public offices that had been acquired through wealth could only be passed on by being sold, whereas offices obtained through diplomas, in a certain sense, became an even more stable inheritance than wealth. Access to education for the offspring of public officials was far easier than for others, thereby laying the groundwork for the emergence of a select administrative class more and more cut off both from the peasantry and from the necessity of interacting with society in general, by dint of being insulated from economic activity by the guaranteed status provided by academic diplomas.

With the new system of recruitment via diplomas, officials tended to become irresponsible, being satisfied merely to implement orders coming down from above. Very much in line with French administrative practice, authority was concentrated in the capital, and the provinces had very little say in decisions concerning them. In the time of the protectorate, the official's chief concern was merely to submit to sanctioned orders without undue display of imagination. Similar behavior was exemplified during the Sihanouk era and, to a degree, even under Pol Pot.

No doubt members of the urban administrative class maintained family ties connecting them to the countryside and would occasionally return there for the more important village festivals. Nevertheless, gradually they found themselves more and more ill at ease with a peasantry they no longer understood. In parallel fashion, to the extent that in previous times the king had kept close to his subjects and continued to share their concerns, he eventually came to know them only through the distoring prism of his administration. Peasants in the main no longer held the opportunity to present their grievances directly to him in the manner they had enjoyed through the first decades of this century.

With the schools came the diffusion of a new culture both patterned on the West and rendered profane and secular. Voltaire, Rousseau, and the heroes of the French Revolution were the models the intellectually fervent young were asked to meditate upon. Contact with the French led to Western role models displacing traditional ones, thereby widening the chasm between the "educated" class and the peasantry. This educated class led a schizophrenic existence, torn between its indigenous cultural roots and the culture the protectorate promoted as that of "civilization." Thus long hair, a disheveled look, loose morals were all capped—at least until 1975—with the term "civilay," meaning "civilized."

Following independence, not wont to be outdone by other Asian capitals, Phnom Penh under the auspices of Sihanouk was further remodeled along Western lines, the thatched-roof shantytown districts being razed and replaced by Western- or Chinese-style buildings. The peasants became gradually excluded from the cities: edicts were passed, for instance, forbidding them to walk about the town either barefoot or stripped to the waist wearing sarongs, as had been customary. Attempts were even made to forbid peasants-turned-pedicab drivers from wearing shorts. Peasant carts could go about the streets only at night and even then only on certain itineraries circumventing the city core. In his films presenting the country to the international community, the prince paraded luxurious limousines, showed sumptuous receptions in Western-style decor and setting, deliberately avoiding the screening of any peasants or pedicab drivers—who yet comprised the majority of his countrymen—as if they were a disgrace to be somehow veiled from public view. Keeping up with the times, the prince had even founded the pornographic review "Pseng Pseng," whose editorship he personally assumed.

It is to this disdain for traditional culture values that certain dialectical conditions for revolution can be traced.[2] On the one hand, schools promoted a fascination for knowledge, progress, and anything foreign. On the other, a reaction set in within part of the educated class, notably among some of the teachers having a moral responsibility for the countryside youth, breeding a form of nationalism that became increasingly exacerbated. One might add that this tendency was facilitated by the prickly nationalism of Prince Sihanouk himself with regard to political issues. The absence of a true anticolonial struggle against the French had the effect of prolonging the foreign cultural influence well past the time of independence.

It was thus relatively easy for the revolutionaries, mostly spawned from the ranks of the teachers, to instill in some peasants an awareness of the cultural alienation in which the urbanities were steeped and to push them to purify their country of these depraved influences. To them, the abstract knowledge disseminated in the schools was no sign of progress. Hence, such knowledge was suppressed just like any other contraption from the cities, a more rustic education taking its place. "You don't need education to cultivate the rice fields." "Paper diplomas" are worthless compared to diplomas earned "on sight," which is to say through good conduct and honest work. "The rice field is the university," "the hoe is the pen." Similarly, to them, the peasants' way of life became synonymous with Khmer culture: the traditional peasant black garb must be worn by all, a colorful attire becoming a sign of attraction to the cities and its foreign influences; the short hair worn in the countryside came to be imposed on all, long hair being synonymous with perversion and idleness, according to radio broadcasts and refugee reports; moral rigor, a constant with all revolutionaries, here was set in opposition to the loose ways of urban life. Likewise, the abolition of currency was viewed as a scandal by the Westernized urban world but not by

---

[2] Of course, the Khmer Rouge also manifested profound disdain for many traditional values. Sequence in time, however, is important to understanding the delegitimization of a ruling elite. The Phnom Penh elite's disdain for traditional values created mass alienation, the very social clay the Khmer Rouge remolded, at first somewhat gently in the period 1970 to early 1973 and then much more drastically from early 1973 to 1979. Finally, the mass social alienation that gave rise to the Khmer Rouge was remolded in revolutionary form by pairing the rejection of tradition with an egalitarian ideology backed by a powerful coercive apparatus. (On the changing tactics of the Khmer Rouge during the 1970–1975 period, see Quinn 1976.)

the rural population, and even less by the marginalized hinterland peoples who, up until fairly recently, had lived in a nonmonetized universe where barter formed the basis for material transactions. Up until 1975 and, indeed, again in 1980, the peasants in Tonle Sap would, in late December and early January, come and exchange their rice for dried fish.

One of the most frequent criticisms that the urbanites leveled against the Khmer Rouge cadres was their ignorance: "They often neither know how to read nor write" and only stubbornly repeat their often ill-understood lessons, sprinkled with new vocabulary derived from Sanskrit roots. The urbanites thus found themselves in the same position as the peasants listening to Radio Phnom Penh before 1970—understanding hardly anything. The use of a language comprised of stereotypic formulas, while tied to the necessity of transmitting ideological referents, also reflects the will on the part of the authorities to prevent any possibility of meaningful exchange among the uprooted peoples even on the level of language.

This criticism of urbanites, quite common in other communist regimes, is particularly edifying in this case: under the communists, oral civilization—typically Khmer—once again is made to take precedence over the written culture brought in from the West. The older generations left their traces in important architectural vestiges, whereas the written Khmer literature is relatively poor and recent. In contrast to their Vietnamese and Chinese neighbors, the Khmers do not feel undue veneration for the "literate," who in the Confucian hierarchy held a place of preeminence. Among the Khmers, power is granted to the "smooth talker," and it was often from the ranks of the vernacularly articulate (*mean voha*) that revolutionary cadres were chosen. Those who knew how to write were chosen as "secretaries," third in rank in the village committee hierarchy. Content was less important than harmony of effect, and something only acquired significance if it was "spoken." For example, Prince Sihanouk held the crowds in rapture for hours with speeches whose content was rather barren; Saloth Sar, alias Pol Pot, while a student in Paris, subdued his fellow students with the magic of his oratory; Hou Youn was a legendary narrator of stories.

Inversely, in such an oral civilization, silence was an absolute rule for subordinates: for instance, no one addressed himself to the prince without being invited to do so; in the queen's chambers, all the women worked in total silence. In like manner, the Khmer Rouge society became a society of silence where cadres held a monopoly over speech.

In the same vein, it is significant that the Khmer revolution was able to function practically without a bureaucracy: no written resumés, hardly any archives, few official texts or periodicals.[3] As in ancient times, decisions

[3] For further details on the administration of Democratic Kampuchea, see Chapter 3 by Timothy Carney.—ED.

fixed collectively were transmitted via messengers. This serves as an explanation for the considerable variation in implementation of directives by local leaders: each acted according to his own understanding, without referring to a text spelling out the details for implementation. We can also better understand the all-embracing authority of the mysterious Angkar in light of the "oral" character of the culture. Just as previously, when in order to convince their subordinates, officials would invoke and hide behind the authoritative "Samdech says . . . ," in the same way, the cadres had only to affirm "Angkar says . . ." without anyone having the gall—either under the Khmer Rouge or, for that matter, under the previous regime—to ask for a written confirmation.

Thus, it is in this ethnic and cultural opposition between peasants and city dwellers that one can search for a partial explanation of some of the revolutionaries' behavior. This antagonism was carried over to the era of foreign occupation and exile. The people of Phnom Penh under the People's Republic of Kampuchea continued to see themselves as the crux of the nation, using up for themselves the flow of foreign assistance, neglecting the countryside. It is the people from the south, vassals to the Vietnamese, who seek to impose their rule over the whole country. In the Thai refugee camps, one frequently hears former city dwellers refer to the peasants and the Khmer Rouge with the same sweeping hatred. This opposition between city and countryside, does it not stem from deeply embedded historical roots? This antagonism appears to superimpose itself on the old opposition between the population of Fou Nan, from the delta and open to outside influence, and that of the Chenla, in the hinterland around the middle Mekong, closed unto itself and hardly permeable to new ideas and techniques. On this point it is significant that Lon Nol's regime saw itself as bearers of the Fou Nan legacy, perhaps intimating that their opponents were descendents of the Chenlas.

It is precisely in these remote Chenla regions that the leaders of the revolution, essentially from 1962 on, lived and recruited the bulk of their troops. Many shared the life of the Pors in the Cardamons, in the Amleang and Samlaut sectors, that of the Stiengs in the Damber region, or that of other ethnic groups in the Stung Treng and Ratanakiri provinces. A latent rancor opposed these ethnic groups to the Khmers of the rice-growing region who had driven them back to the forests and who despised them. The bloody repression by Sihanouk's army of the Samlaut uprisings of 1966 and of the Ratanakiri–Mondolkiri turmoil of 1968–1969 pushed them to enter the ranks of the revolutionary army. The initial phase of the 1970 war had split Cambodia "along historical lines: in the North, on both sides of the Mekong, the mountain regions, corresponding to the Chenla of old . . . to the South, the low country of the old Fou Nan . . ." (Meyer 1971:50–51). According to an engineer who was a member of FUNK (Front Uni National du Kampuchéa), it is among the people of the Kratie district that Pol Pot had chosen his bodyguards and his most loyal cadres, even though they were completely illiterate. Moreover, it is near Kratie where the quasi-magical raised site of Sambaur, the old Chenla capital, can be found. Pol Pot and Ieng Sary, from 1970 on, were the masters of this particular region in the northwest.

Such origins probably had an influence on the leaders of the revolutionary army, who for the most part were either from the cities or from the delta or had undertaken part of their studies abroad. Far from reining in their zeal to innovate, it is perhaps their very bourgeois class origin which, in dialectical opposition to the influences they received from their years in the peasant underground, galvanized their radicalism. These leaders' French culture might have served as a catalytic influence allowing the emergence of the forest people's traditional values. As was true for many Khmers educated in the French tradition, the leaders held in admiration the work of Jean Jacques Rousseau, exalting the "noble savage" corrupted by society. Through contact with the peasants of these remote regions, they harked back to deeper sources and experienced a type of "illumination." "Through close contact with the peasants, we have had to completely remold the knowledge we had acquired in Paris," a member of FUNK confided to a French diplomat acquaintance in 1974. According to the engineer quoted earlier, Ieng Sary, in 1978, held his own case as an example to be emulated by the intellectuals being held in the Boeung Trabek camp, "You have to delve among the people, merge with the people. I have lived with the Montagnards, I became used to their customs. At first I was shocked by their primitive life, but I felt that they should not be dealt with recklessly or made to turn to our ways. One must first blend in with them, and then, little by little, make them understand hygiene. But in order to do so one must act like them: if they don't wear clothes, neither should we; if they file their teeth, we must file ours also." This "illumination" also was experienced by the Phnom Penh residents banished to the countryside after 1975; thus, the manager of the city's largest hotel described his own experience: "I did not know the peasants from the forests. At the start I didn't even understand their language, but they turned out to be very resourceful. And to think that I, a Khmer, thought I knew Cambodia!"

Driven to the conquest of the rest of the country, of the rice-growing plains as well as the cities, the revolutionary troops behaved like men of the forests, like huntsmen, setting their traps, drawing in their quarry through all sorts of ruses including deceit, bringing them down with ebony bludgeons, as was described by Boun Sokha (1979), or with the native pickaxe. Booby traps and concealed pointed bamboo stems, such as were used by hunters, remain to this day the arms heralded by the radio and official propaganda. If eating human liver is a ritual practice widespread among the peoples of Southeast Asia, extracting human bile for the making of traditional medicine appears to be a custom unknown to the people of the plains and practiced only by those of the Khmer forests. Apart from the traditional treatment of vanquished populations, deported and reduced to slavery, the act of smashing consumer goods to pieces seems to correspond to the attitudes of men of the forests: these were useless goods whose very existence they had hitherto been unaware of. Indeed, the men of the forests were more concerned with external flash appeal than with the intrinsic or monetary value of Western goods.

Driving the urban population back into the forests and later into the rice fields was probably inspired as much by a desire to regenerate them by plunging them back into a universe from which they should never have strayed, as by vengence (Meyer 1971:16). The capacity for adaptation and innovation, so much evoked in radio broadcasts, could thus be regenerated. Moreover, one can find kindred themes in Khmer literature. In this literature, the forests represent the "non-domesticated" in contrast to the "domesticated," the "wild" in opposition to the "civilized." It is also the home of hermits and a place of regeneration. "Once you come to live in the forest, as you settle there to take up some line of activity, there is a break with the familiar world, with the domesticated universe of the 'srok,' and you find yourself tied to a world 'where anything is possible' " (Thierry 1978:451–54). Urban dwellers had to transform themselves into "people of the forest," as they themselves used to refer to the revolutionaries. Moreover, most murders were carried out behind bushes or in the forest, a recurrent setting for murder in Khmer literature, and rarely in public view. In the folktales, the act of murder, furthermore, "is not conceived as an evil and uniquely reprehensible act: it assumed a revelatory function, either in the sense that it was a prelude to a rebirth, or in that it triggered acts of salvation, exemplifying the divine or Buddhistic cosmic order" (Thierry 1978:457). The killings of corrupt and irredeemable elements in the forest were a prelude to the birth of a moral and more properly ordered society.

Though the Democratic Kampuchean revolution appears to be the most radical revolution of the twentieth century, the behavior of the revolutionaries is not totally alien to Khmer culture. Many analogies can be traced to Khmer ancestral practices as well as to those of the forest cultures. The Angkorian era forms the conscious reference against which the revolutionaries measured themselves, just as even Prince Sihanouk had done. It is notably the Angkorian model that inspired the carrying out of massive hydraulic construction projects, displaying the same suicidal megalomania. Nevertheless, it is most probably in the far reaches of the Chenla period that it is appropriate to search for traditional models. As in the eighth century, the Khmer Rouge leveled the cities, displaced entire populations, imposed their own earthbound values, cutting themselves off from the world.

Thus, the Khmer revolutionaries stood directly in line with the Chenla conquerors of a bygone age. "To the cosmopolitan and coastal culture are now opposed closed and earthbound values. . . . A civilization is taking form that is bent on being wholly indigenous and which is taking root on purely Khmer soil" (Thierry 1964:54). An analogous judgment could be made on the revolutionary era arising eleven centuries later.

In accord with the image of the old Chenla, resolutely closed to the external world, the leaders of Democratic Kampuchea hardly bothered with international public opinion. Contrary to their Vietnamese neighbors, they did not mount propaganda offensives of any consequence to justify their acts or to beget themselves friends. The very widely held presumption on the part of the Khmer leadership at all levels that they were infallible, that they were the best of all things and, notably, that they were the best communists in the world may also be a legacy from the distant past.

Revolt of the Youth against the Elders

This return to the past—characterized by the destruction of cities, the exclusive attention to agrarian work, the abolition of currency as well as the establishment of a nonbureaucratic society—was accompanied by profound modifications in the social structure, marking a definite break with the past.

While authority is granted to the elders in all rural societies, this was particularly true in Cambodia: grandparents, parents, and elders exercised real authority over younger members of society; the spirits of the earth (the *Neak Ta* or "ancient beings") presided as venerable masters over the destinies of men.

The relationship between youth and elders, even more than that along sexual lines, governed the basic structure of traditional Khmer society. One may note several revealing signs: in the common Khmer language as well as in folktales, men and women are not portrayed in a relationship of tension. One only has to list various pairings of terms granted parity in frequent usage: "ta/yiey" (old man/old woman = grandparents), "eupouk/maday" (father/mother = parents), "méa/ming" (uncle/aunt), "pdei/praponh" (husband/wife = spouses), "koun/cau" (children/grandchildren = offspring), "bank/pauôn" (older/younger offspring = siblings, cousins), and so on. In all these pairings, apart from the last two, which are gender-free, the two sexes are expressed as being on equal terms. Similarly, while aunts and uncles carried considerable weight as parental substitutes, they were not distinguished as being either from the maternal or paternal lineage, as would be the case in an African society, but rather according to whether they were the parents' elders.

While religious attitudes tied to sexuality placed women at a rank below that of men, in daily life—and notably in work—women were held as equal to men, working the rice fields on the same footing as men. Men and women could begin claiming a measure of independence from their parents once they had children, and only acquired authority when they became grandparents. Thus it is hardly surprising, given the relative equality between men and women, that under both the Khner Republic and the Khmer Rouge, soldiers were recruited among the youth of both sexes. The equality in work between the sexes, touted by revolutionary broadcasts as a significant victory, had already attained reality in the social context of the civil war.

On the other hand, it was much more among different age groups that cleavages and relationships of tension prevailed. Filial piety was a virtue that was inculcated within the family, in schools, as well as in pagodas where all rituals at least in part involved acts of gratitude for the blessings provided by the elders (parents, grandparents, masters, and so on), to whom devolved the merits stemming from the ceremony. Young men became monks "in gratitude for the blessings of their parents" (*sang kun eupouk-maday*). In the context of family life, no important decision could be made without submiting the matter and deferring to grandparents, parents, or their substitutes (uncles, aunts, elders). The decisive importance of the elders was felt keenly at the time of marriages, which were arranged (*reap kar*) by the parents as part of their sacred duties toward their offspring. "To love your wife as much as your mother" was the highest vow of love a man could make to his bride. In terms of the common language, the relationship between spouses was that of "elder" and "junior"—"elder" (*bang*) being used to denote the man and "junior" the woman. If a young woman remained chaste, it was "out of gratitude" for her parents, and the like. Among the refugee population, the absence of parents is more keenly felt than that of a spouse or child because one can no longer "bestow upon one's parents the care and blessings" that they provided in one's own youth.

At the village level, the family underpinned the whole social structure: the communal forms of authority that had been instituted by the French protectorate never really took root in everyday life. Most inhabitants of a *"phum"* shared kinship ties, and village solidarity was manifested in the common worship of *Neak Ta* ancestors, who had been founders of the village or initiators of cults toward a particular village tree or rock. These were the "ancestors" who provided a protective shield to the village, insuring at once health, fertility, regular rainfall, and other benefits. While the Khmers, in traditional society, traveled widely outside their village of origin, they nevertheless often returned, at least for the major village festivals, because no place else offered as much protection as the village where the "ancestors" were familiar. Khmer literature, especially folktales, provides countless examples of this feeling of permanence infusing the visible and invisible world. "The village community does not limit itself to its living residents but rather comprises a whole microcosm of *Neak Ta* and the spirits of the dead, peasants and rice, commingling destinies whose ties are constantly being reinforced through community rituals. If one of these 'elements' comes to be lacking, the whole community comes to an end: without water or dry seasons there would be no rice, hence no population, no cult, no *Neak Ta*—and without these no mastery over the waters and hence again, no rice . . ." (Forest 1980:38).

The patriotism of the Khmers emerges first of all by way of attachment to one's family. At a more general level, one could consider the Khmer people as comprising a vast single family: first names were nonexistent in the Khmer language, everyone addressing each other or themselves as "child" or "father," "mother," "nephew," "uncle," "grandfather," "grandmother," "older brother or sister," "younger brother or sister," and so on. These various designations revolved around age differences, and outside of the family were used to stress the social rank or status of the speaker, as well as the relationship in which he or she wanted to be viewed by the person spoken to. Within the family, incorrect usage of such forms of address constituted a serious breach. With regard to the royal family or officials, monks, and foreigners (Chinese or European), use of such familiar forms was precluded—these formed a caste apart. Since the 1960s, those educated in official schools tended to style their language on that of Westerners: *Lauk* (My Lord) became the equivalent of "Mister," *Khniom* (Servant) serving as "I."

If it is indeed family structure that forms the basis of Khmer society, and within the family the relationship among age groups, one may well understand the desire on the part of the revolutionaries to modify family ties and, notably, to substitute themselves for the elders. Nor is it all that surprising that Angkar, or more precisely all adults, came to be addressed as the "dad-mom" (*pouk-mè*) of the people, even if such an expression had not been used in such paired form in the past. The revolutionary era is referred to as "the dad-mom era" (*samay pouk-mè*); the people in the cooperatives are called "dad(s)-mom(s) from the cooperatives." Does this not follow the same logic as when Prince Sihanouk would have himself addressed as "*Samdech Euv*" (Lord-Father), or would himself refer to his subjects as "children-grandchildren" (*kaun-chau*), a form of address frequently used to include all subordinates, all of whom being thus held in a subaltern familial role vis-à-vis authority. The various terms that were used to pin down interpersonal status roles generally have disappeared from common use, though usage varies with region. The elders are generally referred to as "comrade father" (*met pouk*), or as "comrade mother" (*met-mè*), the children as "comrade child" (*met kaun*), as if these categories were sufficient to denote status. The terms "junior uncle-aunt" (*pou, mong, mea*) or "elder uncle-aunt" (*om, eupouk thom, maday thom*) have for the most part been abolished. Military leaders are called "*ta*" (grandfather) irrespective of their age since they are the ones who now have true knowledge and authority. Among peers of the same age the term "comrade" is widely used, even if occasionally one is addressed as "elder comrade" or "younger comrade" or even simply as "elder" or "younger one" as in previous times.

Since Angkar is the "dad-mom" of the people, it hence has the responsibility to determine who is part of the family and who is not. Already in 1973 some cases of children who had joined the ranks of the revolutionaries and had executed their fathers who were enrolled in the republican army had become known: these were not their fathers, they said, they were "enemies." Many such cases have been reported since. Several cases are known of officers' wives grieving over their lost husbands: "Why are you crying over him? He was an enemy!" they would be told scornfully. The revolutionaries, however, were aware of the extent to which people were tied by family obligations. They therefore did not hesitate, in certain sectors, to execute the wives and children of the condemned, especially those of former officers in 1975, and even those of Khmer Rouge cadres after 1977. In fact it was "the application in attenuated form of the 1877 Cambodian penal code which stipulated that sudden death could be meted out to the entire family of the culprit as well" (Meyer 1978). The novel *Tum-Teav*, probably written in the nineteenth century, echoes a certain tradition as concerns forms of punishment: the relatives "to the seventh degree" of the culprits were buried alive, their heads raked off with an iron harrow. In the same vein, since 1975 and especially since 1977, a considerable number of Khmer Rouge cadres were purged and sometimes executed because of their family links with the republican military (*choap ninykar noyobay*).

Since Angkar is the "dad-mom" of the people, it follows that all children belong to it and not to their true parents. Even before the 1975 victory, cases had been reported of families "spontaneously" offering their offspring to Angkar. Parents were not held accountable for reprehensible acts committed by their children, since these belonged to Angkar. Since 1977, with the general extension of "higher-level cooperatives" to the country as a whole, children scarcely lived with their parents any more: those under six years of age were entrusted to the care of grandmothers who cultivated their revolutionary spirit through the narration of heroic tales while their mothers were out at work. Those six to twelve lived apart from their parents, sleeping in separate quarters—called "*monti-komar*"—or else were organized into groups of ten, receiving a type of schooling chiefly geared to manual work. Once twelve, children were enlisted in "mobile troops" and hardly ever had the opportunity to see their parents again.

In a certain sense it could be said that Angkar adopted for its own use certain prevailing social customs, pushing them to extreme form. Previously, it was not uncommon for parents to entrust one or more of their children to the care of a grandmother, an aunt, or to a neighbor who wanted to adopt them and who thus became a foster parent. Furthermore, education was carried out by osmosis within the village, with the children growing up free to all constraints except for those imposed by the village community as a whole, parents hardly intervening more than others in the education of their own offspring. Children were considered a kind of old-age security capital and were expected to provide for their parents in the future, once they were no longer able to work productively. Children, however, were not subject to a great deal of adult attention. Angkar, on the other hand, fulfilling a collective parental role, took diligent care of children—"the future of the nation"—"whose minds aren't tainted like those of their elders." This solicitude is manifested in the terms of deference by which they were addressed—"*komara-komaray*" (somewhat lofty terms for boys and girls). Parents did not have the right to admonish them, let alone beat them, and could be punished for doing so. Since 1977, in the communal mess halls, children were served first, before workers.

Angkar's substituting itself in the parental role is especially significant as concerns marriage. In 1975 several cases were reported of marriages where war invalids were authorized to pick a bride among the population expelled from the cities. This type of union was relatively infrequent, however, and could be viewed in connection with the treatment of prisoners of war. From 1976 on, marriages were carried out according to strict guidelines, applications of which have been traced to all regions. Marriages were allowed only within set categories: young soldiers (*yotheas*), male or female, chose their spouse only from "within the ranks" (*Khnong chuor*)—either other soldiers like themselves, or female guards (*senachon*), or members of district mobile troops (*dambân*), or even staff personnel belonging to various organizations. They were not allowed to wed anyone from the "new people." Members of the "old people" usually married the same, though sometimes they could wed individuals designated as being from the "new people."[4] While in the past, parents played a decisive role in choosing spouses for their children, now individuals made their own choices subject to the approval of Angkar. Thus a liberalization of marriage practices came into effect, especially for young women who now could take the initiative, which would have been unheard of in the past. When a young man wants to marry and has set upon a choice of spouse (or vice versa), he informs his group leader, who in turn informs the village or company head. The latter then refers the request to the female cadre in charge of the girl's unit who then informs the girl in question and, eventually, her parents. The reply is trans-

---

[4] The "new people" constituted those who were "liberated" by the Khmer Rouge on April 17, 1975. These people were considered prisoners of war as well. The "old people," also called the "common people," constituted those who were under the control of the Khmer Rouge since 1970.

mitted via the same channels back to the individual concerned. It is reported that often the cadres discuss the query among themselves, examining the biographic details of both parties before granting or turning down the request. For example, a case was cited near Sisophon where a poverty-stricken youth had asked to marry a girl from a middle peasant background: his request was refused. This is frequently the case when dealing with those from the "new people." Until 1978, furthermore, one could not ask to marry someone living outside one's village or cooperative. During the first post-victory year, however, it was reported that in several instances, Angkar had arranged marriages without even asking the consent of the individuals concerned, future spouses having never before laid eyes on each other. This even led to ridiculous incidents, as when the bride, having lowered her eyes throughout the ceremony, would fail to recognize her bridegroom after the rites had been performed.

Dates for the marriage are set by the authorities who organize the ceremony, just as parents had done previously. If the rites vary in detail from one region to the next, nevertheless they always follow similar general lines: the couple are united "before the people," "vow loyalty to Angkar," "swear never to betray the Way" (*Meakear*). Whereas before marriage constituted a vow made before one's parents and one's community, now it is to Angkar that vows are made. It is significant to note that "to be faithful to each other" has now become synonymous with "to be faithful to Angkar." Adulterous couples are condemned to death for having "betrayed Angkar," betrayed the constitution, or "betrayed the Way," just as previously a young woman who ill-behaved was seen as wronging her parents. The good of the nation takes precedence over individual emotional life, which is akin to Khmer tradition according to which love tended to come after—rather than precede—marriage, the latter being viewed primarily as serving the continuation of the family line.[5]

In more general terms, however, Angkar demands that it receive the same respect and obligation from the population at large that children or younger family members used to proffer to their parents or elders: "recognize the blessings of Angkar" (*deung kun angkar*) is the master theme in the new moral code, just as heretofore, "recognize the blessings of your parents" had been the theme.

While exercising a parental type of authority over the people, Angkar also has knocked down the power of the "ancestors," or spirits of the earth.

In their drive to gain mastery over the world, to make the people "masters of the earth and of water," "masters of the rice fields and plains, of the forests and of all vegetation," "masters of the yearly floods," the revolu-

---

[5] Among refugees, even those under the control of former Khmer Rouge cadres, these marriages do not stand up to the wear of time and are for the most part broken off.

tionaries had to confront the invisible masters who before them, at least in the minds of the peasants, governed over the welfare of the villages. In their will towards a total control over fate and creation of man by man, they had to suppress the "ancestors." It is probably in light of this that one should view the relentless shifts of population since 1975. Beyond economic necessity, these constant shifts destroyed the religious environment surrounding peasant life, thus breaking the vital link between villagers and celestial powers, and obviating all spiritual references connected to the soil. Population shifts were frequent in ancient times, especially during droughts: entire villages would be displaced for a certain time, only eventually to return to the same sector in order to ensure the cult of the "ancestors." Outside their villages, and especially when exiled to the forest, villagers would feel lost, cut off from their customary overseers, and could only therefore entrust themselves to the all-powerful Angkar.

In official or private propaganda, little mention is made of the *Neak Ta*— they are ignored. At most, as some witnesses report, they are said to exist no longer. One might very well be surprised to find that such a belief so deeply embedded in the daily life of the Khmers could so easily be uprooted from the Khmer soul. Trained to fight, young Khmer Rouge soldiers don't necessarily deny the existence of mysterious beings, they only deny their practical efficacy: the soldiers defeated them, just as they defeated the "old people" or the people with whom the spirits shared their existence. A thirty-two-year-old peasant who lived under revolutionary rule for eight years brings the following significant testimony:

Me, I believed in the *Neak Ta*. Once I was keeping watch over some water buffalos, I didn't remove my hat when passing by the *Neak Ta*'s pagoda, and I swore at the buffalos. Then the *Neak Ta* made me so ill I thought I'd die, I had to offer him some cake and alcohol, which cured me. But since the Khmer Rouges rule the country, the *Neak Ta* don't dare do anything, they're afraid of the Khmer Rouges' meanness. When we spoke about the *Neak Ta* to them, they would say: "Where is he, I'm going to shoot him." Even the *Neak Ta* were afraid of them, they didn't dare act up against them. (Compiled by the author in 1976.)

The soldiers behaved in line with traditional Cambodian folklore, where one often comes across tales of spirits being overpowered by courageous men unafraid to face them. For the peasant, only immediate efficacy testifies to the power of the spirits: if they don't punish those who have transgressed their rules, they no longer can be said to have authority or real existence. "Since they didn't do anything against the Khmer Rouge, I don't trust them any more." If people no longer believe in them, what powers do they still hold? "They can only act if people believe in them," the peasant adds. And, thus compelled, the people line up on the side of the more powerful.

In fact, even in 1978, there were numerous indications as to the survival of the ever-present spirits. Witnesses relate the story of the difficulties that some Khmer Rouge soldiers encountered in wanting to displace an Angkorian statue: the spirit embodied in the particular statue was said to have caused the breakdown of two military transport vehicles. Others tell the story of a Khmer Rouge soldier who, quite forthrightly satisfying his bodily needs over a *Neat Ta's* pagoda, became ill in the night and was compelled to make ritual offerings. When they or their children fell ill, some secretly would go present offerings to the spirits or go seek the help of mediums. Those who were caught carrying out such practices were subjected to the taunts of the soldiers but were otherwise left unmolested. If a medium went into a trance, however, he was killed, not so much because he was practicing a religious act as because he wasn't working, or would happen to criticize Angkar, or even because it was felt he was seeking to leave the country by pretending to be crazy.

By attacking the way in which age groups traditionally related to each other, the Khmer revolutionaries modified what was at the core of Khmer society. Doing so, however, was going against the grain of the agrarian society they were seeking to reconstruct. Whereas in former times, recently dispatched officials would take up their provincial posts by making offerings to the local spirits, and whereas the Issaraks[6] sought to become masters of the villages under their control by endowing new *Neak Ta*(s), the Khmer revolutionaries neglected this important spiritual slant and alienated themselves from the people in their deepest impulses. It is not surprising to hear in 1980 peasants blaming them for the poor harvests since 1970: "A country at war cannot have plentiful harvests, there are too many sins committed (*bap* = demerits) and no one in the last five years has honored the spirits." While the peasants agreed to support the revolutionaries in their struggle against urban dwellers, they could not bring themselves to support the destruction of the family and of their religious universe. To bring their project to good end, the revolutionaries relied especially on the support of combatants whose very youth was to strike all observers. Prince Sihanouk already had granted the school-age youth inordinate political status, but they still remained nonetheless under the sway of the elders. From very early on, separated from their family as well as religious environments, they were able to adhere without undue difficulty to those goals that their elders found harder to accept. The uplifted status assigned to youth, in a setting where youth heretofore had low status, no doubt served as a powerful incentive to incite them to transform a society where, henceforth, they would be granted to choice role.

---

[6] The Issaraks, or "free Cambodians," with the aid of the Thais, struggled against the French. After 1947, a group of them collaborated with the Viet Cong and were called Vietminh.

Buddhism and Revolution: Its Conditioning Effects and Its Eradication

It is in the same context—that of the systematic destruction of the symbolic and religious environment—that one should look for initial explanations for the suppression of Buddhism. In conjunction with the spirits of the earth, Buddhism also ensured the fertility of the land and the well-being of its people. At the start of the twentieth century, the monasteries had incorporated and socialized agrarian rituals such that these could be practiced alongside Buddhist rites. In their desire to attain a total mastery over both nature and the population, the revolutionaries could not countenance any rival authority. On the social plane, the pagodas served a key integrative function within the villages: the construction of a pagoda represented the constitution of a true economic and religious community for the grouping of peasants pooled together into a village. It marked the decision on their part to invest their surplus in nonworldly goods so as to guarantee the prosperity of the donors. All villagers defined themselves with respect to the ties that bound them to particular pagodas and would call themselves "servants at the feet of (such and such) a pagoda." The pagoda would break up the flow of daily life through its cycle of festivals, serve as a recreational focus, and mobilize the energy of the surrounding community. The young men of the countryside, who nearly all would serve as novices for an indefinite period of time, would forge common worldviews, the sermons and advice of the monks serving to diffuse a shared ideology. Through the moral authority of the monks and *achars*, key figures in the Buddhist ritual, pagodas constituted a true counterforce. The pagodas represented a possible threat of opposition, an alternative hierarchy of values, a different language as well as leaders and meeting places lying outside the scope of the state's authority. Indeed, often in the past, pagodas had served as the launching point for peasant opposition to established authority.

Rarely had the monks themselves taken an active part in a political revolt, since their spiritual quest turned them away from the cares of this impermanent world. Nevertheless, one can report their frequent participation in the front ranks of political solicitations or demonstrations (as in the case of the Kompong Cham demonstrations for the reinstatement of Sihanouk in 1970). More than being active initiators, the monks provided moral sanction, they represented the weight of Khmer essence, of tradition, of the stable values to which the peasants were tied. It is significant that the only active demonstrations organized by monks were in 1942 when a hundred among them, armed with their umbrellas, protested against the decision to Latinize the Khmer script and to reform the Buddhist calendar. One can readily understand the felt need on the part of successive regimes to court the monks—without much success, one might add.

More than the monkhood itself, it was the pagodas as a whole that could serve as the starting point for political movements: agitators or outlaws being pursued by the French administration could have found inviolable refuge therein, under saffron robes. More than the monks, who were more detached from the world, it was the *achars*—preachers of the faith—who ignited the uprisings, the *achar* Sva between 1864 and 1866, and the *achar* Chieu in 1942, being the most well-known. The *achars*, idealized in the monkhood, in a certain fashion served as secular transmission belts to the Khmer people.[7]

Thus it was logical for the Khmer revolutionaries to do away with the pagodas and the monkhood; this suppression tended to atomize peasant society, the villagers losing the organic and spiritual ties that had bound them together. Buddhism was ill-prepared to resist the totalitarian power of the Khmer Rouge, who did not broach any other influence. Similarly in India, where it had not been able to fend off the advance of Islam, equally totalitarian on the social plane. If the pagodas were able to help promote popular revolts, it is because there existed a minimum of freedom allowing the exercise of their influence, since the national leaders, out of political and moral concern (for the Khmers), shied away from attacking the monks. Little refashioned in its thinking, resolutely guarding the values of the past, Buddhism had come to lose its credit among the youth. A sense of tolerance and aversion to violence rendered the Buddhists helpless against the armed young revolutionaries, who in large part originated in the peripheral zones where Buddhism did not have a strong hold, and who had been trained to kill, paying little heed to national or international public opinion.

Beyond reasons particular to Khmer society, the revolutionaries did not lack classic arguments inspired by Marx's reflections on religious alienation. More than any other religion, Buddhism lent itself to being viewed as "the opium of the people," justifying all social inequalities through the karmic

---

[7] It is particularly interesting to note the importance of pagodas in the Khmer refugee camps in Thailand. At Khao I Dang, a camp harboring 150,000 people, the pagoda, with its thirty or so male and nearly forty female monks—not to mention its *achars*—serves as a pole of resistance to such foreign influences as the Western religions brought in primarily by Anglo-Saxon missionaries. (See James Pringle, *Newsweek*, September 8, 1980, for the comment of a monk, "Buddhism has two enemies, Pol Pot and the Christians.") It is at the pagodas that the Khmers can reestablish contact with their essential Khmerhood. At Sakeo, where refugees living under Khmer Rouge control were regrouped, a pagoda without monks was organized, thanks to the help of international agencies. This pagoda has become the only center of opposition to the Khmer Rouge cadres, who in fact have sought to destroy it. Several hundred men armed with bamboo spears protected the sacred spot every night. Questioned as to their political convictions, several refugees replied that they were "Buddhists," hence implicitly anticommunists. Local authorities had to arrest the four leading *achars* in order to disarm the general opposition and facilitate voluntary repatriation efforts organized by them.

doctrine that continues to permeate deeply the Khmer mentality: poverty and misery are the fruits of sinful actions committed in previous lifetimes, just as wealth and well-being result from merits acquired in the past. Such a karmic doctrine presented a serious obstacle to class struggle and, generally, the poor were insensitive to the injustices they were prey to, since a fatalistic resignation to misfortune was a virtue. "What a karma I'm stuck with!" A mother of twelve children, nine of whom died from mistreatment under the Pol Pot regime, and whose husband was also killed, states quite simply, "I do not hate the Khmer Rouge. Such was our karma." "Wait for the next reincarnation"—these words of consolation in the face of distress well betrays this state of mind.

The world being impermanent, a veil of illusions, what was essential in life was to acquire merit in view of a better reincarnation and, notably, to establish harmony within one's self and with the world. This conception leads to a definite lack of concern to transform the world or to leave one's mark thereon, and was thus in total opposition to the doctrines of Angkar. Furthermore, such a conception of human life fostered an absence of social responsibility. "It is he who eats who is full," "no one can add to the merit or demerit of another," "rely only on yourself," formed key tenets of Buddhist teachings. Thus, notions of the commonweal or of collective responsibility at a class or national level are almost totally absent from Buddhist doctrine. A materialistic conception of merit as acting independently of one's internal states tended even to favor prevaricators, like some chiefs of police or high-ranking officials who, notoriously corrupt, sought to compensate for their extortions through donations for votive rites.

Adding to these ideological concerns, in the eyes of the Khmer intellectuals avid for purity and hankering for the distant past, was the foreign nature of Khmer Buddhism, which indeed dated to the late Angkorian era. In this regard, they are the heirs to the Chenla masters: "the king returning only to better persecute buddhism" (Thierry 1964:56).

In spite of their revolutionary intention to eradicate Buddhism, however, elements of Buddhist doctrine survive as artifacts within the doctrines of the revolution itself. In fact, the limited doctrinal similarities between Buddhism and Khmer communism may have assisted the Khmer Rouge in their drive to dominate Cambodian society. Obviously, one should not overemphasize these connections between Khmer Marxism and Buddhism any more than the connections between fascism and Christianity or communism and Christianity in the European context. Moreover, one should recall that the Khmer peasantry had already reshaped this Buddhism in their own eyes, modifying it for their own purposes.

Buddhism presented itself in Cambodia as a rationalistic religion, capable of providing scientific explanations of the world, in contrast to other religions based on faith. It was, according to intellectuals I encountered, a philosophy that could explain the world and the history of men without reference to a divine presence, basing itself on evidence (*chéak sdèng*). In this regard, the revolutionaries found themselves following similar lines and, indeed, adopted some of the same materialist affirmations with which to explain the world. Just as Marxism emphasizes substantial differences in wealth between classes, the doctrine of karma is founded upon the existence of vast differences regarding intelligence, longevity, and wealth: "And so it is with men! They are not alike because of different karmas. As the Lord said . . . 'Beings each have their own karma. They are . . . born through karma, they become members of tribes and families through karma, each is ruled by karma, it is karma that divides them into high and low' " (de Bary 1972:25). Furthermore, Buddhism—and particularly the doctrine of karma—gives religious sanction to the vast differences between rich and poor, educated and illiterate, and specifically validates the inheritance of privileged positions across generations. Differences in wealth result not so much from the worthiness of present-day activities but from the store of good and evil deeds carried over from former incarnations. Khmer Rouge theoreticians undoubtedly agreed that vast differences in wealth and privilege were inherited rather than earned, and cadres needed only to add that belief in the doctrine of karma was itself a major cause of the perpetuation of the socioeconomic inequalities that were so apparent in Khmer society during the Lon Nol period. Thus, the Khmer Rouge could exploit Buddha's affirmation of the existence of vast social and material divisions and in the next breath explain to the most impoverished sectors of the peasantry that Buddhism was an important cause of their miseries.

In addition, anti-individualist elements exist in Buddhist teachings: man is nothing, the supreme illusion being to imagine that the awareness of self corresponds to the existence of the individual being. In this regard, it is significant that the Khmer language has no equivalent for the word "individual" in the sense of a responsible being in relation to others. Khmer Rouge operatives bent on creating a mass movement into which members would totally submerge their identities were not faced with the necessity of combating powerful arguments about individualism found in Western philosophy. In relation to this, it is interesting to note that the language of revolution refashioned for its own use part of the vocabulary of Buddhist belief: "the wheel of revolution which never stops and which will crush all who place themselves in its path" seems an answer to "the sansara wheel" of successive reincarnations. "Rely only on yourself" (*Khloun ti peung khluon*) changes into "help your own self" (*Khluong opatham khluon*); the Buddhist commandments (*Viney*) become Angkar's commandments (*Angkarviney*), and so on. At least this is the summary explanation that some Khmer Rouge cadres gave, according to several peasants I interviewed.

Cadres espousing radical egalitarianism were wont to recall in their pre-

1975 propaganda that Buddha had said, "All men are equal, princes and the powerful must purify themselves like each and all." The essence of being a monk, a *bikkhu*, is being a wandering beggar with minimal possessions whose collected donations of food are shared equally among monks of the same monastery or temple. Buddha instructed his followers to take their robes from the charnel fields, to dress alike, to live from donations, and to have few, if any, possessions. Certainly the egalitarianism and asceticism of Buddhist monastic life found echoes in the abandonment of home, family, and all possessions practiced by the mobile work brigades of Pol Pot's Cambodia.

Karmic doctrine and the belief in reincarnation, which both underlie the Khmer peasants' vision of the world, can shed some light on the enigma of the massive executions carried out in Kampuchea. To the Buddhist, the greatest "demerit" stems from killing either animals or humans. The example quoted above concerning the treatments inflicted on both culprits in the novel *Tum-Teav* shows that the sentiments of royal mercy towards the two heroes was strictly relative. Sihanouk himself was hardly tender toward captured Khmer Rouge: they were hurled from the top of the cliffs at Bokor and died slowly amidst ineffable suffering. In the Damber region it was not uncommon to see rebels meet their death tied to trees, their bellies slit open. No macabre detail was spared the spectators who watched on film the execution of Chau Bary in 1965 (Meyer 1971:39). Likewise, the Buddhist sentiments of Lon Nol's soldiers were at most relative: one need only recall the massacres of Vietnamese in April 1970 or the proud smiles of some soldiers carrying the heads of slain compatriots, as was shown in photographs transmitted by wire services.

The widespread beliefs in reincarnation gives rise to a relationship to death less tragic than that prevailing in the West since the end of the Middle Ages. If life is precious to Westerners, it is because it is conceived as being unique, beginning with conception and ending in death. In contrast to such a linear conception of life, the Buddhist cyclical concept, stemming from the doctrine of reincarnation, tends to dilute the absolute nature of existence. Thus, during the war, republican troops would justify the insane risks they were willing to take in combat by affirming their absolute belief in immediate reincarnation. A former warrant officer, now a refugee in France, with a memory avowedly stretching back to ten previous reincarnations, doesn't hesitate to proclaim, "He who will deprive me of life shall gain four times greater merit than she who gave me life, since I shall be reborn into a life of happiness." In common speech, moreover, death was constantly being referred to: one would rather die than be disparaged or defrauded; a mother would not hesitate to threaten her child with a beating unto death, and the like. If such a relative respect for life is added to a karmic doctrine which stipulates that "merits and demerits follow one like a shadow," and thus that no conversion is possible, one might expect that considerable excess could occur. The culprit must face the punishment due him for acts committed, without there being any possibility for redemption, in contrast to the Confucian mentality (more prevalent in China and Vietnam) according to which a wrongful act is above all a mistake and hence redeemable. Listening to numerous accounts provided by refugees who escaped massacre, one cannot fail to note a certain complicity between the executioners and their victims, each accepting the tragic rules of the game governing them.

In daily life, internal purification from all desire was held as the supreme virtue of Buddhism. This applied to laymen as well as to monks. The revolutionaries adapted for their use such Buddhist dogma by also stressing renunciation (*lak bang*): "Renunciation of attitudes of cleanliness; renunciation of worldly goods; renunciation of control over personal destiny." The renunciation of attitudes of cleanliness meant that above all else, one should concentrate completely on the task at hand without regard for oneself, just as in Buddhist meditation. Renunciation of worldly goods implied detachment from one's spouse, children, and home just as once Buddha renounced all. Forsaking one's hold over the conduct of personal life meant the eradication within one's self of pride, disdain for others, and the tortuous thoughts of before, just as the monks used to preach. This self-abnegation is particularly stressed as concerns emotional bonds within the family, either between spouses or those of parents towards their children and vice versa, as Pin Yathay relates in numerous examples: "You must purify yourself, free yourself of your emotional ties," or "you still have feelings of pity or of friendship: you must clean your mind of all individualist leanings" (Pin Yathay 1980:222, 227). Many refugees, Pin Yathay included, speak of achieving, through work and ill treatment, a complete extinction of all sexual desires, one of the goals of Buddhist asceticism. The same applies for material goods: to lose all of one's material belongings was inconsequential. Most refugees questioned on the subject admit it straightforwardly: "If we had been provided with food, if there had been no killings, we would have stayed in the country, even after having lost everything." On the other hand, for refugees of Chinese origin, the reaction was quite different, material belongings being viewed as almost an integral part of themselves.

Thus, the various parallels just noted between Buddhism and the principles put forth by the Khmer revolutionaries could have made for a certain connivance between the two intellectual worlds. The revolutionary model, however, did not leave room for the survival of the religion itself. Themselves strangers to the religious climate permeating their own country, instilled with antireligious instruction while in French universities, the revolutionary leaders applied with little discernment the Marxist dogma of the West concerning religion, and thereby laid waste to a structure that in the long run might have helped them to achieve legitimacy among a wider segment of the Cambodian population.

One may nevertheless marvel at how so few leaders with—relatively—a weak army and few cadres, applying so strict a doctrine, could impose so quickly their views on the total population. One may refer to the Buddhist fatalism holding sway over the population, but that cannot explain all. The most pertinent explanation can be sought by examining the traditional structure of Khmer society, and the extraordinary status held by the king within it. The complete lack of full-fledged intermediary structures between the population of peasants and the higher authorities left the way open for the unfettered exercise of dictatorial power.

In the traditional mindset, the king, at national and even universal planes, was "the key for the preservation of harmony with the elements," "it was incumbent upon him to have the power and duty to rule over the broad universal expanses," and even "to master the earth spirits" (Forest 1980:35–57). His legitimacy was tied to his capacity to ensure prosperity, and a bad crop or an overabundant flood, such as that of 1967, would give rise to a decline in royal popularity. The absence of a sovereign implied the lack of effective communication between the celestial powers and the world of men; without him you have complete chaos. Proof of this came in 1970: if the urban intelligentsia cheered at the time of Prince Sihanouk's destitution, the peasantry, who cherished him as the king, were subject to deep and widespread consternation. To them, harmony had been shattered, and they didn't hesitate to heed his appeal and join the underground forces or to welcome the Vietnamese as liberators. Ten years later, peasants interviewed at the Thai border still thought that the absence of the king was the cause of the poor harvests. "Ever since the king left, the sky has been in disarray," or "When the prince will return, the rains will start up again as before," some of them would say.

Lon Nol, true antiking, like Sihanouk had surrounded himself with augurs, a royal court, and had exercised the same type of absolute authority, concentrating all powers of decision on himself. If, following the example of Trasak Paem who had substituted himself for the king six centuries earlier, he had proclaimed himself and been anointed king (apisek), he—or any other member of the royal family—could have fulfilled the symbolic function of the king and thereby united his people. Of all the reasons for the military disaster of 1975, not the least of which was the felt certainty of the prince's return: had this not been the case, both officers and men probably would have continued to battle for some time. Because of this felt certainty, the victors were able to eliminate with relative ease a large number of officers invited to go meet the former monarch upon his return. Even today, despite all of Sihanouk's mistakes, the people from the Khmer countryside still continue to vow him true respect.

Between such a king who held a central place in the symbolic network of Khmer society and the individualistic peasants who were grouped into economic and religious communities around villages, there were no intermediary structures mediating authority. Even in Khmer folktales one notes this absence: the peasant goes directly before the king, and can become king himself without referring to any assembly. Up until the time of the French protectorate, and even beyond, officialdom was but the extension of the king's supreme authority. In a certain sense, the French protectorate strengthened the symbolic functions of the king. Not wont to assail it, setting aside for him the right to sign laws and hold audience for public complaints, the protectorate administered the country through its own corps of officials, often Vietnamese, and required absolute compliance from them. This form of government left no room for the emergence of a mediating political class between the king and the people. This absence continued to be felt after independence, Sihanouk taking up the whole breadth of possible authority, not so much out of his personal charisma but because there was no one else to vie for it. As was the case for officials during the time of the protectorate, elected deputies had no real independence. To oppose the prince was viewed as a crime of lese majesty. In 1970, and again in 1975, similar patterns apply. Lon Nol, and then the anonymous Angkar, barred all possible opposition and substituted themselves in place of the royal function. Under Angkar rule, as under the reign of the Angkor kings, "the people should be happy or else disappear" without their having any say (Thierry 1964:86).

The Cambodian revolution was born in a period when the nation's institutions were blocked: the Westernized official class had lost contact with the people in the countryside and bowed to the exclusive authority of the head of state. Young intellectuals had little opportunity to share even partially in that power. Returning back from a foreign education, and rapidly in breach with the powers that be, the revolutionary leaders fashioned their plan in direct contact with the peasants. Cut off from the outside world, in part even opposed to the Vietnamese and Chinese communists, they developed their ideology to the fullest in their own closed and ingrown world. This revolution, plunging its roots in Khmer soil, is nevertheless the handmaiden of the West that provided it with its mode of analysis. Notwithstanding its anti-Western slant, from the West it brought back notions of justice, equality, progress, and productivity. While antireligious and antimonarchist, it coopted for its own benefit the religious and symbolic functions of Buddhism, animism, and the monarchy. It allowed for the unleashing of tensions accumulated over decades and abolished certain taboos, but the thirst for vengeance that it spawned was not sufficient to give rise to constructive pursuits. The revolution violated the Khmer culture, and it registered itself more in breach than in continuity with the past, which in part explains why it came to be an object of repudiation among the people. Will the new leaders have the wisdom to respect the culture of the Khmers? Only thus can a durable national peace be ensured.

6. The Pattern and Scope of Violence

by Kenneth M. Quinn

The communist military victory in April 1975 brought with it the hope that peace would return to Cambodia and that there would be an end to the dying. There was instead an almost immediate escalation of the level of violence, as Pol Pot moved to impose on all Khmer the radical economic and social system he had introduced in areas he controlled since June 1973.

A review of the pattern of violence in other totalitarian regimes would suggest that this increase in the use of force and terror in Cambodia should not have been unexpected and is indeed characteristic of both communist and fascist revolutionary regimes. Prior to total victory, violence against the population is usually held to a minimum to maintain popular support for the revolution's military effort. Once victory is achieved, however, totalitarian rulers in general resort to fear and terror to achieve unanimous acquiescence in their political program and to destroy any potential challenges to their rule. Communist China, the Soviet Union, and Nazi Germany experienced the greatest degree of terror after Mao, Stalin, and Hitler had achieved power.

Hannah Arendt, in her classic study on the Nazi and Soviet regimes, *The Origins of Totalitarianism*, noted that in the initial period after the seizure of power the major force is directed at obvious enemies—the remnants of the former government and armed forces that might continue to resist. After the remaining elements have been destroyed, the new regime turns on the masses using even greater amounts of terror,

. . . the end of the first stage comes with the liquidation of open and secret resistance in an organized form. It can be set at about 1935 in Germany and approximately 1930 in Soviet Russia. *Only after the extermination of the real enemies does terror become the actual content of totalitarian regimes.* (Arendt 1958:400; emphasis added)

Pol Pot's rule was to follow this pattern, although it took him only about one year to effectively deal with residual internal threats to his rule.

Carl Friedrich and Zbigniew Brzezinski in their work on totalitarianism touch upon another aspect of terror that has relevance to Pol Pot's Kampuchea:

It is a curious and frightening fact that totalitarian terror increases in scope and violence as the totalitarian system becomes stable and firm—terror embraces the entire society reaching everywhere for actual or potential deviants . . . (Friedrich and Brzezinski 1956:137)

179

Totalitarian terror grows by leaps and bounds. It not only . . . [is] . . . aimed at anticipating political resistance—it becomes the fundamental method of achieving the revolution without which the regime would lose its total character and probably also its power. Totalitarian terror is therefore the vital nerve of the totalitarian system . . . Because of the belief of the ideological infallibility of its dogma, the regime is propelled toward an increase in terror by a violent passion for unanimity. Since history tells the totalitarian he is right, he expects others to agree with him. This passion for unanimity makes the totalitarian insist on the complete agreement of the entire population. (Friedrich and Brzezinski 1956:131–32)

On April 18, 1975, Pol Pot had every reason to believe he was indeed on the historically correct path. Just five years earlier he and a handful of loyal cadres had appeared on the verge of oblivion. By following an assiduously cultivated plan for revolution, the Communist Party of Kampuchea had: gained control of the revolution by thwarting the influence of Prince Sihanouk; driven the Vietnamese from much of Cambodian territory; established a nascent collectivized agricultural system; forced the American diplomatic and military personnel to flee by helicopter; defeated the better-equipped Khmer Republican Army; and finally captured Phnom Penh a full two weeks before the North Vietnamese entered Saigon, thereby accomplishing in five years what it took Hanoi thirty years to do.

Flushed with victory and imbued with a sense of righteousness, Pol Pot then set out to implement his plan to radically restructure Cambodian society. In seeking to establish this new social system, Pol Pot employed terror, violence, and purges in a systematic way to accomplish these specific goals:

1. *Breaking the System*—using violence and terror to destroy the old society and its social, political, economic, and cultural infrastructure
2. *Socioeconomic Transformation*—applying violence and terror to force the entire society into new socioeconomic patterns (collectivization, work battalions, abolishing private property and religion, and instituting a new value system)
3. *Political Prophylaxis*—using purges and selected executions to counter revisionism and coups d'etat from within
4. *Defending against External Threat*—seeking to eliminate threats posed by Vietnam and perceived collaborators of the Vietnamese

In each case the target of the violence would be different.

Breaking the System

From April 1975 until April 1976, Pol Pot and his followers concentrated on the steps necessary to "break" the old system: that is, to destroy the patterns of political authority, economic activity, and cultural tradition that had characterized it. To accomplish this goal they sought to: (1) empty all cities and towns and resettle the population on agricultural communes; (2) identify, arrest, or execute officials and military personnel from the Lon Nol government; and (3) neutralize those elements in society perceived as potentially threatening to their rule and desirous of a return to traditional Khmer society. In all three efforts, the party utilized significant amounts of violence and terror to accomplish its objectives.

THE EXODUS FROM THE CITIES

Pol Pot's first move was to empty all of the cities and towns and force the entire urban population to walk to new collective agricultural sites in order to begin new lives as farm workers. Several reasons were put forward by the Khmer Rouge for this radical development: the threat of American bombing; the inability to supply sufficient food to the cities; and the fear of counterrevolution. In an interview in 1978, Pol Pot told journalists that: ". . . the cities were not evacuated through a pre-established plan but were in conformity with the situation at the time, . . . the shortage of foodstuffs, the necessity to solve this problem for the population and the U.S. imperialists and their lackey's plan aiming at destroying our revolution and taking back power" (FBIS IV, March 1978:10).

These reasons were indeed ones that Khmer Rouge cadres used in ordering people to leave the cities. Other statements made by communist cadres, the inclusion of sick and handicapped persons in the evacuation, and the well-established checkpoints in operation along the routes suggest, however, that the evacuation was planned in advance and implemented to achieve fundamental policy objectives rather than for spur-of-the-moment security reasons. In 1977, Pol Pot himself admitted openly that the evacuation of the cities was a carefully planned, premeditated action. "One of the important factors is the evacuation of city residents to the countryside. *This was decided before victory was won, that is, in February 1975 . . .*" (FBIS I, October 3, 1977:A23; emphasis added).

Moreover, it appears clear in retrospect that the evacuation of the cities was not a new concept but a repeat of the policy implemented in June, 1973, when the Khmer Rouge systematically burned rural villages and hamlets under their control in order to force peasants into the new communal agricultural system. The goal of the new Cambodian rulers was fundamentally and drastically to change the nature of Khmer society. Cities were viewed as creations of Western influence, centers of decadence and conspicuous consumption, and impediments to change. Like villages and hamlets, they were a fundamental part of the old order. By literally tearing the great bulk of the country's population from its roots and familiar patterns of work and life, the Khmer Rouge leadership intended irrevocably and irretrievably to move toward a new egalitarian agricultural society.

One communist cadre put it this way in explaining the emptying of the capital: "From now on if the people want to eat, they should go out and work in the rice paddies. They should learn that their lives depend on a grain of rice. Plowing the soil, planting and harvesting rice will teach them the real value of things. Cities are evil. There are money and trade in cities and both have a corrupting influence. People are good, but cities are evil. This is why we shall do away with cities" (Barron and Paul 1977:16–17). Another Khmer Rouge cadre echoed this notion: "The city is bad for there is money in the city. People can be reformed, but not cities. By sweating to clear land, sowing and harvesting crops, men will learn the real value of things. Man has to know that he is born again from a grain of rice" (Ponchaud 1978:21).

Other evidence indicated that the Khmer Rouge also disdained the influences of city life—like long hair on students—and the class distinctions that were maintained by such things as large houses, opulent furniture, automobiles, and fancy clothing.[1] Moreover, cities were centers of commerce where large sums of money changed hands and "greedy" merchants made "unseemly profits" by exploiting the rural poor. Pol Pot may also have been influenced by the Chinese experience that cities are not conducive to communization and were in fact the locus of much political opposition to the Great Leap Forward and the Cultural Revolution. Furthermore, the Khmer Rouge viewed the cities as unproductive economic drains on the countryside, and the revolutionary movement did not have enough cadres to control all the cities. By destroying urban life, Pol Pot sought to wipe out all of these negative features.

The forced march of approximately three million out of Phnom Penh and hundreds of thousands of others out of Cambodia's provincial towns caused a significant number of deaths, particularly among the aged and infirm. This process began when ". . . roughly twenty four hours after the advent of peace, the Communists began routing out the people much more methodically and vigorously. In the name of *Angkar*, parties of four to six soldiers systematically went from door to door, . . . and by mid-morning the streets teemed with hundreds of thousands of people" (Barron and Paul 1977:25–26). One French journalist reported that refugees in Saigon recounted the story of a "Khmer Rouge cadre entering a hospital crying, 'The American imperialists will bomb the hospital—you must evacuate immediately'. Everyone had to leave. Those who could walk helped the crippled, amputees and others, some hobbling, others on their hands and knees" (*Le Figaro* 1976).

François Ponchaud, whose analysis of the social context of these events

---

[1] See Chapter 5 by François Ponchaud for additional interpretation of the anti-urban bias of the Khmer Rouge.—ED.

preceeds this chapter, provided an eyewitness account of this exodus of the walking wounded, "A few moments later a hallucinatory spectacle began. Thousands of the sick and wounded were abandoning the city. The strongest dragged pitifully along, others were carried by friends, and some were lying on beds pushed by their families with their plasma and I.V. bumping alongside" (Ponchaud 1977:6–7).

The largest numbers of deaths along the evacuation route resulted from the heat, lack of food and water, and absence of medical assistance. As one refugee noted:

From noon onwards, the masses in the streets multiplied as Communist troops uprooted more and more families . . . there was a huge crowd of every age and condition, young, old and sick . . . virtually everybody saw . . . corpses rapidly bloating and rotting in the sun. Then the water supply ceased throughout the city . . . No stores of drinking water, no stocks of food, no shelter had been prepared for the millions of outcasts. Consequently acute dysentery racked and sapped life from bodies . . . already weakened by hunger and fatigue . . . we must have passed the body of a child every 200 yards. (Levin 1977a).

The sheer rigor of the march and the lack of sanitation and health care added to the death toll. Unburied bodies accumulated rapidly, aggravating health problems; "an estimated 100,000 people died in a single cholera epidemic that broke out southwest of Phnom-Penh 15 days after the exodus" (*Time* 1976:9).

By interviewing refugees that reached Saigon a month later, one reporter concluded that "hundreds, and possibly thousands, of city dwellers had died on the roads . . . mostly old people and children" (Dawson 1975:17). This estimate concerned only one part of the evacuation. Others estimated that as many as four hundred thousand people succumbed during the entire process of emptying the cities (Barron and Paul 1977:203). Although it will probably never be possible to achieve a precise accounting of the actual number that perished, the evidence strongly points to a significant loss of life during this evacuation.

The Khmer Rouge, in their application of these harsh measures, had extracted a high price from the population, but they had achieved several of their objectives. Through the forced abandonment of the towns and cities:

they had totally cut off virtually the entire population from whatever material connection it had with the old order

all homes, money, cars, bank accounts, and consumer goods were left behind

potential adversaries and opponents were disorganized and separated from places that might serve as centers of resistance, thus maximizing the communist political control familiar social, religious, familial, and economic patterns were shattered, and all evacuees were thrown into a basic struggle for physical survival

Thus, in the first few days of implementing their revolution, Pol Pot and his followers eschewed all gradualism and instead abruptly terminated a thousand years of Khmer socioeconomic history and began the establishment of a radically new order.

SETTLING THE SCORE: IDENTIFYING AND ELIMINATING THE FORMER ENEMY

Concomitant with their destruction of the patterns of urban life, the Khmer Rouge began an effort to identify—and in many instances execute—political leaders, military officers, and civil servants from the republican government. Some were killed at their offices; others were identified at check points along the march routes outside of Phnom Penh; still others surrendered and were taken out in large groups to be killed. In some instances the spouses and children of the officials were killed alongside their husbands and fathers.[2]

The persons most sought after by the victorious communist forces were the top leaders of the former government. Although some escaped before the Khmer Rouge entered Phnom Penh, others remained behind and were subsequently arrested and executed. In November 1975, Ieng Sary confirmed that Sirik Matak, former Prime Minister Long Boret, and Lon Non (Lon Nol's younger brother) were all executed. An aide to Prince Sihanouk in Beijing at the time confirmed the deaths, saying that Lon Non had been lynched by a mob and the other two shot by a firing squad (*Washington Post* 1975).

Other officials were included in this roundup of former government functionaries. For example, here is the story of one female refugee who managed to flee to Vietnam: "Married to a police officer, she lived in Phnom Penh with her four children. On April 18, the Khmer Rouge entered their house and without so much as a word of explanation killed her husband with a stick (right in front of the family). They did the same to the 10-year-old son. The woman immediately fled with her other children. She walked for a month across Cambodia. Her younger two children died along the way of starvation and sickness" (*Le Figaro* 1976).

Most of the killings took place after the officers had been rounded up, often on the pretext that they were going to meet with Prince Sihanouk or to participate in the "reconstruction of the country." Here is a report of

---

[2] See Chapter 5 by François Ponchaud for an explanation of the tendency to kill whole families. See Chapter 7 by David Hawk for evidence that this same pattern was carried out against communist cadres judged to be enemies of the state.—ED.

what a refugee from Battambang Province saw when he was forced to serve on burial detail:

He [Soun Heap] and other men were taken to a place called Arak Bak Kor near Sisophon. There the villagers found a killing ground scattered with the corpses of soldiers who had been beaten to death. As they began to bury them, which they were ordered to do, trucks began to arrive packed with more Lon Nol soldiers, each man individually bound at the ankles and by a rope pinioning his arms at the biceps. The first batch of soldiers were taken from the trucks by the Khmer Rouge Guards and then tied together with a long rope to form an enormous human chain. The Khmer Rouge then beat them to death with pieces of timber in full view of the other victims awaiting the same fate in the trucks. "The men in the trucks began to scream and wail and many fell down unconscious," Soun Heap said . . . (Woollacott 1976)

Ith Thaim, another refugee who had been drafted to drive a Khmer Rouge truck provided this eyewitness account of the execution of some civilian officials and their families:

At Mongkol Borie, the local Khmer Rouge commander . . . ordered . . . a squad of young Communist soldiers to punish . . . a group of civilian officials of the fallen government . . . The 15 Khmer Rouge rounded up ten former civil servants and their wives and children—about 60 people—tied their hands behind their backs . . . and drove them . . . to a banana plantation . . . Scattered about the place were the bodies of people killed one or two days earlier . . . The Khmer Rouge thrust each official forward one at a time and forced him to kneel between two soldiers armed with bayonet-tipped AK–47 assault rifles. The soldiers then stabbed the victim simultaneously through the chest and back . . . As each man lay dying, his anguished, horror-struck wife and children were herded up to the body. The women, forced to kneel, also received the simultaneous bayonet thrusts. The children, last to die, were stabbed where they stood. Of the 60 or so executed, only about six were spared the bayonet. These were very small children, too young to fully appreciate what was happening. In a killing frenzy now, the two executioners each grabbed a limb—one an arm, the other a leg—and tore the infants apart. (*Time* 1976)

François Ponchaud cites the slogans he frequently heard on Khmer Rouge radio broadcasts as evidence that this drive to destroy all these links and kill all the officers and their families was indeed premeditated:

. . . this total purge was, above all, the translation into action of a particular vision of man: a person who has been spoiled by a corrupt regime cannot be reformed, he must be physically eliminated from the brotherhood of the pure. "The regime must be destroyed"; "the enemy must be utterly crushed"; "What is infected must be cut out"; "What is rotten must be removed"; "What is too long must be shortened and be made the right length;" "It isn't enough to cut down a bad plant, it must be uprooted;" those are among the slogans used both on the radio and at meetings, to justify the purge. The authorities of the former regime were enemies and as such had no place in the national community. Several accounts state that in many places the officers' wives and children were killed too: the theme that the family line must be annihilated down to the last survivor is recurrent in such reports. (Ponchaud 1978:50–51)

Executions were usually carried out in locations far removed from the population—sometimes, if villagers were nearby, Khmer Rouge cadre took measures to eliminate the noise associated with mass executions. A former member of the army described the scene as he and his entire family were being taken to be executed:

One evening the Khmer Rouge assembled us. We were to be interrogated. At 2030 hours we were ordered to leave the pagoda where we were waiting. The Khmer Rouge took us to the edge of a forest. My wife held the youngest of our sons in her arms. I held the hands of the other two. Our elbows were then tied. I stretched them as far as possible so that my bonds might be looser. We were blindfolded and I knew we were about to be executed. I was able to untie myself and lift my blindfold. I witnessed a scene of horror. The Khmer Rouge were stuffing the mouths of those they were leading with rags and grass to prevent them from screaming and were cutting their throats like animals—the throats of men, women, old folk and children alike. I managed to escape. (Porlier 1976)

Another report of a large-scale execution came from refugee Chea Sambath, who stated that on April 24 he arrived at Thmar Kaul, where "there were hundreds of bodies lying by the roadside with their hands tied behind their backs. I learned later that they were the non-commissioned officers from Battambang who were supposedly going for retraining" (Ponchaud 1978:44).

Chan Dura, a court clerk in Pailin, recounted how all the municipal officials—eighty people in all—were executed together (Ponchaud 1978:44).

Yon Kim Lanh, a young electrical technician who stayed in Phnom Penh to help run the city's power plant, witnessed the continual disappearance of military officers and had a chance to ask a senior Khmer communist official about it. He was working at a communist headquarters at the Monorom Hotel where he observed:

I saw more than two hundred Lon Nol officers brought in. They were taken away the same night, for an unknown destination. Everyday the Khmer Rouge brought in another hundred or more people, mostly officers . . . [but also including the editor-in-chief of the newspaper Depeche du Cambodge.] One after another they all disappeared, and always at night. I knew a few of the Khmer Rouge—and asked them what had happened to the people who disappeared from the hotel. The answer was: "We kill them all because they're traitors and deserve to be shot." (Ponchaud 1978:28)

Regardless of the source of information, the pattern seems to have been relatively uniform throughout the country during the opening days of liberation: army officers and bureaucratic functionaries (often with their families) were systematically sought out and executed as "traitors." This program, of course, directly contradicted the promises of the revolution before it came to power, when it sought to reassure the population that only the most important traitors would be executed.[3] It, however, represented another clear indication that the success of the Khmer Rouge revolution was premised on the early elimination of all political impediments. The mass of the population was cut off from their cultural and economic roots, and former enemies and (as will be seen) political dissidents within the revolutionary movement were physically eliminated.

SUPPRESSION OF TEACHERS AND STUDENTS

The Khmer communists apparently saw the intellectual community as one of the major threats to their continued rule and to the smooth transition to the new society they were imposing. Thus, while military officers and former civilian officials were the primary target for elimination, the new Cambodian authorities also initiated a campaign to identify teachers, professional people, students, and intellectuals—anyone with an education. In some instances this process led to immediate execution. In others it was the beginning of a process that would culminate with the violent effort a year later to do away with virtually every educated or technically trained person in Cambodia.

During the forced march out of Phnom Penh, Khmer Rouge cadres put up signs requiring all professional people to register along with military personnel. One former army captain, Mam Sarun, told of such a sign at the Kieng Svay Pagoda which read: "All officers the rank of second lieutenant up must register here, in order to return to Phnom Penh. *Professors, students and school teachers must also give their names, but will leave later*" (Ponchaud 1978:27; emphasis added).

Another refugee recounted that in September of 1975 the Khmer Rouge were still rounding up educated persons for review, and then for re-education or elimination. He had been forcibly moved to Sisophon by train and recalled that as he disembarked, a loudspeaker asked "all specialists to step forward: doctors, architects, school teachers, students, technicians and skilled workers of all kinds" (Ponchaud 1978:69).

This refugee went on to describe how he was held in forced detention for months while Khmer Rouge cadres evaluated whether he and the other "397 specialists" who voluntarily identified themselves would be "trouble makers." He described a Khmer Rouge "trick," which they often repeated in other parts of the country. In an effort to make people relax and not feel threatened, they would provide plenty of food and even have a banquet of sorts. After that, people were asked about their ideas on how to make the new society better. Those teachers and students criticizing Angkar (the

---

[3] For confirmation of this point, see Chapter 2, p. 50, by Karl Jackson.—ED.

Khmer party organization) for all of the new hardships were later tied up and taken away, either to prison or to be executed (Ponchaud 1978:68). Numerous other sources confirmed executions of students and teachers alike. Lea Kong Thy, a former high school student at Sisophon said, "I saw with my own eyes the execution of 20 former students of Sisophon High School. They were taken into a field . . . and killed with a blow from a stave at the back of the head. Their hands were tied behind their back with a strip of red cloth. No official explanation was given. Perhaps they were killed because intellectuals are difficult to order about and go in for subversive activities" (Henry 1976).

In another incident, a medical orderly from the same area named Pho Chanta said he helped bury the bodies of nine teachers from a school at Sisophon who had been executed in August 1975, confirming this type of systematic killing of intellectuals. Pho Chanta was working in the fields one day, "when two taxis came along the road from Sisophon and stopped. Two Khmer Rouge got out, dragged some bodies from inside and threw them on the side of the fields . . . The Khmer Rouge said they had been corrupt customs and immigration officers who had been punished. But when we were burying them, I saw that one was Professor Mom Chantana, my old Cambodian language teacher from the Lycée Sisophon (Wollacott 1976).

Like regime critics and a money economy, books were links to the past, to the old society, to the old way of doing things. To the Khmer Rouge, they contained foreign learning that would have no place in the new society. By destroying them and eliminating the intellectual class, the Khmer communists were apparently hoping to ensure that the direction of the new social order would be irreversible.

Since Pol Pot and his closest lieutenants and advisors were almost all scholars and teachers, it would seem an enigma that a revolution with such clear roots in the intellectual community would turn so viciously on its own kind. Yet, it may be that Pol Pot and his ideological companions perceived that the academic world posed an inherent threat: if it had produced them, it could also produce a new dissident group to overthrow them.

Moreover, as Pol Pot later made clear, the Communist Party of Kampuchea saw religious leaders and teachers as playing a key role in "blinding" the peasants to their exploitation and the need for "conflict." In his famous September 27, 1977, speech, Pol Pot said: "This conflict was, however, contained—hidden—because the landowner class, the ruling functionaries and the teachers at the pay of the oppressor classes, forced them and duped them into burying this conflict. Such views as the belief in a former life and the influence of the stars and past deeds were also instrumental in misleading the peasants about the conflict" (Pol Pot 1977:H12).

Finally, Pol Pot probably saw most students and teachers as part of a corrupt class that had no connection to the classes that would provide leaders in his new society. For all these reasons, the Khmer Rouge embarked on a systematic effort to neutralize the Cambodian educational apparatus. They apparently saw it as an essential part of breaking the old system.

Socioeconomic Transformation

The great bulk of the Khmer population, having been uprooted from homes in cities, towns, and villages, was resettled in new communal farms ranging in size from several hundred persons to several thousand. Reports indicate that prolonged work days, short rations, and an absence of most health and sanitary aids were characteristic of life at these centers. The work and living conditions caused a number of deaths and weakened many people, increasing their susceptibility to illness. Persons who lived at these centers indicated that severe punishments were meted out to those who did not conform or seemed less than fully productive.

Much of the remaining populace was organized into 10- to 15-person work teams supervised by armed Khmer Rouge. Their food ration: two small tins of rice per day for villagers already living in zones of long-time Khmer Rouge control; one tin for ex-city dwellers. By August, 1975, as the country suffered shortages, the ration changed: for many it became one can of rice husks every two days; and thousands more died. The captive populations—including rural dwellers and notably any prosperous ones—became slave labor. Men and women were segregated at work. Rules forbade women to marry until age 25, men until 32. People were set to work either in the fields or on irrigation projects employing as many as 25,000 Cambodians at a time. They were treated as so many component parts—used until they gave out, then thrown away. Says one refugee: "If some worker made a mistake or criticized a project, he was taken away, and we never saw him again. They were sometimes flogged to death, other times shot at night . . . The only thing was to work and wait for the day we died." (*Time* 1976:9)

Another account of the hardship of life in the new Khmer communist society and its effect on the people living in the collectives put it this way: "Those from the cities describe the pain of working, with no experience and hardly more food, in the fields. Farmers tell of being moved off their land into new campsites far from home. Many say that young and old still die of disease and starvation as they did on the roads out of Phnom Penh and other towns . . . Some talk of youth so weak that they support themselves on sticks as they labor in the fields" (Shawcross 1976a:25).

Still another description of the effects on a former village of the new regimen went as follows: "By September (1975) . . . the people of Ampil Praum Dacum had stripped the jungles of crabs, snails, bamboo shoots, bindweed and all else edible. People looked like skeletons draped with a thin, sickly cover of skin . . . about 15 percent had died and only 10 were strong enough to do their jobs. Ten men had been executed . . ." (Levin 1977a).

At first, the largest numbers of deaths in the new communes were attributed to the lack of nutrition and vitamins, the long hours and the absence of the most elemental medical care. Yean Sok, a refugee who lived on a new collective farm, wrote: "Everyday 3 or 4 people died at the village in a population of 440 families. There were families that were totally exterminated. For example, the family of Mr. Ben Huot who lived next to me and used to be the judge of Phnom Penh: a family of 18 members from November 29, 1975, till July 3, 1977, were deceased and only six people remained. All of these deaths were caused by dysentery plaudisime, wounds which are untreated, or lack of vitamins. These people died miserably without medicine. The sanitary personnel is very young and have no medical training. Almost every family lost at least 2 or 3 members." Yean Sok added that one "section" of his commune disappeared entirely and that he later learned from one of the local communist cadres that in the year and a half after Pol Pot took over "more than 4,000 people died" in their village (Yean Sok 1978).

Deaths from the physical hardships of the new order were supplemented by efforts to do away with politically undesirable individuals. Toward the end of 1975, a campaign was initiated in the communes that aimed at identifying and eliminating individuals with any attachment to the former regime, including government employees, anyone who had served in the Lon Nol military down to the rank of private, and all students and teachers and all their families. "In October 1975, monitors abroad listened as the Communist commander in Sisophon received radio orders to prepare for the extermination after the harvest of all former government soldiers and civil servants, regardless of rank, and their families. The killing began during . . . 1976. Before the organized slaughter had been largely confined to officers and senior civil servants. Now the lowliest private, the most humble civil servant, the most innocent teacher, even foresters and public health officials, became prey" (Levin 1977).

This type of "Purification Campaign" would be repeated again in 1977 and in 1978, each time seeking out people at the lower levels of society with any connection to the old regime. These purges and harsh treatment of the population on the collective farms was intended to force acceptance of the new economic, social, and cultural regimen, as well as to establish new patterns of work. Moreover, since most of the city dwellers from the "old society" were viewed as tainted by their association with the corrupt former social order, those that might expire would not be considered a loss. In addition, a weakened, dispirited population would be less able to resist the other changes that Pol Pot envisaged for the new Cambodia—the elimination of the most basic features of the Khmer culture and society.

In order to create the "new socialist man" to inhabit his new society, Pol Pot sought to strip away the cultural, religious, and social infrastructures upon which traditional Khmer society was based and to replace them with a new socialist order based on total acquiescence to the "organization" (Angkar) and subjugation of the individual self to the collective good. The new collective farms served as the main instrument for achieving this goal. They represented a tabula rasa upon which the new Khmer culture was to be imprinted. To create a new system, a plan was implemented to eradicate old practices, beliefs, and social patterns. Similar to the Chinese Cultural Revolution's campaign to destroy the "Four Olds" (old thoughts, old culture, old customs, and old habits—Baum 1964:101), this process had several distinct elements, all aimed at destroying the institutions and organizations of the ancien régime.

First came the attack on organized religion. Buddhist pagodas were closed, statues and icons destroyed and monks forced to take up secular work or join the army. The new collective farms had no religious edifices of any type, no monks were allowed, and the practice of religion was proscribed. A Yugoslav journalist quoted Yun Yat, the minister of education and propaganda and the spouse of party leader Son Sen, as she outlined the underlying philosophy for this action: "Under the old regime peasants believed in Buddhism, which the ruling class utilized as a propaganda instrument. With the development of revolutionary consciousness, the people stopped believing and *bonzes* (priests) left the temples. The problem gradually becomes extinguished. Hence there is no problem" (*Des Moines Register* 1978).

Dragoslav Rancic, the journalist to whom Yun Yat made these statements, wrote that based on his two-week tour of Cambodia, "priests were considered social parasites . . . [and] their fate was not known." Rancic added that "we saw pagodas turned into storage houses for rice or into barns for storing farm equipment" (*Des Moines Register* 1978). He stressed, however, that while religious shrines had been attacked, the Khmer Rouge were careful to guard and preserve the Angkor Wat complex as a national shrine, apparently seeing it as a relic of an earlier primitive Cambdodia that they respected.

The second institution that came under attack as part of Pol Pot's revolution was the family. Many young teenagers were separated from their families and sent away for rigorous ideological training. Upon returning to their homes these young people were described by refugees as fierce in their condemnation of the "old ways," contemptuous of traditional customs, and ardently opposed to religious and parental authority (Quinn 1976).

In other instances, families in the new communes were segregated by sex and compelled to live in dormitories with large numbers of other persons. The end result was a severe lessening of parental control, which along with monastic authority had formed two of the strongest pillars in the cultural foundation of the Cambodian village.

The burning of old, long-established villages and the emptying of cities and towns was yet another part of this destructive process, as was the abolition of a money economy and the prohibition of most individual possessions. By these steps, individuals were totally cut off from their previous ways of life and any wealth they had accumulated. In one stroke, every member of Khmer society was to be ineluctably reduced to the same economic and social level. The "contradictions" between rich and poor, educated and illiterate—and rural and urban—built up over the years, were to be wiped out.

Next, and perhaps the most basic change of all, the pattern of land holdings and agricultural cultivation was completely transformed. Individual plots of land and reliance on kinship ties for assistance in planting and harvesting gave way to production brigades and large communal farms. The peasant farmer's direct personal relationship with the land, which had developed and endured for generations as a hallmark of Cambodian society, ceased to exist in a matter of a few days.

The final institution that the Khmer communists sought to eliminate was the monarchy. Prince Sihanouk had his critics and detractors in Phnom Penh, but royalty still retained esteem in the countryside. It is one of the ironies of this entire period that without Sihanouk on their side, the Khmer Rouge might never have attracted peasants to their cause. But, just as the Chinese and the Vietnamese communists were able to espouse popular nationalist themes to attract individuals to join their cause, so too were Pol Pot and his followers able to use the restoration of the prince as a rallying cry during the first years of the united front against Lon Nol (*Asia Week* 1977). When it was clear that Pol Pot was finally in charge, however, Sihanouk was eliminated from any role in the government or society (Quinn 1976). In 1976, with the adoption of the new constitution and the death of Zhou Enlai—Sihanouk's chief supporter in China—the monarchy was abolished.

Thus, in a relatively short time following their April 1975 victory, the Khmer communists dramatically changed the nature of many of Cambodia's oldest and most enduring institutions: religion, the family, cities, natural villages, private property, land tenure, money, and the monarchy. It was upon these structures that Cambodian society had been built. Yet through the application of terror and the establishment of the new communes, all these institutions were extensively changed in a short time.

New York Times journalist Sydney Schanberg described Pol Pot's new Cambodia this way:

The Draconian rules of life turned Cambodia into a nationwide gulag, as the Khmer Rouge imposed a revolution more radical and brutal than any other in modern history . . . attachment to home village and love of Buddha, Cambodian verities, were replaced by psychological reorientation, mass relocation and rigid collectivization.

Families were separated, with husbands, wives and children all working on separate agricultural and construction projects. They were often many miles apart and did not see each other for seasons at a time. Sometimes children were separated completely from their parents, never to meet again.
The practice of religion had been forbidden by the Khmer Rouge; all statues of Buddha had been destroyed; monks had been either killed or made to work in the fields as common laborers. (Schanberg 1980)

But the Khmer communists were not concerned only with the organizational structure of Cambodian society. Their second point of attack was the minds of the Khmer people themselves. Pol Pot's policies aimed at creating a new socialist man whose actions would no longer be based on individual profit, but rather on selfless dedication to the collective well-being. To do this the Khmer Rouge sought to remove all incentives for individual accomplishment: thus the elimination of money, individual plots of land, and any differentiation in housing, clothing, and personal property. But beyond that, they strove to teach each person that any deviation from the general party line—any selfish act—would result in the most severe punishment and probable death. It appears that on the new collective farms they sought a society of automatons carrying out repetitive functions in a mechanistic fashion. Cambodian society was to become a giant agricultural factory with each person filling a distinct, specific function, like a small part of a machine. To accomplish this, Pol Pot created within the new communes an atmosphere of terror in which people were in some cases afraid to even talk with each other and in which families feared to speak even in their own homes or in front of their children for fear of being taken away and never being heard of again. "Fear and suspicion became the essence of existence. To trust anyone was to risk one's life. People stopped having meaningful conversations, even inside their own family" (Schanberg 1980).

What Pol Pot sought to achieve was the obliteration of individualism, for just like Mao, he believed that for communism to succeed it must eliminate individualism (see Pol Pot 1977:H30 and Schurmann 1966:92). Pol Pot saw that to achieve the full socialist transformation he had to strip the concept of individualism from the collective Cambodian psyche. It appears he believed that only by destroying every root, every vestige of individualist thought could a new society emerge consisting of persons totally dedicated to, and knowing only, a collectivist regimen.

After learning about the multitude of executions in Cambodia, many observers concluded that these could only have resulted from irrational, purposeless madness. In fact, the killing had a clear, distinct purpose—the systematic eradication of those persons who embodied or perpetuated the notion of individualism. To Pol Pot it was necessary to kill the professional or well-educated persons, the wives of military officers and government officials, and their children. All of them possessed the ethical and philosophical heritage by which the individualist system operated; Pol Pot evidently feared that, if allowed to live, they would always seek to return to it.

This rationale would also seem to explain the Khmer Rouge emphasis on allowing "poor peasants" to hold positions of responsibility even when technical expertise was required. Among all persons in society, they alone were believed to least embody the most exaggerated aspects of individualism—ambition, achievement, wealth, and avarice. All others in society were deemed untrustworthy. The evidence strongly suggests that from 1975 to 1978 Pol Pot followed a course of progressively executing many people from all but the "bottom level" of the old society. First, right after the fall of Phnom Penh, the senior officials and military officers of the Lon Nol government (as well as in many cases their families) were executed in large numbers. They were followed a few months later by teachers, highly educated persons, and professionals such as doctors and engineers. At about the same time, the lower military personnel were singled out for elimination, and then later (1977), persons who had served in the republican military, even if it was only as a private in the village militia. Finally, the campaign was initiated to identify and eliminate the "new people"—that is, those who had lived in the noncommunist zones at the end of the war.

Apparently, all of the above classes were tainted in the eyes of the Khmer Rouge leadership. To them, the new collectivist, socialist society could only be achieved when a new generation emerged—imbued only with the philosophy that a human being's sole function in society is as an interchangeable part of a large collective entity. Once that occurred, the new socialist man and woman would pass this new value system on their children and the new society would be institutionalized. To insure that this plan would not fail, the Khmer Rouge appeared to have planned to eliminate systematically all those judged as incapable of fitting into the new, or possessing an attachment to the old.

Political Prophylaxis

In addition to being aimed at achieving radical social transformation, Pol Pot's violent policies served to stamp out any remaining remnants of opposition from the old society, while simultaneously insulating him from challenges from inside his own party. Nonetheless, Pol Pot's draconian policies inspired attempts to overthrow his rule. These in turn led the Khmer Rouge leaders to initiate violent, far-reaching purges of the party.

The available evidence indicates that there were two attempted coups against Pol Pot: the first in 1976, from within the center of the Communist Party of Kampuchea itself, and the second in 1978, which was encouraged by Vietnam and led to the defection of Heng Samrin and Pen Sovan and the ultimately successful move to topple Pol Pot through the use of Vietnamese military power. The first coup attempt occurred in September of 1976, and was organized and carried out by military leaders and senior party officials who were dismayed by the continuing level of violence in the country and the stark nature of the new society. These feelings had apparently been building for some time. Hou Yuon, the minister of the interior and cooperatives and one of the most prominent Khmer Rouge leaders during the war, had reportedly resigned in late 1975 in protest over the brutal nature of the forced and rapid communization of the entire country. Evidence of Hou Yuon's departure first came in April 1976, when a new government was announced and his name was conspicuously absent. It later became apparent that he had been executed (Quinn 1977).

Dissatisfaction appears to have spread to a number of other senior leaders who then conspired among themselves to kill Pol Pot and impose a new leadership on the party. According to Khmer Rouge defector Chek Win, planning for the attempted coup began on February 24, 1976, when Mit Soth, the regional commander in Damban (region) 106 (Oddar Meanchey, Siem Reap, and Kampong Thom provinces), called a clandestine meeting in Siem Reap City. Chek Win claims that at this time plans were drawn for an uprising because "all the soldiers wanted to create a rebellion that would allow people to go back and work as they did before the capture of Phnom Penh" (*Asia Week* 1977). April 17, 1977, was set as the date for the liberation, according to Chek Win, who added that he was told about a week before it was to take place that the plot had been uncovered and foiled. Other evidence provides a different chronology, indicating that the attempt to overthrow Pol Pot took place in mid-1976, although word of it did not get out until the spring of 1977.

Little is known with certainty about the actual attempt to kill Pol Pot. According to one account provided by a former Khmer Rouge member who later fled to Thailand, the commander of troops in Phnom Penh, Mit Cha Krey, joined by the military commanders of the Northern and Northeastern regions and of the Battambang and Oddar Meanchey special zones, attempted to poison Pol Pot during one of his regular meals. The poison was added to his food by his cook who was a relative of one of the conspirators. The plot was foiled when one of the guards at Pol Pot's headquarters inadvertently sampled the food in the kitchen and died immediately. Cha Krey and the others were motivated, according to this report, by the "hardships" the people were being made to endure.[4]

In September 1978, Democratic Kampuchea openly confirmed in its own *Black Paper* that Cha Krey had been asked to assassinate the Khmer Rouge leadership in mid-1976—but that "nothing came of it" (Democratic Kam-

---

[4] This account was provided to U.S. Government officials in Thailand in 1977.

puchea 1978a:45, 62).[5] This same document also acknowledged the attempt to poison Pol Pot, but caused some confusion by attributing it to the Vietnamese and putting the date for its occurrence in 1970. The details of the 1970 poisoning attempt contained in the Cambodian *Black Paper*, however, were remarkably similar to those provided for the 1976 incident by the Khmer Rouge defectors. More confusion was added by the *Black Paper* statement that the 1970 plot was not discovered until 1976:

. . . On the occasion of the negotiation of November 1970, the Vietnamese tried to poison Comrade Pol Pot and Comrade Second Secretary Nuon Chea through their agents infiltrated into the very breast of the KCP . . .

The negotiation took place in the Northern Zone, called Zone 304. The Secretary of the Zone, Koy Thoun, organized these negotiations, and it was his wife who prepared the food for the occasion.

Arrested in 1976, Koy Thoun revealed the plot . . . As the KCP took strict surveillance measures one had loyal Party members in the kitchen, this heinous criminal act was unsuccessful (Democratic Kampuchea 1978a:45, 62).

There are several reasons to believe that the poisoning attempt described in the *Black Paper* occurred in 1976 rather than 1970. First, the *Black Paper* account implies that the incident was not discovered by party officials until 1976, leaving one to wonder why the "Party members in the kitchen" who thwarted the attempted assassination would not have told someone about it before then. Second, the relationship between the Khmer Rouge and the Vietnamese communists in November of 1970 was hardly at the point where an assassination would seem called for. Rather, 1970 represents one of the high points of cooperation between the two parties as they fought against Lon Nol.

There is additional evidence lending support to the argument that the poisoning occurred in 1976. On September 26, 1976, Radio Phnom Penh announced that Pol Pot had taken "temporary leave" from his post as prime minister "to take care of his health, which has been bad for several months" (Quinn 1977:46). At the time, this development caused much speculation about whether Pol Pot had been removed from office. In retrospect it seems

---

[5] The *Black Paper* issued by Pol Pot's ministry of foreign affairs detailed two other abortive assassination attempts that the Cambodians attributed to the Vietnamese, but that could reasonably have sprung from the ranks of the Communist Party of Kampuchea itself.

The first occurred in July 1975, at a ceremony in which all military commanders pledged their Kampuchean Revolutionary Army forces to the party central committee. At that time "the enemy . . . was able to implant a soldier, from a unit in the Northern Zone, among the group of security guards responsible for the conference area or room to fire on the leaders of the KCP [Communist Party of Kampuchea] . . . But the plan failed because all weapons were emptied of cartridges prior to entry into the ceremonial room. The enemy plan was only revealed a year later in 1976."

The second attempt came in September 1975, when "a three or four man team from a unit in the Eastern Zone" was organized "to assassinate the leaders of the KCP." This plot also failed because "the three soldiers could not recognize the leaders and consequently did not know whom to fire at (Democratic Kampuchea 1978a:45–62)."

probable that the relinquishing of his governmental duties was directly linked to the assassination attempt. It is possible that Pol Pot actually did become ill as a result of eating some of the poisoned food. What seems more likely is that Pol Pot retreated to a secret, well-protected area where he would be safe from further attacks and from which he could direct the effort to rout out and eliminate all of those involved in the plot to kill him.

Still other evidence confirms that a coup attempt did take place in this general time frame. In mid-1977, Thai intelligence officials revealed information about an abortive overthrow of Pol Pot (*Bangkok Post* 1977; see also Kramer 1977). Another indication came in September 1977, when North Korean radio broadcast Kim Il-Song's message to Pol Pot on the seventeenth anniversary of the founding of the Cambodian communist party, which contained the following paragraph: "the heroic Cambodian people have wiped out some time ago the counter revolutionary group of spies who had committed subversive activities and sabotages, worming themselves into the revolutionary ranks for a long time at the instigation of the foreign imperialists" (FBIS IV, September 30, 1977).

At the time (September 1977), this was a subject of great sensitivity for Pol Pot, since he had just finished announcing openly the existence of the Cambodian communist party and had recounted all of its "positive" achievements.

An indication of the sensitivity of this issue is provided by the fact that references to the internal plot were expurgated from the version of Kim Il-Song's message when it was broadcast over Radio Phnom Penh (Jackson 1978a:81).

Four months later, Cambodian officials were less circumspect. Engaged in an increasingly heated confrontation with the Vietnamese and anxious to excoriate all sympathy for Hanoi from their ranks, Khieu Samphan admitted that in 1975 and 1976 ". . . a small group of traitors at the service of the Vietnamese and the expansionists attempted to overthrow the Phnom Penh government" (*Asia Week* 1978:17).

From all this evidence, it seems relatively certain that an attempt to poison Pol Pot occurred in 1976. The Cambodian communists probably changed the date in their *Black Paper* because they wanted to shift the blame to the Vietnamese and hide the fact that the assassination attempt had come from within their own ranks.

THE PURGE

While there may not be precise information on all the details of the 1976 coup attempt, a great deal is known about what followed in January 1977— a large-scale effort to identify and eliminate all party leaders, governmental officials, and military officers associated with the plot. This purge then expanded to all those whose loyalty might be suspect for other reasons, including any who might be pro-Vietnamese.

This purge took place in several phases. In late 1976 some of the most senior of the suspected conspirators were taken to the Tuol Sleng school in Phnom Penh that was Pol Pot's main "torture and execution center." It seems certain that Hu Nim—the former minister of information—was executed there, as well as Hu Yuon and probably most of the other plotters: "When Pol Pot's former Information Minister Hou [sic] Nim was executed in 1977, his torturers reported to Brother Duch [the Center's head] that they had 'lashed him four or five times to break his stand, before having him filled up with water' " (Newsweek 1980:42).

Public acknowledgment that Hou Yuon was also executed came from four former members of the Khmer communist administration who reportedly told a conference in France that "the former Minister of the Interior and the Minister for Co-operatives in Kampuchea had been accused of 'treason' and 'shot'." (FBIS IV, July 3, 1978:K13)

The executions of these senior officials were followed by many others, according to a prisoner who worked at Tuol Sleng. Documents found after the Vietnamese overran Phnom Penh indicated that thousands of Cambodians were systematically executed at Tuol Sleng. According to one report, the victims: "passed over iron beds on which they were beaten and tortured with electrical shocks, passed through tiny cells where they were left in chains without food to starve and rot, among them Khmer Rouge Ministers, Ambassadors and high functionaries who were accused of 'treason' " (Terzani 1980).

The report revealed that among the records at Tuol Sleng were "more than 16,000 dossiers on victims, dozens of boxes of photographs of people prior to and after execution, among them 1,200 pictures of children, some of them under 10 years of age" (Terzani 1980). Peter White, who visited the prison in Phnom Penh after the defeat of Pol Pot, indicated that "four out of five prisoners brought to Tuol Sleng were Khmer Rouge supporters . . . (White 1982:600)."

Still another report indicated that "Brother" Duch, the head of the "torture center," was a well-educated university graduate from Kompong Thom; he was also reported to be head of Nokorbal, the secret police system in Cambodia and as such "responsible for the deaths of as many as one million people" (Newsweek 1980:42). Duch had "200 like-minded interrogators and torturers" working under him. His right-hand man was Mam Nay, "a former teacher." Another was Peng, "who used a butcher's knife to kill prisoners." "A woman known as 'Yek' was in charge of killing women" (Newsweek 1980:42).

Thousands of prisoners were tortured into making preposterous confessions, often that they were agents for the CIA, the Soviet KGB and the Vietnamese—all at once. Then, ever the schoolmaster, Duch would carefully go through the confessions, "correcting" them with a red pen and suggesting improvements here and there, which meant further torture. Finally the victims would be killed, often in gruesome fashion. (*Newsweek* 1980:42)

Ing Pech, the lone survivor of the Center, said that when Duch indicated someone had made an "error" and had to be re-educated, that meant they would be "crushed to bits after torture" (*Newsweek* 1980).

After disposing of the coup leaders at Tuol Sleng, and learning the names of other coconspirators in the provinces, Pol Pot initiated the next step in his purge, the removal and execution of party leaders who had been implicated in the provinces. Beginning in March 1977, in scenes reminiscent of the roundup of former Lon Nol army officers, "new" Khmer cadres descended upon selected areas and arrested large numbers of party officials, village and hamlet leaders, and, in some instances, even soldiers. For about four months, this purge continued with formerly trusted party cadres disappearing overnight. In some instances, the new leadership, which for the first time included women at some villages and districts, explained that the "old" officials had been removed because they were lax in not executing all the former officials of the Phnom Penh government. Others, near the Thai border, were accused of secret trading relationships with Siamese businessmen or allowing too many people to escape across the border. Still others were more straightforward in saying that the former officials had tried to revolt.

According to one former communist official, Hui Pan, who served as a village chief in Siem Reap Province, the purge in his area began in February 1977, when fifty or so Siem Reap officials were ordered to Phnom Penh. They were soon replaced by "new Khmer Rouge" leaders (Kramer 1977).

Many other changes took place during the time Khmer Rouge leaders were preparing to celebrate the second anniversary of their coming to power. Khem Chhomali, a refugee from Kapong Cham, said that: "Between the 6th and the 17th of April, all of the 'Old Khmer Rouge' were suddenly removed. We don't know what happened but they say the *srok* (district) chief had died and that the old Khmer Rouge had tried to make a new revolution. I heard that 500 village chiefs and 1,000 soldiers were taken away in *Damban* (region) 106" (*Asia Week* 1977). Chuk Han, a Khmer communist military leader who fled to Thailand, added that "In my province of Oddor Meanchey, many people simply disappeared. Five hundred military chiefs and ordinary soldiers linked to the Khmer Rouge had their hands tied up and were taken away for execution. The arrests continued throughout May, June and July" (Chinoy 1977). Khem Chhommali offered additional evidence that many of these "old cadre" were put to death, claiming that he saw a mass grave containing the bodies of about seventy former Khmer Rouge leaders (Kramer 1977).

Refugees Im Vin and Chhoeng Sokhom Theavey from northeastern Cambodia reported that the purge was carried out in that part of the country as well during April and May of 1977. During this time a local party cadre admitted that the commanders of the Northern and Northeastern regions had been executed, along with some senior party officials "accused of revisionism and plotting to overthrow the government" (*Asia Week* 1977). Among them, according to Im Vin, was Koy Thoun. Im Vin went on to recount another experience in which he overheard Khmer Rouge soldiers at Stung Treng discussing the execution of twenty-five party cadres for participation in a conspiracy headed by some "ministers" (*Asia Week* 1977).[6]

One former Khmer Rouge veteran and the chief of a major cooperative in Thma Poek district of Battambang Province—Tuay Mien—provided additional information about the purge. According to him, on June 26, "outside units" of Khmer Rouge moved into his district and arrested the five members of the ruling committee and disarmed the one hundred members of the civil militia. From there, according to Tuay Mien, the new troops fanned out to the district's fifteen cooperatives, arresting the leaders of each. On July 5, Tuay Mien and his subordinates were taken prisoner. Also on that day, it was announced that "of the 70,000 citizens of the district, 40,000 were traitors who had collaborated with the U.S. Central Intelligence Agency and concealed the names of former Lon Nol agents . . ." (Nations 1978).

EXTENDED PURGE

In mid-1977, Pol Pot turned once again to purifying his new society by further efforts at eliminating the remainder of the population with connections to the "old society." To accomplish this, Pol Pot sent many new cadres into the villages to implement his revolutionary programs. Refugee Hui Pan described how the new Khmer Rouge cadres carried out this effort: "Under the old Khmer Rouge, only about 30% of the soldiers who had served in Lon Nol's army had been killed. But the new Khmer Rouge are worse, and under their rule all the Lon Nol soldiers are being hunted down. The new Khmer Rouge is killing all former policemen, soldiers, government officials, teachers, students, monks. If anyone is found to be an agent, he must be killed" (Chinoy 1977).

Refugee Chhoeno Sokhum Theavy, himself a former school teacher, echoed this philosophy. "The Communists would keep telling the people about the Maoist principle that if you want to tear out the weed, you must go for the roots (Asia Week, December 2, 1977). Khem Chhommali added that during meetings, the "new Khmer Rouge" repeatedly emphasized that the leadership in Phnom Penh was dedicated to destroying "the old rich

[6] These "ministers" may have been a reference to Hu Nim, who had not been mentioned publicly since January 1977, perhaps confirming that it was at that time that he was arrested, and, more certainly, to Koy Thoun, whom the Cambodian *Black Paper* identified as the assassination leader.

classes." As one cadre put it, "we must destroy these people in order to destroy the class" (*Asia Week* 1977).

Other evidence of this campaign came from Henry Kamm, who concluded after interviewing numerous refugees that

Detailed narratives of mass killings of enemies give rise to an impression that the regime has lost what inhibitions it may have had in its early stages and is conducting mass slayings without regard to the presence of witnesses. A number of refugees reported that officials were more and more openly speaking of a need to kill great numbers of Cambodians.

Mr. Sen Smean [from Battambang Province's Ampil district] said that Nan, the late district chief, had announced early last year [1977] that of the 15,000 people of the district, 10,000 would have to be killed as enemies and that 6,000 of them had already perished.

"We must burn the old grass and the new will grow," Nan said, according to Mr. Sen Smean. (Kamm 1978)

Kamm pointed out that "the principal targets for extermination continue to be intellectuals, soldiers in the Lon Nol army and former government officials." But Kamm added that

A devastating new element that emerges from the refugees' accounts of the last year [1977–78] is that the regime now appears to be methodically killing wives and children, many long after the husbands were killed.

Mr. San Daravong said that toward the end of last year he had witnessed the killing of 108 wives and children of former soldiers outside the village of Chba Leu, situated about 10 miles east of the town of Siem Reap in the midst of Angkor temple complex.

He said the victims had been led to a dike, their arms tied to their sides and pounded to death with big sticks in groups of 10 by a small group of soldiers. Some of the small children, he said, had been thrown into the air and impaled on bayonets; others were held by their feet and swung to the ground until dead. (Kamm 1978)

Other refugees indicated that even living in proximity to former government leaders could be sufficient cause for elimination. For example,

Mr. Okeum said that he came from the district of Siem Reap Province where former President Lon Nol was born. He said that to celebrate the second anniversary of their victory in April 1977, the communists had killed the entire population of the former leader's village . . . [Okeum] said that the district chief, who was later killed himself, announced that the villagers had been slain because all were relatives of Lon Nol. Throughout the district, Mr. Okeum said, about 350 families had been killed on that occasion, their family names recorded by authorities and displayed at the anniversary rally. (Kamm 1978)

Kamm's analysis pointed out that, in addition to deaths by execution, the constant hunger and disease caused considerable suffering and death in the new, larger agricultural communes with their communal kitchens and poor rice crops. In Siem Reap,

Malaria, cholera, diarrhea, tuberculosis and enfeeblement from pervasive malnutrition took a catastrophic toll in the district of Banteai Srie . . . [A] former [medical] student said that children, particularly infants, suffered the most cruelly from illnesses and died in frightening numbers. He said that infant mortality was particularly high because mothers, as a result of malnutrition, had little milk and no substitutes were available. (Kamm 1978)

Tuay Mien, the commune head from Thma Poek, said that as early as April he was ordered to survey the 999 families in his cooperative to identify "suspicious elements." The list was to include "all individuals and their families—who were former regulars in the Lon Nol army, minor officials, school teachers, village headmen of 10-family units in areas under Lon Nol's control and anyone educated or trained in Thailand or Vietnam." After conducting a house to house census, relying on every third house to cross-check the others, Tuay Mien finished with 700 families on his list (Nations 1978).

Some of the most detailed testimony about this campaign was given by refugees interviewed by U.S. government officials who later submitted their accounts to the United Nations High Commissioner on Refugees. Excerpts from these unclassified State Department cables paint a picture of life in Cambodia during the 1977–1978 effort to eliminate people connected to the old society. One refugee from Oddor Meanchey said:

In 1978, the Khmer Rouge started executing former students, former members of village defense forces or former militiamen. They started with leaders and those who studied to higher grades. In January or February, about twenty students who had studied five years or more—and about 30 former militiamen were killed. I know of 13 young men, some of whom were my friends, who were killed. The Khmer Rouge tied their hands behind their backs and took them to the forests. The next day I saw 13 fresh mounds. No one knew any reason why they would have been killed except that they were former students. (U.S. Department of State 1978)

Another refugee indicated that people would often be killed for being late to work and confirmed that the Khmer Rouge policy was to kill the spouses and children of persons judged to be guilty of an offense.

In 1976–1977 the guilty would be executed alone. After late 1977 and in 1978, the guilty and his family also were executed, even for a minor offense. For example, if you were executed for being late for work, your family would be executed too. This may have been because of the leader. In 1975, the head of the northern sector in Siem Reap, Anmed Sot, was not too strict. Sot was found to be a traitor and was replaced in late 1977 by Se who was more strict. Se followed the policy of killing wives and children of former soldiers and teachers. *Se said that wives were vestiges of the old society and are still corrupt.* (U.S. Department of State 1978; emphasis added)

A resident of Battambang, who said he was so afraid of the pervasive control of the Khmer Rouge that he did not even trust his own children, said: "All the 'New Cambodians' are being eliminated. Buddhists, intellectuals, anti-Communists as well as former soldiers, students and government officials. Everyone even remotely associated with the former regime. I fled because the Khmer Rouge suspected that I was a former official and would certainly have killed me sooner or later. *I did not dare speak to my children about my departure, because the Khmer Rouge spies are everywhere and greatly to be feared"* (U.S. Department of State 1978; emphasis added).

The underlying rationale for this campaign to eliminate the parts of the population that were suspect was contained in Pol Pot's major address on September 27, 1977, commemorating the seventeenth anniversary of the founding of the Communist Party of Kampuchea. In that 299-minute peroration, Pol Pot reminded his followers that certain "contradictions" continued to exist in new Democratic Kampuchea: ". . . we should ask whether there are any more social contradictions in this great new society of ours. We also should want to know more about these contradictions, if any, so that we can work out ways to solve them. We pose these questions in order to correctly assess and define our revolutionary duty for our new revolutionary phase" (Pol Pot 1977:H28).

Pol Pot answered his own question by saying, "Contradictions do exist within the ranks of our people. These contradictions stem from the differences in the nature of the remaining class vestiges. It is understandable that each person can not easily shed the vestiges of the class to which he belonged for generations and which he has just recently renounced for the proletarian nature of the revolution. These contradictions are regarded as contradictions within the people's ranks (Pol Pot 1977:H28). He added that, even more importantly, "These people must be constantly and profoundly instructed and educated in collective, socialist ownership and asked to gradually shed and finally eliminate the idea of private ownership" (Pol Pot 1977:H28).

Earlier in the speech, Pol Pot had given his assessment of how many Cambodians fell into each class in the new Cambodia: "We estimate that workers, peasants and other working people number more than 90 percent of the population, because we know the peasant class alone represents 85 percent of the people . . . among [the remaining] 10 percent are capitalists, landowners or members of other special strata" (Pol Pot 1977:H27).

In his public speech Pol Pot advocated dealing with these "contradictions" through "serious education, criticism, self-criticism and inspection of the revolutionary life style"; however, the overwhelming preponderance of evidence suggests that violence and terror were the preferred means of eliminating the contradictions.

Pol Pot saw other contradictions as well: "The actual situation clearly shows that imperialisms and foreign reactionaries harbor the strategic and fundamental intention of threatening and attempting to grasp our Cambodia. This brings about contradictions, contradictions in which foreign enemies want to violate, want to encroach upon, threaten and annex our Cambodian territory" (Pol Pot 1977:H28).

While this reference appeared directed at the Vietnamese Communist Party, Pol Pot also saw threatening contradictions within his own party and inside Cambodia:

In our new Cambodian society there also exist such life and death contradictions as enemies in the form of various spy rings working for imperialism, and international reactionaries are still planted among us to carry out subversive activities against our revolution. There is also another handful of reactionary elements who continue to carry out activities against, and attempt to subvert, our revolution. These elements are not numerous, constituting only 1 or 2 percent of our population. Some of them operate covertly while others are openly conducting adverse activities. (Pol Pot 1977:H28)

Pol Pot's prescription for dealing with these internal dissidents was harsh and to the point:

These counter revolutionary elements which betray and try to sabotage the revolution are not to be regarded as being our people. They are to be regarded as enemies . . . We must thus deal with them the same way we would with any enemy, that is, by separating, educating and coopting elements that can be won over . . . , neutralizing any reluctant elements . . . , and isolating and eradicating only the smallest number . . . who determinedly oppose the revolution . . . and collaborate with foreign enemies to oppose their own nation. (Pol Pot 1977:H28)

DEFENDING AGAINST EXTERNAL ENEMIES

The Khmer Rouge had been consciously working to reduce and finally eliminate the Vietnamese communist presence and influence in Cambodia since the early 1970s. Many Khmer cadres trained in Hanoi who returned to Cambodia after Sihanouk's overthrow were quickly replaced, and in many cases killed. Radio Hanoi in a 1978 commentary confirmed this: ". . . at the wishes of the Cambodian Revolution, Vietnam sent back to Cambodia cadres that the Cambodian Revolutionary Organization had asked it to form, indoctrinate and train. But it was most heart-rending to learn that almost all these Cambodian cadres have been executed" (FBIS IV, February 15, 1978:K1).

Skirmishes and outright fighting between North Vietnamese units and

Khmer Rouge troops were not uncommon even before the war ended, as the Cambodians sought to eliminate any Vietnamese presence from Kampuchean soil. In 1972, in one area, Khmer Rouge military officials even entered into an informal agreement with South Vietnamese army officers in an effort to reduce the North Vietnamese presence in Cambodia.[7] These disputes, which subsided after 1975, when Vietnamese troops withdrew from many parts of Cambodia, erupted again in 1977 and escalated during that year until early January 1978, when Cambodian military forces took the unprecedented step of attacking into Vietnam and capturing the small Vietnamese coastal town of Ha Tien. Hanoi quickly countered with a large-scale military move into southern Cambodia.

SECOND COUP ATTEMPT

At the same time that Hanoi moved into Cambodia, reports suggest that the Vietnamese began efforts to recruit some Cambodian military and political officials to lead an uprising against Phnom Penh. A communique from the Kampuchean ministry of information issued June 25, 1978, charged that, in early 1978, six political operatives of the Politburo in Hanoi had, ". . . several times sneaked into Kampuchean territory in order to contact and hold meetings with the Vietnamese agents planted in the Eastern Region for subversive activities by Vietnam, concerning implementation of the coup plan and to directly supervise this coup" (FBIS IV, June 26, 1978:H1).

The communique pointed out that secret meetings were held in February, March, April, and May, 1978, in the eastern parts of Kampong Cham and Svay Rieng provinces. The aim of this activity, the communique charged, was to "topple Democratic Kampuchea" or, if that was not possible, to take over and separate the Eastern Region from Pol Pot's control (FBIS IV, June 26, 1978:H1).

Phnom Penh authorities claimed they were successful in thwarting this plan in May of 1978. Although not acknowledged by Cambodian officials, this coup attempt apparently led to a second purge that began in late 1977 or early 1978, and included military and party leaders suspected of sympathy for the Vietnamese.

Evidence for the existence of the purge came from Prince Sihanouk, who wrote in 1980 that Pol Pot, Ieng Sary, and Khieu Samphan all admitted over Radio Phnom Penh that "the CIA, the KGB and the Vietnamese agents made repeated attempts" to overthrow them. Sihanouk intepreted this to mean that "the split within the Khmer Rouge Party and army was widening." When Sihanouk asked Khieu Samphan what in fact was happening, all he

---

[7] The author learned this while residing in the border province of Chau Doc in South Vietnam.

would reply was that Le Duan and Pham Van Dong wanted to replace the Khmer Rouge leadership (Sihanouk 1980:75).

It is unclear whether there was any Vietnamese attempt to undermine Pol Pot in 1976 and 1977, or whether this was a charge Pol Pot used to mask exteme dissension within his own movement. What does seem clear is that Pol Pot did carry out another purge that again reached deep into the ranks of the Communist Party of Kampuchea and the military and civil structures of Democratic Kampuchea. What is further known is that by 1978, Vietnamese authorities were actively urging Khmer Rouge cadres to revolt against Pol Pot.

THE SECOND PURGE

According to Sihanouk, evidence of the second purge came from Phnom Penh radio, which in 1977 broadcast news of "the complete removal of Vietnamese, CIA and KGB agents from every cooperative, administrative department and army unit" (Sihanouk 1980:76). He added that in 1978 a Khmer language broadcast over Radio Peking mentioned "extensive and radical purges in Zone 203" (areas along the Vietnamese border). Curiously, the report indicated that the only survivors of the purge were Heng Samrin, Chea Sim, and Ros Samay, who later would side with the Vietnamese and head the new government that would replace Pol Pot (Sihanouk 1980:76).

There is other evidence that this second purge reached into the upper ranks of the party leadership. Sihanouk said that Von Vet, the vice-premier in charge of economic policy, was reportedly killed during 1978, and implied that other senior leaders were so suspect that by the middle of that year the country was being run by only four people: Pol Pot, Ieng Sary, and their wives, Khieu Ponnary and Khieu Thirith (Sihanouk 1980:79).

This purge also reached down into the party organization, military structure, and governmental organization, particularly in those areas thought to be under any Vietnamese influence. Refugees arriving in Thailand in 1978 reported that "growing numbers of local Communist officials have been killed in what appeared to be an ongoing wave of violent purges" (Kamm 1978).

These refugees noted that in one district in Battambang Province, district chiefs had been removed twice in one year and reportedly "killed as enemies." In addition, "the changes of district chiefs were always accompanied by the disappearance of village chiefs and frequently by the small teams of soldiers who supervise the villagers' work" (Kamm 1978). Similar reports were received from refugees in Siem Reap, Oddar Meachey, and Koh Kong provinces. These reports from western Cambodia were matched by others from the eastern part of the country.

One former Cambodian officer who fled to Vietnam indicated that at the end of March "three truckloads" of cadres and officers were arrested and executed by Pol Pot loyalists. Among those reportedly killed were the political commissar of the 280th Division and members of his staff. By May, this same source stated that the purges were reaching down to the battalion level. In a radio broadcast from Hanoi, this officer called on all of his former comrades remaining inside Cambodia to "rise up and struggle to topple the Pol Pot–Ieng Sary clique of traitors who have betrayed their nation and people and who are henchmen of the reactionary People's Republic of China rulers" (FBIS IV, June 22, 1978:K7–9).

Ironically, it may have been Pol Pot's fear of the Vietnamese and the resulting purges that drove senior Cambodian officers to break with him and side with Vietnam. Sihanouk himself claims that Heng Samrin, Chea Sim, and Ros Samay, who led the rebellion in the Eastern Region (albeit heavily supported by Vietnamese military forces), had been true Pol Pot supporters and only defected after they feared they would be purged (Sihanouk 1980:23). Whatever their true motivation, the three did side with Hanoi and, backed by a Vietnamese offensive launched on December 25, 1978, Heng Samrin and his followers rode into Phnom Penh on January 7, 1979 (almost a year, to the day, after the attack on Ha Tien), and established the People's Republic of Kampuchea.

Conclusion

An analysis of Pol Pot's September 27, 1977, speech indicates that he identified four major contradictions, each of which he dealt with by means of violence.

1. The contradiction between the peasants and ruling strata of the old society that continued to exist even in the new agricultural communes. To eliminate this contradiction, Pol Pot embarked on a campaign to identify and eliminate former soldiers, government workers, intellectuals, and anyone with an education.
2. The contradiction between individualism and collectivism, that is, between private ownership of land and "socialist ownership." Here the targets of Pol Pot's efforts were the peasants, including the poor peasants who had to be forced to accept the new economic regimen and produce goods under it. Pol Pot used terror, executions, and the threat of death to force villagers and peasants to conform to his new collectivized society.
3. The contradiction within his own party, between those supporting him and those opposing his radical revolution. Pol Pot implemented violent purges deep into the party in an effort to resolve this contradiction.
4. The contradiction between Democratic Kampuchea and foreign "imperialists and reactionaries," which presumably included the Thai,

the Americans, the Soviets, and the Vietnamese. To deal with these potential problems, the Khmer Rouge sought self-sufficiency, practiced a constant vigilance to protect their borders, and meted out brutal treatment to those, including party members, suspected of allegiance to foreign powers—particularly Vietnam.

In analyzing the use of terror and violence in Cambodia, it is important to point out that it did take an *external* force to unseat Pol Pot. Heng Samrin could not have accomplished this without Vietnamese military forces. Pol Pot's political plan had largely achieved its goals inside Cambodia. He had destroyed virtually all of his potential and real opposition, although at one point he was only a spoonful of soup away from being deposed. Having weathered this challenge from within his own ranks in 1976, by 1977 he appeared to have the ability to continue to rule for the indefinite future. Without his conflict with the Vietnamese and their long involvement in Cambodia, it would be possible to argue that Pol Pot might still be in power.

With the end of Pol Pot's official reign, efforts were made to estimate the number of deaths and the extent of the suffering that Pol Pot caused, either directly by execution or indirectly through disease, malnutrition, and starvation resulting from his forced mass relocation, harsh working conditions, destruction of virtually all health and sanitary facilities, and the changes in the agricultural and economic distribution systems. It must be conceded that all attempts thus far are rough estimates at best, and range from several hundred thousand to about 3 million.

7. The Photographic Record

by David Hawk

The general outlines of Khmer Rouge rule in Cambodia have become generally known through the accounts of refugees and survivors, as retold and portrayed in articles, books, and recent motion pictures. These accounts tell of the precipitous evacuations of the cities and towns, the forced marches and forced labor, the harsh collectivization of production and the communalization of living and eating, the abolition of money, the attacks on traditional religion and culture, the massive, widespread summary executions, and the starvation and disease.

Following the Vietnamese invasion of Cambodia in 1978, which drove the Khmer Rouge from the capitol of Phnom Penh to the mountainous jungles on the Thai-Cambodian border, and the famine of 1980–1981, Cambodia reopened to foreign relief officials, journalists, and scholars. Vastly more information and evidence became available and it is now possible to document in detail the extreme human rights violations of the Khmer Rouge.

Unknown outside Cambodia until after 1979 was the existence of a nationwide prison-torture-execution system—virtual extermination facilities—and the large number of mass graves that now scar the Cambodian landscape. The physical structures of some prison-execution centers still stand. Elsewhere, the mass grave sites, with their thousands of skulls, are mute witnesses to calculated, large-scale human destruction.

It is now evident that policy and practice in Democratic Kampuchea included systematic torture, extensive extra-judicial execution, and specific programs of genocide against religious and ethnic minority groups, as well as the partial decimation of the Cambodian people themselves.

A System of Killing

Murder-by-government under Khmer Rouge rule was so systemic and widespread that a large bureaucracy was required to eliminate the projected, suspected, and imagined opponents of the revolutionary transformation of Khmer society. The most definitively documented killings are those that took place at S–21, now known as Tuol Sleng, the prison-execution facility in Phnom Penh. Tuol Sleng was an extermination center at the hub of a nationwide system of imprisonment, interrogation, torture, and execution.

When the Vietnamese invaded Cambodia in 1979, Pol Pot's forces retreated so precipitously that they left behind tens of thousands of pages of archives from the S–21 "bureaucracy of death." These meticulously kept records indicate that nearly twenty thousand were executed (literally "smashed to bits") at Tuol Sleng. Only seven persons may have survived—prisoners whose skills were useful to the Khmer Rouge prison authorities.

At any one time, Tuol Sleng held between one thousand and fifteen hundred prisoners. The prisoners were individually photographed upon arrest. They were repeatedly tortured until confessing to be traitors to the revolution, compelled to name their collaborators, and then executed. Those persons named as collaborators were in turn arrested, interrogated, tortured, and executed in an ever-expanding series of purges directed against various sectors of the population. Prison interrogators prepared typewritten summaries of the confessions to pass on to superiors. The confessions provide a chilling glimpse into the political pathology of the regime. Sometimes interrogators noted in the margins of the confession the specific application of the torture technique used. Victims were sometimes photographed after torture and death, documenting that the "wrongdoers" had been eliminated.

Daily arrest logs and execution schedules listing each prisoner's name, alias, sex, position, function, or region detailed each day's work. October 15, 1977—418 killed; October 18—179 killed; October 20—88 killed; October 23—148 killed. The highest figure was for May 27, 1978—582 killed.

The day-by-day records of arrests and executions make it possible to analyze the evolving pattern of massacre—what regions, occupations, political tendencies, or organizational units were being purged during particular periods. Correspondence between the commander of Tuol Sleng and the standing committee of the central committee of the Communist Party of Kampuchea indicate that S–21 operated with the full knowledge, and directly under the command, of the highest political authorities of Democratic Kampuchea.

Most revealing of the macabre, criminal nature of Pol Pot's torture and execution system are the Tuol Sleng "Interrogators' Notes." Alongside mundane admonitions about not smudging reports, not using unsharpened pencils, or not lying down while interrogating prisoners, these documents contain an extraordinarily explicit discussion of the policy, practice, and problems of systematic torture. The "problem" the interrogators strove constantly to solve was that the torture was too indiscriminate and prisoners were dying prematurely, before all necessary information had been extracted from them. This is represented as a "loss of mastery" and "a defeat for the party." Leading interrogation cadres explained that having to revive prisoners the party had already decided to execute was a waste of medicine and doctors' time.

After 1979, the nearly hundred thousand pages of confessions, summaries, entrance forms, authorizations to torture, torture reports, prisoners photographs, signed execution orders, daily execution logs, and the like were stored in former prison rooms on the upper floors of Tuol Sleng. The arrest photographs were displayed on the ground floors, where Cambodians come to search for pictures of missing relatives. The "employment section" of the archives contain the photographs and biographies of the guards, interrogators, and executioners at Tuol Sleng.

Archival fragments and refugee and survivor testimonies indicate that similar prison-torture-execution centers (but without the photographic equipment) operated at the commune, district, and regional levels throughout Cambodia, where local-level enemies of the revolution were imprisoned, tortured, and eliminated by the thousands.

Mute Witness

Mass grave sites, landmarks of large-scale political killings, have been discovered throughout the Cambodian countryside. While some villagers speak of local killing grounds, a number of the larger mass graves were located in remote areas. The grave pits have been opened and the bones and skulls removed in order to estimate the number of dead. Some remains were found still bound and blindfolded. The skulls and bones were collected and piled in enclosures constructed of bamboo and thatch. These were to serve as reminders of the Khmer Rouge period and as memorials where Buddhist funeral rites could be performed to allow the spirits of the deceased a more peaceful passage to the afterlife.

One mass grave site, Cheung Ek, where over eight thousand skulls have been counted, is reported to have been a burial ground for Tuol Sleng. Two other sites, Ta Mon and Tonle Bati, were adjacent to district or regional prison-execution centers. Wat Eik and Wat Samdach Money are two examples of former Buddhist temples converted after 1975 into prison-execution centers.

The mass graves contain those who were deliberately executed—not the old, young, or sick who died along the road during the forced evacuations, nor those who died from malnutrition or from forced labor or other causes. At this writing, comprehensive information about the total number of mass grave sites throughout Cambodia is unavailable.

Acts of Genocide

Khmer Rouge policy and practice also sought, and substantially achieved, the dissolution and elimination of religious and ethnic or racial minority groups.

The constitution of Democratic Kampuchea strictly prohibited "reactionary" religion, and all religious activity was brutally suppressed. The Catholic cathedral in Phnom Penh was removed stone by stone from its former site on Monivong Avenue. Throughout the countryside, Buddhist temples, Moslem mosques, and Protestant churches were demolished or converted to warehouses, workshops, or prison-execution centers.

Before 1975, Theravada Buddhism was the established state religion. For centuries the Buddhist *wat* or temple was the center of village life, the source of learning, the resevoir and transmitter of Cambodian culture. Khmer Rouge policy toward Buddhism constituted one of the most brutal and thoroughgoing attacks on religion in modern history.

Once in power, the Khmer Rouge began to destroy or desecrate Buddhist books, statues, and other holy objects and relics. Worship, prayer, meditation, festivals, were forbidden, as was Pali, the language of Khmer Buddhist scripture. Considered by the Khmer Rouge to be a remnant of feudalism, the organized monkhood, a celebate, mendicant, teaching, and contemplative religious order—and Cambodian's preeminent religious group—was forcibly disbanded and virtually destroyed. The leading, and most venerated, monks, and those who refused to take off their saffron-colored robes, were executed. Thousands more died of exhaustion, starvation, and disease, were forced to marry, or simply disappeared. Before 1975 there were approximately sixty thousand monks. After three years and eight months of Khmer Rouge rule, fewer than one thousand survived and returned to their former monastery sites. Democratic Kampuchea's minister of culture (the wife of the Kampuchean Communist Party central committee member directly responsible for Tuol Sleng) bragged about having "surpassed" Buddhism and rendering it a "thing of the past."

Ethnic, racial, or national minority groups were proclaimed to be dissolved, and their members became victims of repeated massacres. Thousands of ethnic Chinese, Sino-Khmer, Vietnamese, Khmer-Vietnamese, Lao and Thai, Indians, and Pakistanis were summarily killed.

The Cham, an Islamic group of Malayo-Polynesian racial stock, were singled out for especially harsh treatment. Recognizable by their distinctive dress, customs, and language, the Cham lived apart from the Khmer in their own villages and neighborhoods.

The remnants of the Hinduized, later Islamicized, Kingdom of Champa on the central coast of what is now Vietnam, the Cham had migrated to Cambodia after the sixteenth-century to escape the southern migrations of Vietnamese settlers. Khmer Rouge policy and practice nearly brought about their extinction as a people.

The Khmer Rouge ruthlessly suppressed Islamic practices, and Cham religious and community leaders were executed. After 1976 there was a ban on Cham dress, custom, and the Bahasa-Cham language. Communities and villages were broken up. The Cham were subjected to massacre or dispersed among the general population. While the Khmer population was severely restricted in food rations, Cham were forced to eat pork. Cham dead were buried "upside down," that is, not facing Mecca—an extreme sacrilege to the Cham of Cambodia.

Gross Violations

In Cambodia, under Khmer Rouge rule, a well-documented program of destruction took place against religious and ethnic groups. Such a program is a clear violation of the United Nations Convention on the Prevention and Punishment of the Crime of Genocide, which defines genocide as "acts (including killings, mental and physical harm, the infliction of conditions of life calculated to bring about physical destruction in whole or in part . . .) committed with intent to destroy in whole or in part, a national ethnic, racial or religious group." As many as one-quarter or even one-third of the Cambodian people died at the hands of their government in less than four years—from massacres, executions, torture, and the debilitating conditions of life to which the populace was subjected. Those conditions included exhaustion, from forced labor and forced marches; starvation, resulting from the government's complete restructuring of agricultural production and food distribution; and disease, following the dissolution and decimation of medical and health professions and the restriction of medicines to the army and cadres of the regime. A strong case can be made that suffering and death on this scale and proportion constitute, in the terms of the Genocide Convention, the partial destruction of the Cambodian "national" group itself.

In 1950, Cambodia became a state party to the Genocide Convention, a treaty obligation that the Khmer Rouge never abrogated. Yet, Khmer Rouge policy and practice constituted a consistent pattern of gross violations of internationally recognized human rights that was amply documented by the 1978 submissions to the United Nations Human Rights Commission. The 1979 U.N. report analyzing the 1978 submissions determined that the violations were "the worst to have occurred anywhere in the world since Nazism."

There is no statute of limitation on crimes against humanity, including genocide. Democratic Kampuchea's failure to punish, or even remove from positions of authority, those responsible for acts of genocide is a breach of international legal obligation. In 1988, the international community's disregard of this egregious violation lay, along with foreign military occupation, at the core of the Cambodian people's tragedy.

One of four indentical buildings—formerly a school and classrooms at Tuol Sleng. On the ground floor were interrogation and torture rooms. The second and third floors contained cells for women prisoners.

First floor outside corridor of prison building at Tuol Sleng.

Inside Tuol Sleng many of the former classrooms were broken up into tiny cinderblock cells.

Above: Cinderblock cell. Prisoner was shackled to the floor by leg irons. *Below*: Prisoner photographed in interrogation cell. (From Tuol Sleng archives.)

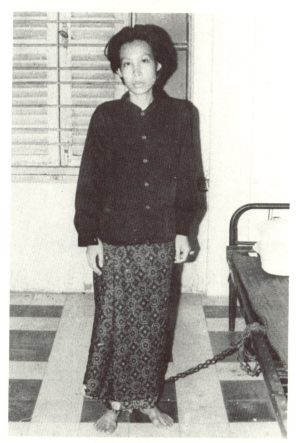

Prisoner mug shot arrest photographs taken by the Khmer Rouge prison officials.
Over 5,000 such individual photographs have been hung in groups on the walls of
Tuol Sleng.

Interrogation room. (Photo courtesy of Joel Charney.)

Files at Tuol Sleng containing prisoners' confessions, entry records, and execution schedules.

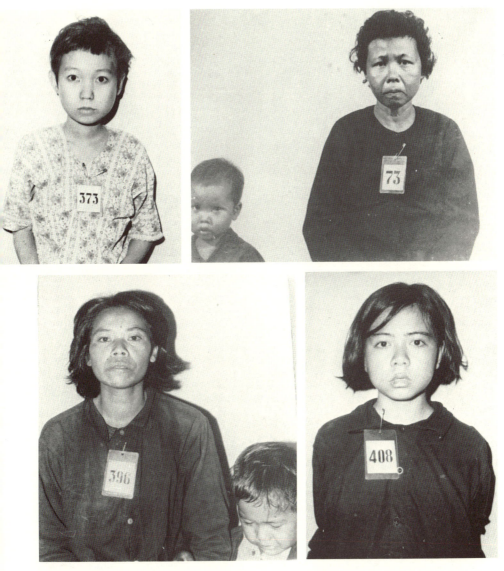

Arrest photographs from Tuol Sleng. Often the wives and children of prisoners were also arrested. Certain days, July 1 and 2, 1977, for example, were set aside for the execution of the families of men previously executed. (From Tuol Sleng archives.)

Brother Duch

Measures in the Interrogation of IX which resulted in he himself confessing on 26.9.76 (in the afternoon).

1- In the morning Brother Duch came in for a neck massage and to scrub the dirt off his body

2- We received our instructions from Brother Duch:
- ask him about the medicines for which he has a personal need
- remind him about the welfare of his wife and children: does he know that his wife and children have been detained; now that he's here does he know what's become of his wife?

3- Our interrogation:
- before he was taken into custody and brought here, did he realize what was about to happen; what aspects of the situation made him suspicious.
- what had the organization disseminated about the question of 20 September 1976; IX said the matters of security measures for the one named VIII and the removal of Brother Khoun from his posts inside and outside the Party for moral reasons; he put pressure on him: "Your face is going black with terror, just as if you were marking yourself clearly for the Organization to see".
- the threat was made: there's no avoiding torture if you don't confess

4- In the afternoon: we proposed to Brother Duch that he give permission for us to use both hot and cold techniques; after having received authorization, towards the early evening we went to intimidate him, telling him to prepare himself at eight or nine p.m. for the torture to be continued.

5- At about almost ten p.m. we went in to get ready to carry out torture with our bare hands; IX started to confess by asking us to clarify what all he was to report; we clarified as follows: "Please write a systematic account of your treasonous activities from beginning to end."

Brother Duch,

Previous Measures in the Interrogation of IX

1- On 23 September 1976, we received instructions from the Organizatio to use torture. We started using torture in the morning with about 20 whippings with fine rattan; in the afternoon there wer about 20-30 whippings with electrical wire instead.

Reduced photocopies and translation of cover notes to the confessions of Hou Nim. Brother Duch was the commander of Tuol Sleng. Pon was an interrogator. Hou Nim was a popular dissident Khmer Rouge leader and longtime member of the Communist Party of Kampuchea. He, like many others, was tortured to confess falsely to being a CIA (or KGB) agent, and then executed.

ហូ និម = ភាស
II

សារភាពច្រកាត់ឲ្យ គ្រាន់

ដំរាប បង ឌុច

នេះ ចម្លើយ ភាស់ ពេលបើយវាយ ៤-៥ ដៃ
បត្រាក់ដំហោ មុនឃស្សាកោវត្រេក្ជីក

ដោយគោរព
16.6.77
ប៉ុ
1

HOU NIM alias PHAS

II

CONFESSION GIVEN AS AN EXCUSE

Dear Brother Duch

This is Phas' answer while we beat him four or
five times. He was humbled by the
beatings and then the water torture.

With respect
14.4.77
(Signed) Pon

ដំរាប បង ឌុច

អំពីជួបសារៈច្រើយសរុបការបេប់ ភាស់ សើរៈ ស៊ីលាក់កម្លំង្លង់នៃ
ស៊ី កវិលលាលវា វាជាភ្ញាក់ងារសើម័ុក ឯករាជ ឌាលលង្ខ័្ប ខ្លួ ឈ្មូលវិ?យូថ
កុំដ្រើយលោមុភាពប្រនិងបក្ស ភាក្រោហស់ ឆុ?ុក្ក ង ឈ្មូន ហាយ៉ៈ។
រូ?ុរ?ដ្ឃែតលោកកុ ឲ្យកសរលោមុ?ឃ?ុយថៃ៖

ដោយគោរព
ថ្ងៃ ២២ មេសា ឆ្នាំ៧៧
ប៉ុ
1

To Brother Duch,

   This time the gist of Phas' confession is that
he hid other traitorous forces...He said that he is an
independent CIA officer who buried himself for a long
time, and did not carry out any impetuous anti-party
activities, like those of the wicked Khoun and Ya groups.
   I have tortured him to write it again.

With respect
22 April, 1977
(Signed) Pon

Reduced photocopies and translation of interrogation and torture records from the
Tuol Sleng archives.

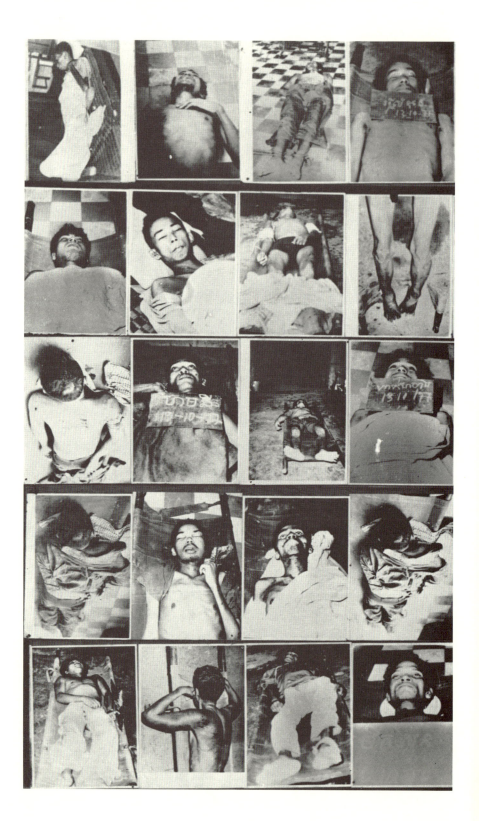

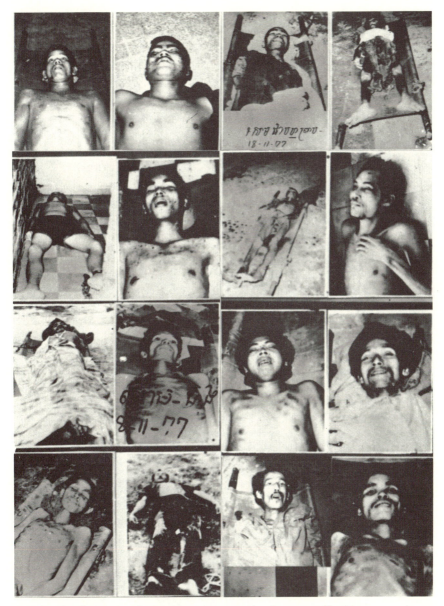

Photographs of prisoners after execution. Pictures taken by prison officials were sent to party higher-ups to show that "traitors" and "wrongdoers" had been executed.

Below: Two opened mass graves at Cheung Ek, Kandal province, 1981. More than 8,000 bodies were discovered here. By 1982, remains from the Cheung Ek grave site had been collected in a wooden shed as a memorial (*above*).

Above: Collected remains at Ta Mon, from one of several mass grave sites of the Angkor Chey district prison-execution facility in Takeo province. *Below*: Tonle Bati, 1981. More than 2,500 bodies were discovered at this site.

The collected remains from Tonle Bati mass grave, 1982.

On facing page: At top, the former site of Wat Preach Mean Bon in Phnom Penh, and below it the site of the Catholic cathedral in Phnom Penh that was wholly dismantled and leveled by the Khmer Rouge. (Photo courtesy of Kris Buchner.)

Above: Krapuchaet, "the temple of the satisfied crocodile," in Kandal province. This gutted building was the temple library. *Below*: Scene of destruction at Ampil Bey temple near the old capital of Oudong.

8. Explaining the Terror

by Kenneth Quinn

What did Pol Pot seek to accomplish with the extensive use of force and terror in Democratic Kampuchea? What were Pol Pot's overall goals in emptying the cities and establishing rural communes? and What set of moral or political beliefs permitted the Khmer Rouge to execute or otherwise cause or allow the deaths of perhaps millions of their compatriots?

Early Theories

A number of possible answers to these questions have been put forward. One early theory was that the Khmer Rouge had been so brutalized during the war that they were radicalized and turned into "savages"; upon achieving victory, their pent-up passion was turned loose upon an unsuspecting populace. Writing in 1970, shortly after his release from Phnom Penh by the Pol Pot authorities, Sydney Schanberg, the *New York Times* correspondent who covered the end of the war, wrote:

. . . many people have asked me: how could the Cambodian peasant whom we had always regarded as gentle and charming and smiling and civilized turn into the kind of tough and grim and even brutal revolutionary who entered Phnom Penh on April 17? I have no easy answers. One partial explanation is that the Cambodian peasant's sense of exploitation by the land owners and city merchants and the urban system in general may have been much deeper and much more bitter than we had perceived. But there is a more complete, though perhaps, oversimplified answer—the war. Cambodians were carpetbombed by American B–52s, shelled by both sides and kidnapped as their villages were overrun by the Khmer Rouge. *The war hardened them.* (emphasis added)

Schanberg then went on to speculate that if the United States had not supported Lon Nol in 1970, the communists would have achieved victory immediately, and ". . . some more moderate form of socialism or Communism would surely have been the result. The irony of American intervention in Cambodia is that it created the very kind of Communism it set out to contain" (Schanberg 1975). Schanberg thus argued that in 1970 the Khmer communist leaders were not disposed to perpetuate such a violent revolution, but were, in fact, so brutalized by the war that this radical transformation of the totality of Cambodian society was the result.

The idea of the Khmer Rouge as an enraged group of soldiers intent on vengeance has been suggested by several other observers as well. William Shawcross wrote:

215

All wars are designed to arouse anger, and almost all soldiers are taught to hate and to dehumanize their enemy. Veterans of the combat zone are often possessed of a mad rage to destroy, and to avenge their fallen comrades. It does not always happen, however, that victorious armies have endured such punishment as was inflicted upon the Khmer Rouge. Nor does it always happen that such an immature and tiny force comes to power after its country's social order has been obliterated, and the nation faces the takeover by a former ally, its ancient enemy. In Cambodia that did take place. In the last eight years, degree, law, moderation had been forsworn. The war and the causes for which it was fought had brought desolation while nurturing and then giving power to a little group of zealots sustained by Manichean fear. (Shawcross 1979:389)

In another article, Shawcross noted: "The victors were a very small army that had suffered appalling casualties. In any war, veteran soldiers who have experienced terror often become possessed by fury." He then goes on to quote J. Glenn Gray's description of soldiers in the heat of battle: "Blinded by the rage to destroy and supremely careless of consequences, they storm against the enemy until they are victorious, dead or utterly exhausted. It is as if they are seized by a demon and are no longer in control of themselves" (Shawcross 1978:25).

The theme of the brutality of the war and its effect upon the Khmer Rouge was echoed by two other commentators as well. The French sociologist and journalist Jean Lacouture offered two reasons for the "derailment" of the Cambodian revolution and its extreme violence: "Two important explanations can be given. First of all the total isolation of the revolution. It developed in the jungle, led by a guerrilla who had been cut off from the rest of the world. It has been based on peasants without real ideological control and without serious revolutionary cadres. Such a revolution is very difficult to keep within sensible limits and to guide in a sensible direction" (Lacouture 1978). During Congressional testimony on May 3, 1977, Gareth Porter of the Institute for Policy Studies in Washington contended that "the postwar bloodletting which took place was not a consequence of an ideological perversion, but of the savagery of the war itself." Porter then went on to quote a journalist's account which speculated that "apart from the thirst for vengeance, the 'political experience' and 'lack of organization' contributed to the incidence of reprisals" (U.S. Congress 1977a:26).

The above theories may be useful in helping to explain the executions of the political leadership of the Lon Nol government and reprisals against selected military leaders immediately after the surrender of Phnom Penh. A number of other factors would suggest, however, that they fall short of offering a full explanation for the violence that permeated Pol Pot's entire rule and that was directed at vitually every level of Khmer society.

First it must be pointed out that the brutality and terror did not start only after the Khmer Rouge achieved total victory in 1975. Khmer Rouge cadre began implementing their radical policies as early as 1972, and while the violence that occurred after the fall of Phnom Penh in 1975 was the most publicized, it was not the first instance of force and terror by Khmer Rouge forces.

Second, Khmer Rouge violence was not directed only at opposition military forces, but also at students, teachers, and peasants—groups that had not fought against them.

A third point is that the terror and purges lasted for more than three years *following* the April 1975 victory. This would seem strong evidence that the violence was not just a spasmodic excess of enraged, vengeful, triumphant troops, but rather a systematic implementation of a comprehensive, premeditated national policy.

Fourth, the fact that the same type of violence occurred at roughly the same time in all parts of the country, again would indicate a planned campaign of terror rather than random, spontaneous occurrences.

A fifth point is that virtually all evidence suggests that rather than being a leaderless pack, the Khmer Rouge military was a tightly disciplined, well-controlled force that carried out the instructions of its superiors. These leaders, moreover, had not spent years of isolation in the jungle, as Lacouture suggests, but rather had spent significant amounts of time in Paris, Beijing, and Phnom Penh. Pol Pot, Khieu Samphan, and Ieng Sary were urbane revolutionaries who spent almost as much time in capital cities as in the jungle, as were many of the officers in their army. Journalist Schanberg, who was in Phnom Penh when the Khmer Rouge forces arrived, noted that "Their officers, however, were no longer village boys. Though they spoke only Khmer in our presence, it was clear that they were educated men and could speak French, the colonial language of Indochina" (Schanberg 1975:49).

The experience of neighboring Vietnam would also seem to cast serious doubt upon the argument that the savagery of the war so brutalized the Khmer Rouge that they eliminated up to a third of their population. After all, if anyone was to be radicalized by the war, surely it should have been the North Vietnamese, who endured several decades of war and a much longer and more intense air bombardment. Yet there were few reports of extreme violence emanating from Vietnam following the capture of Saigon.

Finally, the Cambodian communists themselves offered the strongest refutation of the theory that American bombardment, which had ceased in 1973, had turned them into radical extremists. In its September 1978 *Black Paper*, the Pol Pot government wrote that: "The air war bombardments of the American Imperialists against the Kampuchean revolution did not achieve the anticipated results. The American planes could not inflict any great damage on the Kampuchean Revolutionary army because it was constantly on the move" (Democratic Kampuchea 1978a:49).

A totally different explanation for the violence in Cambodia was offered by John Barron and Anthony Paul, who hypothesized that Khieu Samphan, driven by personal neuroses and sexual impotency, was the virtually "insane" architect of these policies. While conceding that the "fundamental program adopted was a collective creation," Barron and Paul speculated that:

. . . the origins of some of the more extreme policies may lie in the impotent ideologue Khieu Samphan. Transient impotence can be the result of many mundane causes, but numerous psychiatrists consider that chronic impotence, unless inflicted by physical factors, is the product of profound hostility. Certainly, Khieu Samphan, the sickly, bullied child, the friendless, tormented youth, the meek, persecuted man, had reason to be hostile. Perhaps some of the deathly hostility *Angka Loeu* was to visit upon the Cambodian people, such as the savage slaughter of women and children as well as men, the ferocious assault on the Khmer traditions of love, courtship and family, the draconian punishment of extra marital sex was spawned by the hostility of the unloved and unloving Khieu. (Barron and Paul 1977:60–61)

Yet neither does this explanation seem to fit. The killing appears to have been too systematic and coordinated to have simply been the result of the mental excesses of one man. Moreover, we now know what Barron and Paul did not know when they wrote this passage—that Khieu Samphan was not the top man in the organization and did not give the final orders for the implementation of these programs of violence and terror.

Lacouture offered a third hypothesis—namely, that Cambodia was experiencing a "genuine peasant revolution" in which the long-oppressed rural poor rose up against their "oppressors." The violence that ensued, he argued, was only the natural reaction to generations of exploitation. But this thesis, too, falls short of satisfaction. Cambodia's peasantry has a long history of ownership of its own land, as was pointed out by Jean Delvert in his classic study of rural landholdings in Cambodia (Delvert 1961). Moreover, the history of the Pol Pot regime has been one of peasant resistance to the imposed changes, rather than active or even grudging support and involvement.

It is possible that all efforts to date to supply a satisfactory explanation of what occcured in Democratic Kampuchea have fallen short because answers have largely been sought by looking inside Cambodia, endeavoring to find some factors in the background of the Pol Pot leadership and their experience as wartime revolutionaries, or in the political and social makeup of traditional Cambodia that could account for the radical nature of the Communist revolution.

While some of these factors may offer help, it may be that the best overall explanation of what happened in Cambodia is not to be found inside the country, but rather from without.

Radical Left-wing Chinese Communist Underpinnings of Cambodian Communism

There is strong evidence that the radical Communist programs in Cambodia were derived almost in toto from left-wing Chinese communism and that, in particular, they were patterned after Mao Zedong's Great Leap Forward and the Cultural Revolution. Pol Pot's policies, it may be argued, were designed to achieve transistion to a "pure Communist" society in the shortest possible time frame by utilizing violence, terror, and purges to overcome all impediments, obstacles, and inhibitions (that is, the contradictions that were enumerated at the end of Chapter 6).[1]

Almost every element of the radical Cambodian revolution has an antecedent in Mao's China. Moreover, it appears that the terror and purges that took place in Cambodia were utilized to ensure that the elements which prevented "success" in achieving the transition to pure communism in China would be successfully overcome in Democratic Kampuchea.

Transition and contradiction thus may be two key concepts that go far in explaining what happened in Cambodia. Both the Soviet Union and the People's Republic of China, it could be argued, have thus far failed to make the final transition to pure communism, because of a number of internal stumbling blocks, such as the peasants' desire to retain individual plots; the emergence of a new "intellectual class" within the Communist Party; and the difficulty of communizing the cities. Cambodia's communist leaders sought to overcome, by force and fear, these "contradictions" that kept their ideological patrons from reaching this final plateau.

There is significant evidence establishing this connection to Chinese communist ideology and the thesis that Pol Pot was embarked on an effort to make the transistion to pure communism as rapidly as possible. At a press conference in Beijing in late 1977, Pol Pot himself publicly acknowleged an early link between the development of the Cambodian Communist Party's line and the thought of Mao. Pol Pot revealed that shortly after his return from France, "We set up a committee in 1957 to formulate the line and policies of the party" (FBIS I, October 3, 1977:A20–21). This at a time when the Pracheachon Party (as the Communist Party was then known) was still more concerned with winning seats in the new National Assembly then fighting a guerrilla war in the countryside. According to Pol Pot, the committee decided that

. . . the parliamentary road will get nowhere. We also learned from the experience of the world revolution and in particular *Comrade Mao Tse-tung's works and the*

---

[1] See the conclusion of Chapter 6 by Kenneth Quinn.—ED.

experience of the Chinese revolution played an important role at that time. After summing up the concrete experiences of the world revolution, particulary under the guidance of Comrade Mao Tse-tung's works, we have found a road conforming with the concrete conditions and social conditions in our country. Therefore, the committee for formulating our Party's line has worked out a program concerning the Party line and submitted it to the first Party Congress held on September 30, 1960 for examination and adoption." (FBIS I, Oct. 3, 1977:A20–21; emphasis added)

While it does not indicate specific programs that the party was advocating, Pol Pot's 1977 statement would seem clearly to indicate that in 1957, as Mao was implementing the Great Leap, his thoughts and ideas were also having a direct and significant impact on the development of Cambodian communist ideology.

Pol Pot acknowledged the key role of Mao's thought in those early years as well as later in other public statements. Addressing a banquet hosted by the central committee of the Chinese Communist Party in the fall of 1977, he said: "In the concrete revolutionary struggle of our country, we have creatively and successfully applied Mao Tse-tung's thought—from the time we had only empty hands to April 17, 1975 . . ." (FBIS I, September 29, 1977:A19).

Further evidence of this Chinese influence is offered by Prince Sihanouk, who described Pol Pot and his senior advisors as "intellectuals (with) a passionate love for the People's Republic of China and a boundless admiration for Chinese Communism in its most extreme and terrible form (the Cultural Revolution)" (Sihanouk 1980:7). Ith Sarin, who spent five months with the Khmer Rouge in 1972, confirmed this. "Most of the higher cadres of the Party are pro-Chinese socialists" (Carney 1977:39).

Sihanouk recounted two incidents that he believed revealed the philosophical basis of the Khmer communist programs. The first came in Beijing in 1975 when he and other Khmer Rouge leaders visited Zhou Enlai in his hospital room. Zhou advised Khieu Samphan and Ieng Thirith not to try to achieve total Communism in one giant step, emphasizing, rather, the need to move "step by step" toward socialism. Zhou told them, Sihanouk said, that China itself had suffered devastating setbacks by trying to move too quickly into pure Communism. Zhou told the Khmer Rouge leaders: "Don't follow the bad example of our great leap forward. Take things slowly: that is the best way to guide Kampuchea and its people to growth, prosperity and happiness." Sihanouk said that Khieu Samphan and Ieng Thirith did not reply or argue with Zhou but that from the looks on their faces it was clear they would ignore his counsel. The second incident followed shortly thereafter:

Not long after we got back to Phnom Penh, Khieu Samphan and Son Sen told me their Kampuchea was going to show the world that pure Communism could indeed be achieved in one fell swoop. This was no doubt their indirect reply to Zhou Enlai. "Our Country's place in history will be assured," they said, "we will be the first nation to create a completely Communist society without wasting time on intermediate steps." (Sihanouk 1980:86)

In his eulogy, after Mao's death, Pol Pot also indicated his close affinity to Mao's teachings. He described Mao as "the most eminent teacher . . . since Marx, Engels, Lenin and Stalin." In an earlier message, Pol Pot praised the Cultural Revolution against the "counter-revolutionary headquarters of Liu Shao-ch'i [Liu Shaoqi] and Deng Xiaoping" (*Far Eastern Economic Review* 1976).

Further evidence came a year later, in 1977, when Pol Pot journeyed to Beijing, just after formally announcing that Cambodia was in fact being ruled by a communist party. From his arrival on, all of the actions and words exchanged between the Cambodian visitor and his Chinese hosts indicated a special and close relationship. As one observer noted: "In a rare show of warmth, a top trio of the Peking leadership, Chairman Hua Kuo-feng and Vice Premiers Teng Hsiao-ping [Deng Xiaoping] and Li Hsien-nien, turned up at the airport to receive Pol Pot and Vice-Premiers Ieng Sary and Vorn Vet. The next five days of their stay were also marked by signs of unusual comraderie and solidarity in which Peking repeatedly affirmed that the friendship with Cambodia is 'Unbreakable'—a description so far reserved for Albania in the heady days of that relationship" (Chanda 1977).

Other statements during the visit further confirmed the influence of Mao and radical left-wing Chinese ideology on Pol Pot and his followers. For example, in his welcoming speech at a banquet, Chairman Hua complimented his Cambodian guests for being equally good in "destroying the old world" as in building the new, and complimented them on "smashing the disruptive schemes of enemies at home and abroad." A *People's Daily* editorial repeated this congratulatory theme in noting that the Cambodians had overcome "the conspiratorial activities of enemies both at home and abroad" (Chanda 1977). These statements were seen by some observers as an indication of an inner party struggle where the "opponents of Pol Pot's overtly pro Mao Tse-tung line might have been defeated" (Chanda 1977). They were almost certainly references as well to the attempt on Pol's life in 1976 and his subsequent purge of those implicated in the plot.

Still more evidence linking him to Maoist thought emerged during Pol's 1977 visit to China. In response to Hua's speech, Pol Pot termed Mao's thought a "brilliant beacon" for revolutionaries and "the most precious aid" that was provided by China. It was also revealed that Pol Pot had secretly visited Mao in Beijing in June 1975, just two months after the capture of Phnom Penh (Chanda 1977).

Still additional indications of the link between the Cambodian communist revolution and Mao's thought came in a 1978 Phnom Penh radio commentary following the June 1978 visit of Deputy Prime Minister Ieng Sary to Beijing. In it, Ieng Sary was quoted as saying that "China and Kampuchea are comrades-in-arms sharing weal and woe." The commentary concluded by stating that "The great Kampuchean-Chinese fraternal, revolutionary friendship and militant solidarity . . . are based on Marxism, Leninism, and Mao Tse-tung thought . . ." (FBIS IV, June 22, 1978:H1).

Finally there were several private statements by Chinese officials to an American Congressional staffer that would tend to confirm a close philosophical and ideological link between Pol Pot and Mao's Cultural Revolution. Two representatives of the Chinese Marxist-Leninist Institute reportedly told this Congressional committee official that Pol Pot and his followers were "following the Gang of Four" and "implementing the Cultural Revolution" in Cambodia.[2] Apparently Mao was well pleased with what Pol Pot was able to achieve; upon Pol Pot's arrival in Beijing after the fall of Phnom Penh Mao reportedly told Pol Pot, "You have achieved in one stroke what we failed with all our masses."[3]

Mao also reportedly told Vietnamese Communist Party First Secretary Le Duan that his party ought to "learn from the Khmer Rouge how to carry out a revolution."

Mao's death and the subsequent attack on the "Gang of Four" led to a loss of Chinese support for Pol Pot's policies. In a 1979 meeting with a delegation of American governors, Deng Xiaoping said, "We don't agree with some of Pol Pot's policies. Frankly, some of those policies were unpopular."[4]

Earlier in 1979, when Pol Pot and Ieng Sary flew into Beijing after being deposed by the Vietnamese, they reportedly told Deng, "Our mistake was following the line of the Cultural Revolution and the Gang of Four."[5]

Whether Pol Pot and Ieng Sary were entirely sincere in that statement or just seeking to please the new power elite in China, their words confirm that in carrying out their radical revolution in Cambodia they were indeed using the Cultural Revolution as their model.

All of the above information when, combined with the fact of the relationship between the Cultural Revolution Group and the Phnom Penh branch of the Sino-Khmer Friendship Association and the numerous trips Pol Pot made to China during the period of the Cultural Revolution, provide

[2] The author obtained these quotes directly from a Congressional staffer who visited China often, speaks Mandarin, and has established contacts with the Chinese officials involved.

[3] Ibid.

[4] The author attended the meeting that took place in Beijing in Deng's office in late October 1979.

[5] Congressional staffer.

strong evidence of a direct and close ideological partnership between Pol Pot and Mao and the Cultural Revolution.[6]

Understanding what Mao sought to accomplish in the Great Leap and the Cultural Revolution illuminates Pol Pot's goals for Cambodia. Mao's dream—which became Pol Pot's—was to transform the peasant into a modern producer with a commitment to the collective good and the elimination of selfish individualism. Mao saw this revolution taking place in essentially three steps:

1. Destruction of the old rural elite and landlords through the land reform program;
2. Removal of the peasant attachment to individual plots of land and private property through the establishment of cooperatives;
3. Massive restructuring of the way work is carried out and rewarded, which came in the communization of the Great Leap (Schurmann 1966:xliii).

Mao felt this drastic change in Chinese agriculture was necessary because he believed that output would sooner or later reach its limits and stop expanding, although population would continue to grow. In his view, only by transforming the traditional system of work organization and placing each peasant into a "rationally designed work team" could Chinese society hope to meet its goal of feeding its masses (Schurmann 1966:471). In short, the commune aimed at becoming an agricultural factory with each proletarian worker carrying out a set mechanistic but efficient role. In order to accomplish this, Mao realized he had to uproot the peasant from his own land, his traditional kinship ties, and his established role in the village. Therefore, Mao sought to alter the peasants' traditional patterns of work, thought, and behavior (Schurmann 1966:24).

Mao at first seemed content to feel that his dream of a totally changed society could be attained gradually. For example, the General Line of the State introduced in 1952 provided for the completion of the socialist transformation over a period of 15 years within the framework of three "five year plans" (Hughes and Luard 1961:21)." The new Chinese constitution adopted on September 20, 1954, reinforced this notion: "From the founding of the People's Republic of China to the attainment of a socialist society is a period of transition. During this transition, the fundamental task of the state is to, step by step, bring about the socialist industrialization and . . . the socialist transformation of agriculture" (Hughes and Luard 1961:21).

This was changed dramatically by Khrushchev's secret speech to the Twentieth Soviet Communist Party Congress in 1956 and subsequent eco-

[6] For a full discussion of the involvement of key Khmer Rouge leaders in the Sino-Khmer Friendship Association and its links to the Cultural Revolution, see Leifer 1969, Smith 1968, and Quinn 1982:32–46.

nomic reforms. Mao was horrified to see that Khrushchev was halting the inexorable march toward complete socialist transformation that had been Stalin's life's work, in favor of increased short-term industrial and agricultural production:

In the final analysis, the question of training successors for the revolutionary cause of the proletariat is one of whether or not there will be people who can carry on the Marxist-Leninist Revolutionary cause started by the older generation of proletarian revolutionaries, whether or not the leadership of our Party and our state will remain in the hands of proletarian revolutionaries, whether or not our descendents will continue to march along the correct road laid down by Marxism-Leninism or, in other words, *whether or not we can successfully prevent the emergence of Khrushchev's revisionism in China. In short, it is an extremely important question, a matter of life and death for our Party and our country.* (Mao Tse-tung 1965:477–78, and MacFarquahr 1966:113; emphasis added)

Looking around him, Mao saw the seeds of "revisionism" everywhere in China. "Rich" and middle-level peasants were still present in large numbers in the villages despite the land-reform program, and they were more and more responding to individual production incentives. Moreover, a "new class" of educated managers was developing within the party itself, a new "conservative elite" that Mao feared would not seek to achieve the final transistion to socialism (Pye 1967:24). No longer could Mao feel secure that his followers would carry out his dream of full socialist transformation after his death. Haunted by the fear that almost forty years of revolutionary activity would be in vain, Mao immediately set out to shorten drastically the transition period and to attempt to achieve full socialism in one or two years. His vehicles to attain this goal were the Great Leap Forward and the Cultural Revolution (Karol 1967:28).

Many had understood the Great Leap Forward to mean a large increase in economic output and production or a great effort to make China into a modern industrialized society. The more precise meaning, rather, was that Mao wanted to make a major jump forward in the process of socialization. He wanted to skip over the long transition period and move immediately to a pure communist society.

Mao's view of this new socialist society was clearly set in 1958 when he began the Great Leap. All citizens would live in large production communes organized along military and industrial lines. No longer would the traditional village be the organizational framework in rural areas. In its place would be the commune, involving several thousand families and several "natural" villages. Peasants would not work their own individual plots of land, but instead would be part of production brigades assigned to do specific set jobs. Individuals would be assigned to work on the basis of their age and sex and not family or kinship ties. Private land holdings and most private property would be confiscated and living would be on a communal basis with common dining rooms and in some instances, segregated dormitories (Schurmann 1966:363–80). It is not without significance that this could also serve as a description of Cambodia in the period 1975–1978.

The Great Leap was marked by a number of other distinctive programs, many of which would also be emulated years later in Cambodia. In 1957, Mao initiated the *Hsiafang* movement in which millions of city people poured into the villages to work in the new communes (Schurmann 1966:465). Agricultural programs were characterized by an intense effort to build water conservation projects such as canals and dams, and by an emphasis on the collection and use of natural fertilizer (canal digging and dam construction were two of the most important emphases in Pol Pot's Cambodia). Imported technology and expertise were disdained in favor of traditional native approaches to problems—particularly in medicine, with the famous "barefoot doctors." Former "experts" from the cities were sent to the countryside to be reindoctrinated in the ways of the people. Factories, particularly those emphasizing local approaches to manufacturing using lo-cal materials, were established. These steps were almost paralleled eighteen years later by Pol Pot, although Mao never emptied cities the way Pol Pot did.

As we know now, the Great Leap was a great economic failure. Chinese agriculture was devastated and the economy nearly ruined. Until recently, the West has not known the full extent of the damage caused by Mao's ill-prepared, ill-timed attempted transformation of the agricultural production system. In the spring of 1981, however, a startling revelation was made by a Chinese economist from the People's Republic of China. Writing in the Chinese journal *Economic Management*, the economist stated that the death rate in China jumped from 10.8 per 1000 people in 1957 to 25.4 per 1000 in 1960 as a result of the famine in those years (*Des Moines Register* 1981). Although not referring to Mao by name, the article clearly indicated that the author was linking these results to the programs started during the Great Leap Forward. If these figures are correct, the famine and devastation caused by Mao's policies resulted in about ten million starvation deaths in 1960 alone and perhaps twenty million total during 1959–1962, the period considered affected by the upheaval in 1957–1958. The parallel with Cam-bodia in terms of large-scale deaths is so obvious as not to need restating.

Under heavy attack by the pragmatists and moderates in the party as a result of this debacle, Mao resigned from his position as Chairman of the Republic in December 1958. Undaunted, however, by this failure and still set on achieving his goal of a full transformation to socialism in China, Mao in 1962 began a new effort, which was to culminate in the Cultural Revo-lution. Using his position as chief theoretician of the party, Mao began slowly to pave the way to remove the obstacles he perceived had prevented him from achieving success in the Great Leap—the cultural structure of the country and the intellectuals and revisionists within his own party—thereby advancing his vision of a new society and a new Chinese citizen. According to a commentary in the *People's Daily*, "The proletarian Cultural Revolution is aimed not only at demolishing all the old ideology and culture and all the old customs and habits which, fostered by the exploiting classes, have poisoned the minds of the people for thousands of years, but also at creating and fostering among the masses an entirely new ideology and culture and entirely new customs and habits—those of the proletariat . . . This great task of transforming customs and habits is without any precedent in human history" (MacFarquheur 1966:123).

One other observer summarized the intent of the Cultural Revolution this way:

It is a thorough housecleaning, the fundamental aim of which is to wipe out the influence of the bourgeoisie, to destroy the old thought, old culture, old customs and old habits and to remove all those superstructures which were felt to be unsuitable to the foundation of the Socialist economy. It aims to eliminate possible restoration of the old economic system and the rise of revisionism, and to create and establish new thought, new culture, new customs and new habits; in short, to transform spiritual energy into material force by indoctrinating and mobilizing 750 million people for Socialist construction. Mao probably believes that the failure of the commune was due to the people's deep seated belief in traditional culture and thought. Thus, he plans to remove the obstacles so as to prepare a new political and social environment for another "leap." (Hsueh 1967:182)

By removing the obvious reference to China, this analysis could just as well have served as a description of Cambodia under Pol Pot in 1976.

To carry out the cultural revolution, Mao entrusted great authority to Zhen Boda and appointed him to head the "Cultural Revolution" group (also included were Mao's wife Chiang Ch'ing, Yao Wenyuan, Zhang Zhun Jiao, Gang Sheng, and Ji Benyou), an ad hoc body designed to overcome the resistance of the unwieldy government bureaucracy. It is possible that this powerful, unstructured committee was the prototype for the Cambodian Angkar—the mysterious "Organization" that directed the Cambodian revolution until the official emergence of the Communist Party in September 1977.

Several other elements of the Cultural Revolution were also replicated by the Pol Pot regime, lending further credence to the philosophical link between them.

The Critical Role Played by Youth. Mao formed the Red Guards and sent them to the universities, the government offices, the provinces, and even the villages and hamlets to propogate and implement his programs. In like manner, the Cambodian communist revolution drew upon extremely young cadres, often taken from the poorest sections of the country, who were then sent to replace older cadres who were viewed as settled in their ways and laden with vested interests in continuing the old system.

The Attack on Vested Interests. Following Mao's cry of "fight self-interest, establish the public interest," the Cultural Revolution group directed its attack on four groups in China that it believed were opposed to the revolution and interested in maintaining the status quo:

1. The majority of rural cadre who had reached accommodations with the peasants or were afraid of losing their positions;
2. Low-ranking officials whose loyalty was to their bosses;
3. Ordinary peasants with kinship ties or other ties to village leaders, which gave them a favored position;
4. Peasants with an economic stake in the status quo, such as the "rich peasants" who by 1962 were reemerging in the villages as the government's emphasis turned to increased production (Robinson 1971:16–17).

To be strong enough to stand up to the Soviet Union, the Cultural Revolution Group believed China must "adhere to the principles of strict self-reliance; weed out hidden revisionists and capitulationists within China; and vigilantly guard against ideological deviations and eliminate those responsible for undermining the domestic unity needed to oppose revisionism" (Gottlieb 1977:22).

To uproot these "opponents" of the revolution, the Chinese again turned to young cadres from distant places, who were then interjected into a commune, factory, or university. With no stake in the preservation of the status quo, they were uninhibited in their attacks on the institutional infrastructure.

Likewise, in Cambodia, as early as 1971, hitherto unknown young cadres were showing up in villages in southwest Cambodia with a mission to purge local cadres, particularly those considered loyal to Hanoi, and then to implement the tough new Pol Pot programs. It was these "outsiders," moreover, who in June 1973, led the way in establishing the new communes, which involved the systematic burning of all hamlets and villages and the forced relocation of thousands upon thousands of Khmer. The new communes were seemingly patterned after those in the Great Leap.

The purges of party cadres and the elimination of intellectuals, students, and persons connected to the former government by these Khmer Rouge cadres after 1975 would seem also to be rooted in the ideology espoused by the Cultural Revolution Group.

The Primacy of Politics. A third similarity between the Cambodian and Chinese revolutions was the preference both had for those who were "red" over those who were "expert" ("better red than well read"). Mao had actually revealed his antipathy for, and fear of, the intellectual elites during the Great Leap. His 1957 speech "On Contradictions" contained his analysis that Chinese society was comprised essentially of three elements: workers, peasants, and intellectuals (by which he meant those in the party and society who were educated professionals or had technical training). Mao saw the "contradiction" between the intellectuals and the peasants as one of the key stumbling blocks to achieving full socialism. Mao's great fear was that these "experts" were too conservative—too interested in maintaining their own elevated place in society (Schurmann 1966:92).

The problem in China was that this new elite had emerged prior to the completion of the socialist transformation and thus had no stake in seeing the process completed—and indeed were interested in the maintenance of the *status quo*.

The Chinese antirightist campaign of 1957 was thus aimed at jerking these intellectuals from their elite status and replacing them with peasants with greater political loyalty to the party's ideology. In 1958, just as would occur later in the Cultural Revolution, administrators, managers, and technicians were attacked for their lack of revolutionary zeal. Their punishment was to be sent to the countryside to be indoctrinated into the rigors of communal life. Their places were to be filled by peasants trained at "worker-peasant universities" and inculcated with the notion that they could master the intricacies of technology by virtue of their political ardor (Schurmann 1966:97–98).

The aim in Pol Pot's Cambodia was to avoid this problem by achieving the complete socialist transformation prior to the emergence of this new elite. Thus the need for speed and the total break with the past. Once the new socialist order was established, the new elite that emerged would have a stake in preserving the new system. Just as in China, the desired end result of the Cambodian revolution was to break down these "artificial" class distinctions and create a homogeneous population. Pol Pot waged an anti-intellectual campaign in 1976 and 1977 rivaling that in China, which extended fully throughout Khmer society. Persons with any education or a managerial background were singled out for harsh punishment or were subject to execution. In emulation of the Chinese, Pol Pot also allowed only "poor," usually semiliterate, peasants to participate in administrative and technological functions—a policy that greatly accelerated the crumbling of the Cambodian economy.

Elimination of Individual Incentives. Still another similarity between Mao's and Pol Pot's revolution, was the elimination of individual incentives and in some cases the use of money. Mao saw a sharp contradiction in Chinese society between individualism and collectivism. He believed that individual incentives, favored by the economic pragmatists like Deng Xiaoping and Zhen Yun, were leading to "vested-interestism" and away from socialism (Schurmann 1966:97). Social mobilization, Mao felt, could better motivate people to do work, and during the Great Leap Forward and the Cultural Revolution there was movement toward collective rewards. In 1958, in some areas, wages were done away with and workers were paid with part of their work product. Later, the Cultural Revolution saw the initiation of the *Ta Chai* system whereby collectives would accrue work points rather than monetary profits, as well as a system of red flag awards to communes making special economic achievements.

Again emulating their ideological patrons, Pol Pot and his comrades sought to eliminate all individuality within their new economic system. The total destruction of the money economy, along with the establishment of a completely communal work organization meant that a Cambodian now had no way of accruing any type of material wealth or even being rewarded for good or extra work. A "red flag honor program" was established in Cambodia, but in order to ensure complete compliance and to achieve top performance from the peasants, Pol Pot added terror and the threat of violence (FBIS IV, July 19, 1977:H2).

Anti-City, Anti-Western Self-Reliance. At the heart of Mao's espousal of self-reliance during the Cultural Revolution was his view that Asians could reach inside themselves to find a path to modernization and development. Implicit in this was the renunciation of the views held by Marx, Lenin, Liu Shaoqi, and others that Asia could develop only by learning from Europe (Schurmann 1966:26–38).

Anti-urban bias was exhibited in other ways in China during both the Great Leap and the Cultural Revolution through the programs to send millions of people back to the countryside. During the Great Leap, the cities had proved themselves to be inhospitable to the communal process since they were structured on the basis of residence rather than production.

Pol Pot rigorously pursued all three policies. The anti-Western aspect of his regime could be found in the rejection of virtually all foreign influences and technology. Cities were viewed as unproductive centers created by "imperialists" and not part of the indigenous Khmer society he wished to recreate. As such, they were all emptied in a few days time, with all of the population sent to the countryside where they could be placed in production brigades.

Many of the public statements by Democratic Kampuchean officials are laden with anti-Western emphasis and filled with slogans exhorting self-reliance. In sharp contrast to their neighbors in Hanoi, who were receiving aid from many foreign sources, Pol Pot and his followers rejected outside assistance, except from China and North Korea.

There were numerous other similarities between the Cultural Revolution and Pol Pot's Cambodia: a similarity in foreign policy; the same restrictive rules on the age of marriage and the relationship between the sexes; the same categorization and emphasis on poor and lower-middle-class peasants as the basis for the new society; the same disdain for long-haired students and those affecting Western dress; and even the involvement of the wives of Pol Pot, Ieng Sary, and Son Sen (Khieu Ponn, Ieng Thirith, and Yun Yat, respectively) who, while not as powerful or instrumental as Chiang Ch'ing or Ye Zhun (Lin Piao's wife), clearly played important roles in the revolutionary organization.

At the same time, it is obvious that the Cultural Revolution was distinctly different from the Cambodian revolution in several critical ways. For example, even though large numbers of people were forced back to the countryside, Chinese cities were never totally emptied the way Cambodian cities were. Moreover, China never experienced the scale and scope of violence and death that occurred under Pol Pot. Yet these differences may still indicate the philosophical connection between Mao and Pol Pot. It may be argued that, since Pol Pot was present in China during at least part of the Cultural Revolution, he had the opportunity to see why it did not "succeed." In formulating his own plans for Cambodia, he may have added elements necessary to ensure success: the emptying of the cities and more generalized use of force and violence.

The reasons why the full transition to pure communism was not achieved in China would have been evident to Pol Pot, particularly during his trips to China in the wake of the Great Leap Forward and the advent of the Cultural Revolution:

the near impossibility of establishing communes in the cities;
the strong opposition of the peasants to losing their individual plots of land;
the tendency to rely on the profit motive and the rich peasants to spur agricultural production at the expense of emphasizing social change;
the emergence of a new "intellectual" (that is, educated) class within the party itself, which having attained status by virtue of its technical expertise became satisfied with the status quo and drifted toward "revisionism";
the dissidence of families or members of the old ruling class;
the loss of energy and momentum and the emergence of new vested interests wherever the transition followed a gradual process.

In China, the Cultural Revolution failed in part because of the opposition of key party leaders, the enduring strength of Chinese social and economic institutions, and the sheer size of the country, which made control and implementation of the revolutionary process in the provinces extremely difficult.

Much smaller Cambodia, with a more delicate social structure and with no Zhou Enlai or Deng Xiaoping to provide a moderating influence, provided fewer obstacles to Pol Pot's implementation of the Maoist strategy. Still, Pol Pot was faced with opposition to his plan from virtually every level of Cambodian society: the Lon Nol government in Phnom Penh; noncommunist allies in his coalition against Lon Nol; the Khmer Hanoi; Prince Sihanouk; urban dwellers; the peasants; and eventually cadres from within his own party.

To overcome each of these obstacles, Pol Pot devised a plan to eliminate every locus of resistance, achieve the acquiesence of the peasantry, and completely change Cambodian society within the fastest time possible. He did so by adding two factors that were absent in China—the use of violence on an unprecedented scale and totally emptying the cities. By taking these two extraordinary steps, Pol Pot seemed to believe he could succeed where the Cultural Revolution and the Great Leap Forward had failed.

The Roots of Violence

It is one thing to identify Pol Pot's model in revamping of Cambodian society. A separate question, however, is what ideological and cultural factors permitted, caused, or justified the extensive use of violence by the Khmer communists. Pol Pot, Ieng Sary, Khieu Samphan, and other Khmer communist leaders were, after all, men and women who had been exposed to many elements of liberal education. Moreover, they were products of a relatively tranquil, harmonious society that, despite their perceptions of it, was not beset by the social problems that existed in China, Russia, or even Vietnam. How then can the policies, by which hundreds of thousands of people were killed and millions forced to endure extreme hardships, be explained?

There is certainly no single answer to this quesiton, but a series of factors that led to the use of violence and then permitted it to escalate.

One factor in understanding the Khmer Rouge penchant for violence was the educational experience they received in France. There the Cambodian students were exposed to the basic tenets of communist philosophy and soon came to view social situations in terms of the exploitation of the workers and peasantry. It is clear from their written papers that several of the young Cambodian intellectuals came to view their country in a new light after spending several years at the University of Paris. Hou Yuon's doctoral dissertation, for example, described an oppressed and exploited Cambodian peasantry and recommended creation of "semi-social types of agricultural production cooperatives" (Hou Yuon 1955:145). Khieu Samphan's thesis prescribed a coordinated cooperative effort to uplift the rural poor (Khieu Samphan 1959). While neither came close to advocating the extreme violence they were eventually to put into effect years later, these papers provide strong evidence that their time in Paris started them on their radical course of thinking.

The second and related factor may have been the position of education and educators in Cambodia. Both Mao and Pol Pot started out as normal school teachers, and in both the Chinese and Cambodian Communist Parties a large portion of the early membership came from the teaching profession (Lewis 1964:114). Khieu Samphan, Son Sen, Khieu Thirith, and Ieng Sary all were secondary school teachers turned radical revolutionaries, as were numerous other members of the communist hierarchy. It is not unreasonable, therefore, to ask if there was something in their experience as educators and intellectuals that alienated them sufficiently to become radicalized.

The alienation of the intellectual class is not a new concept. In his introduction to Georges Sorel's "Reflections on Violence," Edward Shils wrote:

The modern intelligentsia in all countries except Great Britain have, ever since the 18th Century, been in various forms of opposition to the prevailing society and the authorities who rule it. Their opposition has derived from a feeling of being outside the existing society. They have felt little or no kinship with the rest of society: they have not felt themselves to be members of it in the sense of being guided by moral rules and standards which are shared by the other members of society. They have stressed their isolation from society. (Shils 1950:16–17)

Based upon their writings while students in Paris and their later actions while holding teaching positions in Cambodia, it may be argued that Pol Pot, Khieu Samphan, and others were so alienated from their society, so disturbed by the pervasive corruption they perceived and so motivated by their belief in the cause of liberation of "oppressed peasants," that they had not the least hesitation in destroying the existing order.

It is not known if any of the Khmer Rouge leaders read the works of Georges Sorel while studying in France, but if they did they may have found there the philosophical underpinnings for the violence they eventually perpetuated. Again quoting Shils:

With Pareto and Michels, Sorel argues that large-scale organization necessarily leads to the formation of a group of leaders, who will act only for self-aggrandizement and who will be prey to the enervation and corruption always produced by the exercise of power and opportunities for advantage . . . [Sorel] thus concluded *that violence and deception must be the only procedures which can be used to bring the actions of individuals into concert.* In the life of a society, there were for Sorel only two possibilities: one *decadence,* in which the ruling class of politicians and property owners, lacking in self-esteem, corrupted by the niggling procedures of the pursuit and exercise of office, and too cowardly to be violent, resorts to fraud and cunning to control a mass lost in hedonistic self-gratification and individualism; and the other *renascence,* in which the aspirants to rule or those already ruling, inflamed with enthusiasm, their minds on remote goals, caring nothing for the immediate consequences of any action but performing it because it is morally imperative. (Shils 1950:16–17; emphasis added)

Even though Sorel put forward his ideas half a century before young Pol Pot, Khieu Samphan, Hou Youn, and the others journeyed to France to study, both the description of decadent society and his suggestion that only violence could cure hedonistic individualism would have struck close to their own view of court politics and aristocratic society in Phnom Penh. Imbued with a sense of ethical rightness in their revulsion against what they saw as the injustices of Cambodian society, they then sought an appropriate response to try to change the situation. Here, too, Sorel provided a guiding philosophy—the establishment of a tightly knit group, separate from community and dedicated to achieving a more just society. The already alienated academic was thus Sorel's most logical revolutionary. But, as Shils points out, Sorel

. . . went even further in regarding political separation as the morally most appropriate form of social and politiical organization. Only where a group drew sharply defined boundary lines around itself could it lead a moral life. Only where it regarded itself as bound by no moral obligations to other sections of the population could it perform its moral duty. For moral duty entails, in substance, hostility towards those outside one's own group, not just hidden rancor and bitterness, but aggressiveness . . . [for Sorel] the very content of moral action lay for him in the aggressive affirmation of the group's integrity and solidarity against an outside group. Heroism and a sense of the sublime are the highest virtues . . . they raise the dignity of the individual and endow him with the pride which dignity requires. All attempts to reconcile differences between groups by compromise and negotiation, by the discovery of a common standard, through discussion or by joint renunciation were repugnant to Sorel and contrary to his ethical system. In his whole life—there is one common theme: *the highest good is the heroic (i.e. aggressive) action performed with a sense of impersonal consecration to the ends of a restricted, delimited group bound together in fervent solidarity and impelled by a passionate confidence in its ultimate triumph in some cataclysmic encounter.* (Emphasis added) Sorel's ethic is the ethic of the political sect living in the midst of a continuous crisis, with all the stress on purity and all the fear of contamination by the affairs of this world which mark the sect. It is the ethic of crisis, and it is of a piece with the expectation of an ever deepening crisis *which is resolved ultimately only by an apocalyptic transformation in which everything is totally changed.* (Shils 1950:14–15; emphasis added)

So much of what Sorel put forward in 1906 and 1908 aptly describes the way the Khmer Rouge conducted themselves seven decades later: the totally separate society they created for themselves within Angkar, their hatred for the "decadence" of the old society, and their fanatical sense of purity. All of this was clearly described by Ith Sarin, who spent nine months with the Khmer Rouge in 1972. The ideology and lifeways he described in his *Regrets for the Khmer Soul* mirror the theories of Georges Sorel:

The Organization continually guides them [the cadre] to try to get rid of "personal traits," individualistic aspects which they denounce as "reactionary traits," that in order to attain the highest, one must hold firm "an overall image" of the principle of "collectivity" and concentrate on the greater rather than on personal interest . . . All of these traits are regarded as opposed to the revolution, as traits of the oppressor class, traits of the reactionaries. (Ith Sarin 1977:47)

Another discipline of the Khmer Rouge [cadre] is keeping secrets. Members of the Bureaus must keep confidential their personal information . . . This is why each person must have a new name and must hide his former name . . . (Ith Sarin 1977:48).

So the picture that emerges is one of a small, totally dedicated group of intellectuals, alienated and driven by their perception of an unjust society, and possessing a belief that a new, just social system can be formed only by an enormous act of violence.

A third factor in explaining the brutality of Democratic Kampuchea may be exposure to Stalinist methods. It is important to remember that virtually the entire top leadership of the Cambodian communist movement came under the influence of the French Communist Party at a time when that party was adhering to an extremely hard line. Stalin was still the world communist leader in 1949 when Pol Pot arrived in France and when most of the Cambodian students were being inducted into the communist-controlled Khmer Student Association in Paris. Pol Pot and his fellow students "learned their socialism from the French Communist Party in its most Stalinist period" (Shawcross 1978a:25). Moreover, violence, terror, and secret police tactics were still being practiced in the Eastern bloc countries to which Pol Pot was exposed during his work with the International Youth Brigade and his visits to East Berlin and Yugoslavia in the early 1950s (Democratic Kampuchea 1978b).

While Pol Pot did not in his writings or speeches acknowledge any influence of Stalin in the formulation of policies for Democratic Kampuchea, there are enough similarities between Pol Pot's methods and those employed in the Soviet Union in the 1930s to suggest a relationship between them:

1. Both Stalin and Pol Pot moved with brutal swiftness in seeking to collectivize the rural agricultural sector (Dmytryshyn 1965:168; Dallin and Breslauer 1970:65–77). Stalin was committed to the simultaneous destruction of traditional authority, reintegration of the peasantry into one dominant type of organization, and economic exploitation (Dallin and Breslauer 1970:65). Pol Pot may have benefited from Cambodia's much smaller size as well as the lesson Stalin learned in 1930 when he was sharply criticized

and almost removed from office because of resistance to his collectivist policies.

2. The levels and scope of violence and terror during both the Stalinist peasant mobilization phase and the one in Cambodia were quite similar. Whole classes of people, including spouses and children, were marked for elimination in both. Between 1929 and 1936, the Kulaks "were exterminated wholesale with their families; whole regions suffered famines caused both by nature and the government . . . estimates [of] deaths [were put] at more than 10 million men, women and children" (Adams 1980). Pol Pot likewise followed a policy aimed at eliminating those who had been a part of the old society.

3. In both Cambodia and the Soviet Union, the number and type of persons who were viewed as potential members of the new society was sharply limited: ". . . whereas Maoist strategy defines outgroup . . . so narrrowly as to leave open the possibility of re-educating most class alien elements, the Stalinist is marked by a far narrower definition of the in group; those who can be trusted as, and those who can be made into 'good communists' " (Dallin and Breslauer 1970:7).

In this respect Pol Pot followed closer to the Stalinist model than to the Maoist, which held that the urban bourgeoisie and landowners could be transformed into useful members of society (Dallin and Breslauer 1970: 51). But there was a political price to pay for this more lenient Chinese approach: "The Chinese failed to eliminate potentially rival elites before embarking on its major mobilization tasks . . . Once the Maoist failed, in key spots within society there remained . . . alienated survivors whose counterparts elsewhere in the Communist world would have been purged" (Dallin and Breslauer 1970:79).

To ensure that these elements did not survive to challenge his authority, Pol Pot appears to have turned to the more encompassing Stalinist approach to eliminating potential dissidents and enemies.

4. A fourth similarity between Pol Pot's regime and that of Stalin was the extensive purges of top party cadres and the use of false confessions to justify political executions. During the Great Purge about two-thirds of the Communist Party of the Soviet Union's Central Committee "was liquidated: and about half the office *corps* was arrested" (Dallin and Breslauer 1970:29). One estimate put the number of party members "sent to the Gulag" in the millions, with about 1.4 million executed (Adams 1980). Within this process, Stalin made extensive use of false confessions and contrived conspiracy plots to justify these arrests and executions.

The party purges in Cambodia, particularly in late 1976 and 1977, show a remarkable resemblance to the Stalinist model. It should be recalled that many of those tortured and killed at the Tuol Sleng jail were party officials and cadres and that before execution each had to write and sign a confession.

Moreover, by 1978 Pol Pot's purges of senior cadres had been so extensive that policy decisions were essentially handled by "The Gang of Six" (Pol Pot, Ieng Sary, Son Sen, and their wives Khieu Ponnary, Ieng Thirith, and Yun Yat), with Southwestern Region Commander Ta Mok and Khieu Samphan in an auxilliary role.

What emerges is a Pol Pot exhibiting some of the more violent measures he may have learned in Europe in the early 1950s. There can be little doubt that Pol Pot and his followers were adherents of Maoist ideology, but it appears that early Soviet practices influenced their behavior regarding the use of violence. In short, Pol Pot was implementing Mao's plan with Stalin's methods.

THE IMPLEMENTATION OF VIOLENCE

Pol Pot, Khieu Samphan, and the handful of other Khmer students that studied in Paris could not carry out all of the executions and harsh practices by themselves, so a final question has to be asked about who it was that actually implemented these policies that cost so many people their lives.

The answer seems to be that the Khmer Rouge turned to the youngest members of the poorest levels of Cambodian society to recruit cadres who would willingly destroy the old society because they resented it and had little stake in it. In much the same way that Mao turned to youthful cadres and Red Guards in carrying out the Great Leap Forward and the Cultural Revolution, Pol Pot sought out those from the bottom rung of society— those who were so envious of persons with more wealth that they would willingly strike them down.

Pol Pot may have found such a group in the hill people and poor Khmer living in northeastern Cambodia.[7] In the 1960s, Pol's main base of operation was in this area and he, by his own admission, sought to exploit many of the grievances these people felt toward the central government. As Pol Pot himself said: "My backing base was in the regions of the national minorities, that is in the Northeast region. I know perfectly these national minorities. They were very miserable" (Democratic Kampuchea 1978:22–23). Pol Pot described them as ". . . completely illiterate people who did not have even the slightest idea of cities, automobiles and Parliament [but who] dared to fight under the guidance of The Party" (FBIS IV, September 27, 1977:H14).

The possibility of recruiting hill tribes of northeastern Cambodia was noted before 1970 by one observer who wrote: "The Cambodian Government is correct to be concerned about the possibility that Pathet Lao and Vietnamese forces are stoking the fires of resentment and antipathy among the hill tribes. But the elimination of genuine grounds for resentment seems the only sure way to avoid the current situation in which all indica-

---

[7] For a similar observation, see Chapter 5 by François Ponchaud.—ED.

tions suggest a readiness on the part of the tribal groups to respond to suggestions that they are underpriviledged and disadvantaged and, on occasion, to respond by the use of violence" (Osborne).

Gerard Brisse, in his introduction to Prince Sihanouk's book, *War and Hope*, added to this evidence by writing that the Khmer Rouge had been

. . . cleverly playing on old historical grudges of the minority population in Cambodia's high plateaus (the Khmer Loeus). This was a fairly nomadic population planting burnbeat fields (in Ratanakiri, Mondolkiri), or picking cardamom pods (in Pursat, Koh Kong, Kompong Speu, and Kampot). They envied the much more prosperous inhabitants of the plains (Khmer Kandal). The people of the high plateaus were much sought after, much worked on by special services of every variety; *they formed the pool from which the Khmer Rouge found its future cadres. They were uneducated cadres, used to moving around. Instructed in hatred, they behaved like brutes.* (Sihanouk 1980:xxix; emphasis added)

Sihanouk himself echoed this point by stating that "the most fanatic Khmer Rouge soldiers were from the mountain and forest regions." At another stage in the same volume, Sihanouk advanced three reasons why the Khmer Rouge were so successful in developing fierce soldiers and cadre:

The Method of Recruitment: Poor peasants, mountain people, the inhabitants of forest regions, and the most remote villages, those most "neglected" by the old regime, were exclusively recruited. To what end? Clever propaganda filled their hearts and minds with a seething, unquenchable hatred for the "upper classes": those who were well housed, clothed and fed; who could send their children to school, not needing them at home to help in the fields or tend the cattle or buffalo; who owned real and personal property, had servants, etc.; who could easily pay their taxes or who collected them; those who administered or governed—in a word, the "oppressors."

The Use of Children: Once they were enlisted in the revolutionary army, these children were separated from their families, removed from their home villages to Pol Pot's indoctrination camps. They began their military careers at the age of twelve. Taken in hand so young, these *Yotheas* (youth) were convinced before long that the Party was doing them the greatest of honors by naming them *Oppakar Phdach Kar Robas Pak*, literally, "the dictatorial instrument of the Party."

The School for Cruelty: . . . Pol Pot and Ieng Sary quite rightly thought that if they trained their young recruits on cruel games, they would end up as soldiers with a love of killing and consequently war. During the three years I spent with the Khmer Rouge under guard, (I saw those guarding) my "camp" constantly take pleasure in tormenting animals . . . The Khmer Rouge loved to make their victims suffer as much as possible. (Sihanouk 1980:27–30)

Later in his book, Sihanouk provided details of the kinds of cruelty practiced by those young cadres and how they got that way:

As early as the 1960s, Pol Pot, Ieng Sary, Son Sen and Khieu Samphan had made up their minds to eliminate any obstacles in their path toward total domination of

Kampuchea. Torture games became their principal training tool. Young recruits began "hardening their hearts and minds" by killing dogs, cats and other edible animals with clubs or bayonets. Even after their April 17, 1975 victory, the Khmer Rouge kept in practice with a game consisting of throwing animals into "the fires of hell," since they had no human victims handy.

These young cadre put their torture to work on humans as well, as Sihanouk explains:

Khmer Rouge atrocities in Thailand from 1975 through 1977, involving the innocent inhabitants of border villages, can be explained by the fact the *Yotheas* were *addicted to torture.* For years their chief entertainment had been the physical suffering of men and animals. (Sihanouk 1980:83–84; emphasis added).

[Simultaneously on the Vietnamese border] Khmer Rouge soldiers would rape a Vietnamese woman, then ram a stake or bayonet into her vagina. Pregnant women were cut open, their unborn babies yanked out and slapped against the dying mother's face. The *Yotheas* also enjoyed cutting the breasts off well endowed Vietnamese women. Vietnamese fishermen who fell into the hands of the Khmer Rouge were decapitated. (Sihanouk 1980:83–84)

Other evidence tends to support the thesis that the Khmer Rouge used very young, often illiterate cadres to carry out their programs. Peang Sophi, a Cambodian refugee who escaped to Thailand, described most of the Khmer Rouge cadres he had contact with as "real country people, from far away"— illiterate, out of touch, and ill at ease (Chandler, Kiernan, and Lim:3). To make his point, Sophi indicated that the cadres were so unused to even the most rudimentary aspects of modern life that "they were scared of anything in a bottle or tin can. Something in a tin can had made one of them sick, so they mistook a can of sardines, with a picture of a fish on it, for fish poison, and one of them asked a friend of mine to throw it out. I saw them eating toothpaste once, and as for reading, I remember them looking at documents upside down" (Chandler, Kiernan, and Lim:3).

A long-time European observer of Indochina echoed Peang Sophi's observation of the background of these Khmer Rouge cadres when he reported that refugees said "red guards [who guarded the new agricultural communes under Pol Pot] . . . are very low-level cadre, summarily indoctrinated; most of them come from the poorest, most backward regions . . . Incapable of carrying on a discussion with better-educated and more perceptive people, they tend to take to hitting rather than discussing. They envisage a physical liquidation of the 'class enemy' . . . The guards are, indeed, very conscious of the general hostility of the population, which they cannot manage except through terror" (Barre 1976).

Yean Sok, another refugee, described the *chlorbs*[8] (those who ensure se-

---

[8] *Chlorb* is also a term used to designate soldiers, militia, and defense forces at different levels of organization. The "old" population Sok mentions refers to those under Khmer Rouge control before April 17, 1975—those people were the most trusted by the Khmer Rouge.

curity) and their power this way: ". . . they have complete supremacy over people [in the village]: children, women, young girls and boys. Most of the chlorbs are themselves boys less than 15 years old and belonging to the 'old' population" (Yean Sok 1978).

Dith Pran, an employee of the *New York Times* in Cambodia who remained inside the country during the entire rule of Pol Pot, reinforced the contention that these young Khmer Rouge cadres were the most brutal. Sydney Schanberg, with whom Pran worked prior to the fall of Phnom Pen, reports,

> Pran says he was always most afraid of those Khmer Rouge soldiers who were between 12 and 15 years old; they seemed to be the most completely and savagely indoctrinated. "They took them very young and taught them nothing but discipline. Just take orders, no need for a reason. Their minds have nothing inside except discipline. They do not believe any religion or tradition except Khmer Rouge orders. That's why they killed their own people, even babies, like we might kill a mosquito. I believe they did not have any feelings about human life because they were taught only discipline." (Schanberg 1980)

Schanberg recounts that Dith Pran told of other ways in which the senior Khmer Rouge made use of the young cadres: "Children were encouraged, even trained, to spy and report on their parents for infractions of the rules. 'The Khmer Rouge were very clever', Pran says. 'They know that young children do not know how to lie or keep secrets as well as adults, so they always ask them for information. Informers, old and young, were everywhere; betrayal could be purchased for a kilo of rice' " (Schanberg 1980). To demonstrate just how much control the Khmer Rouge had over these youths, Schanberg tells more of Dith Pran's tale: "Sometimes Khmer Rouge youths were ordered to kill their teachers or even their own parents. Some carried out these acts without apparent qualm. Others were devastated. Pran remembers a case in his district in which a man was identified as an enemy of the commune and his son, a Khmer Rouge soldier, was told to execute him. He did so, but later alone, he put the rifle to his own head and killed himself" (Schanberg 1980).

All of the above information strongly suggests that Pol Pot and his highly educated followers in the Communist Party of Kampuchea relied on the youngest and least literate elements of Khmer Society to impose their programs and policies. Furthermore, these young cadres, as a result of strict indoctrination and discipline and a minimum stake in the existing society, were willing to use terror, violence, and execution to enforce their will and carry out the orders given them by their superiors.[9]

[9] For additional comments on the revolutionary dynamic involved in elevating those who formerly had no authority whatsoever to a position of life-or-death authority in the dictatorship of the proletariat, see Chapter 2 by Karl Jackson.—ED.

What thus emerges as the explanation for the terror and violence that swept Cambodia during the 1970s is that a small group of alienated intellectuals, enraged by their perception of a totally corrupt society and imbued with a Maoist plan to create a pure socialist order in the shortest possible time, recruited extremely young, poor, and envious cadres, instructed them in harsh and brutal methods learned from Stalinist mentors, and used them to destroy physically the cultural underpinnings of the Khmer civilization and to impose a new society through purges, executions, and violence.

9. Intellectual Origins of the Khmer Rouge

by Karl D. Jackson

Chapter 2 described Khmer Rouge ideology while neglecting its roots, portrayed its content without locating its intellectual origin. Among the questions raised about the Khmer revolutionaries are: Were they genuine communists? If they were genuine Marxist-Leninists, where did their ideas come from—Cambodia itself, Mao's China, Stalin's Russia, the France of the late 1950s and early 1960s, or an amalgam of all of these influences with genuinely indigenous influences?[1] Much of what follows concerning the roots of this radical ideology remains speculative because of the dearth of direct testimony from the founding ideologues themselves. One cannot, however, understand this century's most radical revolution unless one attempts, albeit tentatively, to trace the revolutionary ideology back to its source.

In the postcolonial era, regimes define themselves as socialist, or even Marxist-Leninist, although analysis of government policies and social patterns often does not substantiate these symbolic claims (Jowitt 1979). Pol Pot publicly revealed that Democratic Kampuchea was a communist country in late September 1977, and yet, repeatedly, Khmer Rouge leaders emphasized that their revolution was indigenous and followed no foreign model. Opponents within the communist movement around the world have tried to deny the Khmer Rouge their communist credentials by labeling Democratic Kampuchea as "rabidly fascist" and as a form of "medieval barbarity" (Vasilkov 1979:44–45). Even Cambodian observers have questioned whether the ideas of Khieu Samphan had anything "to do with socialism or communism" and portrayed him as driven by extreme nationalism bordering on xenophobia (see Boun Sokha 1979:218).

From the discussion of Khmer Rouge ideology in Chapters 2 and 8, it should be evident that the Cambodian revolutionaries were communists. They were communists of a peculiar sort, however, a post-Leninist amalgam of nostrums of the left, a union derived from sources previously thought to be incompatible, namely Mao and Stalin, Frantz Fanon and Samir Amin, as well as indigenous Cambodian sources.

Model Leninist regimes emphasize ideological correctness and collective leadership as an ideal, rather than the cult of personality.[2] Part of the rela-

---

[1] See Chapter 8 by Kenneth Quinn, who also attempts to trace the intellectual heritage of the Khmer Rouge.

[2] The generalizations about Leninist regimes depend heavily on the work of Kenneth Jowitt (see Jowitt 1978, 1979).

tive stability of communist regimes stems from the enhanced integrative role played by shared ideology, whereas the political integration of many noncommunist authoritarian states in the Third World is largely a function of the personal, inherently ephemeral, authority of a paramount leader. The Khmer Rouge partially adhered to the model of collective leadership. The movement was never wholly dominated by a single figure, and the charismatic appeal of Sihanouk was rapidly jettisoned in early 1976. Pol Pot may have lost effective political power between October 1976 and April 1977; in the interim, Nuon Chea served as acting prime minister and Khieu Samphan may have held the real power (see Boun Sokha 1979:216–21). Furthermore, when international political pressures mounted, in December 1979, Pol Pot was formally replaced by Khieu Samphan.

Finally, as an underground movement before 1975, Khmer Rouge leaders adopted noms de guerre, making it difficult even to identify the top leaders. Even after 1975, these pseudonyms continued to be used, and in the absence of mass media, refugees escaping to Thailand and Vietnam before 1977 could not identify the names and faces of world-famous personages such as Pol Pot, Ieng Sary, and Khieu Samphan. Angkar, the revolutionary organization, was inherently faceless, and its leadership was collective rather than personalistic. An overriding set of ideological goals rather than a single leading personality set the course followed by Democratic Kampuchea. This image of an anonymous collective leadership must be modified, however, because the Pol Pot clique also followed Asia's age-old tradition of concentrating power within a small number of families through intermarriage.[3] Pol Pot's foreign minister, Ieng Sary, was also his brother-in-law, and their respective wives occupied powerful positions in their own right; Pol Pot's spouse, Khieu Pennary, was chair of the association of democratic women during the war against Lon Nol, while her sister was minister of social affairs in Pol Pot's government. The minister of defense, Son Sen, was also related to Pol Pot, and his wife, Yun Yat, became the minister of culture and education (see Eads 1977). In essence, the concept of collective leadership was infused into the tradition of Khmer family power. Rivals within the communist movement (as well as earlier competitors from the deposed Lon Nol regime) were tortured and executed in large numbers along with their spouses, indicating the degree to which the Khmer leadership perceived power as flowing along family lines; to destroy an important political opponent it apparently was perceived as necessary to root out the entire family (see David Hawk's photo essay in Chapter 7).

If revolutionary regimes characteristically utilize violence to enhance systematic social and political transformation, no one has outdone the

[3] See Ben Kiernan for a description of the struggle among factions within the communist movement. Kiernan indicates that a cult of personality may have been growing in 1978 when the Vietnamese army extinguished the Pol Pot government (Kiernan and Boua 1982:227–317).

Khmer Rouge.[4] Within days of their victory, they altered the entire organization of the country. Cities were emptied, villages were moved, and
whole social categories began to be exterminated. Obviously, noncommunist regimes have also used violence on a large scale. The defining element
is not violence alone but the goals for which violence is used, for example,
collectivizing agriculture and establishing the dictatorship of the proletariat.

A third characteristic feature of communist governments is the political
and social mobilization of the entire society. Most noncommunist, authoritarian regimes in the Third World remain content with being quietly
obeyed by their preparticipatory citizenry, whereas communist states seek
to mobilize all sectors of society through party organization, political education, and the influence of the state-controlled mass media (see Inkeles
1969). In the matter of social and political mobilization the Pol Pot regime
deviated from standard Leninist practice. Khmer Rouge policies fostered
far-reaching social mobilization by collectivizing production, abolishing private property, and completely reorganizing traditional villages; however,
political mobilization was far less evident in Kampuchea than in neighboring Vietnam. According to refugees, political indoctrination sessions were
infrequent and irregular, and when conducted they were led by such unso-
phisticated cadres that their effect was certain to be negligible. The most
striking Khmer Rouge deviation from the Leninist tradition was the exces-
sive reliance on raw physical coercion in preference to ideological persuasion. While they sought social mobilization through organizational transformation of the entire society, they did not expend much energy on using
the party, the schools, or the mass media to inculcate revolutionary values.
Largely absent were the mass rallies, banners, heroic photos of the leader,
and blanket mass media coverage that have characterized communist regimes in other parts of the world (see Pool 1963). Instead, there was a steady

---

[4] The Third Reich's policies prove that Marxist regimes hold no monopoly on the utilization
of violence to achieve rapid social change. However, collectivization in the Soviet Union, the
antilandlord campaign in China, and the Cultural Revolution epitomize the intentional, systematic use of violence to achieve revolutionary ends. Collectivization, with its attendant violence and resistance, is the standard rural institutional arrangement sought by communist
regimes everywhere (Dallin and Breslauer 1970:57–80). The principal reasons for adopting
such an economically dubious form of agricultural organization are political and social; collectivization is meant to replace traditional objects of peasant loyalty (the extended family and
the corporate village) with new loyalty objects (the collective and the organs of the one-party
state).

Although Vietnam was more pragmatic, it was nonetheless quite Leninist in its use of violence or the threat of violence to achieve political and social transformation (see Desbarats and
Jackson 1985). The Vietnamese leadership moved slowly toward socialization of the economy
until March 1978, when all businesses were nationalized and the expulsion of the Vietnamese
and Chinese began. In spite of the relatively more leisurely pace, Vietnamese communists
executed many of their opponents, imprisoned tens of thousands, forced a million citizens to
endure one or another form of reeducation, sent potential opponents to the New Economic
Zones, and created police-state conditions that led more than one million people to flee the
country.

stream of executions for even the most minor infractions, such as tardiness, complaining about the food, premarital sex, questioning the wisdom of work plans, or criticizing the government (see refugee interviews in U.S. Department of State 1978).

Leninist regimes, by definition, emphasize class analysis as the primary means for understanding and organizing society. The working class and particularly the industrial proletariat are the premier socioeconomic grouping. The Khmer Rouge elite certainly perceived Cambodian society through the lens of class analysis, albeit one that Lenin might not have recognized. The magnetic attraction of class analysis for the Paris-educated Khmer Rouge elite is indicated by the creation of a myth of massive class division at the rural level, even though most anthropologists and other observers found an utter absence of rural class distinctions. The fact that the Khmer Rouge sought to eliminate many skilled laborers inherited from the Lon Nol era and emptied the cities indicates a fundamental antipathy for the very urban proletariat in whose name most Leninist parties frame their policies and rationalize their monopoly of power. The Khmer Rouge emphasized the interests of the poor peasants and eliminated existing factory workers, who were regarded as an aristocracy of labor, an artifact of the superficial industrialization promoted by Cambodia's involvement in the international capitalist system.

Whether one looks at their extreme reliance on violence, family-oriented collective leadership, or the denial of the rights of the industrial proletariat, the Khmer Rouge seem to deviate sharply from standard Leninist practices. This is because Pol Pot's Cambodia was not a copy of any single philosophical system, be it Mao's, Stalin's, Fanon's, or Amin's. Instead this post-Leninist movement drew eclectically from all of these sources.

It is clear that Mao's Great Leap Forward and Great Proletarian Revolution supplied many Khmer Rouge concepts: Cambodia's great-leap-forward rhetoric; the forced movement of people from the cities; large communes, communal dining halls, and nurseries; labor surpluses that were expected to produce massive production gains; the emphasis on rice and irrigation; the attention to basic manufacturing in each commune; the desire to abolish personal interest as a prime motive for human behavior; the puritanical reaction against bourgeois consumerism; the primacy of willpower over weapons and machines; the superiority of common sense over academic and technical learning; the overwhelming power of heroic labor; and manual labor as a means of self-rectification.[5]

Regardless of these similarities, it is patently obvious that Maoism in China was never carried to the extremes reached in Democratic Kampuchea. Mao never emptied Beijing, never sought to liquidate all officials of the old

---

[5] For an affirmation of Khmer Rouge devotion to Chairman Mao, see the eulogies following his death (FBIS IV, September 20, 1976:H1–10).

regime, never elevated bloodshed to a national ritual, and never engaged in simultaneous military conflicts with all bordering nations.

Although Maoist goals guided many of Democratic Kampuchea's economic and social transformation schemes, other intellectual antecedents were responsible for the uniquely extreme character of the Cambodian revolution. In a 1980 interview Khieu Samphan was asked: "What made you a revolutionary?" He replied,

This dates to my time as a student in Paris where I was in the same situation as many students of our country. We debated the future of our people and ways of realizing our goals such as national independence, economic progress, and prosperity for everybody. Already at that time all my activities had been aimed at the fulfillment of these ideals. My studies as well as my experiences convinced me that the only way of implementing our ideals in general, and of building up our backward agriculture in particular, is socialism. *Thus, I became a communist.* I did so out of objective conviction and not out of daydreaming. After our victory of April 1975 we hoped to be able to put our ideals into practice. (Pilz 1980; emphasis added)

Khieu Samphan's Paris connection certainly included the early writings of Samir Amin and probably at a later date the writing of Frantz Fanon. Samir Amin is a well-known, French-educated Marxist theorist of economic development (see Amin 1974, 1976, 1977). The most important citation in the bibliography of Khieu Samphan's dissertation is to Amin's 1957 dissertation on the structural effects of international integration on precapitalist economies. Amin's work is the probable source of many of Khieu Samphan's ideas about the pernicious effects of integrating Cambodia's precapitalist economy into the international economic system and the wholesome effects of partial autarky. Amin's later works echo many of the same themes found both in Khieu Samphan's early writing and in the policies of Democratic Kampuchea:

. . . the principal contradiction of the capitalist system tends to be between monopoly capital and the over-exploited masses of the periphery. (Amin 1977:109).

In the underdeveloped countries the traditional economic system has been gradually destroyed by its integration into the world capitalist system. The handicrafts have almost disappeared due to the competition of manufactured goods, and the system of agricultural production has deteriorated due to external pressures which have forced it to adjust to the requirements of the world market. (Amin 1977:163)

. . . underdevelopment results from development in the center, the center's domination of the periphery—destruction of handicrafts, dominant role of agriculture—and, at the same time, from a belated and inadequate industrialization based on technological and consumption models borrowed from the advanced world which therefore cannot produce work for the majority of the producers it "marginalizes." (Amin 1977:164)

In addition, Amin labels the Soviet model a Western model because it, like its capitalist counterpart, gives too much emphasis to mass consumerism. Amin praises the Chinese model because it has rejected capitalism's "models of consumption and labor organization" (Amin 1977:90). Amin sees the import substituting economies of the Third World as a bogus form of development, denounces their workers as a labor aristocracy, and describes the services sector as "parasitic" (Amin 1977:131). He manifests the same cultural alienation from Westernization as the Khmer Rouge leaders (see Amin 1977:101, 151–52).

In a short chapter, evidently written in late 1975 or early 1976, Amin discusses the Cambodian revolution in glowing terms that duplicate in some ways Khmer Rouge analyses of their revolution. Amin describes the revolution as an ideal model for Africa and praises the Khmer Rouge as "better Marxists" (1977:152) than the Vietnamese and Chinese. Amin supplies an intellectual justification for Khmer Rouge policies directed against those who were connected in any way with the international economy—the businessmen, factory workers, plantation owners, and peasants producing for the international market (Amin 1980:149): "The revolutionary experience of Cambodia demonstrates a correct assessment of the hierarchy of contradictions specific to that type of society. The principal contradiction here is between the peasantry as a whole and the capital which dominates it—symbolized by the town" (Amin 1977:150).

For Amin and the Khmer Rouge, society is divided neatly between those associated with international capitalism in the towns and the long-suffering rural peasants whose energies would be liberated if they were only freed to develop spontaneously; that is, if they were freed from contact and domination by the forces of international capitalism.

Samir Amin provides only a part of the French connection. The intellectual ancestry of the Khmer Rouge most probably included Frantz Fanon, the French-educated apostle of violent revolution. Even though we cannot prove from dissertation footnotes that the Khmer Rouge leaders read Fanon during or after their student days in Paris, Khmer Rouge practices of the 1970s are foreshadowed by Fanon's writings of the 1960s.

The unrelenting rage (exercised against all who had been associated with either Lon Nol or Sihanouk), the desire for complete and total revolution, and the romanticization of wholesale violence are all prominent in Fanon's writing. Furthermore, he emphasizes that the primary contradiction in colonial and postcolonial society is between working peasants and all other social classes. Fanon, like the Khmer Rouge, is antiproletarian and anti-intellectual as well as being antibourgeois and opposed to nationalist politicians.[6] Just like the Khmer Rouge, Fanon uses geographic location as a most important criterion for identifying class enemies (see Jowitt 1978:20–21).

---

[6] Fanon, in turn, is related to an older apostle of apocalyptic violence, Georges Sorel. The

Frantz Fanon's *The Wretched of the Earth* is replete with passages that give the impression of having been drawn from either official pronouncements or a daily operating manual of Democratic Kampuchea:

. . . decolonization is always a violent phenomenon. . . . To tell the truth, the proof of success lies in a whole structure being changed from the bottom up. (Fanon 1963:35)

To break up the colonial world does not mean that after the frontiers have been abolished lines of communication will be set up between the two zones [of the colonizers and the colonized]. The destruction of the colonial world is *no more and no less than the abolition of one zone, its burial in the depths of the earth or its expulsion from the country.* (Fanon 1963:41; emphasis added)

. . . the native can see clearly and immediately if decolonization has come to pass or not, for *his minimum demands are simply that the last shall be first.* (Fanon 1963:46; emphasis added)

. . . *the same know-all, smart, wily intellectuals. Spoilt children of yesterday's colonialism* and of today's national governments, *they organize the loot of whatever national resources exist.* (Fanon 1963:48; emphasis added)

It cannot be too strongly stressed that in the colonial territories the proletariat is the nucleus of the colonized population which *has been most pampered by the colonial regime.* The embryonic proletariat of the towns is in a comparatively privileged position. In capitalist countries the working class has everything to lose; . . . it includes tram conductors, taxi drivers, miners, dockers, interpreters, nurses, and so on. It is these elements which constitute the most faithful followers of the nationalist parties, and who because of the privileged place which they hold in the colonial system constitute also the "bourgeois" fraction of the colonized people. (Fanon 1963:108–9; emphasis added)

The people are suspicious of *the townsman.* The latter dresses like a European; he speaks the European's language, works with him, sometimes even lives in the same district; so he is considered by the peasants as *a turncoat who has betrayed everything that goes to make up the national heritage.* The townspeople are *"traitors and knaves"* who seem to get on well with the occupying powers, and do their best to get on within the framework of the colonial system. (Fanon 1963:112; emphasis added)

The *national bourgeoisie of underdeveloped countries* is not engaged in production, nor in invention, nor building, nor labor; it is completely canalized into activities of the intermediary type. Its *innermost vocation seems to be to keep in the running and to be part of the racket.* (Fanon 1963:149–50; emphasis added)

---

morality of class violence, the rejection of consumption as hedonistic, the anti-intellectualism, and the desirability of total revolutionary transformation are all found in Sorel (1950). See Chapter 8 by Kenneth Quinn for additional comments on Sorel.

In its beginning, the national bourgeoisie of the colonial countries *identifies itself with the decadence of the bourgeoisie of the West.* (Fanon 1963:153; emphasis added)

Because it is *bereft of ideas,* because it lives and cuts itself off from the people, undermined by its *hereditary incapacity* to think in terms of all the problems of the nation as seen from the point of view of the whole of that nation, *the national middle class* will have nothing better to do than to take on the role of the manager of Western enterprise, and it *will in practice set up its country as the brothel of Europe.* (Fanon 1963:154; emphasis added)

And it is clear that in the colonial countries *the peasants alone are revolutionary,* for they have nothing to lose and everything to gain. The starving peasant, outside the class system, is *the first among the exploited to discover that only violence pays.* (Fanon 1963:85–86; emphasis added)

For the native, this violence represents the absolute line of action. The militant is also a man who works . . . to work means to work for the death of the settler. This assumed responsibility for violence allows both strayed and outlawed members of the group to come back again and to find their place once more, to become integrated. *Violence is thus seen as comparable to a royal pardon. The colonized man finds his freedom in and through violence.* (Fanon 1963:85–86; emphasis added)

For the native, life can only spring up again out of the rotting corpse of the settler. . . . for the colonized people this *violence . . . invests their characters with positive and creative qualities.* The practice of violence binds them together as a whole, since each individual forms a violent link in a great chain, a part of the great organism of violence . . . (Fanon 1963:93; emphasis added)

Fanon clearly moves well beyond Leninist or Maoist concepts of the dictatorship of the proletariat. Whereas both Lenin and Mao indicated that socioeconomic class origins could be overcome by correct attitudes and behaviors toward the revolution, Fanon resembles the Khmer Rouge by indicating that whole groups are irredeemable class enemies because of their past association with the colonial state.

The only historical precursor for such a stringent definition of class enemies is found in Stalin's dekulakization campaign against the Kulaks, the wealthy peasant class. The rapid and brutal process of collectivization in the Soviet Union is in several ways quite similar to the transformation of the Cambodian countryside under the Khmer Rouge. In the Soviet Union after the abandonment of the New Economic Policy, Stalin sought "rapid and simultaneous destruction of traditional authority [that is, "dekulakization"], reintegration of the peasantry into one dominant type of organization (the *kolhoz*), and economic exploitation through forced and at times impossible deliveries of produce to the state" (Dallin and Breslauer 1970:65). The Khmer experience with immediate rural transformation was similar to the Soviet experience in the weakness of spontaneous support for the transformation among the peasants. The Khmer Rouge in 1975 and the Communist Party of the Soviet Union (CPSU) in 1930 were numerically weak among the rural masses, and their minority status resulted in much heavier reliance upon coercion than was apparent in the more carefully prepared and slow-paced transformation of the Chinese countryside.[7] In addition, whereas according to Maoism redemption was theoretically possible for class enemies (through self-criticism and thought reform), Stalin's strategy of rural transformation was similar to that of the Khmer Rouge because both practiced elimination and forced migration of whole social groups rather than relying on "the demonstration effect of selective elimination" (Dallin and Breslauer 1970:63). Finally, the proportion of crops extracted from the villages through forced deliveries in both instances contributed directly to the massive death toll through famine and famine-related fatalities.

Even though I know of no evidence indicating that Khmer Rouge leaders actually thought of themselves as emulating Joseph Stalin's techniques for rural transformation, there exists at least a superficial similarity, especially in the rapidity of the transformations and the willingness to liquidate entire social groupings. It may well be that the methods of Stalin became mixed with the goals of Mao in the context of the French Communist Party, which was the most Stalinist communist party in Western Europe when several future Khmer Rouge leaders were members of it in the 1950s.

No revolutionary ideology is entirely imported, and regardless of the substantial intellectual debts owed to Mao, Amin, Fanon, and perhaps Stalin, the Khmer Rouge's concept of total national independence springs primarily from the centuries-old Khmer fear of foreign invasion rather than from any twentieth-century foreign ideology.[8] The economic and organizational self-reliance stressed by Mao were largely the product of necessity resulting from the party's geographic isolation during the early Yenan years and the deterioration of trade relations with the Soviet Union at the time of the Sino-Soviet split. The Chinese Communist Party never sought isolation for isolation's sake and would probably have preferred to continue international aid and trade relations if the circumstances had been more favorable. In contrast, the Khmer Rouge carried self-reliance to an extreme by cutting off virtually all relations with the outside world in the 1975–1976 period. Blockading themselves from the outside world and adopting extremely aggressive tactics toward all of their neighbors probably flowed primarily from traditional Khmer fears of being swallowed by Vietnam or Thailand and

[7] The CPSU at the start of collectivization lacked rural roots to such an extent that the coercion had to be carried out almost entirely by urban party cadres. Although the Khmer Rouge were almost entirely rural in origin, they nonetheless constituted only a very small minority within the traditional Cambodian peasantry.

[8] On traditional sources of Khmer ideology, see Chapter 5, pp. 161–62, by François Ponchaud.

from the realization of just how tenuous their own grip on power was within Cambodia immediately following the capture of Phnom Penh. Neither Lon Nol nor Sihanouk shared ideological bearings with the Khmer Rouge, and yet, both made national survival, particularly vis-à-vis the Vietnamese, a first priority for which they were willing to run almost any risk. Although Soviet policymakers depict the anti-Vietnamese policies of Pol Pot and Ieng Sary as mere offshoots of Chinese foreign policy, it is much more plausible to ascribe the anti-Vietnamese goals of the Khmer Rouge to the traditional Khmer motive of national survival in the face of expansive neighbors.

The intellectual sources of Khmer Rouge ideology included Maoism, European Marxism, Fanonism, perhaps Stalinism, and certainly Khmer nationalism. No single theorist minted the ideology and horrific reality of Democratic Kampuchea. The intellectual coinage of each theory was debased as it became amalgamated with the others and was refined in the crucible of circumstances besetting the Khmer Rouge as they came to power. A tragedy of massive proportions derived from the unique alloy forged from the combination of foreign ideological elements and Cambodian revolutionary circumstances. Khieu Samphan and the Khmer Rouge elite followed Amin, Fanon, Stalin, and Mao down a road that ineluctably led from student idealism, through recruitment to revolution, to the final degradation of idealism in the torture chambers of revolutionary Phnom Penh's Tuol Sleng prison. The economic, cultural, and political autarky was too extreme and abrupt, the violence too debilitating, the economic revolution too extensive, and the destruction of traditional values too rapid and complete. In Cambodia the back of a nation was broken by an excessively literal application of untried romantic revolutionary schemes that were too facile to succeed given the absence of mass support, the premature nature of revolutionary victory, and the imminence of international strife.

Appendix A

Summary of Annotated Party History

[Copy of the original text, by Eastern Region
military political service.]

On the occasion of our Nth anniversary, it is good to take note of the following points:
— Subsequent to the 1966-1967 decision of the Central Committee and the Committee of Liberation, we took 30 September 1951 as the Party's date of founding.

The reasons were as follows:
— 30 September 1951 was the date of opening of the first conference during which the decision to form the Party was made justifiedly and decisively.
— Also, 1951 was the year organization of central committees was begun; the mission of these committees was to set up the Party.

In order to understand this commentary easily, reference must be made to the following points:

1. The importance of each Party anniversary for committees' cadres and Party members.

2. Brief Party history.

3. A certain number of important experiences, according to the observations in the Party history.

4. Summary of past and present victories and activities of the bitter revolutionary struggle, to joyfully celebrate the Nth anniversary of the Party; and the duties of each Party member.

5. Conclusion.

6. Slogans.

I. THE IMPORTANCE OF EACH PARTY ANNIVERSARY FOR COMMITTEES' CADRES AND PARTY MEMBERS

1. The object of the anniversary of our party, a Marxist-Leninist party, is to guide the revolution to destroy imperialism and its lackeys, and feudalism and its rich reactionaries; to destroy the old society and to rebuild it according to the current people's and democratic revolution. Its object is to direct the socialist-communist revolution in the future. This is a very important political event in the lives of the people, combatants, committees' cadres and each Party member.

This is why on each anniversary of the Party's founding, combatants, party members, committees' cadres and our entire people must be informed regarding the birth and history of the Party, in order to study the progress and faults of our Party, class organization, cadres, committees and members. Let us study the [good] qualities and faults, so as to move our Party better and better into the future and to improve each one of us, to suit the age of the Party.

2. Our party is at the age of a man in his prime, capable of directing the revolution

251

by itself, with satisfactory support. If we say that our Party has so far passed through a very arduous period of the revolution, in armed as well as political struggle, we are admitting that our Party is experienced and is capable of directing itself and of gradually improving in quality within the framework of the People's revolution under Party direction. Within the framework of the revolution of the peoples of the entire world, we will be able to transform ourselves into a high-quality communist people, day by day, month by month and year by year, to adapt ourselves to our era's revolutionary movement.

II. BRIEF PARTY HISTORY

To comment easily, it is best to divide the Party history from 1951 to 1967 into two periods: *The first period* is the Party history in armed revolutionary struggle from 1951 to 1954. *The second period* is the Party history in political struggle from 1955 to 1967.

1. History of the Cambodian People's Struggle before the Birth of the Marxist-Leninist Party

a. In Cambodia's national society there exists a natural contradiction between the oppressors and the oppressed. From this was born the people's struggle.

b. In the French colonialist period, our people, especially the farmers, arose continually and everywhere against the French imperialists and their lackeys. This was a bitter struggle against the expansionist enemy and his lackeys by all inhabitants, minorities as well as major ethnic groups. For example, the PO KAMBOR, ACHAR SVAR and VISSES NHOV movements; the ROLEA and PHEA EAR [presumably ROLEA PEIR] inhabitants' movements; the KOMPONG SPEU, KAMPOT, BA PHNOM, KOMPONG SVAY and KRAING LEAV farmers; the "EN CHEY" [Entrachey] farmers' anti-tax movements; the Kratie and STUNG TRENG people's movements, etc.

Actually, our people are a nationalist people who are truly angered at the enemy aggressor and his lackeys. They joyfully and courageously consented to struggle firmly against the enemy. Several centuries ago our people, especially the farmers, had a history of audacious struggle.

c. However, our people 's struggle did not win victory over French imperialism and feudalism with its lackeys, because our people did not have a policy, a just and scientific proletarian class policy. The enemy was thus able to eliminate our people's strength little by little, until it disappeared. This occured because of the lack of a policy or a proletarian class policy plan, and the lack of scientific direction by the Marxist-Leninist Party.

d. This is why we base the following basic historical lessons on the experience of the audacious struggle already passed through by our people:

If we speak of strength, we see that our people, especially the farmers, the backbone, are a very powerful force. However, this force did not win victory over the enemy because it did not receive direction from the Party and did not have a proletarian class army, proletarian class policy and proletarian class strategy in the struggle against the enemy.

Therefore, we can clearly conclude that after the experiences resulting from the struggle of our people, especially the farmers, the factor leading to victory was the Marxist-Leninist Party.

Based on these experiences, we continue to wage our people's and democratic revolution by uniting the strength of the people, especially the farmers, with the Marxist-Leninist Party and the proletarian class. These two factors will certainly bring about the victory of the revolution.

2. Party History in the Period of Armed Revolutionary Struggle from 1951 to 1954

a. After World War II followed by the second invasion of Indochina (including our country) by the French and other imperialists, our people, like the other Indochinese peoples, never accepted the French imperialist yoke. So our people rose up in increasing numbers everywhere against the French imperialists and their lackeys, aggressors of our well-beloved Cambodia.

b. Based on the experiences of the unrelenting struggle by our people, especially the farmers, at the end of as well as after World War II [as published], we note that if the Marxist-Leninist Party with a good proletarian class does not direct the people's revolutionary struggle, that struggle will not win out over the enemy.

History has clearly shown that after World War II, the French imperialists and their lackeys employed all means, policies, methods and maneuvers to destroy the force of the people's struggle. At the time existed the DAP CHHUON, KAO TAK, CHANTARAINGSAY, SAVANGVONG, PUTH CHHAY, and ACHAR YI etc. movements against the revolution and the revolution's force. The people were separated from the revolution's ranks, according to the degree of control the enemy imposed on them.

c. Based on the above, to bring the movement and direct the struggle to victory over the enemy, it is necessary and it is sufficient to have the proletarian class Marxist-Leninist Party as the leader. It is necessary to cultivate certain other qualities to form a proletarian class Marxist-Leninist Party in our country, in conformity with the slogan: "IT IS THE PEOPLE WHO CARRY OUT A COUNTRY'S REVOLUTION."

d. What qualities were necesary to form the party at that time? There were then few proletarians in our country. So, their struggle was weak. Because of this, was it or was it not possible to form the proletarian class Marxist-Leninist Party?

So, we were not able to form it in our Cambodia because the number of proletarians and their [good] qualities were insufficient to direct the revolution at that time. Meanwhile, we based ourselves on our concept of our national society to form it in our country. This concept was as follows: Our country is an underdeveloped agricultural country. It was under the French imperialist colonialist yoke. In the colonialist and semi-feudal society, there were two basic conflicts: the first conflict was between the people and the French imperialists, that is, between the proletarian and French colonialism. The second conflict was between the feudal lords and the people, that is to say, between feudalism and the farmers. In sum, the basic contradiction in both of these cases was the contradiction between the farmers and the French imperialists, and between the farmers and the feudal lords. From this was born a very powerful proletarian class revolutionary movement. However, if it had been left alone, it would have failed. Therefore, direction by the proletarian class Marxist-Leninist Party was necessary.

e. From where does the proletariat arise? From where does Marxism-Leninism derive? Proletarian class Marxism-Leninism was injected into our revolutionary movement by the international communist movement and the Vietnamese communists. It is certain that our communist combatants were a number of Cambodians who were trained in the Indochinese Communist Party, about 40 men in 1951; in the French Communist Party, 10 men in 1951; and in the Thai Communist Party, 3-4 men in 1951.

f. These Cambodian communists took the following path in forming the proletarian class Marxist-Leninist Party in Cambodia:

— To give impulsion to the revolutionary movement of our people, especially the farmers, against the French imperialists, with the firm support of the Indochinese Communist Party (new name: Vietnam LAO DONG party), we held a conference in 1951 and decided to organize a committee to teach Marxism-Leninism in the revolutionary movement to our people (the farmers). From this committee came the leaders of our proletarian class party and our new communist combatants.

Parallel with the formation of the proletarian class Marxist-Leninist Party by communists trained in the Indochinese Communist Party, there was also the movement of communist combatants trained in the French Communist Party and the international communist movement. These persons derived from military trainees and students in France. They collaborated closely with the party formation movement committee toward the end of 1953.

The communist combatants trained in the Thai Communist Party had also participated in the country's revolutionary movement since prior to 1952.

It was these communists who brought Marxism-Leninism and proselytized it among the people, above all the farmers, according to their level of instruction.

The certain evolution of the formation of our party in the period of armed revolutionary struggle from 1951 to 1953 was the following:

— In 1951 a Party propagation and formation committee was set up, made up of [Comrades Ng. M., S. H., T.S.M. and Ch. S. M.], the plan of action of which was:

— to draft provisional statutes;

— to draw up a political program; and

— to carry out a survey of conditions and sufficient good qualities (?) [as published]

— Then a conference of representatives from the whole country was organized in order to form a just and durable party. From the progress and evolution of the formation of the party in our country as related above, it can be observed that the party was formed little by little, adopting the following two factors: It was a people's revolutionary movement of all social levels, above all the farmers; and education in proletarian class Marxism-Leninism by the nucleus trained in the Indochinese, French and Thai communist parties and with the support of the Vietnamese Communist Party. Therefore, during the period of armed struggle, the history of our party clearly showed that the basic factor in its formation was the revolutionary movement of the people, especially the farmers, and the spirit of the proletarian class

Marxist-Leninist doctrine, which brought the international communist movement to our country.

The conditions for the formation of the party in our country were not different in principle from those of the revolutions which formed the world's Marxist-Leninist parties. To the best of our knowledge of France, England, the USSR, China, Vietnam, etc., all followed the same principle of revolution, that is the people's revolutionary movement; and the people are the workers (in the industrial countries) or farmers (in the underdeveloped agricultural countries).

The formation of the Party was certainly according to Marx and Engels' "declaration of the Communist Party" [Communist Manifesto ?], Lenin's disciples' Party, the Great October Socialist Revolution, China's people's democratic revolution, and revolution throughout the world.

During the period from 1951 to 1954, our party developed the [good] qualities to build the party bit by bit. It directed the revolutionary movement little by little. It surmounted obstacles to win victory over the French imperialists and their lackeys at the 1954 Geneva Conference, with the party and people of Vietnam, Laos, and the entire world.

What Was the Degree of Forming [Good] Qualities to Build Our Party in the Armed Revolutionary Struggle

From 1951 to 1954, counting the months and days, it lasted about 3 years.

For the period of forming [good] qualities to build our party, let us sum up the following principal experiences, both [good] qualities and faults.

In principal [good] qualities, we see:

Regarding ideology and politics, we aroused the spirit of nationalism and independence against the imperialists to a large degree. During this period, we accomplished the utmost in the areas of ideology and politics. However, the accomplishment remained minimal; it was like a shadow. There existed only the organization of a committee and the education movement to form the [good] qualities to organize the party. We also strengthened a number of party members and a number of party committee cadres to [be able to] direct the revolutionary movement. However, the principal experience, deemed an important quality of our party during this period, was waging the armed revolution until the 1954 Geneva Conference.

If we speak of the party's conduct in the armed revolutionary struggle, it can be seen that the leadership qualities were like "rather raw" meat. Even for a short period, this revolutionary struggle was a basic experience and great capital for the party in our people's and democratic revolution, capital which is not easy to find elsewhere.

— In faults, we see:

From the ideological point of view, we have not yet won the support of the revolutionary class, which is the real master of the country and the perpetrators of the revolution. We have not educated it in the idea of "SELF HELP." We had not asked enough for aid for our people and party. The nationalists had not acted enough like professionals. They asked for aid from abroad and looked with contempt upon their compatriots' national force.

From the political point of view, we did not have a political line, strategy, stratagems and independence.

From the organizational point of view, the composition of the party was still not adapted to the various social classes. Its organization had not yet achieved unity throughout the country. Direction in each "region" was in the form of "monopoly," contrary to democracy. A great number of leaders were above all profiteers, and a certain number of others were worse. It was these persons who destroyed our achievements to a large degree, above all during the period of political revolutionary struggle from 1955 to 1959.

These faults are normal in all parties, above all for our party, born just 3 years previously. During this short period of time, we had not yet had all sorts of experiences. We did not understand the Marxist-Leninist doctrine very well. Several reviews [revisions] were necessary to understand them little by little.

We can clearly see the exactitude of these experiences in both principal [good] qualities and principal faults.

When we see the state of the party clearly, we can develop the [good] qualities and correct the faults so as to build the party, better and better and more and more depending on the path of Marxism-Leninism. However, if we think only of the faults without taking the [good] qualities into consideration, or vice versa, we can in no way build our party on the path of Marxism-Leninism, as in the case of SIV HENG from 1955 to 1959.

III. *History of the Party's Political Revolutionary Struggle from 1955 to 1959 [as published]*

So as to comment easily, we will again divide this period into two parts: from 1955 to 1959, and from 1960 to 1967.

PERIOD OF PARTY FORMATION FROM 1955 TO 1959

a) After the 1954 Geneva Conference, a temporary central committee, not in conformity with the party's conditions, was set up. It was composed of S. H., T.S.M., Ng. M., S. V. and N.T.Nh., with SIV HENG as secretary. After Geneva, we transformed armed struggle with the enemy, above all during the 1955 election and with regard to the Cambodian-American military agreement (sweeping away the American strategic bases), to introduce the policy of neutrality to Cambodia. We fought unarmed behind and within the enemy's center of power. However, our party, only 3 years old, lacked the following three things: ideology, policy and organization.

With this state of affairs, the temporary central committee, with SIV HENG as secretary, foundered. Around 1956, this committee headed in the direction of urban movements; some bad activities took place and a second committee was formed.

This gave rise to a rural committee, responsible for rural action throughout the country. It was composed of three persons, with SIV HENG as chairman. The urban committee, secretly or overtly responsible for all cities throughout the country, was composed of four persons, with Comrade T.S.M. as chairman.

b) After the armed struggle, the party engaged in political movements in the countryside and in the cities. The combatants' bitter struggle against the enemy became very intense. The party firmly directed the political struggle, above all in the press and during the 1954-1955 elections. This changed the political atmosphere in the country and at the levels of the people.

c) However, according to our observation, the movement to form the party in the cities and the countryside showed that from the end of 1954 to 1959, the committee in charge of the urban movement, with T.S.M. as chairman, continued its revolutionary activities against the enemy either secretly or overtly. Although this committee acted capriciously because of its lack of means, it succeeded in forming a few committees in cities which did not yet have any, and in infiltrating the enemy government, thanks to its efforts. The workers', students', intellectuals' and mass movements progressed quickly and took up increasingly numerous places alongside the revolution.

In addition, from the middle of 1956, the committee in charge of the rural movement, headed by SIV HENG, committed worse misdeeds after its betrayal of the party.

From the ideological and political point of view, SIV HENG taught the people that there were no social classes in our Cambodian society. This meant that there was no struggle between the social classes; and that the people, above all the farmers, did not wage revolution. They had to follow the ruling class with SIHANOUK at the head, like SIV HENG had followed it. SIV HENG betrayed the principles of the party struggle, such as the policy of the committee in charge of the urban movement, which decided to combat SAM SARY and the DAP CHHUON groups.

From the organizational point of view, it is very sad and regrettable to see the temporary central committee and the rural committees in disagreement on ideology, policy and organization. As secretary, SIV HENG thought only of money and traded with circles which the party deemed counter-revolutionary. Because there had not been any indoctrination, criticism and self-criticism sessions and no directives on organization, liberalism was born in each individual, which had a bad influence on the masses. We feel that this is why from 1955 to 1959 the rural committees lost about 90 percent of their cadres and party members because of the organization's inability to combat the enemy. They had become passive, and carried out no heroic acts. Only 10 percent of the revolutionary movement remained active and persisted in struggling against the enemy in bitter and respectable fashion, against all obstacles. Comrade T.S.M.'s temporary central committee remained active, and was responsible for the urban movement. A number of regional committees from various sectors, organized toward the end of 1954, were traitors and submissive to the enemy. As secretary, SIV HENG bowed to the enemy and betrayed the revolution and the people in 1959.

d) *What Were the Party's Principal Experiences from 1955 to 1959*

What were the causes of the progress in [good] qualities? And what were the causes of the loss of 90 percent of the rural movement?

We can sum up the [good] qualities in the formation of the party from 1955 to 1959, as follows:

1. The [good] qualities to progress in forming the party had two basic parts:

— From the ideological and political point of view, the urban movement and a minority of the party organization in the countryside led the people in the struggle against the enemy secretly or overtly in the elections in 1955, 1958, 1962, etc., and in the press against SEATO, the Cambodian-American military agreement of 16/5/55, and the traitors SAM SARY, SON NGOC THANH and DAP CHHUON.

The movement continued the struggle in 1955 and influenced the Cambodian people in the future struggle against imperialism and feudalism, and for peace and revolution throughout the world.

— From the organizational point of view, a number of party members and cadres in the cities and countryside strengthened the revolutionary base above all among the people, students and intellectuals. During this period, the workers' movement as a revolutionary class was completely in favor of the revolution.

2. Regarding the party's destruction through its faults, we see that from the ideological and political point of view the principal faults are: lack of awareness to let itself be the master of the country and perpetrator of the revolution; lack of responsibilities in carrying out its duties; lack of confidence in the people's support; and requests for foreign aid.

Another serious disadvantage was the influence of revisionism abroad, which gave rise to confusion of political ideas and weakened the revolution's situation.

It was the period of revisionism which destroyed our party.

— Concerning rural organization, the loss of 90 percent caused regret and sadness to the party and the people. It was the fault of organization lightly carried out with reference to just any so-called revolutionary movements. The worst is that the leader was a profiteer and traitor who did not have support (from the people); then the indoctrination, criticism and self-criticism sessions on organization were suspended, and the party's situation was no longer absolutely stable. When indoctrination was not carried out, the party's organization was condemned to being subject to eventualities and without support.

These experiences are called experiences "against the mainstream." However, if studied and analyzed well, they are the most profitable experiences. When we study them correctly, we will push our party movement toward victory.

Period of Party Organization from 1960 to 1967

The great faults during the historical period from 1955 to 1959 were a lesson which the party learned seriously in 1959, at the very moment SIV HENG's treason was taking place.

The committee in charge of the urban movement was named the committee in charge of the country's general affairs. It was composed of four persons, with Comrade T.S.M. as chairman. The committee was responsible for continuing the revolutionary movement and developing the party's organizational situation in the countryside, where the party had suffered a 90-percent loss of strength. It had to organize and draw up a political line, a strategy and party stratagems, and establish the party's Marxist-Leninist statutes to organize the second general assembly toward the end of 1959.

However, toward the end of 1959 the enemy violently attacked the revolution in the countryside. Numerous bases were invaded by the enemy, who slaughtered everyone there. In cities where activities were overt, a great number of members were apprehended and killed quietly and savagely; the Cambodian and French-language newspapers were seized and closed down. The second general assembly had to be delayed until 30/9/60. Subsequent to an important decision by the designated organizing committee, it was opened from . . . to . . . (sic) [as published] with the participation of representatives from all branches of operations, overt as well as secret, in the cities and the countryside.

The second general assembly approved a political line, strategy, stratagems and Marxist-Leninist statutes for the party. It decided to form the Marxist-Leninist Party in Cambodia, to continually wage the Cambodian revolution, and to form a party central committee plenipotentiary (?) [as published] to operate as leader. The committee was composed of eight persons, with Comrade T.S.M. as secretary.

The preparations for and opening of the second general assembly were carried out in a spirit of complete independence, of energetic self-help, and with the awareness of being the perpetrator of events and the master of one's own destiny and of being certain of final victory even in the situation where the enemy was attacking violently. That is to say, it was with the second party general assembly that the party began to lead a new life in a truly revolutionary atmosphere.

During this period of time, the party's main activities were indoctrination, proselytizing and carrying out the political line, strategy, stratagems and the party's Marxist-Leninist statutes. From this was developed internal unity in all areas. This attitude was the first step, and served the basic position [as published]. It was a problem of [having] a nucleus very necessary for the time. It gave rise to the people's revolutionary struggle movement in all countries, and helped it progress.

— It was to make the organization of the front forces and the organization of the party force proper, progress.

— It was to reorganize and straighten out the situation of the first-priority organizations in the countryside, purifying, strengthening, enlarging and reorganizing them. This straightening out activity, which began toward the end of 1959, permitted the establishing of a correct organization, initially for the whole country, subsequently for the first-priority locations in 1962 [as published]. (It was during this period, on 20/7/62 to be exact, that Comrade T.S.M., secretary of the party, was kidnapped by the enemy, leaving no trace. This was great grief for the party which had just been reorganized.)

At the beginning of 1963, on the 20th and 21st of the second month (February?) [as published], the third party general assembly was opened to study past activities and draw experiences from them in order to rectify and improve the political line, strategy, stratagems and party statutes, and to approve a decision for a new operational direction which would correspond to the situation at that moment.

The third party general assembly was an important new step in accelerating building the party in order to set forth once and for all the party's ideology, policy and organization. Starting with the basic position and the decision of the third party general assembly, the central council and all party organizations carried out activities to build the party and direct the revolution, and they advanced from victory to successive victory, transforming the party into one which now played a leading role in the revolution, which had a solid revolutionary position, and which had arrived at a stage where, as of 1964, the party had a great deal of influence. In parallel, the party gradually attracted interest on the international level, according to the correct revolutionary attitude.

Thus, as of 1964, the party was organized to launch itself into organizing the working class in a correct manner, based on Marxist-Leninist doctrine. It now had an absolutely revolutionary nature and played an absolutely revolutionary role even on second-priority battlefields. The working class and the Cambodian people placed all their confidence in our party. At the same time, the organization of our party contributed its part to the international revolution in the resolute struggle against the imperialists, especially the American imperialists and their lackeys, in defense of world peace. Meanwhile, in organizing the party from 1960 to 1967, parallel with the principal [good] qualities were also numerous large faults regarding which the party had to demonstrate its flexibility in order to study correctly to accelerate the speed of party organization in the future.

The principal [good] qualities of party organization during the period from 1960 to 1967 were:

— From the ideological point of view, the party was formed progressively, aware of being the perpetrator of events and in the spirt of self-help and having confidence in oneself, a spirt of independence. It became aware of the class (proletarian) position and this class's struggle. This position is absolutely revolutionary, a position of responsibility in waging the revolution, a nationalist and internationalist workers' position. Although ideological indoctrination had a few awkward points and faults, it progressed ceaselessly according to the political line to make the party into a workers' and revolutionary party; this permitted the various party echelons to have a generally firm revolutionary attitude. This gave them confidence in the party at all times, at present as well as in the future.

— From the political point of view, the party introduced and developed in the revolutionary movement the questions of strategy and stratagems, to a large degree. Despite a few successive faults in developing its political position, the party was nonetheless able to arrive at a stage where its strategic position was fairly solid, and became master of events in the political strategic field in a fairly stable manner, as, in the political field of stratagems, it was able to attack the enemy. The party built its revolutionary force with a view to overthrowing the enemy regime and building the people's revolutionary regime. From this, it created the struggle movement to combat imperialism and feudalism, and it has always been able to contain the enemy.

— From the organizational point of view, the party strengthened and enlarged the organizational system throughout the country, strengthened and enlarged the base organizations and central ruling organizations according to the principles of the policy designed to make the party revolution a worker's revolution within the framework of the real revolutionary movement. The organizational system throughout the country had a unified nature from top to bottom, from the central [as published] to the lower echelons in the countryside and the cities. This system applied the democratic principles, rallying and directing the masses and making criticisms and self-criticisms within the party. Internal unity developed increasingly in all areas. The movement to build the revolutionary concept and revolutionary views was also evolving toward a better state of affairs at all party echelons, above all among the youth, who had been forged by the revolutionary movement severely and arduously.

The three points—ideology, policy and organization—were injected into all the ruling organizations, and were developing in depth in the base organizations, although faults still existed in the party and injured the revolutionary movement in a few places and at certain periods of time, causing a certain bad influence within the party. It was because of the large faults that the revolutionary policy was shaken: the revolutionary spirit became less active, hardly distinguishing the lines between the classes, forgetting the duty of combating imperialism and feudalism to seize state power, forgetting the duty of directing the party, and not taking into account the importance and role of the masses in the revolution. Because of this, the ardor of the revolutionary struggle and the fury and bitter struggle of the class (proletarian) against the enemy to carry out its revolutionary nationalist democratic duty against imperialism and feudalism regressed, and became very passive in a few places and during certain periods of time. Moreover, according to the ideological, political and organizational conditions (of each place), a few missteps were also committed, for example, indifference to the composition of workers and farmers in organizations from the base to the central. The various committees still had a few weak elements. While the ideological, political and organizational situations were occurring, bureaucratism, lack of control of activities and non-completion of construction still existed to a great degree.

During the period of party organization from 1960 to 1967, many [good] qualities were acquired through experience, which allowed the elimination in time of the principal faults so as to make the organization of the Marxist-Leninist Party in our country progress toward a firm position according to the policy of making it into a worker's organization. These [good] qualities were:

— The spirit of endurance, national honor, awareness of the party's people's revolution, individual responsibility, the spirit of self-help, self-confidence and the awareness of being master of the country and the perpetrator of the revolution. These qualities had a leading character and gave patience, which engendered other rather numerous advantageous factors.

— Knowing how to gain experience, then study it and learn lessons from the good as well as the bad experiences during the period of armed struggle as well as during the period of political struggle after 1955. The fact of gaining experience from the organization of the party in its revolutionary movement, studying it and learning lessons, had great imporance for developing Marxist-Leninist doctrine in the party as well as ideological, political and organizational questions, because these lessons are obvious and something concrete which every person can see for himself.

— Another important point was the fact of having launched once and for all an absolutely revolutionary movement in all its branches, whether the movement is large or small. According to the principle, "THEORY FOLLOWS PRACTICE," this struggle movement will be the flame which continually fires the party to expand it. It is the only well-purified source which will apply increasing fruitful ideology policy and organization to the structure of Marxist-Leninist doctrine. It is through this revolutionary struggle that exposition, explanation, carrying through to completion and application with flexibility of the party's Marxist-Leninist political line and principles could be accomplished. The ruling organs, above all the ruling organ at the party's highest echelon, are chosen and named by applying democracy during meetings, and based on the principles derived from the above-mentioned revolutionary struggle movement. From that, the quality of leadership clearly improves. By following the points listed above and the party principles, the party can surely take charge of the revolution and achieve internal unity. The states of disunity and unity are two opposite things which still exist internally (in the party). The great problem is to take this internal contradiction well in hand and resolve it, and to build internal unity. During the period from 1960 to 1967 in its history, the party successfully confronted numerous and serious obstacles to building internal unity in all areas. Doing so is one of the party's principal achievements.

III. [AS PUBLISHED] A FEW OF THE PRINCIPAL EXPERIENCES, ACCORDING TO OBSERVATIONS IN THE PARTY HISTORY

By observing the convolutions and fortunate and unfortunate evolutions of the party's history from 1952 to 1967, we can briefly note a number of principal experiences which will serve as basic lessons for organizing the Marxist-Leninist party in our country and further strengthening it in future, and for leading the revolution toward brilliant successes, successes which will succeed each other ceaselessly until the final victory of the national and democratic revolution now, and the socialist revolution in the future.

1st experience: To have the correct political line and the political base point for the correct strategy and stratagems, and to take these well in hand. Our party's primary and [most] important question is to really have a strategic political line to determine the revolution's direction, responsibility, real structure, goal, enemy, force, ruling organ, etc. These factors must then be taken in hand and used as base, foundation and support factors so as to advance correctly on the path, the way, or the determined direction. The party's experience has clearly demonstrated that the lack of a strategic political line, the bad handling of this strategic political line, and the lack of control over strategic events inevitably cause shakiness and vacillation according to eventualities, when the enemy uses cold war methods; when the enemy uses hot war methods, we are buffeted by the tempest. In any case, we drift without knowing where we are going, and we thus easily fall prey to the "rightist" or "leftist" tendencies.

Thus, from the beginning, to lead the revolution to victory, the revolution's direction must be determined, and this direction must be taken in hand for always. The revolution's direction is none other than the strategic line. At the same time, along this strategic line there must be political base points, which are the stratagems, so as to progress toward successive victories over the enemy. (The strategic line must be followed and there must be stratagems) [parentheses as published] in each campaign, on each battlefield, and for short periods of time, to lead to final victory.

2nd experience: To develop ideology, so that there is always the revolutionary attitude and the class (proletarian) attitude in the party. Another problem in organizing the party is to conduct internal ideological indoctrination so that the initial attitude taken is conserved firmly, and the Marxist-Leninist class leaning and devotion to the class struggle is retained always to win power by annihilating the enemy regime and setting up workers' and farmers' regime, and to create class ardor and fury. This ardor and fury must be aroused according to the contradiction of the day, whether it be large or small. Thus, ideological force will be converted into a burning material force which will dare to engage in struggle, attack the enemy and win final victory over the enemy even if he is very strong.

3rd experience: To note the good as well as the bad experiences of the party and its revolutionary movement, and to learn lessons from them. One of our party's experiences demonstrated that if the past good as well as bad experiences of the party and its revolution are not analyzed and learned, we can not only not build, enlarge and strengthen the party in the ideological, political and organizational areas, but we will also lead the party to disaster, and the revolution will encounter numerous difficulties. Because when error and justice are discerned in confused fashion, we do not know exactly which is the bottom and which is the top, in order to head in that direction. We would make the same mistakes as in the past because we were still following a personal idea.

4th experience: The organization of the party in its armed and political movements. An important problem being reflected upon, studied and learned is the building of our party during the periods of armed and political revolutionary struggle. What is the effectiveness of this building for waging these armed and political struggles? Building the party and the organ directing the revolution during the armed and political struggles, and the two struggles themselves, the two faces of revolutionary violence, are altogether very important activities which we must carry out; we must seriously learn how to do so so as to always play the role of master of events in accelerating the revolutionary movement.

5th experience: Burning ardently and actively, the revolutionary movement is the very spirit of Marxism-Leninism. The progress of the party organization clearly showed that, when we want to organize, strengthen and enlarge the party according to what we have learned from books and empty theories which are without action or real struggle movements against the enemy, no good results can be obtained. We only succeed in making the revolutionary spirit rigid. The party members and committees' cadres have no [good] qualities except for a few qualities without pracitical value.

6th experience: Take care to choose qualified leaders. One important experience in organizing the party is the choice and organization of the various organs, above all the ruling organs; and the higher the ruling organ, the more important this is. This care attempts as much as possible to keep out profiteers, opportunists and those who approach other ruling elements. Thus, to choose leaders, their ideological conditions, political attitudes and organizational abilities must be determined, and factors for judging must be based on the work completed and their real and sustained accomplishments.

7th experience: Take care to include working class ideology and organization in the composition of the party ranks. Our party was formed in an underdeveloped agricultural country. The party was thus born out of a basically agricultural movement. Our country's farmers are greatly oppressed by the imperialists, the feudalists and the bourgeois. The revolution's structure is thus well founded. However, our farmers still do not have a working class nature; they still have a special farmers' agricultural nature. The party is composed of elements from the middle class and intellectuals, a large number of which still retain the structure and nature of their origins.

Thus, to make the party more working class in nature, it is necessary to concentrate to the maximum degree on the working class spirit and on establishing the Marxist-Leninist ideology within the ranks of our party. This ideological education work must be carried out, repeated and always perfected in order to insure that the party has a communist structure and to guarantee that the conduct of the revolution will always be successful. In parallel with education in the working class spirit, it is also necessary to set up a working class organization. The party's ruling ranks must have a majority working class composition.

8th experience: The problem of building internal unity well. It is important to build absolute internal unity which will give force to the Party to conduct the revolution correctly and successfully. Regarding the problem of unity, above all internal unity, our party's experience has shown that disunity on the political point of view, with the personnel divided into partisan groups, should be a cause for alarm, and is a danger for the party. These problems cause anxiety and suffering, because instead of attacking the enemy outside, we are offering our own flesh as prey for the enemy.

9th experience: Learn from the experiences of foreign parties in order to perfect our own party, building it according to the real situation of the Cambodian revolution. In learning from the experiences of foreign parties and the international communist and workers' movement, we must also take into account the complex present-day problem, the principles of independence and the spirit of being master of events, and also remember the idea of studying good as well as bad cases and considering whether or not they could be utilized, according to the real state of our party and country. It is very necessary to develop the above-mentioned experiences. This learning and its application helped greatly in building our party in the past, above all during the period from 1960 to 1967. Now we must still follow the learning principles and methods. In parallel, however, the party also has numerous bad experiences resulting from the learning and copying of foreign experiences. This learning often had bad results for the party with regard to both large and small problems. On the one hand, it made us completely ignorant; on the other hand, it hindered and even sometimes destroyed the revolutionary movement and progress in organizing the party.

In this case, it is better to learn nothing from foreign experience

IV. SUMMARIES OF PAST AND PRESENT VICTORIES AND THE PRESENT STATE OF THE REVOLUTIONARY STRUGGLE MOVEMENT: AND SUMMARY OF THE RESPONSIBILITIES OF ALL PARTY MEMBERS AND COMMITTEES' CADRES TO WELCOME THE PARTY'S NTH ANNIVERSARY JOYFULLY

In the past:

— During a 9-year period of struggle, the party led the nation to fight in the revolution and chase the French colonialists out of Cambodia.

— In 1954, it aroused the struggle in the country against the "CAMBODIAN-AMERICAN" military treaty.

— It launched the press campaign to attack "SEATO."

— It forced the feudal, bourgeois and reactionary class, the landowners, to follow the policy of neutrality.

— It led the nationalist movement, attacking the traitors SON NGOC THANH, SAM SARY and DAP CHHUON.

— It led the nationalist struggle movement which forced the feudal class in power and the imperialist lackeys to refuse the American imperialists' poisonous aid in 1963.

— It aroused the attack movement against the American Embassy and other Free World embassies.

— It led the nationalist struggle movement which forced the class in power, lackey of the American imperialists, to break diplomatic relations with the American imperialists.

— It led the nation to overthrow the government of the traitor LON NOL, lackey of the American imperialists, and destroyed the plan for the so-called legal coup d'etat in 1970.(?) [as published]

— By facts obvious on battlefield in our country, our party played the role of leader in the revolutionary struggle movement, that is to say, conducting politics with support of arms, as it has solemnly proclaimed since 1968 (?) [as published].

Beginning with the example of BATTAMBANG, the revolutionary movement with politics supported by arms expanded brilliantly from province to province, as in the provinces of RATTANAKIRI, MONDOLKIRI, STUNG TRENG, KOMPONG CHAM, KOMPONG THOM, KOMPONG CHHNANG, KOMPONG SPEU, PURSAT, KOH KONG, KAMPOT, PREY VENG, SVAY RIENG, etc.

Our region (Eastern Region) worked to cooperate with this political movement supported by arms in the country from 1968 to 1970, to raise higher the banner of struggle to destroy the mortal enemy of our nation and people, to tear them into pieces, as in the case of SANTE, TEADAK, KANDOL CHRUM, etc.

In short, the political movement with support of arms won successive, numerous and great victories which scared the imperialists, especially the American imperialists and their feudal, bourgeois and reactionary lackeys, to tears.

These latter were evidently tormented in every area and never found a way to get out.

At present:

The year . . . (sic) [as published] is the Nth anniversary of the party's birth; our people, combatants, and members of party committees are currently conducting a campaign under party direction to fight actively, violently attacking the American imperialists and their lackeys THIEU [and] KY (sic) [as published] and THANOM [and] PRAPHAT, the foreign aggressors, and the traitors LON NOL, SIRIK MATAK, CHENG HENG, IN TAM and SON NGOC THANH, our people's internal mortal enemies.

During this period, through its perspicacity, the party advanced the revolutionary situation in Cambodia by modifying it, and thus turned a new page of history. This was a step by the Cambodian revolution toward a brilliant victory over the worst kind of enemy.

The obvious proofs of the party's victories are:

— directing the revolutionary movement, liberating 9/10 of the territory and governing 5 million inhabitants.

— thanks to party direction, our Cambodian revolution formed the new regime of farmers and workers, now the masters of 9/10 of the territory.

Our revolutionary regime is organized systematically and in measured fashion from the hamlets to the provinces throughout the country, to administer this regime in a large area of territory. *Politically speaking*: In all countries, the revolutionary regime is sincerely and actively supported by the great majority of patriotic people at all levels of society who support the cause of independence, peace, integrity, liberty, democracy and the country's brilliant life.

Abroad, the reputation of the Cambodian revolution is influencing the entire world, and the revolution is very actively supported by the peoples of the entire world who love peace, justice and humanity. They are happy to see that the National United Front of Cambodia under party direction is becoming fruitful.

Militarily speaking: The strength of our three branches of forces is winning brilliant and repeated victories over the enemy on all battlefields. Our forces are on the attack and are master of events. They have besieged and contained the enemy. Our enemy, the boss as well as the lackeys, is weakening and can do nothing to prevent the blows falling upon his back, while awaiting total defeat.

Economically speaking: Over a large area of 9/10 of the territory, the revolutionary regime has controlled economic resources, the nucleus of man's life, such as rice, corn, vegetables, meat, fish, wood, etc.

The other areas have been and are in the process of changing about, and becoming even better, in parallel with the three areas cited above.

In sum, thanks to party direction, the Cambodian revolution has won increasingly greater victories over the enemy, weakened and isolated him, and reduced him to a state of no return and no salvation. His head is continually bowing lower. He sees no way or means to come about. He has no hope of aid or salvation before his certain fate.

It is because of this that we have concluded:

At present: — We can defend our revolutionary regime.

   — We can strengthen our revolutionary regime.

   — We can enlarge our revolutionary regime.

All this demonstrates that the state of our revolutionary regime has currently arrived at a stable position.

The party took the position of strength, attacking firmly and chasing absolutely the third force which was the obstacle; this third force tended to split our country's political forces in three or four directions. The party took the position of strength, rejecting absolutely the game of negotiations and arrangements under any method, form and trick.

The party raised the banner to struggle absolutely, in no way deceiving or confusing peace and independence in the people's hands with peace and deceitful independence (impure) in the hands of the imperialists, feudalists and reactionary bourgeois.

At the same time, the party is playing the role of active leader in the revolutionary war, and continuing the attack against the enemy on all fronts, political, military and economic; it stands on its position of independence, master of events, having firm confidence in itself that we will win total and final victory over the enemy of the revolution to accomplish our present revolutionary, nationalist and democratic duty and to organize a socialist and communist society in the future on Cambodian territory, our beautiful country.

On the party's Nth anniversary, all committee members must compete to:

— combat the external enemy, the imperialists, above all the American imperialists and their lackeys THIEU [and] KY, THANOM [and] PRAPHAT the aggressor pirates; combat the traitors LON NOL, SIRIK MATAK, CHENG HENG, IN TAM and SON NGOC THANH, who are selling our country and people; and combat the feudalists, bourgeois and reactionaries absolutely and violently on every battlefield the party names.

— study well the circular giving directives on celebrating the anniversary [21st] on "30/9/73" [as published], and promise to and take on themselves the responsibility of carrying out these directives.

— combat and chase out the revolution's enemy and everything which is not of the working class within our organization. Then, as soon as possible, arouse in our organization the ardor for struggle, party spirit, working class attitude and the spirit of abnegation for the revolution. Put the common interest over personal interest. Cultivate the revolutionary reflex, the spirit of sacrifice, optimistic confidence and revolutionary heroism.

— use revolutionary prudence ten times more, to destroy the ruses of the enemy who is attacking the party by all cold war and hot war means.

It is for us to warmly celebrate the party's Nth anniversary, and to be ready to welcome the subsequent anniversaries in the 1970s energetically and satisfactorily.

V. CONCLUSION

1) This presentation of a summary of the party history, the first of its kind, naturally lacks many things. We must correct and embellish it, and add to it even more (victories). However, this summary of the party history can still serve as a basis for discussions and studies in the regions, from which lessons can be drawn to organize the party in the future.

2) This presentation of a summary of the party history shows that during this period each year [as published], our party was formed and has evolved progressively, and this was not easy.

It was a revolutionary, difficult, mortal, harsh and complex struggle for the nation, combatants, party members and committees to apply the Marxist-Leninist doctrines.

The external enemy is attacking the party savagely by both hot war and cold war methods. The internal enemy is also attacking the revolution. The building of internal party unity has encountered many bad experiences. All this demands physical and moral strength, intelligence, revolutionary spirit and a spirit of responsibility on the party of party and committee members, to resist the tempest.

Today, the party has arrived at a fairly good state in all ideological, political and organizational areas. However, the party's 22-year march has been very circuitous. We must understand well that the party history was written with the flesh, blood, bones, sweat and physical, moral and intellectual strength of the people, combatants, party members and committees' cadres, both dead and still living. They made many sacrifices to organize the party. Thus, on this anniversary, as on any other anniversary, even an ordinary one, we must correctly evaluate the party history at its true worth.

It is because of this that we must seriously learn the party history so as not to commit the same faults as in the past. We must follow the right path, which the party has laid out for us, to consolidate the building of the party as fast as possible.

In parallel with this, we must love the party, adore it, and serve it sincerely with no reservations or preconditions, to repay the efforts with which the party had educated us to be unreservedly revolutionaries and communists. Nothing is more precious and honorable than to belong within the party's ranks, and nothing is better than to be a communist.

We must all defend this honor and become ever worthy, throwing ourselves into the flame of the greatest movement to make ourselves into "workers and revolutionaries," to attack the external enemies, the imperialists and their feudal, bourgeois and reactionary lackeys, and to attack the internal enemies who have no revolutionary quality.

SLOGANS

Long live the party's Nth anniversary!

Long live the brilliant Cambodian Communist Party!

Long live Marxist-Leninist doctrine, the strongest force!

Long live the Cambodian people's great revolutionary movement under the direction of the party!

Down with American imperialism, the warmonger!

Down with the traitors LON NOL, SIRIK MATAK, CHENG HENG, IN TAM and SON NGOC THANH, lackeys of American imperialism!

Down with the lackeys THIEU [and] KY, unscrupulous lackeys of American imperialism!

Appendix B

Sharpen the Consciousness of the Proletarian Class to Be as Keen and Strong as Possible

Revolutionary Flags
Special Issue, September–October 1976
pp. 33–97

[Translated by Kem Sos and Timothy Carney.]

On the occasion of the celebration of the very great, victorious 16th founding anniversary of the Communist Party of Kampuchea, I would like to elaborate a basic and strategic document on consciousness in five articles in order for comrades in the party; all revolutionary ranks; and the Revolutionary Armed Forces to scrutinize, consider and regularly study, to strengthen standpoints of political consciousness and management in the new period of Socialist Revolution and Building Socialism. Concretely, that is, it is in order to have a strong and everlasting force of political consciousness and management to assault (vay samruk) and finish the requirements of the 1976 Plan, and to prepare resources to strongly assault even further to fulfill the party's 1977 Plan's requirements with great and bounding success.

I. CONCERNING SOCIALIST REVOLUTION IN EVERY AREA

AIM

To grasp the correct traits (dhatu) of the Socialist Revolution which stands on class struggle (kar da suv vann) between the proletarian and capitalist classes; between the proletarian class and the various oppressing classes; between the collective property (kammasiddhi samuhabhap) of the proletarian class and the individual property (Kammasiddhi ekajan) of various oppressing classes; between the socialized goods and the individual ones. Based on this understanding, we wish to build our party, our cadre and our party members continually struggling to destroy and extirpate the traits specific to the capitalist class and the traits specific to the various oppressing classes; and the traits specific to all kinds of individual property, and by struggling to build at all costs and nurture to be strong, the traits specific to the proletarian class, the traits specific to collective property, socialist property in every area.

EXPLAINING THE AIM

We study documents of the Socialist Revolution in all areas in order to absorb (jruat jrap) the Socialist Revolution. In order to build ourselves, the sine qua non is understanding the correct traits of the Socialist Revolution.

We must understand which fronts (mukh bruan) the Socialist Revolution has to strike at in order for us to strike at the right target. The direction to strike is all traits specific to the capitalist class in all areas: economy culture, society sentiment (mano-sancetana), . . . etc. If we know this clearly, we can prepare our weapons to strike on target and burst it open. If we have not correctly calculated the objective of our blow or it is unclear, we will not strike for a day, a year or ten years.

Therefore, this issue is not beyond the capacity of the base class. In fact, it is within the capacity of the base class. It does not have any heavy either material or intellectual property; therefore, it can easily destroy them. The strength of property in the base class is weak.

However, the Socialist Revolution is conducted in other classes that have material and intellectual property; for example, such as capitalists, intellectual capitalists which is difficult because they have a property that obstructs the understanding and the absorption of the Socialist Revolution. No matter how we explain it, the struggle cannot break it out. Only when we gather artillery, strike it hard and relentlessly can it be broken out.

Therefore, in the Socialist Revolution, the objective that must be struck does not exist only on the capitalist class, but also in the working class. But striking the working class is easier. Striking in the capitalist class is difficult.

The objectives that must be built: build the stand of the proletarian class; build collective property, socialist property.

Thus, we have grasped this problem; we are building ourselves; we are building our party in this framework. We are not wandering or marking time. We are striking right on the problem.

ESSENCE OF THE DOCUMENT

1. Specific traits of the Socialist Revolution
2. What must we struggle to eliminate and what to build?
3. Who must we struggle to eliminate and who to build on?
4. Why must we struggle to eliminate the capitalist class and the oppressor class and private property and strengthen the stand of the proletarian class and the collective stand?

1. Specific Traits of the Socialist Revolution

The specific traits of the Socialist Revolution are the specific traits of class struggle between the proletarian class and the capitalist class. It is different from the specific traits of the National Democratic Revolution which is class struggle between the people and the imperialists, feudalists and reactionary capitalists. This is the fundamental meaning of the Socialist Revolution.

However, in the present society of Kampuchea, there is still class struggle between the proletarian class and various oppressing classes, between the collective property of the proletarian class and private property of various other classes. That is why we increasingly strike various other oppressing classes and strike private property.

Thus the specific traits of the Socialist Revolution are class struggle between the proletarian class and the capitalist class and various other oppressing classes and between the collective property of the proletarian class and private property.

Is this presentation right or wrong? Are there still imperialists in our society? Are feudalists and capitalists gone or not? The imperialists are shattered, but they are still causing us trouble. The feudalists and capitalist classes are, in fact, overthrown, but their specific traits of contradiction (tamna's) still exist. They still exist in policy, in consciousness, in standpoint and class rage. Therefore the points we have raised are not wrong. And private property still exists. In the working class private property still exists. We struggle to eliminate this private property in order to have collective property and socialist property.

If we only strike the capitalist class, we will not be the masters. For we will not only regard that which is of the capitalist and we will not be wary.

Another Experience: In the world, that which is revisionist [soeroe] comes from striking only capitalism; [it is being stymied] like a blocked chesspiece. That which is not capitalist is not seen and not hit. But, as for private property, which is aberrantly created in the party, in the armed force and in the people, if we cannot see it, we do not fight it. Therefore, the private property increases and strengthens. If private property is growing, collective property is more and more shrinking.

That is why we are fighting private property. This fight must be fought without ceasing. And we are fighting it over a long time. Private property cannot be destroyed immediately. It needs a tough and relentless fight continuously.

We have raised this in this way following the concrete experience of our revolutionary movement. We have raised it this way because we want it to be tight. Otherwise, our workers, our farmers, and our petty bourgeoisie [qanudhan] will strengthen and expand their own private property. Private property is a specific trait of the capitalists. When private property is strong and widespread, there will be opportunities taken to steal collective goods to sell. So it is a specific trait of capitalists. The only question about these capitalists is whether they are little capitalists or big ones.

Is this rightism by raising it this way? In general, it is not rightism.

Is it leftism? This question has been overtaken by circumstances, because we have done it already. We have already put down the capitalists and feudalist classes and we continue to strike them further. And we are also hitting the private property of the petty bourgeoisie, the peasants and the workers. We are not fighting it in disarray, we are fighting it by means of a collective regime. We are building. As for those who charge leftism, they have made the accusation for a long time now. In the time of Political Struggle, when we were struggling with Sihanouk, we were also charged with leftism. When we were in Armed Struggle, the time of Internal War, they charged that we were left, that we were adventurist [prathuy prathan]. But on reexamination, we see that struggle in this way enabled us to protect our force, strengthen and expand our force, and prepare the view and standpoint of people, of the party and of the armed forces in order to oppose the 1970 coup. When we did not negotiate in 1973, they accused us of leftism. We took the people out of the cities and stopped using money, and they accused us of leftism. But we had our own reasons. And the movement has affirmed that we were right. And, now, everyone admits that we were right.

Therefore examine our line. Left or not left, we must stand by the movement. We must not stand by the Scriptures.

2. What Must We Struggle to Eliminate and What Must We Struggle to Construct?

Over all phases: over worldview (our comprehension); life-view [jivadassen] (visualizing about our life); over our economy in all areas; over culture; over art; over literature; over feelings; over ideology; over thought.

What to Stuggle to Eliminate: Eliminate the capitalist class worldview; eliminate the worldview of other classes. Eliminate the individual worldview.

What to Construct: Construct the worldview, the life-view of the proletarian class; construct the economy of the proletarian class; construct the sentiments of the proletarian class; construct the morality of the proletarian class.

THE CONCRETE MEANING IN IMPLEMENTATION

It is normal in our party, speaking generally, that there are accomplishments and deficiencies. It is an accomplishment that there are proper socialist traits up to a certain degree already. We have struggled to eliminate that which is capitalist, what is of the oppressing class; what is of the standpoint of private property to a certain important limit already. However, areas exist that are still lacking: [that have] worldview, life-view, economy, morality of the various classes. That is why there have emerged manifestations of material property in some trivial problems. This problem is still small, but it is one manifestation of private property. It is one manifestation that is not yet fully consistent with the Socialist Revolution either. It is not clean and smooth yet. If we are based on the socialist standpoint, we see it clearly. We see ourselves and we see our organizational unit [qangabhap] as well. Therefore, the Socialist Revolution, building socialism, is not sleek yet. There is still some sluggishness.

Some property of authority [kammasiddhi khan qamnac] still exists. Besides this there are deals made about daily living; the life-view; our worldview is not yet clean and smooth either. Deals are wrong regarding the collective, are wrong as for socialism. Deals are finding a way to manage, are mixing up the private and the collective. Sometimes they are clear; sometimes unclear. They are not clean.

In carrying out work: Leadership work, other work, joint work, separate work in general are very strong. But there is an aspect that we must examine: There are some deficiencies and some slowness, too. This is because some of our comrades do not pay much attention to the Socialist Revolution movement. Maybe each of us still has these two aspects as well.

Among our workers, a socialist character [nissay] already exists, but some deficiencies are still there. For example: the character of being thrifty; of machine utilization, utilization of other things. Our workers are not thrifty yet; they do not take care of things yet. Therefore, this affects the building of socialism. One effect: there is nothing to use in the future. Another effect: Is to require purchases. Workers of this kind are not an important problem for workers; this is a problem for the party.

Taking this example shows clearly that there are still contradictions, contradictions between socialism and non-socialism. It is not a strong contradiction, but it is a hindrance to the Socialist Revolutionary movement and the building of socialism. We have made many tools, but we have broken many knives forming them on a lathe, which is because the Socialist Revolution is not yet good. If socialist consciousness is good, we are able to progress from not knowing how to do it, to knowing how to do it and to be able to take care of collective goods. In the various Ministries it is the same. In cooperatives, it is the same. If the party is solid, there will surely be good influence reaching the masses in cooperatives. Therefore, how do we organize and care for draft animals, hoes, knives, axes? Not by yourself. It is done by assigning persons to be responsible for it and educating, nurturing, and building them continually.

As for the problem of slowness, is it serious or not? In the party, in the offices, in factories, in cooperatives, some are bounding quickly, some are bounding well enough; some are uncaring; some are lazy. The ones that are bounding quickly must be pushed further by providing [pamba'k] them with the stand of the Socialist Revolution. As for those bounding well enough, they must also be pushed into accelerating even more. As for the ones that are uncaring, this is because the flame of the Socialist Revolution lacks intensity. If we leave them this way, it will affect our Socialist Revolution movement; it will affect the life of our revolution and affect the defense of our country. For example, if rice farming nets only 1 1/2 tons of paddy, not 3 tons per hectare, the defense and the construction of our country are affected. Do not allow this aspect to continue if it is noticed. We must light their flame even hotter. Is this problem too late to solve? No, it is not over, because the '76 plan is not yet finished. We have transplanted rice into most of the fields. But 20% are left. What can we properly do in order to help first the 80% [sic] that are short. Second is to take care of the 80% to be good. Pull out weeds, add water and fertilizer by pushing the Socialist Revolutionary consciousness and stance. If we just go along and are not careful, do not take care of the 80% that we have finished transplanting, it will be even further reduced.

3. Who Must We Struggle to Eliminate and Who Must We Struggle to Build On?

That is, we must struggle to eliminate and build in the entire party; in the whole Core Organization; in all revolutionary ranks; in all peasant collectives; in the whole national society; and especially we must struggle to eliminate and to build each individual; of further importance, each cadre and each party member.

We must rid in each party member, each cadre, everything that is of the oppressor class, of private property, of stance, view, sentiment, custom, literature, art . . . which exists in ourselves, no matter how much or how little. As for construction, it is just the same: we must build a proletarian class worldview, proletarian class life; build a proletarian class stand regarding thinking, in living habits, in morality, in sentiment etc.

Construction Program: There must be a clear dividing line between private property and collective property; private stand and collective stand. [What] do we consider private or collective? Anything that is tilted toward private must be eliminated. Normally, for some problems, we stand on collectivism, but some problems we stand on the private. If we stand on the private, we are at odds with collectivism. No matter what, whether thinking or doing, we should not stand on the private but stand on that that is of collectivism. Work out internal quarrels of the party, of the people, by standing on the collective in order to think and find solutions to a problem. Stand on the collective to manage. Stand on the collective in order to manage. If you stand on the dividing line, you will be mixed up and not firm. If an objective [?] [satyanumati] attracts even a little bit, the private has already come to the fore. If we stand on collectivism, even if some objective attracts us, we will have the time to consider. Having thought about it, we realize that we are about to slide into the private; we run back immediately to the collective.

We must stand on the collective even when we are listening to a report. Even when we settle contradictions between our nation and other nations, we must stand on the collective, looking for profit or loss for our united revolutionary movement. We must do likewise when we settle a quarrel between individual and individual. If we stand on this individual or that indivdual in order to affect this individual, the other individual will suffer a loss. Concerning each individual, if we mistreat and criticize, do not see his good qualities, do not raise his good qualities in order to build them, we are wrong.

Therefore, we must hasten to stand on collectivism immediately. And do not stand on the dividing line. Stand deeply in collectivism. Get ouselves ready, immediately sit on collectivism's chair. Scrutinize each problem. We must scrutinize ourselves; is there a stand on collectivism yet? Sometimes we say we are aleady standing on collectivism, but the result of solving the problem affects collectivism. There, this stand is not yet correct; our line of solving is not yet valid. We must reevaluate our stand.

Morality is the same. For example, if we are living with a woman. As time goes on, the material atmosphere leads to the development of sentiment. If we stand on the collective, we must manage the solution immediately. But if we just expand and strengthen the management, remaining attached to this woman, this is a strong private stand. A strong private stand by a certain point will have affected morality.

And do not put the blame on the [?] objective. And say that someone offered the private chair to us to sit in. No one gave it to us. Because the private chair is everywhere around us. We must look for the collective chair and grasp it tightly.

4. Why Must We Struggle to Eliminate the Capitalist Class and the Oppressor Class and Private Property and Strengthen the Stand of the Proletarian Class and the Collective Stand?

In order to construct socialism to be strong. Only unless we eliminate that which is of the capitalist class; that which is of the oppressor class that which is private can we cause to burst forth the movement to construct socialism quickly and well. In factories, in cooperatives and in offices, thrift is good; utilization is good; and the work is good. And the construction of socialism is good; the defense of the nation is good; and safeguarding the fruit of the revolution is also good. And our good influence will be spread abroad. We can also resolve the lifestyle of the people well. The popular forces will be increasingly strong. The forces of the revolution will be increasingly stronger.

Therefore, the source which is the important root and stem is the specific traits of the Socialist Revolution which must struggle to eliminate that which is of the capitalist class, of the various oppressor classes, and of private property. This is a summary. However, it is the same in specifics. In a cooperative, even if there is only one party member, if his proletarian class standpoint is good and clear, the Core Organization can be built according to the standpoint of the Socialist Revolution and the socialist revolutionary movement will be pushed to be strong in the cooperative.

. . . . .

SUMMARY

1. We must tightly grasp the specific traits of the Socialist Revolution. What do we fight? The Socialist Revolution must have its specific traits to fight the capitalist class, fight various oppressor classes, and fight private property. We have been fighting already. And we will continue to fight under the leadership of our Communist Party of Kampuchea at all costs.

2. What do we build? We build the collective of the proletarian class.

3. Any method of eliminating and any method of constructing should be used that gives effective [sakdi saddhi] results. We must have a clear dividing line between private property and collective property, between the private standpoint and the collective standpoint of the proletarian class of the party.

II. ABOUT CLASS CONTRADICTIONS IN THE PRESENT SOCIETY OF KAMPUCHEA. CLASS STRUGGLE AND RESOLVING CLASS CONTRADICTIONS IN THE PRESENT SOCIETY OF KAMPUCHEA

AIM

To set forth the specific traits of class contradiction that exist in the present society of Kampuchea; what are some of the class contradictions? At this point, how must the class struggle take place and how must we resolve class contradictions to have clarity so that there is no mistake in the revolutionary life and death contradiction between us and the enemy, and in the internal contradiction which exists in our own interior and our people. And we must know how to solve anti-party contradictions correctly as well as contradictions within the party and among the people, too.

The class composition in the present society of Kampuchea is different from that of the society of Kampuchea in the period of National-Democratic Revolution. And class contradictions are also different from those of the period of National-Democratic Revolution. It is looked at this way in order to separate clearly the anti-party contradictions and the internal contradictions so we can strike the right target. It is looked at this way in order to develop the advance view which says that class contradiction and class struggle will remain for a long, long time in order that there is no confusion that the party holds power throughout the country, that the worker-peasant class holds power throughout the country and so there is no more class struggle, in order to have the view that class struggle will be long, hard and tough.

ESSENCE OF THE DOCUMENT

1. The division into classes in the present society of Kampuchea

2. Catagories of class contradictions in the interior of the present society of Kampuchea and the contradictions coming from outside

3. Class struggle in the present society of Kampuchea and with the enemy from outside

4. Solution to the categories of internal contradiction in the society of Kampuchea of today and from outside

5. View of class struggle as long, hard and tough

1. The Division of Classes in the Present Society of Kampuchea

1. THE DESCRIPTION OF CLASS DETERMINATION

In the present society of Kampuchea, what is the class composition like in the description and definition? It is as follows:

1. There is a worker class which has some kind of stand. We have not focused on it yet. We are only concerned about their occupation.

2. There is a peasant class whether of old peasants or new. Besides these two classes, what else is there? Are there feudal-landlords? No. As far as we can see, there are none. Are there capitalists? There is no class defined as making a living as capitalists. Are there petty bourgeoisie? Petty bourgeoisie intellectuals as professors,

civil servants, high school students and university students do not exist either. Speaking from the defining in detail.

[sic] There are only workers; there are only peasants and our revolutionary ranks which are the Party, Core Organization and fighting men and women of our Revolutionary Armed Forces. We decided in the ninth month of 1975 not to have other separate strata than the worker-peasant class. Those who were working in the framework of labor are considered as workers. Those who were working in the framework of farming are considered as peasants. As the base, we decided this correctly. However, we must not forget that besides the worker-peasants, there are the revolutionary ranks. These revolutionary ranks are a strata too. It is a power-holding layer. We must not forget it; it will be hidden. Then, it will expand and strengthen as a separate strata, considering itself as worker-peasant; in fact, it holds power over the worker-peasant.

If it is like this already, where do we want to build these people towards? We do not want them to expand and strengthen themselves to hold power outside of the worker-peasants. Someday they will oppose the worker-peasants. Up to now there is an aspect which united them with the worker-peasants, but there is an aspect which has contradictions with the worker-peasant class. We must eliminate the aspect that opposes, that breaks from the worker-peasant, that affects the worker-peasants. Therefore, whatever section that is working in the framework of worker-peasant must be as the flesh and blood of the worker-peasants. It must be selected from within the worker-peasants; it resolves problems in the standpoint of the worker-peasant, and serves the interest of the worker-peasant.

Concrete Meaning

Furthermore, we must educate our ranks in each locality, in factories and cooperatives. After having been selected, one must stay among the worker-peasants in the sense of sharing weal and woe with worker-peasants while performing labor with them.

That is why the planning of our bases has been increasingly better in this aspect toward this end for some time. We dissolved the committees serving people of hamlets [bhumi] and incorporated them into cooperatives instead.

Along with this idea, bases in general have appointed these village cadre as cooperative members or as cooperative cadre. This is a good aspect.

As for subdistricts [ghum] throughout the country, a goodly number of them have turned into cooperatives or have not remained as committees serving people of subdistricts any more; that is, they became cooperative members or cooperative cadre. This is a good evolving direction.

Besides this, a goodly number of district cadres have involved themselves in cooperatives. Doing so is very profitable.

Cadre in contact with cooperatives:

— see problems in the cooperative report and solve them in a timely manner;

— join their feelings with cooperatives;

— have mastery over enemies.

Therefore our ranks will not develop and strengthen themselves into separate strata. This [would-be stratification] has been continuously weakened.

The Revolutionary Army is also our ranks. How do we organize it? If we organize it independently, it will become a separate strata. If we incorporate it with the co-operatives, we will not be a separate strata. Therefore, its activities must be mixed with those of workers or peasants wherever its operations occur. It will be helping to plow, gather rice seedlings, transplant, and build rice paddy dikes. It will help work, but not join in cooperatives. It will remain in its own organizational units because the army is the dictatorial instrument of the proletarian class of the party. But it has to help the cooperatives to work. As for farming, it only works in what-ever framework that supports itself.

If we organize in this way our ranks will be at ease. Therefore a separate layer will not be created.

In short, according to the description definition, there are only two classes in our society: workers and peasants. Alongside these, we should note that there are rev-olutionary ranks. We must solve these ranks so that they will engage in production-increasing activities with worker-peasants. If we do not follow this path, there will be contradictions for sure.

These ranks, if they develop and strengthen themselves into a separate strata, apart from worker-peasants, will lead worker-peasants into being capitalist. This is a current reality [paccuppannabhap] in the world.

2. ESSENCE OF CLASS

As examined, in our society there is the essence [khlim sar] of the worker class; there is the essence of the peasant class. And, at the same time, there still is the essence of the petty bourgeoisie and still the essence of the capitalist class; still the essence of the feudal-landlord and governing class. The essence is the class stand-point, class character [nissay], sentiments, habits reminding it of the desire to op-press; it is the influence of the petty bourgeoisie class, of the capitalist class and of the feudal class that exists in worker-peasants, in our ranks of fighting men and women and in ranks of the Revolutionary Army. Moreover, the capitalists that are dissolved, the feudalists that are dissolved, their specific class traits and essence re-mains. There are still many of them. They remain with socialism because of man-agement itself, by means of being selected, they are compelled into staying. Can consciousness become clearer and clearer immediately? Some compositions can be-come clearer at once. However, some compositions, they oppose. But they have no economy, no management, and remain under the class dictatorship of the worker-peasant class.

2. Categories of Class Contradictions in the Interior of the Present Society of Kampuchea and the Contradictions Coming from Outside

Internal class contradictions within the society of Kampuchea: What class con-tradictions exist in the society of Kampuchea at the present time? By examining the descriptive determination of classes, essence of class in the society of Kampuchea, we have found the following class contradictions: basically, there are contradictions between the proletarian class and the capitalist class. In addition to this, there are class contradictions with the feudal class, which is landlords, which is governing (subdistrict chiefs, district chiefs, provincial governors, civil servants, policemen, military personnel).

Therefore, in the descriptive sense, there are only the worker class and the peasant class. However, peasants include old peasants and new peasants. In old peasants, there are poor peasants, lower-middle peasants, middle peasants, upper-middle peasants and rich peasants. In new peasants, there are petty bourgeoisie, capitalists, feudalists; there are workers, and other productive forces. Therefore, in the old farmers there are also contradictions starting from the middle peasant up. Especially with the rich peasants, there are life and death contradictions. Among the new peasants, there are also contradictions. Contradictions with the capitalists and the feudalists are life and death contradictions. If an individual corrects himself, the contradiction is not life and death. But it is not easy to correct [themselves].

These contradictions are hidden. Because the dictatorial force of the proletarian class is stronger, they cannot break out. It is possible that some compositions can correct themselves. But many of them can not. If they die, they will have instructed their children to keep struggling against communists.

We have revolutionary dictatorial statepower over these people and we are developing and strengthening the worker-peasant alliance. These people are being isolated and exhausted immediately.

In the bases, the majority of opponents whom we have arrested are mostly civil servants, policemen, soldiers and students. This is because capitalists, landlords, do not show themselves. They are the masterminds, but they do not show themselves. When they were in power, they did not show themselves either. They only showed their money, and had government agents show their persons.

Besides the revolutionary struggle with the capitalist, the landlord classes, there is also internal contradiction that comes from the awakening of low politics and awakening of high politics. We must solve this by education.

In sum, in the present society of Kampuchea there are:

1. Secondary internal contradictions

2. Revolutionary life and death contradictions between worker-peasants on one side and capitalists, feudalists on the other.

The specific traits and contradictions remain the same: Before, the feudal, capitalist classes were over the worker-peasant class. That is why the worker-peasant class made the revolution to strike and bring down the feudal capitalist classes. At this time the worker-peasant class is on top instead. But if the worker-peasant class forgets itself, the feudal, capitalist classes will emerge again.

Contradictions from outside are:

— secondary contradictions

— life and death contradictions

3. Class Struggle in the Present Society of Kampuchea and with the Enemy from Outside*

There also are two internal contradictions in the society of Kampuchea:

— secondary contradictions

— life and death anti-party contradictions

There are likewise two contradictions from outside:

— secondary contradictions

— life and death contradictions

* Note: This section apparently includes the topic listed under item four in the description of the document above.—TRANS.

Manifestations of class struggle in the society of Kampuchea: Outbreaks of slaughtering cattle, buffalo, distributing propaganda leaflets and of demonstrations are not numerous, but are signs of class struggle. The destruction of the collective goods of the cooperatives and propagandizing against the collective regime are acts of gathering various forces in order to fight the revolution; in order to fight the proletarian class.

As for us, do we have class struggle? Yes, we have class struggle. We evacuated the people from the cities which is our struggle of class. We develop and strengthen cooperatives as class struggle in order to disperse the forces of the capitalists, feudalists. If they stay independent, they have strength. If we establish collectives of the proletarian class, we have strength.

We look at it this way in order that we strengthen the standpoint of class struggle further and not to think that class struggle is ended.

The manifestations of class struggle coming from outside are also numerous and continuous.

Therefore, how do we solve them? We resolve them by grasping tightly the view and the standpoint concerning the common aspects of contradictions which exist in our national society and by having a very clear standpoint and view about the common contradictions which come from outside, and by not allowing ourselves to be mistaken that these contradictions only are created once in a while and will disappear afterward. We must see that these contradictions are common and continual. Regarding this view and this standpoint, we must see clearly that there are secondary contradictions and life and death contradictions. Internal contradictions must be resolved according to whether internal contradictions are as flesh and blood, not anti-party opposition, not boring into the revolution, but rather contradictions coming from a lack of understanding. These must be resolved by continuous education.

As for anti-party contradictions, there are two methods of solving them.

One is educate, do the work of politics, consciousness and management in the overall framework of the masses in order to ease the contradiction or delay the contradiction from becoming focused all the time.

At the same time, we must have careful management measures, all kinds of careful measures. Of all these measures, one is basic, implement the dictatorship of the proletarian class over these groups of people. We make the proletarian class dictatorial meaning that regarding these groups of people, we are not confused. Give freedom to the worker-peasant people. As for the capitalists, feudalists, there must be a tight framework. Freedom must be given to some and withheld from some. We must be clear. Be careful so that the feudalists, landlords cannot wander about. Whether on the way to seek salt, to seek roots for medicines or going to tend cattle. If these people wander at will, they will get together. We must educate our cooperatives to be wary of these people.

Regarding anti-party contradictions coming from outside: We must have measures to educate people at all times; careful measures to organize defense forces; a foreign policy to gather friends at all times. According to the experiences of our revolution, the basic plan is secrecy. Take secrecy as the base; we can defend our forces; enemies fail to strike us. We both take a stand and keep secrets, but standing on secrecy is the base.

4. View of Class Struggle as Long, Hard and Tough

We raise this view in order to let it be seen that class struggle will be further long, hard and complicated. This comes from within the society of Kampuchea as well as from outside. In politics, in the military, in subversion, in erosion.

Since we already have this view, we can estimate which way they will come from and gain mastery first.

. . . . .

SUMMARY

We must always closely grasp the standpoint and the view that contradictions are created in an ordinary and continuous way in our country; if we have this standpoint and view, we will certainly always have firm and careful measures.

III. ABOUT STATEPOWER AND ABOUT THE DICTATORSHIP OF THE PROLETARIAN CLASS OF THE PARTY

AIM

To grasp the specific traits of revolutionary statepower of the party and the specific traits of the dictatorship of the proletarian class of the party in order to have an even clearer view of the problem of revolutionary statepower and of the defense and the strengthening of revolutionary statepower of the party; according to the dictatorship of the proletarian class of the party in all circumstances in order not to allow at all costs other classes and enemies to wrest away revolutionary statepower of the party.

ESSENCE OF THE DOCUMENT

1. Specific traits of revolutionary worker-peasant statepower under the leadership of the party.

2. Specific traits of the dictatorship of the proletarian class of the party.

3. View, Standpoint and various measures for defending and strengthening the worker-peasant statepower of the party under the dictatorship of the proletarian class of the party to be as strong and hard as possible.

1. Specific Traits of Revolutionary Worker-Peasant Statepower Under the Leadership of the Party

The specfic traits of worker-peasant statepower under the leadership of the party is that this statepower is the statepower of the party, of the proletarian class to serve the interests of the worker-peasant class. It is not a correct class trait to serve classes other than that of the worker-peasants. We must grasp this problem tightly so that we are not confused into using this statepower to serve other classes such as petty bourgeoisie, feudalists, capitalists. Otherwise, they will claim their rights and we will keep helping them. They have to transform into worker-peasants before they can be served with this statepower. If we use this statepower to serve them, it is wrong. It is not an ordinary mistake, but it is developing and strengthening their force.

As for the compositions who are capitalists, feudal-landlords, who have now become new peasants, we must educate them, build them so they transform into worker-peasants. For a number of them, we have had results correcting them. A number of them cannot be corrected. The latter continuously seek occasions to oppose the revolution.

Where does this statepower come from? This revolutionary statepower of the worker-peasants of the party was not created by itself; nor was it born through elections through a Parliament; nor was it created by collusion [kar sumgralum] with any class; nor did it come by negotiation. It came from fighting which was complicated, difficult, with suffering; ranging from weapons to politics to weapons again, in open and in secret, legally and illegally; with political violence and with armed violence, and with the sacrifice of many lives, including the people, party ranks, and many of our Revolutionary Army. The various oppressing classes, with the capitalists and feudalists as the base, joined with the imperialists to fight the people and against the revolution in the hardest possible way, by using all forces of all kinds, using all kinds of tricks, using all kinds of diplomatic activities. However, by our violence, we won this statepower. We saw the aspect of tough fighting in order to wrest away this statepower, in order to realize the value of statepower. The statepower in cooperatives, the statepower in factories, all of it came from fighting that shed blood and went on for a long, long time.

We have wrested away statepower; now what duty do we toward it?

We must defend it. We must improve it, strengthen it so that at all costs, enemies outside the country cannot take it away; so that the various oppressing classes that are already dissolved will not be able to wrest it back. Standing on our statepower, we can organize the defense of our country; we can organize to build our country into a prosperous happy one. If we do not have statepower, we are unable to build our country; we are unable to resolve the people's lifestyle and change it into an impressive and a sheltered one either. Only revolutionary statepower in the hands of our party can build our country quickly, raise the living standard of the people fast. Therefore, at all costs, we must defend statepower. We must strengthen statepower; we must improve statepower to have ever better compositions following the stand of the party, following the party line: Statepower in cooperatives; statepower in factories; and statepower throughout the whole country. Sometimes, when enemies cannot fight throughout the country, they fight in cooperatives, in factories. Sometimes, they fight in both cooperatives and factories and, at the same time, in the entire country. Therefore, raise high the spirit of revolutionary vigilance everywhere. Protect statepower so it becomes strong and vigorous. Do not let this statepower fall back into the enemy's hands.

2. Specific Traits of the Dictatorship of the Proletarian Class of the Party

The dictatorship of the proletarian class of the party is:

1. The free, democratic right of the worker-peasant people.

2. The dictatorship of the proletarian class over the capitalist class and the other various oppressing classes.

The revolutionary side which is worker-peasant has the right to power [qamnac]. Standing on this right to power, we are dictatorial over the oppressing classes so that they will have no free right to strengthen and expand their forces again and strike the statepower of the proletarian class. Therefore, we are not afraid of being dictatorial over these classes. Allowing them to have freedom, freedom according to their heart's desire like worker-peasants is sure to enable them to develop and strengthen their forces in order to destroy our revolution, making us miserable and shattered again. This is our standpoint. Thus, we are not standing on the morality of the capitalists, feudalist classes. We are standing on the morality of the proletarian class.

In selecting cadre of cooperatives and factories, we are not selecting capitalist composition or composition from various other classes. This too, is included in the dictatorship of the proletarian class. If we select them, they will have rights to allocate material, and, even more dangerous, they will have the right to enter the leadership committees of cooperatives and factories.

3. *View, Standpoint and Various Measures for Defending and Strengthening the Worker-Peasant Statepower of the Party Under the Dictatorship of the Proletarian Class of the Party to Be Strong at All Cost*

This worker-peasant class statepower we won by shedding blood over a long period. And the oppressing classes both outside and inside the country are holding anger against us; they are holding grudges and will try to take back statepower. Standing on this view, we must have a standpoint that we must defend statepower at all costs by using the dictatorial weapon of the proletarian class. Using this dictatorial weapon of the proletarian class is to prevent the oppressor classes inside the country from joining with enemies from outside the country to fight us.

There must be a correct view and standpoint to serve as the basis for correct measures. We are worried only that the view is not yet provided; we are worried that the standpoint has not yet been provided. If they are not correct, if they are flimsy and loose, there will be danger. Therefore, there must be a standpoint and view which is firm and tight at all times.

At the same time, there must be management measures to purify [samrit samramn] our statepower so that it is clean, tough and strong.

To purify out the enemy among the people, to be clean, to be good, to be tough, to be strong.

Measures to change the lifestyle of the people. Military measures to strengthen the armed forces as the dictatorial armed instrument of the party.

Internal factors are the determining factors. If there were no internal factors, the enemy from outside could do nothing to us. If our measures are correct and careful in this way; they can do nothing. In order to have careful and correct measures, the party line must be grasped in all its ramifications.

We look at the aspects of contradiction and solve contradiction continuously. Therefore, management does not stay at a dead end. On some occasions, sometimes, some compositions are able to fulfill duties. However, in these new times, some compositions are unable to fulfill new duties; and not only are they unable to do so, they sometimes actively oppose new duties, too. Therefore, we must dare improve management in order to improve our movement with the times. It is not possible that old assets can serve in new duties. Only if new assets are brought in continuously from the National-Democratic Revolution can new duties be served. If there are no new assets, no new elements, there will be contradictions. Contradictions are of many kinds: in some they do not really care; in others they actively are in opposition.

If immediately after liberation we did not continue the Socialist Revolution, we would already be slaves. If we were not American slaves, we would be somebody else's. Because their compositions were mixed in. If we did not establish cooperatives, our National Democratic Revolution would not have been successful. But some compositions do not accept this new situation.

Enemies fight the cooperatives in order to dissolve them. [They want] only work exchange groups [krum prava's tai]; to allow markets to resume. If there were no cooperatives, the true revolutionary traits would be gone. The true imperialist traits would come back. Revisionism would come back. There would be markets, there would be cities, confusion. Slavery.

IV. ABOUT THE STRUGGLE BETWEEN PRIVATE PROPERTY OF VARIOUS CLASSES OPPOSING COLLECTIVE PROPERTY OF THE PROPLETARIAN CLASS

AIM

Separately nurture further, efforts to be even clearer about the specific traits of private property and its aspects dangerous to the collective stand; to the socialist stand; to the Socialist Revolution; and the building of socialism; and that which enables or paves the way for various oppressing classes and external enemies to fight to wrest victory over the revolution. Therefore, we must have a clear standpoint and view about the contradictory aspects between all kinds of private property of various classes in opposition to the collective property of the proletarian class; and we must fight to eliminate at all costs this private property, no matter what shape it may take.

EXPLANATION OF THE AIM

This document is the continuation of the three documents above. However, we have the separate aim concerning private property in order that it stands out. This private property is everywhere, in every place. And in the places it exists, it obstructs the Socialist Revolutionary Movement and the building of socialism. We bring it up in order to make ourselves more aware of it that we are wary and fight to eliminate it continuously so that it keeps on diminishing, in order that collective property can keep on growing. We ourselves must be wary; the collectives must be wary; we must fight; the collectives must fight continuously. Our leadership standpoint must be fixed [bamba'k] on this problem. This is the way that things must be done so that we do not fall into revisionism. Otherwise, private property will muffle the party little by little; and then we will not be able to break free.

ESSENCE OF THE DOCUMENT

1. Specific traits and manifestations of private property of various classes other than the proletarian class

2. Bad factors [baccay] and dangers of private property

3. The struggle to eliminate private property according to measures of political-consciousness and management in order to build, strengthen and expand the collective property of the proletarian class

1. Specific Traits and Manifestations of Various Classes Other than the Proletarian Class

The specific traits of private property are the specific traits of the capitalist class. They are the essence or the vital part of capitalist class activities. The capitalists stand on the base of private property in order to live and work. Private property is the soul of the capitalist class. If there is no private property, the capitalist class will be out of soul. They sell, make their living independently. And by means of private property, they profit, oppressing workers, oppressing peasants and oppressing various other middle classes. They oppress by using their private laws, by their commercial artistry.

Other classes also have private property. For instance, the feudal-landlords also stand on private property. The capitalists are individual too, but they do private trade. The feudal-landlords stand on private property in the form of exchange, usury and land rent. Their private property is not as modern as the capitalists. The specific traits of rich peasants are semi-capitalist, semi-landowning. Therefore they stand on private property. These three groups base themselves on private property as their foundation.

Besides this, are there any others who have private property in their role of oppressing others? There are the upper bourgeoisie; the urban upper bourgeoisie include big and small peddlers in the markets and the rural upper bourgeoisie include the upper-middle peasants. These stand on an important level of private property in order to make profit in their professional occupations. Therefore, they are big or small oppressors.

The lower-middle bourgeoisie also have private property. The poor and lower-middle peasants also have private property. Workers-coolies also have private property. But their private property is not the base. These classes are satellites of the others. They do not stand on private property. They live in the regime of private property which is opppressing them. They do not use private property as a weapon to oppress or fight others. But they live in the regime of private property which is oppressing them. Therefore, their dealing, living and working habits are in the framework of private property. Therefore their dealings seek to obtain individual wealth, to live individually, work individually, and make merit individually. But this private property is the influence of the regime of private property of the capitalist class. Therefore, when we attack private property in order to build collective regime instead, these classes are at ease. Therefore, disregard some of their contradictions regarding the cooperativization movement [or] anti-party struggles. As for the private property of the capitalist, landlord and rich peasant classes, they are thick. We demand a tenacious fight at all costs. We demand class dictatorship.

This can be condensed in the following chart:

Private Property	I.	1. Capitalist 2. Landlord 3. Rich Peasant	10 [percent]
	II.	4. Upper Bourgeoisie Upper-middle Peasant Upper Peddler	4 [percent]
	III.	Lower Bourgeoisie Middle Bourgeoisie Poor and Lower-middle Peasants Workers-Coolies	Receive Influence

Manifestations of private property: Sectionalism, organizationalism are manifestations of private property. Bureaucratism [naya miniyam], authoritarianism [qajnaniyam] are manifestations of private property.

Individualism, vanity, rank, boastfulness are all manifestations of private property.

There are more: character and customs in living are private; life working individually; making a living individually are common problems.

Sometimes private property exists in collectives. If a unit thinks only of itself, thinks only of its own accomplishments, although the Region or Sector advises it to regard units around itself, the Sector surrounding it, but it does not do so. This is a manifestation of private property.

Some other manifestations: Private property is management, managing following personal sentiments, family, clique, not standing on the political-consciousness, management line of the party. Therefore this is wrong.

In the cooperatives as well as in factories, it is the same. How should the composition be appointed? A loose one? Which compositions should be brought into the leadership composition? Standing on oneself, this is private property.

Cooperative management, living, working are done in the collective manner; that is, according to the party line. But if the manner strengthens and develops privately, following an individual direction, this is wrong, this is according to its own private property.

Everything is related to private property and collective property. They are always fighting one another. Consciousnesses are fighting together, policies are also fighting one another. Managements are also fighting one another. Management in the party, outside the party; management of living and working come from the collective standpoint or from the private standpoint.

2. Bad Factors and Dangers of Private Property

Private property has never provided any good factors. It was so even in the National-Democratic Revolution. From the beginning of our struggle, whether during the political or during the armed struggle, or during the war, private property affected the interests of the revolution. For instance, those who thought of their family interest, always separated from the revolution. They abandoned the revolution, lived apart, seeking well-being in their family instead of in the party. At some point, they would change their traits, struggling against the party. Enemies would draw some compositions to their side; with a bit of private property most do not work for them, but just stay quietly, but some compositions work for the enemy and betray the party.

On entering the Socialist Revolution and the building of socialism, there exists contradictions between private property and collective property. Contradictions are of vanity, rank, duty positions. Besides these, there are big contradictions that arise, for example, from those who are in violation of morality systematically [ja khsae sanva'k]. Struggling by oneself will not succeed; the collective struggling together cannot help because of this heavy private property. Therefore they must fall. This is a bad factor for the individual and a bad factor for the cooperative.

Another number, because of thick private property, confesses. They will not go to join the enemy as before they are not the enemy. But they keep on struggling. Until they develop into anti-party contradictions; then they join hands with the enemy from outside to strike the party. To speak in general, it is a class contradiction. But to speak specifically, this really comes from private property. It is a danger for the person and to the revolution.

3. The Struggle to Eliminate Private Property According to Measures of Political Consciousness and Management in Order to Build, Strengthen and Expand Collective Property of the Proletarian Class

Having seen the bad factors of private property, we must have measures:

1. Political-consciousness measures are strategic measures, are basic measures. That is, measures to awaken, to understand about the specific traits of each class that is struggling with one another in the society of Kampuchea today. Contradictions are permanent. Private property is the private property of the oppressor classes that are in anti-party contradiction. As for our private property within the party, it is not anti-party contradiction. However, if it strengthens and expands as time goes by, it will become anti-party.

Even if it does not become anti-party, it will hinder our progress. If private property is small, our progress will be great. If private property is more, collective property is less; thus, progress is slow. And not only is it slow, the work of revolution will be hindered. And if we do not struggle to eliminate it, it will change its quantity [pariman], and at some point change its essence into anti-party contradiction. Sometimes we have no intention to betray the revolution, but private property that keeps on expanding evolves toward that way. It can only expand and one day become self-sustaining [qattabhap] and then becomes an anti-party contradiction.

Therefore, we must see the dangers of private property in order to understand them. Wherever we march to, we understand it. We ourselves understand. The collective understands and helps to build. That is the reason why we must provide to the Party Central Committee, provide to the entire party, provide to the army, provide to the Core Organization, in order for automatic struggle and to have a struggle weapon by shedding a clear light. Doing this will make the internal unity of the party very strong. If any individual walks contrary to the party line, the masses will see. No need to have other measures because the masses are united with the party.

2. Management measures have two categories. The first category of management measures is an important one. That is to establish collectives, strengthen, expand, improve, purify our collective management. We cannot do 100-percent all at once. But, we take it step by step according to collective procedures. Live collectively, manage collectively, work collectively, lead collectively. Some compositions who are not used to living collectively have difficulties. However, they will be used to it as time goes on. The collective regime expands increasingly, the masses see the self-sustaining nature of the collective regime; eating is easy; working is effective; raising children is easy; security is assured. Therefore, the combination of political work and consciousness makes our collective regime increasingly stronger and wider spread; private property keeps on shrinking, soon it will be finished.

By organizing the collectives this way, we are the masters. Assault private property, keep on pushing private property. It will not have time to breathe, strengthening and expanding itself. This way of fighting is a strategic assault. This is a strategic measure, a basic measure.

The second category of management measures is a supplementary measure: small mistakes must be straightened out by political-consciousness, by warnings, criticism and education. Secondly, the person's party position must be removed; his duty must be changed according to the degree of the mistake up to the point of management measures of a high limit. This measure is a measure of confrontation. It is a tactical measure.

In order to have mastery, we must concentrate on political consciousness measures and the first category of management measures.

SUMMARY

The party has raised this document in order to show again our view about private property, what specific traits it has; what dangers are, in order for the entire party to take strategic and tactical measures to eliminate them entirely.

V. REVIEW OF DIALECTICAL MATERIALISM [SAMBHAR IYAM PATICC SAMUPPAD]

AIM

Further to nurture about the four laws of dialectical materialism in order to upgrade the quality of view and analytical stanpoint about various problems of all kinds that exist in our revolutionary work. Unless there is a view and an analytical standpoint according to the science of Marxism-Leninism following dialectical materialism, only then will that analysis be correct as a base; and if analysis is valid as a base it will lead to the presentation of similarly valid basic measures.

Dialectical materialism is the most basic document of the doctrine of Marxism-Leninism. It is the origin of the doctrine of Marxism-Leninism. Grasping this document leads to a valid analytical standpoint in all facets. An analysis valid on all facets leads to measures valid in all facets.

ESSENCE OF THE DOCUMENT

1. Everything is interrelated
2. Everything undergoes transformation (evolution)
3. Everything undergoes transformation from quantity [parimah] to quality [gunabhab]
4. Everything has contradictions

1. Everything is Interrelated

This means that all things always have influence on one another. It further means that nothing can exist by itself and has never existed by itself.

Observe activities in our revolution or problems outside of the revolution. They are all in the domain of this law.

Example: A person cannot live by himself. He must have various relations [prasray] and labor force ties, too, whether few or many.

Example: Economic problems cannot exist in isolation; military problems cannot exist in isolation. There must be mutual interacting factors. By defending the country are we enabled to build the country. By building the country are we enabled to defend the country.

Domestic policies cannot exist in isolation; they must have mutual relations with foreign policies. Foreign policies also cannot exist in isolation; they have to conform to domestic policies.

Industry must also have contact with agriculture. Agriculture must also have contact with industry.

Regarding our leadership matters. How do we analyze each problem? We must also stand on the first law. When we see any problem, we must relate it to the prior matters. Therefore, we must search for other matters that have contact with the matter at hand. It has contact with various others. Do not only look at this matter alone. If we only look at it alone, our analysis will not be clear. This is the standpoint, the spinal cord that must be examined. This is the analytical habit.

Example: In the situation of a person who has injured a buffalo's leg. We must analyze. If we do not, the buffalo will be put in the stable and the next morning it will be let out to pasture. We must ask if the child or the old man who tends the animal injured it, or who else did; and if it was done, why? Was it unintentional, or was it to oppose the cooperative. Look for a person who has something to do with this matter, the person who tends the animal and the places where he tended the animal in order to find out if other than the cowherd himself could have injured the animal. The cowherd, what composition is he, what class stand, what political stand, which milieu is his stand in contact with? If the cowherd did not injure the animal, ask him if anyone came to the place where the animal was, etc. We follow up. Following-up is a measure. If we cannot find out in one or two days, we will find out in three or four days.

A skinny cow is handled similarly. We must find out what is wrong with it. Why is it skinny, what material reason, what reason of consciousness?

We raise this matter in order to illustrate the law of dialectical materialism in order to accustom our analyses to follow this law.

Another example: Two cooperatives: the first cooperative reports that the second cooperative has created such and such problems. The second cooperative reports that the first cooperative has caused such and such problems. Following these reports, the branch [sakha] grasps that, at bottom, there is a contradiction between the two cooperatives. If we analyze by standing on the report of the second cooperative, we stand on a subjective [qattanomati] standpoint; do not stand on the law that everything interrelates. We must stand on the reporting of both cooperatives in order to analyze. Not only that, we analyze what is the class composition of the second cooperative; what strong points, what are the weak points? We look at the specific traits of the second cooperative: it has many bad compositions; over a long span it has had disputes. The first cooperative has a mostly good composition. Analyzing this way, we can raise measures to purify the second cooperative.

If we do not stand on the first law, we analyze subjectively, by personal sentiment which is very dangerous. The bad factor comes from our not being able to analyze the problem thoroughly. The quality of our analysis, correct or incorrect, will have influence on the quality of our leadership correct or incorrect.

Battlefield situation: The enemy breaks our line of defense. Some commanders analyze seeing only that the enemy is strong, not seeing their weak points. Therefore, their troops were overrun. Other commanders analyze the strong points and the weak points of the enemy and our strong points and weak points. So they find opportunities to strike them, restoring the situation. So, two equal forces, two different measures. This comes from an analytical standpoint that was not founded on the first law.

During the Political Struggle, the enemy conducted many seizures, once in a while they made secret arrests: some were terrified, seeing only that the enemy was strong. But we analyzed according to the standpoint of the first law: the enemy were strongly looting. We were having difficulties. But the people had strong rage toward the enemy. We had the measures to explode a mass struggle.

The year 1973: B-52s struck us heavily. The objective situation was strongly pressuring us. This was a difficulty for us. How did we analyze? We analyzed by standing on the first law. We analyzed the strong points and weak points. We analyzed the good factors and the bad factors of negotiations; we saw the dangers of negotiations: the danger that the enemy might destroy us. The danger of slavery. We fought at all costs.

The March 1976 Meeting: We were of the situation in the year 1975 that we worked the rice fields very well but we would have only a limited crop. Some would run out of rice by March; some would run out of rice by April; in general rice stocks would be gone by June. This was a difficult point for us. But we did not only look at the difficult points. We looked at our strong points: party, people, land, maize, roots, etc. We prepared tactical crops to cross the gap in order to assault in the rainy season. Therefore, most were able to resolve [the situation]. A certain number in one area were able to solve it too, but they did not solve it very well. This came from analysis of bridging tactics that were not adequate. In May and June the situation began to ease itself, but it was a little too late.

Therefore, in thinking about problems, we must think about many angles: good aspects, bad aspects, profitable aspects, wasteful aspects; sometimes profit can be tactical but losses are strategic; sometimes gains are both tactical and strategic.

But each of us, whether we analyze following the first law and however we grasp it, are not finished. Therefore, we must analyze collectively.

2. + 3. Everything Undergoes Transformation (Evolution)
Everything Undergoes Transformation from Quantity to Quality

Everything undergoes transformation (evolution). Anything at all may not remain quiet; may not remain immobile. That is, it is evolutionary; it always changes. Sometime it changes to progress; sometimes it changes to non-progress, but it always is changing.

Example: Our party since its creation has always been changing. It is not still. To speak in general, is evolving to progress, to be fat, both in quantity and in quality to become a party leading statepower throughout the country; achieving its National-Democratic revolutionary duty, and carrying on to make the Socialist Revolution. If we speak of the personnel in the party, they too are changing. A large fraction have evolved into solid, strong progressives. Another number has evolved not up to the movement and opposed the movement, betrayed the revolution. Each party member, speaking of party members means those who have three traits: first policy; second trait is consciousness; third trait is management of work.

Party members undergo transformation of policy as follows:

Some personnel evolve progressively quickly; some personnel progress slowly. Sometimes, some compositions evolve by regressing as well. Some personnel evolve always going forward: this is a good evolution. Beware of personnel who evolve by regressing; however little we must beware. Ourselves, too, we must watch out for. Because we cannot say, I will not betray the revolution and [sic] will not try to devote myself in order to progress greatly forward. Because each one of us can only and always evolve, cannot stay still. If we evolve by regressing a little; then he would drop a step and then fall another step until he becomes the veritable enemy, betraying the revolution. Therefore, in the leadership view, at every level, we must monitor evolution. If it is evolving progressively already, we must push it. If it is regressing, we must be wary.

Example: A person has evolved progressively. But he has a property regarding morality. This property is evolving. At some point, it will not stay correct with consciousness; it will become a concrete action. If he is constructed, trying to face up to it a little, but at some point this property consciousness pressures him again and he commits an act against morality again.

Even ourselves, if we have a consciousness of any sort, we must beware because according to the second law, this consciousness will not remain still; we must grasp this law in order to monitor the party, monitor the party members and monitor ourselves. If we see that it is evolving to the bad, we must immediately eliminate it so that it cannot grow further.

Another Example: Two individuals have some hard feelings toward each other. It is a manifestation of contradiction. Will this manifestation evolve? It will evolve. Sometimes, it will evolve into increasing contradiction, the pair split and are unable to live together. Therefore, we must look at it in perspective. If there are good manifestations, we strengthen them. If there are bad manifestations, we must struggle to resolve them immediately.

Another Example: Before, our revolution was weak. But it did not remain quiet, either it expanded progressively, or it dissolved away. It would not stay the same. We grasped this law we arranged policy, consciousness, management in order that it progressively expanded. If there was something which affected the movement we resolved it immediately. Therefore we did not remain as observers.

In each organization unit, in each Sector, in each Region, in each branch it is likewise. If we do not arrange the attributes of quality well, we will shatter solidarity. Therefore, if there is any category of consciousness that is not correct, we must struggle and eliminate it immediately. If we have any sort of incorrect management, we must struggle immediately. We must do political work, the work of consciousness until they understand. Organizing this regime is not correct according to the party management line. Organizing the regime is correct according to the party management line. Make them understand so that they can correct themselves.

Leading a branch is the same. There are things which are wrong in consciousness, politics, management, we must struggle to resolve them immediately. If we do not, things will be mixed up and confused. Confused internally, confused in the movement. The only method to resolve this is education, construction, study together, doing criticism-self-criticism together.

As for ourselves it is the same. If we have something that is not easy, do not pamper it. For instance, a bud of material property; do not nurse it. Eliminate it immediately. Therefore, we will be masters over ourselves and will have a level joined with the collective; we will be increasingly strong. We cannot decide that it is up to them. For sure there will be contradictions, confusion.

4. Everything Has Contradictions

1. The permanent state of contradiction. If you see that there are contradictions do not be surprised.

2. Contradictions are of two categories:
— secondary internal contradictions
— life and death anti-party contradictions

What is an internal contradiction and what is an anti-party contradiction? This problem must be clarified. Sometimes we have a heavy property standpoint, a slight contradiction becomes an anti-party contradiction. Going just a bit further becomes an anti-party contradiction. Therefore, we must grasp the aspect of contradiction. Internal contradictions must be resolved by internal opposition.

3. Resolving contradictions according to the aspect of category of contradiction, internal or life and death contradiction.

This problem touches on the problem of leadership. In a branch, in an organizational unit, if we analyze contraditions incorrectly, and resolve incorrectly, we have a mix-up.

On the contrary, if we have a life and death contradiction, we cannot think it is an internal contradiction. We must analyze contradictions clearly in order to have clear measures.

In order to analyze clearly, in one way, each of us must grasp the fourth law tightly. In another way, we must analyze with the collective.

SUMMARY

These four laws of dialectical materialism touch on the leadership of our Socialist Revolution. In leading, we grasp and analyze big and little problems according to these four laws, we will be able to raise the quality of our leadership.

Appendix C

Pay Attention to Pushing the Work of Building Party and People's Collective Strength Even Stronger

Revolutionary Flags
No. 3, March 1978
pp. 37–53

[Translated by Kem Sos and Timothy Carney.]

I. BUILDING THE PARTY'S STRENGTH

From July 1977 to this point in time, many bases have brought a fair number of new members into the party. This is a great victory for these bases and also means an expansion of membership for the whole party.

We call this a great victory because in these past few years we had closed the door, stopping the growth of party membership, and, futhermore, we not only closed the door, we have been able to screen and drop bad composition, too. Therefore, the work of building new party membership encountered many difficulties in these two, three years due to the complications over composition. But, since July 1977, many bases have expanded party membership by a fair number. This, in fact, is our victory. In addition to this, we have even been able to make an effort and expand the Core Organization somewhat and the Progressive Masses to a much greater degree.

Wresting victory in building the Party, the Core Organization and the Progressive Masses means that we have expanded the party's leading ranks in the bases. Party members, the Core Organization and the Progressive Masses as well have leadership responsibility. We combine these three categories into the framework of leadership of our party. However, the party members are the leaders in the party itself. And the key cadres of the progressive people or the Yuv KK [Communist Youth of Kampuchea] Alliance, are cadre outside the party, not yet being part of the Core Organization nor yet entering the party. But, all of these have been already established in the leadership of the revolution. We have taken care to build these three compositions, the Party, the Core Organization, and the Progressive Masses, that the leadership force of each base increasingly strengthens. If we deal only with the party members, who are in small number, we will be very strong. The number of our party members is not enough to lead people in the various bases; therefore, we must have many more hundreds of the core; many more hundreds, many more thousands of the progressive masses, before we can develop a strong relationship force in the cooperatives, districts, sectors, regions, offices, ministries, armed forces, etc.

We see this scenario: that is, for the future we must pay attention to expanding the party membership, the Core Organization and the Progressive Masses. We must concentrate on these three categories. If these three forces do not exist, we will not be able to gather enough mass force. And, if we have few of these categories, we will gather less mass force; but if we have enough of them, we will gather enough. If we have many we will gather even more and will be strong. We will have our core on every front. We will have our party members, our Core Organization; our Progressive Masses on every front. In order to have our slogans fulfilled, we can push the great revolutionary movement of the masses in magnificent leaps and bounds into every domain, only provided that we have our core in those domains: Our core on the status of Party Members; the Core Organization and Progressive Masses. Otherwise, we are not strong and successful. For instance, a given job is finished in three days by the masses. But, if there is leading core, it is done in a day, or even a half day. This is indeed strong. This is indeed a great bound. Thus, there must be a core; a core, that is, as a Party Member, Core Organization, Progressive Mass.

We must pay attention to this matter. We must closely follow it everywhere, in cooperatives as well as in Districts and Sectors. Especially in cooperatives, it must be understood. We want to build cadres of our bases to understand it in order not only to gather together people to grow rice, to dig canals, to build water reservoirs and dams, to transplant rice, to harvest rice, etc., but to select compellingly at the time of performing any job Party Membership, Core Organization and Progressive Masses, strengthen and increase them. Therefore, during work performance, do not think only of the technique and the job itself, do not gather people just to transplant rice, to harvest rice, etc., we must also look for the good composition and the bad. We turn good composition into progressives. We make an effort to build the bad ones into progressives. And, for those who are already progressive, try to build them to be even more progressive so that they are transformed into the Core Organization and try to build the Core Organization even more in order to transform it into party membership.

We must build increased numbers of progressives and more cores who are as strong as possible by emphasizing the importance of quality, not merely quantity. Are we able to form these three categories to have quality? We are. This is because our masses have good revolutionary traits [dhatu]. We must strive to build, adding to the leadership organization, and to strengthen and expand the existing leadership organization.

Among the three categories, we must consider the Progressive Masses as the foundation, as the base; next comes the Core Organization and finally the Party Membership. We describe it as in the shape of a stupa, its base is the progressive masses; its bell is the core organization and its tip is the party membership. The party is strong provided that this formation exists. This party already has strong masses of the bases, progressive masses of the party who are close to the party's ordinary masses. A stupa, having only the tip, but no bell or base, is not connected to the leadership organization, and to strengthen and expand the existing leadership party does not connect to the masses.

We have already studied the correct traits of the party. It had correct, forward-looking traits. It had highly correct command traits. It has correct traits of main military forces. It has a correct trait of relations with the masses. It always has the masses with it. The masses will only be with the party if it has its own progressive ranks. If there are only four–ten party members, how can we grasp all the masses? We cannot, unless there are many more. Can fifty party members handle the salt fields? They are not sufficient. There must be many hundreds of people in the Core Organization. Can these hundreds of core, can they take care of many tens of thousands of people? They are insufficient. There must be many thousands of progressive masses before we are able to grasp the masses everywhere. If we are in this position, the party is strong and it has the masses as its strong roots and stem.

We raise this matter in order to further clarify the view about building leadership strength. Only with much leadership strength can we successfully lead in the fulfillment of the party's duty. Only thus will the party be strong. Our party is strong because we have Party Members, the Core Organization and Progressive Masses that are close to the ordinary masses.

According to the experience of these past months, [we] see that we have made much progress in building progressives. If, in the course of the past months, we have enjoyed this asset to expand greatly the number of progresssives, from now on in '78 we will further this aspect, expanding the Core Organization greatly and, standing on this base, we will further develop this aspect, expanding Party Membership greatly. And the seedbed to raise our progressives is now good. Therefore, [we] guarantee that the construction of our party will be good. We must carefully nurture this seedbed of ours to be ever better. This is the view regarding construction.

How can we form strong party members, core organization and progressives? We want the veteran and newcomer strong and those who join later to be strong, too. We would like to bring up a number of party principles as follows:

A.

We must pay attention to political consciousness. This means that education must be firm. Educate as we have been doing. If we do no educational work, we will not be able to produce leadership strength because they will not know the enemy from the revolutionary comrades and from the non-revolutionaries. They will not yet be clear. What the oppressing class and the base class means will not yet be clear. Understanding will come after having been through schooling. Therefore, we must educate people over and over and yet again. And the essence which forms the educational base is not new; it remains bearing down on the class problems, class struggle, problems of the revolutionary situation, the problems of the fight between the enemy and ourselves: which are the enemy's devious tricks in the country and outside: what the oppressing classes were before. Now we hold statepower. How do enemies fight to wrest it from us? How must we protect the statepower of the worker-farmer class, etc.? We educate and build unceasingly, and we work on the tasks of political consciousness until it is firm. What is the educational program? There are meetings, listening to radio broadcasts, studying short documents, by word of mouth itself, by documents from the Regions or the Sectors. The study can be half day, one day or two to three days depending on the concrete situation.

We must pay attention to educate others. Note that our comrades who are party members in branches in cooperatives do not think only on technical work. Do not just gather people to do this or that. Before leaving for work, there must be an education meeting; for instance before setting out to work in any particular place, the significance of the work must be understood. That is, for what? What significance does water control play in solving the people's lifestyle and what in rice farming? It must be clearly understood. Besides, there is another problem: it has to do with the enemy which they must be educated to understand, too. In doing work on political consciousness, in order not to waste time in doing concrete work, there must be a regimen; for example, a meeting once a month. Education on some type of problem every ten days. If possible one education session per month, or attending class once every three months; or attending a two-day class every six months. And the full rights and probationary members of cooperatives and even the depositees, might study and watch and draw experiences as well. However, the full-rights members study apart first, in order to unite together; and the probationary and depositee members study together, drawing experiences, making corrections over and over— they will all progress. We educate and build the full rights members into progressives, which are in turn built into cores. When there is a leadership core, there will be strength. Therefore, we must pay attention to educating; that is, educating according to the party line.

B.

We must pay attention to the problem of organization [jat tamn] especially and basically pay attention and scrutinize autobiographies meticulously. Monitor concrete activities continuously in order to select the good, the average and the weak. This matter must be dealt with at all times. Eliminate the view, the subjective standpoint that autobiographies have already been grasped, that there is no problem; and that is nonchalant, not paying attention to checking them over.

C.

We must undertake the work that is called "fight in the movement, test in the movement" [prayuddha knun jalana sakalpan knun jalana]. In the movement it shows the strong, the average and the weak. At this point, note that we are already party members; we are already the core organization; in each cooperative we must involve ourselves before the rest play more roles and are more active fighters. If we move, it is sure that other people will. If the party members go, it is sure that the core organization will, as will the progressive masses and the ordinary masses. In addition, our ranks will be ever better organized, not fragmented. On the contrary, if the party members do not move, how can the core organization move. This is already ruin. If the fragmented core organization will not move either, the progressives will be fragmented. If these three categories are fractured, the whole organizational unit [qanggabhab] will be in ruins. Therefore, in this organizational unit, no one will be moving forward, no one will be the core. Therefore, in this matter, in order to build strong new party members, a strong core organization and strong progressives, the party members, especially comrades who are responsible for leadership in this cooperative, must be the core; it is important that they be a model. Party members in the front line of plowing should be model plowmen, are miserly at setting work times and careful at dispatching work forces. Party members in rice transplanting are also careful models. In this way we will be strong. Being a model does not mean that we know everything. Discuss with the masses; ask the masses for their opinions. The masses in the party. The masses outside the party. The ordinary masses. Doing it this way is required before we can gather the masses. For example, there is already paddy, only tools are needed to turn it into polished rice. We should discuss with the masses: the masses in the party; the people outside the party and the ordinary masses as well. Raise the topic of discussion that there is paddy, but we are busy reaping, busy doing this, doing that, now we need some help in order to make some polished rice. Is it possible? Discuss collectively. This way, the masses will be pleased, will trust the party branch in the cooperative. It is in this way the the masses will believe in the party and the revolution. However, if we do not resolve problems, the masses will have no belief. They will not trust our leadership. If the masses lack belief in us, it means that we will not be able to preempt the leadership duty in cooperatives. Therefore, do not hold meetings just for the sake of it and return home without solving concrete problems for the people, they will not feel warm toward us. We must do whatever is necessary so that the people are warm toward us, thus we can build forces well and strong and lead successfully.

II. BUILDING THE FORCE OF THE PEOPLE'S COLLECTIVE

In building the force of the people, we must grasp the line or the principles of the party, which is trying to build in what manner?

In the National-Democratic Revolution, the line of building the people's force in rural areas stated:

1. Take the force of poor and lower-middle peasants as the foundation [panqaek].
2. Make close solidarity with midddle peasants.
3. Cooperate or unite with rich peasants and small landowners.
4. Separate out reactionaries, those who would be neutral; those who might be converted; those who are cruel, we must strike these latter.

This was the line of gathering and building force of the National-Democratic Revolution.

However, how do we gather and build force now? Now it is as before, except that there is a wider meaning than before because we hold power throughout the nation already.

First, lean on poor and lower-middle peasants in rural areas. In the cooperatives, we must base ourselves firmly on this force at all times. Do not be distracted. This is our foundation force. There is no better.

Second, close solidarity with middle peasants. In this way middle peasants are allies of the poor and lower-middle peasants. If we are talking about them, they are the second force.

Third, gather all forces of the petty bourgeoisie, capitalists and small landowners; move them toward the revolution. They are the third force. Take everybody. Gather anyone; gather them all, no need to select. It is all right if they have joined the revolution for only one or two days.

Fourth, separate out the small number of reactionaries. We separate them into three categories:

Category 1. [Those who can be] drawn to the revolution.

Category 2. Neutralists, who do not oppose the revolution.

Category 3. The savage ones who cannot be reeducated [kasan].

However, this third category has a small number.

Some cooperatives have none.

We must have the view of gathering forces. Why do we gather them? We gather them in order to isolate enemies and to maximize the forces of our revolution. With many forces come strength. We reduce the enemies' forces to an absolute minimum. The enemy will not be able to draw the people's forces. At this time, we keep expanding and strengthening our forces; in revolution we are stronger. Our party's strength is increasingly stronger; our armed forces strength is increasingly stronger; our economy's strength is increasingly stronger. We do not push away forces.

We gather the people's forces to have this high number in the interest of defending the nation, serving the Socialist Revolution and building socialism. Therefore, we must scrupulously apply the political line of gathering forces. In order to be able to gather the maximum forces by taking poor and lower-middle peasants as base support and middle peasants as allies and other forces, there must be education. The full rights members, the probationary and the depositees must be educated separately and together in order for full rights members to help comrades build others. Education is prime.

Secondly, select and assign by dividing into separate categories the full rights, probationary and depositee members; we must clearly distinguish the good and bad.

Thirdly let them join in the movement. Only if they involve themselves in the movement will we be able to see who is good and who is bad.

The first year is still complicated. The second year is a little better, but still somewhat complicated, The third year is increasingly better. For example, this year is better than the year '75; the year '76; the year '77 because we have continuously educated the political consciousness although it is still not enough. However, we have educated people continually and they have awakened accordingly. Along with this, we have taken care of their lifestyle problems and carefully refined management. Enemies have been refined out [samrit samramn] by us. Good people, we have built and they are even better. This is why our people have higher and higher revolutionary traits compared with the years '75–'76 and '77. We must continue education. We must strengthen and improve management further. Deal with eroding, hidden enemy composition further. At the same time, pay attention to improving the people's lifestyle more and more. In this way, we will surely build up a strong people's force.

In short, if the party's force is strong, the force of the people's collectivity is strong. And if the leadership force is strong we can decide anything. Therefore, we must pay attention to pushing harder the building of the party's force, the force of the people's collectivity even stronger.

Appendix D

I. THE LAST PLAN

A. INTRODUCTION

1. Summary of answer by Chhuk, secretary of sector 24 on 23 September 1976 and of the 19th answer by the same person personally written on 23 September 1976. This summary constitutes the basis.

2. The answer of Isoup Ghanty of the ministry of Foreign Affairs has some similarity regarding an assault from outside and a collusion between the Vietnamese, Soviets, Lao, Thais and the U.S. imperialists.

In brief, we should say:

B. SUBSTANCE OF THE SUMMARY

1. The Soviets are the head of the treasonous machination.* The Vietnamese were the implementers.

2. The U.S. imperialists collude with the Soviets by compelling the Thais to provide supplies to the Khmer Serei in Thailand.

3. Inside the country, the CIA agents and particularly the Vietnamese expansionists cooperated to implement the same scheme in constant contact with outside.

EX.: Chhuk was connected to Be Mab. The group of Khuon connected with the Vietnamese and particularly the Thais through Sot, secretary of sector 106 and through the group of Say in Northwest. The group of Say related directly to the Thais. The group of Hang were in touch with the Thais, the Vietnamese and also through the Lao.

C. IMPLEMENTATION OF THE SCHEME

1. Secretly by murdering or abducting members of the Organization during festivities or during the trips, and so on.

If this succeeded, they would replace the Organization nationwide by secret local appointments,** thus avoiding turmoil both inside and outside the country.

2. If this first case was not successful, they would resort to spreading rumors, sabotage, manifestation, banditry which would lead to partial insurrection.

EX.: — spread rumor on existence of tiger as a superstition for insecurity in Kompong Som;

— Chakrei group exploded grenades behind the royal palace, fired on the national museum in early 1976;

— banditry of the groups of Nhem and Nhek, in sector 37, western region, and of the group of Sreng in the central region;

— manifestation staged in muk kampoul district in November 1975.

---

* The Lao would openly join hands with the Vietnamese in case of need.
** Legally, they used the trick of sending people to further study when arrest was needed, or they caused insurrection by a string of traitors at any one place, or they simply attacked, in accordance with the local realities.

3. If the 2nd case still did not succeed, the VN troops and the traitorous forces outside the country would brutally invade Kampuchea and install their administration on the way.

— swift attack followed by swift withdrawal—as in Angola and the CSSR in order to avoid criticism from the world opinion.

— If they did not completely succeed, the eastern side of the Mekong River would be chunked off and Svay Rieng town proclaimed as temporary city while continuing the total takeover.

— If the operation totally failed, the faction which was uncovered should go abroad while the other part, still intact, should continue to take cover in the CPK.

4. Their desire was to at least hamper, harass and destroy the economy and slow down the national construction of our revolution if they did not succeed.

II. INSTALLATION OF THE NETWORK AND BUILDING OF THE CIA AGENTS AND VN ANNEXATIONISTS

1.

They used the legal means of placing their agents in order to take over the revolutionary power to occupy ranks and functions in the party and administration, which enabled them to carry out activities to protect their men already exposed.

EX.: The groups of Chhuk and Chakrei operated that way in sector 24, and division 170.

The line of Koy Thuong, former secretary of the northern region, also did the same.

According to part evidence, wherever the traitors had been in control long, they set up their network in clumps.

2.

All forces—which had had some sort of conflict with the CPK both in the management, the individual duty and so forth were rallied.

EX.: As contained in the answers by Veng Ky, alias Net, worker in the rubber transportation in the eastern region, on the statute of the Laborers' Party (document dated 9 July 1977).

3. Mode of Operation

A. PERIOD BEFORE 18 MARCH 1970

They managed to control the leading machinery so as to be able to dismiss revolutionary cadres or organize various treacherous activities. Among other things, they cooperated with the ruling class by tipping off information that led to the arrest of revolutionary cadres or by recoursing to assassination.

EX.: Sophan said that Chhuk ordered the imprisonment of Rat in order to facilitate the management of the affairs in sector 24. After 17 April 75, Rat came to the foreign ministry.

EX.: The groups of Keo Meas and Ya competed for the control of the Pracheachon group and sent Vinh In to control Kampujbotr lycee.

EX.: Sreng was in touch with Prey Chor district governor S. Hok in order to carry out suppression drive against revolutionary localities and rally demoralized elements to build up anti-revolutionary forces.

EX.: In their propaganda, they showed the enemy's superiority and that the revolution was in difficulties that would never end. They said that one should walk with its two feet and look to the winning party. This was the CIA propaganda.

In their part, the VN agents called for foreign support. For instance, they said that before long those who were trained in Vietnam will return—who were skillful in various techniques—that the VN army was great and strong, that we should wait until the VN army fought for us, and that we could not fight as we had nothing.

B. THE 5-YEAR PERIOD OF NATIONAL LIBERATION

1. Their main strategy was to control the army.

EX.: The groups of Koy Thuon, Chhuk and Tum planned that way.

2. Using various pretexts, they used their rights to dismiss revolutionary cadres at will, sent them to death or had them assassinated on the battlefield. This occurred in the areas where the traitors were in complete control. Then they replaced them with bad elements such as former bandits, security workers, soldiers, and hooligans in the army and the localities.

EX.: They made all necessary preparations to take power after Lon Nol was overthrown.

C. PERIOD OF NATIONAL DEFENSE

1. Anytime the Angkar asked for cadres, they took the opportunity to send their agents.

EX.: The group of Chakrei sent his men into the air force and artillery. The group of Khuon took control of the trade ministry.

2. Rank, honor and class differentiation were vaunted.

EX.: They said that after waging a long revolutionary struggle you will remain combatants; they frightened those who had relatives in the bad elements; they did not undertake orientation course for the combatants, etc., but turned them into traitors.

4. Summing Up: Percentage of the Traitors

A. COUNTER-REVOLUTIONARY BASES BEFORE 18 MARCH 70

1. The Pracheachon group: Keo Meas, Ya and Norn Suon were the chieftains. They rallied a number of the former Khmer Issarak executives such as Chhuk, secretary of sector 24; Hang, secretary of sector 103; Nhek, secretary of sector 37; Sok Boutchamroeun, sector 25. Keo Neas (generally called as bang Achar) was very influential. He was a VN lackey—to him, anything Vietnamese smelled good.

2. The group of former combatants trained in Hanoi: The chieftains were Son Ngoc Minh, Mey Pho alias Yat and Keo Mouny. They became 100 percent Vietnamese and had nothing left as Khmers. They were subservient lackeys of the Vietnamese.

3. The Khmer Serei or the People's Movement:* This group was dispersed everywhere but was constantly organized by the CIA.

1. A faction lived in South Vietnam and in Thailand, headed by Son Ngoc Than.

2. Another faction was inside the country and led by Hang Thun Hak. It was subdivided into two sections:

— one, already exposed, was composed of Hang Thun Hak in the administration, and Khieu Chum and Pang Khat among the monks; they lived under Sihanouk's administration.

— a second section, still remained underground, took cover in the revolutionary ranks at the secret arrangement of Hang Thun Hak, through the network of Tiv Ol—which included Koy Thuon, former secretary of sector 304 and new men such as Ke Kim Huot, Khek Pen, Chea Huon, San and Hoeng in Northwest, and Saing Rin in sector 33 for example.

The network of Khieu Chum included achar Ven of monastery Kamsan, achar Hay El—a man of Chakrei—of monastery Stoeng Slot.

3. The Vinh Kinh faction—based at the onnalom monastery—was in close and constant contact with the Vietnamese. This faction was the oldest of all. Vinh Kinh was, as Son Ngoc Thanh, one of the main Khmer Serei leaders. It was made mainly of people from Kampuchea Kraom and was also subdivided into three sections:

— one section stayed with the Viet Cong such as Vinh Kinh;

— another section, led by Ya, took cover in the CPK and included Ly Phen and achar Kang in Southwest, and Sophan in (?sector) 170.

— still another section infiltrated the Hanoi-trained group and included Son Sary, alias Prev, and Son Sovat.

4. Another faction of Son Ngoc Thanh group was in France and was also mixed with the group trained in Hanoi. It included Roat Samoeun, alias Ros and Haing Narin, alias Rat.

Stand of the Hanoi-trained group and Keo Meas group toward Khmer Serei or the People's Movement.*

According to the answers given by Son Sary alias Prev and by Chhuk, secretary of sector 24, since before the Geneva Conference, former resistance groups had always accounted that Son Ngoc Thanh group was a nationalist one. They had purported to rally them. They had always been impregnated with this thinking.

EX.: Son Sary, introduced by Vinh Kinh, wrote about his relation with Haing Narin that they had relations with Son Ngoc Thanh. Through this contact Haing Narin also grasped the depth of the matter.

EX.: Chhuk's group cooperated with the Khmer Serei in Thailand. Vinh Kinh, on behalf of the VN, rallied Son Ngoc Thanh. Through this contact Haing Narin also grasped the depth of the matter.

EX.: For his survival, Norn Suon agreed to join the CIA while in jail—according to his answer.

4. *The intellectuals*: This group coexisted with Sihanouk's administration. Some who had been formerly progressive did this for fear of death.** Others, the CIA agents, pretended to be progressive and infiltrated the revolution to gather information. They included Toch Phoen, Uch Ven, Mey Phat, Hou Yun, Hou Nim, Ham former secretary of sector 15, Tum, secretary of sector 22, Sok Krong, Som at the general staff. The party found out since May 1977 they were CIA agents.

5. The officers—CIA agents—who were trained in the United States and then

---

* In his answer, Bun Sany talked about this view expressed by Mey Pho, Son Ngoc Minh, Keo Mouny and others.
** When the revolution was in power, these people rushed in to compete for title and function.

ordered through the repatriation to return in order to spy on the Kampuchean revolution following the liberation on 17 April 1975. They included Phuong Phanh, colonel; Sim Silena and Ung Veng Huor.

Their mission was to establish contact with Koy Thuong, Norn Suon, Phok Chhay and Cheng Sayumborn. (As we can recall it, they were also bang Lin and Li Phen.)

6. The capitalists such as Chong, former deputy secretary of southwestern region, were CIA agents infiltrated since before 1954. He was a Thai national living in Koh Kong province and was uncovered in 1974.

7. The pro-Soviet overseas students: agents of the KGB, they returned home in order to join hands with the Vietnamese.

In 1965, they established a Khmer Communist Party with Hak Sieng Lay Ni as the secretary but failed. They were from various countries such as Hak Sieng Lay Ni and his group from the Soviet Union, Toch Kham Doeun and his men from France, Aing Chou Bi from the CSSR. Some of them under strong pressure from the ruling class became CIA agents, such as Ieng Seiha and Aing Chou Bi. The party exposed them in 1977.

8. Apart from this, there were also agents from other countries: Sien An SDECE France; Boun Sany—a former resistance man and an agent of the French rubber plantation; Chhong Phean FDGB East Germany.

9. The Chinese residents: originated from the KUO MINH TANG, they came as expatriates from China. Their origin went back to before 1944. KMT men controlled, managed and established all Chinese associations, schools and hospitals.

Before 1956—that was before ties were established with China—they operated in the open. After Sihanouk's forbidance in 1956, they went underground and conducted seemingly revolutionary activities.

They had, in the main, close association with the VN revisionists while pretending to have contact with the Chinese embassy for the sake of their business. Main instructions were passed from Taiwan through Hong Kong.

Later, the majority of the KMT members turned into CIA agents. This was first discovered by the party in Feb-March 1978 while they were plotting to overthrow the party on 17 April 1978 together with the VN assault from outside.

Their principal bases in Phnom Penh were Tuan Hua and Chin Hua schools, the Chinese hospital, and others. Beside these, they also had bases in Battambang, Kompong Cham, Kampot and other provinces. But most important of all was Tuan Hua school—which was the largest school and was connected to all other bases in Phnom Penh and the provinces. Teachers were all sent from Saigon.

B. THE LAST COUNTER-REVOLUTIONARY BASES ESTABLISHED BY THE TRAITOROUS NETWORKS

1. The line of Chong, deputy secretary of western region
   a. sector 11 liquidated in 1974

2. The network of Saing Rin, secretary of sector 33, Southwestern region, eliminated in early 1975

3. The string of Noun Soun alias Chey, secretary of sector 25, southwestern region, wiped out in late 1975. Also included Leat, San, Soeun of division 703; Chamroeun, Huot Se and Sok, in sector 25

4. The network of Ham-Keo-Neou, committee of sector 15, Western region, eliminated in early 1976

6. The line Kap-Kandor-Yim of achar Ven, sector 31, Western region, eliminated in early 1976

7. The network of Koy Thuon, former secretary of Northern region, eliminated on 17 Feb. 1977

a. division 310, 450 and 920 (100 percent of the battalion level, some of the company level), tank unit

b. region 304, division 117 (100 percent of the district members and colonels upward)

c. sector 106, division 335 (100 percent of communal and colonel level upward)

d. the former trade ministry

e. sector 505, Ap Kang, deputy secretary of the sector

f. sector 105, Mey and Khamphoun, sector committee

8. The network of Say, member of the northwestern region (Ros Mau alias Say [Khmer script]), eliminated in June 1977

a. division of the Northwestern region: San, Neou, Khleng (Norng Sarim alias San), committee "Kor"

b. sector 1: Chea Huon, Vanh secretary

c. sector 5: Men Chun, Hoeng, secretary

d. Ke Kim Huot alias Sot alias Man, secretary of sector 7

e. sector 4: Khek Pen alias Sou, deputy of sector

f. sector 6: Oum Chhoeun alias Me, sector member

9. The network of Tum, secretary of sector 22, liquidated in April 1977

a. sector 22: 100 percent of the sector and district committees

b. regiment 152: 100 percent of the regimental, battalion and company level

10. The line of Ya

11. The line of Hang, secretary of sector 103, wiped out in Jan. 1978

12. Various ministries of the Angkar:

— Toch Phoeun, alias Phin, secretary of the Public Work Ministry,

— Hou Nim alias Phoas, secretary of information, eliminated on 10 April 1977

— Sin Dara alias Sok, former secretary of the city, former secretary of electricity, liquidated on 7 March 1977

13. The network of the Chinese residents, wiped out in Feb. 1978

— Nget alias Hong, chief of the Chinese community

— Ko Min, in Kratie, Chinese from Saigon, combatant during Son Ngoc Minh time

— So Chea alias Sar, trade ministry

— Khmau, industry committee

The KMT big shots in Phnom Penh were:

3. for the KMT group

Before 1944, only the KMT party existed. After the Japanese defeat in 1944, Chiang Kai-Shek group founded a three-principle youth organization, similar to the Communist Youth of Kampuchea.

In Cambodia, before 1956, they existed in the open. Later when Sihanouk established relations with China, they operated under the VN revolutionary brand. In 1958, they wore the Kampuchean revolutionary tag.

In China, men from Taiwan infiltrated since after 1949 when the CCP took over the mainland.

Summary regarding the planning will be presented in section IV.

III. INFILTRATION IN AND DEVIATION FROM THE LINE OF THE CPK

A. Long-Standing Infiltration

1. ORIGIN OF THE INFILTRATION PLAN

a. From the answer given by Son Sary alias Prev—which we summarized on 16 May 76—we noted that between 1952 and 1954, Vinh Kinh travelled to Dangrek range to meet Son Ngoc Thanh personally or through messenger. First, Vinh Kinh obeyed Son Ngoc Thanh very much. Later, he opposed him and designated Son Sary and Son Sovath to infiltrate the Vietminh in 1954 entrusting them with keeping contact with Roat Samoeun and Haing Narin, former students from France and also Son Ngoc Thanh's men.

Through this connection, it was clear that the CIA had this plan since Roat Samoeun and Heng Narin joined the Vietminh in 1954 or even before.

b. Concerning the Vietnamese: after the Geneva Conference, some former resistance men went to Hanoi while commander Sim Sat was assigned as a messenger between the VN at the border and Keo Meas in Phnom Penh. He carried both messages and gold. In 1957, Sim Sat brought in two Vietnamese.*

As far as we can recall, referring to answers given by Chhuk and Ya in Oct 76 on bang Phim's treason: "following the Geneva Conference, bang Phim undertook a training in Hanoi as the other fellows. After a while, the VN party sent him back to take control of the party in Kampuchea because the VN did not trust ta Tou Samut who was in close and permanent contact with the brothers who had returned from France (particularly bang I). Bang Phim then returned with Boun Sany—who did not say so—in 1956.

We do not conclude on the truth of this answer. It was beyond our understanding. But we note that the VN might have a plan for infiltrating their elements in the CPK in the aftermath of the Geneva Conference.

SLOGANS FOR THE INFILTRATION STRATEGY
— the way the weevils bore the wood, or
— the way oil permeates.

2. TRUE NATURE OF THE INFILTRATION PLAN

According to the enemy's successive answers, those who talked more clearly about this plan were the Khmer Serei or CIA agents such as Chakrei, Sophan, Li Phen, Son Sary alias Prev and Koy Thuon. The name of the VN network still evaded us as we had no document to certify it. Both documents on the VN henchmen showed the founding of another party—summary of which will be given in section V.

3. THE CIA STRATEGIC LINE (INDEFINITE PERIOD)

* to Phnom Penh, who persuaded Sim Sat to join the Pracheachon group. Achar Kang also declared that they were constantly in touch with Ti Kam in Phnom Penh. Chhan said that while in jail his father introduced the VN to him.

The group of Sophan, subdivision 170, admitted this strategic slogan: "the buffaloes hide themselves to sharpen their horns and will come out when the water submerges the reed," meaning that they were hiding and building up their strength to introduce it in the CPK. When Kampuchea will become prosperous, revolutionaries will get excited and increasingly do away with their proletarian position. Then the inside men will rise up and crush the revolution from within.

This goal—based on the answer given by Son Sary alias Prev—was to infiltrate all conflicting parties, to create scuffle to split each of them, to rally the strength for CIA, to incite quarrels between various factions in order to weaken them all, and finally, their men who were hiding inside joined hands to smash all sides thus winning the power forever, particularly definitely abolishing communism.

EX.: The strategy drawn up by Vinh Koeung when he infiltrated the Vietminh in 1954 was to hide in the Vietminh, in the Sihanouk administration and in Saigon. Whenever the opportunity arises they should simultaneously rise up to gain the power absolutely from the Khmer Serei.

EX.: According to the plan drawn up by Li Phen and passed on to Son Sary in 1974, elements should hide in both the CPK and the VN newly-founded party, and rally forces to launch an assault in conformity with the aforementioned slogan of injecting poisonous substance in all the nervous system.

4. SUBSTANCE OF THE INFILTRATION PLAN

a. While the Kampuchean revolution had no power, a number of their elements worked as commune headmen in order to first protect their groups and also cooperate with the ruling class to persecute, disperse and then get rid of genuine revolutionaries thus leaving room for apparently-revolutionary men.

EX.: Chhuk denounced Roat

EX.: In 1967, bang Phuong persuaded Chhaom Savat to become a village headman to protect bang Phuong's men and get rid of other components (based on answer by Chhaom Savat, secretary of Chhlong district, sector 21)

b. At the same time, they fomented economic sabotage against Sihanouk's administration thus causing budget crisis (such as the import of non-utilitarian commodities) and compelling Sihanouk to ask for US aid. In this way, they would advance toward taking over from Sihanouk—according to Toch Phoeun's answer.

c. If the Kampuchean revolution failed, they would unite to search and smash all revolutionaries for good as was achieved in the aftermath of the Geneva Conference (Koy Thoeun's answer)

d. If they failed, they would turn to their own strategy

5. LONG-TERM PLAN

To oppose communism from one generation to the next, continue to do it in successive generations. If it does not succeed in one generation, do it in another.

B. Deviation from the CPK Line

In general, the CIA enemy talked about the deviation from the party's line to the left or to the right in order to create trouble to or hamper its implementation thus preventing the progress by great leap forward.* Their slogan was to learn from the revolution and strike it back.

Their strategic aspirations were:

* Details of the tactics will be presented in section IV.

1. overthrow the CPK and install in lieu a free regime.

2. if this did not succeed, distort the CPK line and deviate it into revisionism like that of the VN and the Soviets.

These were the CIA abject goals.

Apart from this, they also followed many less important slogans such as: grow rice both in the dry season and in the rainy season, obtain the rice from the Angkar and the seed from the people.

In summary, the VN and CIA used the same deviationist strategy. According to the answers given by Koy Thuon, Chakrei and Tum, we had the following periods:

1. BEFORE 18 MARCH 70

The group of Koy Thuon engaged in the struggle using noisy means in order to alert the enemy thus giving it the opportunity to destroy the revolutionary movement. Apparently very revolutionary, these means actually led to the suppression of the revolution by the enemy. According to the answers provided by Chhuk, Chhaom, Savat and Tum, the traitors' networks in the eastern region strived to build up their bases by using revolutionary means. Their true action was to cooperate with the ruling class through replacing village and commune headmen previously discarded by various methods.

2. THE 5-YEAR PERIOD OF NATIONAL LIBERATION

The group of Koy Thuon in sector 304 created an atmosphere of pacifism, luxury and excitement entertained by arts, girls, reception and festivities; fostered house alignment and planting of banana trees along the streets; stimulate prestige, ranks and relation with the enemy.

It gathered tens of thousands of people to dig a canal down from Phnum Kulen, to clear the bush for planting banana trees while giving no thought to the battlefield.

The traitors' networks in the eastern region deviated from the lines and used the slogan of burning to calcination and pulling back raw.

EX.: Chakrei ordered Prayuth to launch the units against the enemy's bullets during an attack and retreated without considering properly the conditions which resulted in great losses. He said:

The group of Tum in sector 22 first established a cooperative at the village level and then collectivized all goods without educating the people. When told to relax, they stopped working.

3. PERIOD OF NATIONAL DEFENSE

At the Angkar directive to launch offensive in rice production, the groups of Oeun and Suong slowed the provision of rice to the combatants, carried the sick to work the land; mixed seeds; improperly transplanted; etc.

Chakrei's group said: "transplant in the dry season and the rainy season" etc.

1962: Sieu Heng, Say and Ta Chea killed Tou Samut.

1956: The Soviet party publicized the resolution adopted at the 20th congress. The CPK opposed it. Toch Phoeun, Chi Kim An, Keo Meas, Ya, Sien An, Chey Suon and others fully supported it as they believed that the Soviet party was older and thus was more experienced. Class division in the Kampuchean society was nonexistent. The Kampuchean people need peace and should not be led to war. Sihanouk was a progressive king with whom we should continue to unite. They conferred disorderly to pick up one of them to be the secretary of the party.

1964–65: Hou Nim, Hou Yun, Phok Chhay, Vann Tipsovan at the trade youth founded a new party.

4. THE KMT PLAN

1949: Chiang Kai-Shek fled to Taiwan. One year later, he prepared a strategy to reconquer China with the assistance from the United States, Japan and the Philippines—countries around Taiwan. They attempted to close sea lines in the China Sea with the US 7th Fleet. They caused trouble in Korea to create more difficulties to China, particularly in solving the people's livelihood. This was aimed at sapping the people's confidence with the CPC and thus creating opposition to it. They would launch attack from outside while the Taiwan remnants fought from inside. But this design failed.

1972: Nixon and China issued the Shanghai joint communiqué in an attempt to establish diplomatic tie. Taiwan then announced relation with the Soviet Union in preparation for the American withdrawal. The Soviets agreed with this strategy of surrounding China. Taiwan has long understood that itself and the revisionists could coexist and together with them would win the power back.

After 17 Apr 75: Kampuchea was liberated. Taiwan was again interested in Kampuchea because of its importance. If Kampuchea collapsed, the revolution in Southeast Asia will lean toward the VN. For this reason, Taiwan cooperated with VN against Kampuchea.

This KMT plan was uncovered in March 1978, which set 17 Apr 75 as the day for attacking the party. This plan was exactly similar to that of the CIA and the VN.

IV. THE CIA AND VN PLANS AT DIFFERENT STAGES OF OUR REVOLUTION (BASED ON KOY THUON'S ANSWERS)

In all stages, each traitors' network attempted to assassinate our brothers who were the standing members of the CPK central committee, particularly brother I and brother II.

A. Before 18 Mar 70

1. THE CIA PLAN

— Before Koy Thuon moved to Kompong Cham, Hang Thun Hak asked him to report on the brothers' names and their meeting places. At that time, the infiltration plan had this goal only.

— In 1960, immediately after joining the party, Hang Thun Hak and Phoc Kly asked Koy Thuon to establish a people's revolutionary base in Kompong Cham. The task was to struggle hard, infiltrate deep in the leadership and seek means to destroy the revolutionary strength.

— In 1964, the meeting of the party's central committee decided on the readiness to counter any eventual coup mounted by the Americans. Koy Thuon's men then intensified their activities against the revolution to help the coup.

— One month before the coup was carried out, Hanh Thun Hak summoned Koy Thoeun, Doeun and Sreng to a meeting with Siruthy—a CIA agent in Phnom Penh—in order to prepare for motivating the masses to support the coup, to arrange for wiping out the revolutionary forces by persuasion and by force, and to drive the Vietcong troops out of Kampuchea.

Tum also admitted receiving directives from bang Lin on this question.

2. THE VN PLAN

Answers given by the trainees from Hanoi served as a basis. In his answer, Koy Thuon also mentioned about this plan. But we had no proper documents, because compiling documents and interrogations conducted at that time were not designed for the future but only to serve the present. The VN group, just as the CIA, planned to hinder our revolutionary movement. They said that they will help us after liberating South Vietnam. In this way, it will swallow up Kampuchea by giving power to the Hanoi-trained people in cooperation with the VN army, just as during the time of struggle against the French.

The inside-men also conducted activities to undermine the revolution, build their bases and made propaganda on an attitude of waiting for the guys from Hanoi *and* waiting for the help of the VN troops, and to despair from the line of independence prompted by the CPK. The chief-executants of the VN plan were Son Ngoc Minh and Keo Meas—the latter moved to Hanoi in about 1968.

3. THE SOVIET PLAN

Answers given by the students from the USSR—KGB agents—provided the basis:

— The Soviets planned to control the students sent there during Sihanouk's time through the Marx-Lenin club.

— In 1965, the KGB founded a Khmer CP with Hak Sieng Lay Ny as secretary. They sent some of their elements* to fight Sihanouk, who were instead closely watched by his administration. Therefore, their activities consisted only to rally the students in various countries, including Toch Phoeun in France and Aing Chou Pi in the CSSR. They also approached Thiourn Mumm.

B. The 5-year War of National Liberation

1. THE CIA PLAN

— Following the coup d'etat on 18 Mar 70, the anti-coup demonstrations were tumultuous. Men of Koy Thuon and Tum could not check this movement and let it go as they were afraid of being exposed. Koy Thuon and Preap met Hang Thun Hak and were given the following plan:

— expand Lon Nol's sphere of influence; cooperate with the governors of Kompong Cham, Kompong Thom, Siem Reap provinces.

— establish the traitors' cells in the VN army and the Kampuchean revolution and establish a new traitor state power.

— organize spying networks in the liberated zones, snipe at cadres, lob grenades into significant installations.

— cause the conflicts between the people and the VN army, between the revolutionary forces and the VN army, and take control of the revolutionary army.

— establish relations with Ba Nge, chairman of the VN public relations of region 304—a veteran CIA agent in the VCP central committee.

— in the United States, CIA sent Huot Sambat to penetrate the GRUNK in Beijing.

EX.: Koy Thuon was uncovered, dismissed and replaced by another traitor. Therefore, the traitors were continuously dismissed and replaced.

* such as Ieng Seiha

EX.: In 1971, during the CPK central commitee meeting, Tum talked bang Phim (?) to become VN satellite because of the directives from bang Piem to oppose the VN, etc.

— In early 1974, Koy Thuon worked with Hang Thun Hak who asked him on the relation with Keo Meas, Ya and Chong—presented as CIA agents in 1964. He then presented a plan for the founding of a new party in lieu of the present CPK. Through this new party, CIA will introduce the VN-type revisionism and the United States will provide support. Koy Thuon was told to work with Keo Meas, Ya or Ba Nge.

Another plan was to expand the enemy's control.

— In June 1974, the battlefield situation changed. Hang Thun Hak was frightened. He ordered Koy Thuon to counter it vigorously, to report on the military installations, on the number of divisions and on the resident of our brothers. Koy Thuong gave incoherent report which delayed the end of the traitorous clique. He made some impediments and launched some attacks. As the battle in other fronts was raging, he launched his men in the assault in early April 1975, as he was afraid of being exposed.

— *Plan in the case of a defeat*: According to the answers given by technicians, public servants and soldiers in Phnom Penh, they were prepared to use the (?third force) in particular to smash us while our army was entering Phnom Penh. But this plan failed because wherever we reached we immediately evacuated the population thus dispersing their forces among the populace.

2. PLAN OF THE VN PARTY*

a. Before returning home, the men trained in Hanoi were told by the VN party to

— make effort to control the army and the localities; three VN divisions will back them; plan the action as during the time of struggle against the French

— not to forget the party outside the country (namely Son Ngoc Minh and Keo Meas)

— establish with former resistance men such as bang Phim, bang Nhim, bang Si Ya and Chong, but first meet Ya. These are summarized from the incoherent answers given by Son Sary alias Prev on 13 May 76.

b. During the coup d'etat, Koy Thuon worked with the Angkar. Later, Ya gave him two introductory messages to contact Sau Hoeung and Ba Nge. Khuon provided the party's documents to the VN steadily. In 1973, Ya told Koy Thuon that the VN helped found a new party with Keo Meas as the president.

On 5 Apr 74, Ya told Khuon that the Hanoi's men such as Mey Pho, achar Vorng, Chhan, Yos, Phim and Vi held a meeting with Ya to oppose the CPK. Son Sary alias Prev also admitted that in Jun 74 and Aug 74, Haing Narin met Mey Pho in Kompong Thom to discuss the founding of a new party.

c. In mid-1974, the party's central committee met to formulate a plan for the final assault in early 1975. Following the meeting, bang Phim met Tum and told him that (according to the recorded answer by Seat Chhe alias Tum on 3 Nov 77 at end of pp. 26 and 27):

— the CPK was short of ammunition; chance for the liberation was slim and it

* More answers will be added in section V.

was not possible to completely liberate the country by the 1975 dry season. In this case, the traitors' networks should absolutely protect the liberated zones in order to maintain their influence in preparation for the complete liberation. Attacks should be so arranged as to delay the liberation until 1976 when the VN party will join in. The VN troops will launch their assault as in 1970.

If the revolutionary army could liberate the country in the short term, then the traitors should accommodate themselves and continue their hiding.

— On this plan, Tum should report to Khuon.

d. *Scheme to take power from the CPK immediately after its victory.* Basis: answer from the group of Sok, sector 25. As we recall it, during our interrogations, the network in the North and the group of Chakrei also mentioned this.

They would take advantage of the army's relaxation to foster a demonstration from sector 25 into Phnom Penh, supported by the traitors hidden in sector 25 and in division 703, to be ready to abduct our brothers in Phnom Penh and proclaim the power of their group. This will be carried out with the cooperation of sectors 24, 15 and others.

The men from sector 25 talked and gave no ground for analysis.

3. THE SOVIET PLAN

Immediately after the 18 Mar 70 coup, the Soviets would send Hak Sieng Lay Ni to join the FUNK. They introduced him to Ney Saran alias Ya and to the Hanoi-trained men. Reports to the KGB should be transmitted through the VN, Cuban and other embassies.

C. The Period of National Defense

We have earlier summarized the enemy's last plan on pages 1 and 2. Now we give the details of what we have grasped.

1. THE OUTSIDE FRONT

— CIA: they sent Lon Nol's officers—who were trained in the United States—back to Kampuchea through the 'repatriation of patriots' label. These officers included Phuong Phanh, Ung Veng Huor, Sim Silena and Kim Phoeuc Toeung, who should contact the CIA network inside the country—composed of Koy Thuon, Norn Suon, Phok Chhay, Cheng Sayumborn, Li Phen and so on. First it was to infiltrate and then to collect information and pass it on to outside. Thailand also sent men steadily through various ways.

— The VN did the same thing.

EX.: They sent back Li Bun Chheang—who had fled Kampuchea in Apr 75—on 9 Sept 76 through the refugee repatriation. Li Bun Chheang was a CIA agent and a soldier. Nguyen Yang Lay sent Li Bun Chheang with the mission of carrying the plan of a VN aggression and other directives to the men inside to be ready for making propaganda in support of the VN troops during their invasion. These inside men included (Toch Phoeun: Phin), minister of the public work.

According to the aggressive plan, the VN used the CIA men in VN and Thailand to first cause trouble and, once they got deeper, the VN troops would assault and control Kampuchea as the savior.

2. INSIDE THE COUNTRY

All traitors' networks were ready to plot against the CPK.

a. After the liberation, while the party asked for manpower to establish various ministries, Koy Thuon and Chakrei took the advantage to send in their men, thus placing them everywhere, at various extents, around the party's leading machine in Phnom Penh.

In addition, they rallied agents—who were formerly evacuated from Phnom Penh. Men such as Soeu Vasi alias Doeun did the job.

b. At various sectors and regions under their control, they did the same thing.

In Northwest, Khek Pen alias Sou and Men Chun alias Hoeng noticeably gathered the evacuees, all CIA agents, to run various technical services, control mobile units, etc. (? according to the investigation committee on the CIA network). In so doing, they tried to establish a treacherous state administration within the revolutionary state power or to create a state within a state, according to Chhuk's words.

c. At each place, special force was created to carry out assassination or subversion. Banditry, vices, pacificism, rumor spreading and frightening were boosted so as to create a feeling of insecurity among the people.

d. In implementing their scheme, they resorted to intensive, hasty, all-time activities using every means in line with their saying: if we cannot do much do a little and act according to the abilities.

3. OBSERVATIONS ON THE PLAN

1. As to the extent of the cooperation between the Soviets, the VN and the CIA we are not yet able to grasp it for lack of evidence. But based on the information provided by the enemy's answers such as:

— that of Son Sary alias Prev, infiltration was made both in the CPK and the new VN-established party in order to strike down both organizations.

— that of Koy Thuon: he did not like the VN, but he must cooperate with them to found a new party because their interests met.

— that of Lem Sim Hak alias Sei who said that lately the United States used the VN with the Soviet agreement because the United States had no troops to fight in Kampuchea.

— that of Li Bun Chheang saying: the VN planned to use the remnant CIA forces in Thailand and VN to launch the first attack, and then they launched their assault in line with the thought: let the others dry up the water, and the VN pick up fish or dry fish still spawn.

All these answers provided that the Soviets, the VN and the US were cooperating and tried to play up against each other through various pressure against each other but not through negotiations at all. A victory scored by any side will benefit all according to their contribution.

2. The situation was now such that the VN were going to grossly invade the country. Thus, their last scheme became obsolescent. We had no light yet regarding this new plan.

(?) the problems of the Indochina federation and the CP of Indochina.

D. The Leaders of the Coup d'Etat

1975: they were Liev Sutsophonta, Norn Suon and Sok, sector 25
1976: they were Chhuk and Li Phen.

proxy leader: Ya

Direct executants were Chakrei, Sophan of division 170

In Apr 76, Chakrei was uncovered

on 28 Aug 76, Chhuk was uncovered
on 20 Sep 76, Ya was exposed.
Apr 77: the leaders were Khuon, Doeun, Sreng, Toch Phoeun, Say from Northwest
on 30 Sep 77 they were Tum,
proxy: bang Lin and bang Si
Apr 78: leaders were bang Si, bang Lin. The clan included Hang, Chan, Chea, Yi, Hong, Chen and Say from the industry (?ministry).

V. ON THE OTHER PARTY FOUNDED BY THE VN AND CIA

A. The Name

The enemies admitted many names such as the New CP, the CP of the Revolutionary Kampuchea, the Workers' Party, the People's Party, the Socialist Party and the Laborers' Party. The majority said it was the Laborers' Party of Kampuchea.

B. The Founding Date

1. In November 1961, Keo Meas asked Um Neng to convene Norn Suon to a meeting at the residence of achar Sieng alias Ya. Present were:
a. Keo Meas
b. Norn Suon (who admitted to be the secretary for agriculture)
c. Ya
d. Um Neng alias bang Vi, now in the Northeast.
At the meeting, Keo Meas declared the the Pracheachon group will be reorganized into the Pracheachon Party with himself as secretary, Norn Suon as deputy secretary, Ya as a member of the standing committee, and bang Si and bang Vi as members. Bang Si was not present but had explicitly advised him beforehand.
Keo Meas set 1951 as the founding year.
2. The groups of Son Ngoc Minh cared for by the VN and that of Hak Sieng Lay under the Soviet auspices, were staying outside the country, and had no contact with the people. They entered the country with the assistance provided by the traitors inside the country and Ya as the contact.
3. But according to the situation in 1974 and from the answer given by Koy Thuon, Son Sary alias Prev and Tum (see pp. 17 and 18 of our summary) the new party was only about to be founded.
4. The intellectuals such as Toch Phoeun, Hou Yun, Hou Nim, Phok Chhay and Vann Tipsovan also organized a grouping in 1964–1965. But after 18 Mar 1970, the CPK was very strong. The people rushed to join the party, so did the intellectuals who then worked in the party's ranks. In Sophat's words: they were acting in the CPK gloves.
We noted that the establishment of so many groups was due to the ambition of various persons who actually did not enjoy the people's support, and thus failed.

C. The Line of the Treacherous Party

In general, they claimed that the party followed the revisionist line of the VN, listened to them and followed them as their professor. On 9 July 77, Veng Ky alias Net, responsible for the river transport of the rubber plantation in the Eastern region, said about the statute of the party as follows:

1. Those who actively opposed the CPK will be given the membership of the Laborers' Party of Kampuchea;

2. The soldiers, commando members, CIA agents who actively opposed the CPK will also be taken as the party's members.

D. The Leaders of the Treacherous Party

1. Until now, we have no document on the matter.
2. High-ranking leaders of this party—arrested or dead—were:
   a. Son Ngoc Minh, dead in VN in 1973
   b. Keo Meas, arrested on 25 Sep 76
   c. Ya, former secretary of the Northeastern region, arrested on 20 Sep 76
      bang Vi
      bang Chea
      bang Se
      bang Soeung
   d. Koy Thuon alias Khuon, former secretary of region 304, arrested on 25 Jan 77
   e. Norn Suon alias Chey, former secretary of sector 25, arrested on 1 Nov 76
   f. Suos Neou alias Chhuk, former Secretary of Sector 24, arrested on 28 Aug 76
   g. Prasith alias Chong, former deputy secretary, region 201, arrested in 1974
   h. Soeu Va Si alias Doeun, former member, region 304, arrested on 16 Feb 77
   i. Chor Chhan alias Sreng, former deputy secretary, central region, arrested 17 Feb 77
   j. Bou Phat alias Hang, former secretary, sector 103, arrested in Jan 78
   k. Seat Chhe alias Tum, former secretary, sector 22, arrested on 30 Apr 77
   l. Pa Phal alias Sot, former secretary, sector 106, arrested on 21 Feb 77.

In addition, they also incriminated incoherently such persons as:
   a. bang Phim
   b. bang Nhim
   c. bang Si.

Bibliography

Adams, J. 1980. "How Did 13 Million Russians Disappear?" *Des Moines Register.* July 28. Reprinted from *Wall Street Journal.*

Allman, T. 1982. "Cambodia: Nightmare Journey to a Doubtful Dawn." *Asia* (April).

American Mission Saigon. No. 598. Translation of Telegram No. 749 S.D.C.S. of October 1952, from the Committee of Current Affairs of the Committee of Cadres in Cambodia to all Zones, Phnom Penh, and the Cadres Contacting the Chinese.

Amin, S. 1974. *Accumulation on a World Scale: A Critique of the Theory of Underdevelopment.* New York. Monthly Review Press.

———. 1976. *Unequal Development: An Essay on the Social Formations of the Peripheral Capitalism.* New York. Monthly Review Press.

———. 1977. *Imperialism and Unequal Development.* New York. Monthly Review Press.

Andelman, D. 1977. "Refugees Depict Grim Cambodia Beset by Hunger." *New York Times.* May 2. A7, A14.

Anderson, B. 1972. "The Idea of Power in Javanese Culture." In C. Holt et al. (eds.), *Culture and Politics in Indonesia.* Ithaca. Cornell University Press.

Arendt, H. J. 1958. *Origins of Totalitarianism.* Cleveland, World Publishing Co.

———. 1969. *On Violence.* New York. Harcourt, Brace, Jovanovich.

Ashford, Douglas E. 1972. *Ideology and Participation.* Beverly Hills. Sage Publications.

Asiaweek. 1977. "Cambodia, How True?" December 2.

Asiaweek. 1978. "An Undeclared War." January 13.

Bangkok Post. 1977. "Khmer Regime Snuffs Out Coup Attempt." August 20.

Barre, J. 1976. "Le Cambodge au pouvoir de tout petits chefs" (Cambodia in the Hands of the Little Chiefs). *Journal de Geneve.* March 4.

Barron, J., and Paul, A. 1977. *Murder of a Gentle Land.* New York. Readers Digest Press.

Baum, R. 1969. "Revolution and Reaction in the Chinese Countryside: The Socialist Education Movement in Cultural Revolutionary Perspective." *China Quarterly* 38 (April–June).

Becker, E. 1978a. "Cambodia: A Look at Border War with Vietnam." *Washington Post.* December 27.

———. 1978b. "The Cambodian Experiment: Great Change of Heavy Cost." *Washington Post.* December 29.

———. 1981a. "An Innocent Abroad." *Far Eastern Economic Review.* August 7.

———. 1981b. "The Death Chambers of the Khmer Rouge." *Washington Post.* August 2.

———. 1986. *When the War Was Over: The Voices of Cambodia's Revolution and Its People.* New York. Simon and Schuster.

Boun, Sokha. 1979. *Cambodge: La Massue de l'Angkar*. Paris. Julliard.

Brown, R., and Kline, D. 1979. *The New Face of Kampuchea*. Chicago, Liberator Press.

Callison, C. 1981. *Land-to-the-Tiller in the Mekong Delta: Economic, Social and Political Effects of Land Reform in Four Villages of South Vietnam*. Berkeley. Center for South and Southeast Asia Studies. Monograph No. 23.

Carney, T. 1977. *Communist Party Power in Kampuchea (Cambodia): Documents and Discussion*. Ithaca. Cornell University Southeast Asia Program. Data Paper No. 106.

————. 1979. Interview with a Family from the Northeast Regions. Typescript.

————. 1980. Interview with a Revolutionary Army of Kampuchea Regimental Commander. Notes.

Cassella, A. 1971. "Interview with Prince Sihanouk." *Far Eastern Economic Review*. December 25.

Central Intelligence Agency. 1979. *National Intelligence Factbook*. Washington, D.C. U.S. Government Printing Office. July.

————. 1980. *Kampuchea: A Demographic Catastrophe*. Washington, D.C. U.S. Government Printing Office. March.

Chanda, N. 1977. "Pol Pot Plays Up to Peking." *Far Eastern Economic Review*. October 14.

————. 1978. "The Bloody Border." *Far Eastern Economic Review*. April 21.

————. 1986. *Brother Enemy: The War after the War*. New York. Harcourt, Brace, Jovanovich.

Chandara, M. 1975. A Khmer Issarak Leader's Story. Translated by Timothy Carney. Typescript.

Chandler, D. 1977. "Transformations in Cambodia." *Commonweal*. April.

Chandler, D., Kiernan, B., and Lim, M. Undated. *The Early Phases of Liberation in Northwestern Cambodia: Conversations with Peang Sophi*. Melbourne. Monash University Centre of Southeast Asian Studies. Working Papers, No. 10.

Cheng, Chu-Yuan. 1966. "The Power Struggle in Red China." *Asian Survey* 6 (September).

Chinoy, M. 1977. "Killings Mark Cambodia Power Struggle." *Los Angeles Times*. November 16.

Chomsky, N., and Herman, E. 1977. "Distortions at Fourth Hand." *The Nation*. June 25.

————. 1979. *After the Cataclysm: Post-War Indochina and the Construction of Imperial Ideology*. Boston. South End Press.

Dallin, A., and Breslauer, G. 1970. *Political Terror in Communist Systems*. Stanford. Stanford University Press.

Daubier, J. 1974. *A History of the Chinese Cultural Revolution*. New York. Random House.

Dawson, A. 1975. "High Khmer Toll is Cited in Saigon." *Washington Post*. July 2.

de Bary, W. (ed.). 1958. *Sources of Indian Tradition*. Volume 1. New York. Columbia University Press.

———. 1972. *The Buddhist Tradition in India, China, and Japan.* New York. Vintage Books.

Debré, F. 1976. *Cambodge: La Révolution de la forêt.* Paris. Flammarion.

Delvert. J. 1961. *Le Paysan cambodgien.* Paris and the Hague. Mouton.

Democratic Kampuchea. 1972. Bulletin d'Information. Mission du gouvernement Royal d'Union National du Cambodge. Paris. August 11.

———. 1973. Summary of Annotated Party History by the Eastern Region Military Political Service. Translated by U.S. Government. Appendix A of this volume.

———. 1976. Communiqué de presse de la première session plénière de la première législature de l'Assemblée des représentants du Peuple du Kampuchéa. Mimeo. Paris. April 14.

———. 1978a. *Black Paper: Facts and Proof of Vietnam's Acts of Aggression and Annexation Against Kampuchea.* Phnom Penh. Ministry of Foreign Affairs.

———. 1978b. Interview of Comrade Pol Pot to the Delegation of Yugoslav Journalists in Visit to Democratic Kampuchea. Phnom Penh.

———. 1978c. Edited collection of Handwritten Confessions of Vorn Vet. Typescript. Phnom Penh. (December).

———. 1978d. The Last Plan. State Security Service (Pon?). Translated privately. Phnom Penh. Appendix D of this volume.

Department of the Army. 1973. *Area Handbook for the Khmer Republic (Cambodia).* DA Pamphlet 550–50. Washington, D.C. U.S. Government Printing Office.

Desbarats, J., and Jackson, K. 1985. "Vietnam 1975–1982: The Cruel Peace." *Washington Quarterly* 8 (4).

Des Moines Register. 1978. "Cambodian Priests Gone, Temples Turned into Barns." April 1: A12.

———. 1981. "Up to 30 Million Deaths in Famine Blamed on Mao." May 18.

Dittmer, Lowell. 1974. *Liu Shao-ch'i and the Chinese Cultural Revolution: The Politics of Mass Criticism.* Berkeley. University of California Press.

———. 1980. "The Radical Critique of Political Interest, 1966–78." *Modern China* 6 (4).

Douglas, M., and Wildavasky, A. 1982. *Risk and Culture: An Essay on the Selection of Technological and Environmental Dangers.* Berkeley. University of California Press.

Dmytryshyn, B. 1965. *U.S.S.R.: A Concise History.* New York. Charles Scribner's Sons.

Dudman, R. 1976. "No Way to Confirm 'Bloodbaths,' 'Pogroms' in Cambodia." *St. Louis Post–Dispatch.* April 25.

———. 1979. "Report by Richard Dudman on His December 1978 Visit to Kampuchea." *Congressional Record* (Senate). January 18.

Eads, B. 1977. "Cambodian Hierarchy Linked by Blood, Marriage and Shared Schooldays." *Bangkok Post.* November 10.

Ebihara, M. 1964. "Khmer." In F. M. Leber et al., *Ethnic Groups of Mainland Southeast Asia.* New Haven. Human Relations Area Files Press.

Fanon, F. 1963. *The Wretched of the Earth.* New York. Grove Press.

Far Eastern Economic Review. 1972. "Au Revoir Sihanouk." August 5.

————. 1976. "When the Killing Had to Stop." October 29: A26.

FBIS (Foreign Broadcast Information Service). Springfield, Va. U.S. Department of Commerce. Volume I (China), Volume III (Soviet Union), Volume IV (Asia and Pacific). Published daily.

Le Figaro. 1976. "Cambodge: La 25ᵉ Heure de Doum Uch." Paris. May 26.

Fisher, C. 1964. *South-East Asia: A Social, Economic and Political Geography.* London. Methuen.

Forest, A. 1980. *Le Cambodge et la colonisation française: Histoire d'une colonisation sons heurts (1897–1920).* Paris. L'Harmatton.

Friedrich, C. J., and Brzezinski, Z. K. 1956. *Totalitarian Dictatorship and Autocracy.* Cambridge. Harvard University Press.

Gelman, H. 1966. "The New Revolution." *Problems of Communism* (November–December).

Girling, J. 1981. *Thailand: Society and Politics.* Ithaca, N.Y. Cornell University Press.

Gottlieb, T. 1977. *Chinese Foreign Policy Factionalism and the Origins of the Strategic Triangle.* Santa Monica. Rand Corporation.

Guillermaz, J. 1976. *The Chinese Communist Party in Power 1949–1976.* Boulder, Colorado. Westview Press.

Heder, S. 1980a. *Kampuchean Occupation and Resistance.* Bangkok. Chulalongkorn University Institute of Asian Studies. Asian Studies Monograph No. 027.

————. 1980b. Stephen Heder on Cambodia 1979 (draft). U.S. Department of State unpublished monograph.

————. 1980c. Thirty-eight Interviews in February–March. Typescript.

————. 1981. "Kampuchea 1980: Anatomy of a Crisis." *Southeast Asia Chronicle* 77 (February).

Henry, J. 1976. Refugees Cited on Continued Executions. FBIS IV. May 20. (Reprinted from *Le Monde,* May 15, 1976. "Des Réfugiés font état de récents massacres dans la Province de Battambang.")

Hinton, H. 1973. *An Introduction to Chinese Politics.* New York. Praeger.

Hobsbawm, E. 1959. *Primitive Rebels.* New York. W. W. Norton.

Hobsbawm, E., and Rude, G. 1968. *Captain Swing: A Social History of the Great English Uprising of 1830.* New York. Random House.

Hoffer, E. 1963. *The True Believer.* New York. Time, Inc.

Hou Yuon. 1955. "La Paysannerie cambodgienne et ses problêmes de modernisation." Ph.D. diss. Paris. Sorbonne. (Reprinted in Kiernan and Boua 1982.)

Hsueh, C. 1967. "The Cultural Revolution and Leadership Crisis in Communist China." *Political Science Quarterly* (June).

Hudson, G. 1960. *The Chinese Communes: A Documentary Review and Analysis of the "Great Leap Forward."* New York. Institute of Pacific Relations.

Hughes, T., and Luard, D. 1961. *The Economic Development of Communist China, 1949–1960.* London. Oxford University Press.

Hu Nim. 1965. "Les services Publics économiques du Cambodge." Ph.D. diss. University of Phnom Penh. (Reprinted in part in Kiernan and Boua 1982.)

Huntington, S., and Dominguez, J. 1975. "Political Development." In F. Greenstein and N. Polsby, *Handbook of Political Science*. Volume 3. Reading, Mass. Addison-Wesley.

Ieng Thirith. 1977. Ieng Thirith to Lao Women's Group. FBIS IV. April 26.

Inkeles, Alex. 1969. "Participant Citizenship in Six Developing Countries." *American Political Science Review* 63 (4).

Ith Sarin. 1977. "Life in the Bureaus of the Khmer Rouge (3 January 1972 to 15 January 1973)." In T. Carney, *Communist Party Power in Kampuchea (Cambodia): Documents and Discussion*. Ithaca. Cornell University Southeast Asia Program. Data Paper No. 106.

Jackson, K. 1978a. "Cambodia 1977: Gone to Pot." *Asian Survey* 18 (1): 79–90.

———. 1978b. "Bureaucratic Polity: A Theoretical Framework for the Analysis of Power and Communications in Indonesia." In K. Jackson and L. Pye (eds.), *Political Power and Communications in Indonesia*. Berkeley. University of California Press.

———. 1979. "Cambodia 1978: War, Pillage and Purge in Democratic Kampuchea." *Asian Survey* 19 (1).

———. 1980. *Traditional Authority, Islam and Rebellion: A Study of Indonesian Political Behavior*. Berkeley. University of California Press.

Jowitt, K. 1978. *The Leninist Response to National Dependency*. Berkeley. University of California Institute of International Studies.

———. 1979. "Scientific Socialist Regimes in Africa: Political Differentiation, Avoidance, and Unawareness." In Carl G. Rosberg (ed.), *Socialism in Sub-Saharan Africa: A New Assessment*. Berkeley. University of California Institute of International Studies.

JPRS (Joint Publications Research Service). 1976. "Terror in Cambodia." No. 641. Washington, D.C. U.S. Department of Commerce. Pp. 59–64 (May 19, 1976). (Reprinted from *Paris Match*, April 24, 1976. "Terreur au Cambodge.")

Kamm, H. 1978. "Cambodian Refugees Depict Growing Fear and Hunger." *New York Times*. May 13.

Karol, K. 1967. "Why the Cultural Revolution?" *Monthly Review* (September).

Khieu Samphan. 1959. "The Economy of Cambodia and its Problems with Industrialization." Ph.D. diss. Trans. U.S. Department of State.

———. 1979. *Cambodia's Economy and Industrial Development*. Ithaca. Cornell University Southeast Asia Program. Data Paper No. 111.

Khmer Peace Committee. 1952. Khmer Armed Resistance. Pamphlet. October.

Khmer Republic. 1970. *Documents on Vietcong and North Vietnamese Aggression against Cambodia*. Phnom Penh. Ministry of Information.

Khmer Republic Military Intelligence. 1972. "Synthèse Particulière: Objet: Organisation et développement des infrastructures communistes locales." May.

Kiernan, B. 1976. *The Samlaut Rebellion and Its Aftermath 1967–70: The Gains of Cambodia's Liberation Movement*. Parts I and II. Melbourne. Monash University Centre of Southeast Asian Studies. Working Papers, Nos. 4 and 5.

———. 1981a. "Khmer Bodies with Vietnamese Minds: Kampuchea's Eastern Zone, 1975–1978." Forthcoming in David Chandler (ed.).

———. 1981b. "Origins of Khmer Communism." In *Southeast Asian Affairs 1981*. Singapore. Institute of Southeast Asian Studies. 161–80.

Kiernan, B., and Boua, C. (eds.). 1982. *Peasants and Politics in Kampuchea, 1942–1981*. New York. M. E. Sharpe, Inc.

———. 1985. *How Pol Pot Came to Power: A History of Communism in Kampuchea, 1930–1975*. London. Verso.

Kirk, D. 1971. *Wider War*. New York. Praeger.

Kissinger, H. 1979. *White House Years*. Boston. Little, Brown and Company.

Kramer, B. 1977. "Cambodia's Communist Regime Begins to Purge Its Own Ranks while Continuing a Crack Down." *Wall Street Journal*. October 19.

Lacouture, J. 1977a. "The Bloodiest Revolution." *New York Review of Books*. March 31.

———. 1977b. "Cambodia: Corrections." *New York Review of Books*. May 26.

———. 1978. *Survive le Peuple cambodgien*. Paris. Seuil.

Leifer, M. 1962a. "The Cambodia Election." *Asian Survey* 2 (7).

———. 1962b. "The Cambodia Opposition." *Asian Survey* 2 (2).

———. 1969. "Rebellion or Subversion in Cambodia." *Current History* (February).

Levin, B. 1977a. "Incredible Detail: The Worst Death March the World Has Ever Seen." *Times* (London). March 29.

———. 1977b. "The Madness and Unforgiving Cruelty that Struck Cambodia." *Times* (London). March 30.

Lewin, M. 1968. *Russian Peasants and Soviet Power: A Study of Collectivization*. New York. W. W. Norton.

Lewis, J. 1964. *Major Doctrines of Communist China*. New York. W. W. Norton.

MacFarquahr, R. 1966. "Mao's Last Revolution." *Foreign Affairs* 45 (October).

Mao Tse-tung. 1965. *The Polemic of the General Line of the International Communist Movement*. Peking. Foreign Languages Press.

Mayer, J. 1979. *Cambodia Action Update*. Indochina Refugee Action Center. October 29.

Meyer, C. 1971. *Derrière le sourire khmer*. Paris. Plon.

———. 1978. Communication au Hearing d'Oslo. April 20.

Migozzi, J. 1973. *Cambodge: Faits et Problèmes de population*. Paris. Centre National de la Recherche Scientifique.

Mihovilovic, M. 1978. Kampuchea Three Years after Revolution. Translated by U.S. Embassy Belgrade. *Vieshik*. March 21.

Nash, M. 1965. *The Golden Road to Modernity*. New York. John Wiley & Sons.

Nations, R. 1978. "Another 40,000 'CIA Traitors'." *Far Eastern Economic Review*. August 25.

Newsweek. 1980. "Pol Pot's Hatchet Man." September 8.

Nixon, R. 1978. *The Memoirs of Richard Nixon*. New York. Grosset and Dunlap.

Osborne, M. Undated. *Regional Disunity in Cambodia*. Monograph.

Paringaux, R. P. 1977. "Evadés du Cambodge." *Le Monde Hebdomadaire*. September 8–14.

Parish, W., and Whyte, M. 1978. *Village and Family in Contemporary China*. Chicago. University of Chicago Press.

Paul, Anthony. 1977. "The Bitter Fate That Awaits Those with 'Old Dandruff'." *Bangkok Post*. September 3.

People's Republic of Kampuchea. 1979. Documents for the Phnom Penh People's Revolutionary Tribunal for Judging the Crimes of Genocide Committed by the Pol Pot–Ieng Sary Clique.

Permanent Mission of Canada. 1978. *Human Rights Situation in Democratic Kampuchea.* Submitted to the U.N. Human Rights Commission, Geneva, Switzerland. September 8.

Pike, Douglas. 1978. *Vietnam–Cambodia Conflict.* Report prepared at the request of the Subcommittee on Asian and Pacific Affairs, U.S. House of Representatives Foreign Affairs Committee. Washington, D.C. U.S. Government Printing Office.

Pilz, Christel. 1980. "Khieu Samphan: Giving Up on Socialism?" *Asia Record* (October).

Pin Yathay. 1980. *L'Utopie meurtrière.* Paris. Laffont.

Pol Pot. 1977. Speech at 27 September KCP Anniversary Meeting. FBIS IV. October 4. H1–37.

Pomonti, J., and Thion, S. 1971. *Des Courtisans aux Partisans.* Paris. Gallimard.

Ponchaud, F. 1976. "Le Kampuchéa Démocratique: Une Révolution radicale." *Mondes Asiatiques.* August.

———. 1978. *Cambodia: Year Zero.* New York. Holt, Rinehart and Winston.

Pool, I. 1963. "The Mass Media and Politics in the Modernization Process." In Lucian W. Pye (ed.), *Communications and Political Development.* Princeton. Princeton University Press.

Porlier, C. 1976. "Terror in Cambodia." *Paris Match.* April 24.

Porter, G., and Hildebrand, G. 1976. *Cambodia: Starvation and Revolution.* New York. Monthly Review Press.

Pye, L. 1967. "China in Context." *Foreign Affairs* (January).

———. 1968. *The Spirit of Chinese Politics: A Psycho-Cultural Study of the Authority Crisis in Political Development.* Cambridge. M.I.T. Press.

Quinn, K. 1974. The Khmer Krahom Program to Create a Communist Society in Southern Cambodia. U.S. Department of State Airgram A–8 from Consulate Can Tho. February 20.

———. 1976. "Political Change in Wartime: The Khmer Krahom Revolution in Southern Cambodia, 1970–1974." *Naval War College Review* 28 (Spring).

———. 1982. "The Origins and Development of Radical Cambodian Communism." Ph.D. diss. University of Maryland.

Réalités cambodgiennes. 1971. Phnom Penh. October 29 and December 31.

Reddi, V. 1970. *A History of the Cambodian Independence Movement.* Tirupati, India. Sri Vankateswara University.

Revolutionary Flags (Dung Pativatt). Phnom Penh. Communist Party of Kampuchea Central Committee. Monthly.

———. 1975. "Long Live the Glorious Revolutionary Army of the Communist Party of Kampuchea." No. 8. August.

———. 1976a. "Guiding Views of the Comrade Party Organization's Representative at a Regional Congress." No. 6.

———. 1976b. "Sharpen the Consciousness of the Proletarian Class to Be as Keen and Strong as Possible." Special Issue. September–October.

———. 1976c. "Setting Forth the Exposition of a Party Representative at the Occasion of the 16th Victorious Anniversary Celebration of the Birth of the Communist Party of Kampuchea." September–October.

———. 1977. "Exposition by a Party Representative Concerning a Few Guidelines to Building, Strengthening and Expanding the Leading Party on the Occasion of a Western Region Cadre Congress." 25/7/77. No. 8. August.

———. 1978. "Pay Attention to Pushing the Work of Building Party and People's Cooperative Strength to Be Even Stronger." March.

Riggs, F. 1966. *Thailand: The Modernization of a Bureaucratic Polity*. Honolulu. University of Hawaii Press.

Robinson, T. 1971. *Cultural Revolution in China*. Berkeley. University of California Press.

Rude, G. 1964. *The Crowd in History, 1730–1848*. New York. John Wiley & Sons.

Schanberg, S. 1975. "The Enigma of Khmer Rouge Purpose." *Saturday Review*. August 23.

———. 1980. "The Death and Life of Dith Pran." *New York Times Magazine*. January 20.

Schurmann, F. 1966. *Ideology and Organization in Communist China*. Berkeley. University of California Press.

Shawcross, W. 1976a. "Cambodia Under Its New Rulers." *New York Review of Books*. March 4

———. 1976b. "Cambodia: The Blame." *Times* (London). December 12.

———. 1978a. "Paradise Lost." *New Times*. November 13.

———. 1978b. "The Third Indochina War." *New York Review of Books*. April 6.

———. 1979. *Sideshow: Kissinger, Nixon and the Destruction of Cambodia*. New York. Simon and Schuster.

Shils, E. 1950. "Introduction." In Georges Sorel, *Reflections on Violence* (below).

Sihanouk, N. 1980. *War & Hope: The Case for Cambodia*. New York. Random House.

———. 1981. *Memoires Doux et Amers*. Paris. Flammarion.

Sihanouk, N., and Burchett, W. 1973. *My War with the CIA*. London. Penguin.

Simon, S. 1975. "The Role of Outsiders in the Cambodian Conflict." *Orbis* 19 (1).

———. 1978. "New Conflict in Indochina." *Problems of Communism* (September–October).

Smith, R. 1968. "Cambodia: Between Scylla and Charybdis." *Asian Survey* (January).

Sorel, G. 1950. *Reflections on Violence*. New York. Macmillan.

Southerland, D. 1976. "Cambodia Becomes One Great Work Camp." *Christian Science Monitor*. February 4.

Spiro, M. 1970. *Buddhism and Society*. New York. Harper and Row.

Stanic, S. 1978. Cambodia: A Path without a Model. Buddha is Dead! Long Live the Revolution. Belgrade Domestic Service. FBIS IV. April 24.

Steinberg, D. 1959. *Cambodia: Its People, Its Society, Its Culture*. New Haven. Human Relations Area Files Press.

Summers, L. 1975. "Consolidating the Cambodian Revolution." *Current History* (December).

———. 1976. "Defining the Revolutionary State in Cambodia." *Current History* (December).

———. 1982. "Cooperatives in Democratic Kampuchea." *Bulletin of Concerned Asian Scholars.*

———. 1987. "The CPK Secret Vanguard of Pol Pot's Revolution." *Journal of Communist Studies* 3 (March).

Swain, J. 1976. "Diary of a Doomed City." *Times* (London). May 11.

Talmon, J. 1952. *The Rise of Totalitarian Democracy.* Boston. Beacon Press.

———. 1960. *Political Messianism: The Romantic Phase.* New York. Praeger.

Terzani, T. 1980. "I Still Hear Screams in the Night." *Der Spiegel.* April 14. (Reprinted by FBIS IV. April 18. H15.)

Thierry, S. 1964. *Le Khmers.* Paris. Editions du Seuil.

———. 1978. "Etude d'un corpus de contes traditionnels." Ph.D. diss. Lille.

Thion, S., and Kiernan, B. 1981. *Khmers Rouges: Matériaux pour l'histoire du communisme au Cambodge.* Paris. Hallier-Michel.

Thion, S., and Vickery, M. 1981. Cambodia Background and Issues. Phnom Penh. Church World Service Kampuchea Program. Mimeo.

Time (Asia edition). 1976. "Why Are the Khmer Killing the Khmer?" April 26.

U.K. Government. 1978. "Human Rights Violations in Democratic Kampuchea: A Report Prepared by the United Kingdom Government." July 14.

U.S. Congress. 1974. Senate Committee on Foreign Relations. *Background Information Relating to Southeast Asia and Vietnam.* Washington, D.C. U.S. Government Printing Office

———. 1977a. House International Relations Subcommittee on International Organizations. *Hearing on Human Rights in Cambodia.* May 3, 1977. Washington, D.C. U.S. Government Printing Office.

———. 1977b. House International Relations Subcommittee on International Organizations. *Hearing on Human Rights in Cambodia.* July 26, 1977. Washington, D.C. U.S. Government Printing Office.

U.S. Department of State. 1971. Vietnam Documents and Research Notes. No. 88. Mimeo. January.

———. 1978. *Human Rights Situation in Democratic Kampuchea.* Submitted to U.N. Commission on Human Rights. Geneva, Switzerland. July 6.

Vasilkov, Ye. 1979. "Kampuchea: The Maoist 'Experiment' That Failed." *Far Eastern Affairs* 3 (21).

Vickery, M. 1981. "Democratic Kampuchea: Themes and Variations." Forthcoming in David Chandler (ed.).

———. 1984. *Cambodia: 1975–1982.* Boston. South End Press.

Wain, Barry. 1981. "Cambodia: What Remains of the Killing Ground?" *Wall Street Journal.* January 29.

Washington Post. 1975. "Cambodia Executions Confirmed." November 2.

Whitaker, Donald P., et al. 1973. *Area Handbook for the Khmer Republic (Cambodia).* Washington, D.C. U.S. Government Printing Office.

White, P. 1982. "Kampuchea Wakens from a Nightmare." *National Geographic* 161 (May).

Willmott, W. 1967. *The Chinese in Cambodia*. Vancouver. University of British Columbia Press.

Wise, Donald. 1977. "Counting the Casualties." *Far Eastern Economic Review*. September 23.

Wivel, P. 1978. "Cambodia Tusindarsrige." *Aktuelt* (Copenhagen). April 5.

Woollacott, M. 1976. "Life and Times under the Khmer Rouge." *Manchester Guardian*. February 9.

———. 1977. "When the Reporters Laughed Off a Bloodbath." *Manchester Guardian*. September 6.

Yean Sok. 1978. Letter to Mrs. Gaetana Enders. March 2.

Contributors

TIMOTHY CARNEY, born in Missouri in 1944, has been a U.S. Foreign Service officer since 1967. He graduated from the Massachusetts Institute of Technology in 1966 and later attended Cornell from 1975–1976 as a special graduate student in Southeast Asian studies. He served in Vietnam from 1967 to 1969, Cambodia from 1972 to 1975, Thailand from 1978 to 1983, and worked on Indochinese affairs at the Department of State from 1976 to 1978. He took part in three separate congressional visits to Phnom Penh between 1979 and 1981. Mr. Carney speaks and reads Khmer, French, and Thai. His publications include: *Communist Party Power in Kampuchea (Cambodia): Documents and Discussion*, a photo essay on Khmer refugees, and contributions to *Asian Survey*. He is currently Counsellor of Embassy in Jakarta.

DAVID HAWK, born in Pennsylvania in 1943, was educated at Cornell University, Union Theological Seminary, and Magdalen College, Oxford. Formerly United States Director of Amnesty International, in 1980 and 1981 he was director of the Khmer Program (Bangkok, Thailand) and the World Conference on Religion and Peace, a nongovernmental organization in consultative status with the Economic and Social Council of the United Nations. Mr. Hawk first visited Cambodia in 1981 as a relief official. In 1982 and 1984, he returned to Cambodia as a freelance journalist to collect photographic and archival documentation on the Khmer Rouge. The resulting exhibit, Cambodia Witness, toured widely in Europe and North America. His writings on Cambodia have appeared in *The New Republic*, *Index of Censorship*, and *The International Journal of Politics*. Currently Mr. Hawk is an associate of the Columbia University Center for the Study of Human Rights and Director of the Cambodia Documentation Commission.

KARL D. JACKSON, born in Massachusetts in 1942, was educated at Princeton University and the Massachusetts Institute of Technology. He is a professor of political science at the University of California, Berkeley. His main field of research is Southeast Asia, with special emphasis on Indonesia, Cambodia, Thailand, and the Philippines. His publications include: *Traditional Authority, Islam, and Rebellion: A Study of Indonesian Political Behavior*, *Political Power and Communications in Indonesia* (co-edited with Lucian W. Pye), *ASEAN Security and Economic Development* (co-edited with M. Hadi Soesastro), *ASEAN in Regional and Global Context* (co-edited with Sukhumband Paribatra and J. Soedjati Djiwandono), and *United States–Thailand Relations* (co-edited with Wiwat Mungkandi). From 1986 to 1989 Professor Jackson served as U.S. Deputy Assistant Secretary of Defense for East Asia and the Pacific before becoming Special Advisor to the President and Senior Director for Asian Affairs on the National Security Council staff in 1989.

FRANÇOIS PONCHAUD was born in France in 1939. As a member of the Society of Foreign Missions he spent ten years in Cambodia as a priest. For the first five years, he shared the life of the Khmer peasants, learning their language, customs, and religion. Father Ponchaud was forced to leave Cambodia with the last convoy of foreigners on May 8, 1975. In 1978, he authored *Cambodia: Year Zero*. Presently, Father Ponchaud lives in France where he works with Cambodian refugees.

KENNETH QUINN was born in 1942. A career U.S. Foreign Service officer since 1967, he served for six years in Vietnam. As a result of two years in Chau Doc Province along the Cambodian border, in 1974 he wrote the first extensive report predicting the tragedy imposed upon the Khmer people after the capture of Phnom Penh in April 1975. He has served on the National Security Council staff, as Special Assistant to the Assistant Secretary of State for East Asian and Pacific Affairs, Deputy Executive Secretary of the State Department, and presently serves as the Deputy Chief of Mission in the Philippines. He was educated at Loras College and Marquette University, and holds a Ph.D. in International Relations from the University of Maryland. His 1982 dissertation was entitled, *The Origins and Development of Radical Cambodian Communism*.

CHARLES TWINING, born in 1940, was educated at the University of Virginia, the Johns Hopkins School of Advanced International Studies, and at Cornell University. Since 1964 he has been a U.S. Foreign Service officer serving in Vietnam, Thailand, and several countries in Africa. In Thailand he was the State Department's first post-1975 "Indochina watcher" and interviewed the initial wave of Khmer refugees who fled Pol Pot's Cambodia. At present, he is the Office Director for Vietnam, Laos, and Cambodia in the U.S. Department of State.

Index

achars, cultural importance of, 170–71
adultery, intolerance of in Khmer Rouge regime, 167
agriculture: Chinese modernization of, 223; glorification of, 118; Khmer Rouge modernization program, 58–66, 109; mutual aid teams, 125–26; production cooperatives, 85; role in economic development, 123–32; solidarity groups, 125–26; work requirements and productivity, 130–32. *See also* collectivization
American Military Equipment Delivery Team Cambodia, 26n.17
Amin, Samir, influence on Khmer Rouge ideology, 241, 245–46
Angkar. *See* Communist Party of Kampuchea; Khmer Rouge
Angkor era, 58; influence on Khmer Rouge ideology, 109–10; parallels with Khmer Rouge revolution, 161
animals, torture of, 237–38
antirightist campaign (China), 228
Aranyaprathet, as foreign trading center, 133, 147–48
"armed propaganda teams" (Vietnamese), 22
arrest logs at torture-extermination centers, 210–11
asceticism of Cambodian culture, 175–76
autarky: Khieu Samphan's theory of, 43; Khmer Rouge policy of, 47–48, 250

background: cadre membership and, 87–88; class divisions and, 50n.10, 51–55, 79–80, 82–84; PKK-defined acceptability, 50–55
banks: demolition of in Democratic Kampuchea, 49. *See also* money
bannheu social class, 52, 55
Barron, John, 218
bartering, Khmer Rouge reinstitution of, 62, 120–22
"base people" (mulethaan): economic role of, 121–22; position in work teams (kemlang), 126–29; role in Khmer Rouge

power structure, 79–80, 82–84. *See also* new people
Battambang province: peasant revolt in, 19; railway operations in, 139–41
ben siddhi status, 84
Black Paper, 15n.2, 195–96, 217–18
blacksmithing, importance of, 121
blood symbolism in Khmer Rouge revolution, 4, 72–73
bonzes. *See* Buddhist monks
books, destruction of in Democratic Kampuchea, 188
Buddhism: influence on Khmer Rouge, 68–69, 170–77; Khmer Rouge elimination of, 33–34, 191, 212; pervasiveness of in traditional Cambodia, 5, 68–72
Buddhist monks (bonzes), Khmer Rouge purge of, 51–52, 69–70, 75–76, 170–77, 212; in traditional Cambodia, 33–34, 68–72
bureaucracy: Cambodian political culture and, 5–6, 158–59, 176–77; Khmer Rouge eradication of, 50–52, 53n.13, 79, 176–77, 184–87; for prison-torture-execution system, 209–11

cadre education, 87–88
Catholic cathedral in Phnom Penh, destruction of, 49, 211–12
Central Committee of PKK. *See* Communist Party of Kampuchea, Standing Committee
Chams (Khmer Muslim minority): dominance of fishing industry, 135–36; persecution of, 50, 212–13
Chan Chakrey, 89
Chan Samay, 18
Chea Sim, 206–7
Cheng Heng, 30
Chenla peasants' revolt, 152–62
Cheung Ek grave site, 211
chhlop spy system, 70
Chiang Ch'ing, 226, 230
child care, 61